Under the General Editorship of

GORDON N. RAY

The University of Illinois

THE NATURE

Part Two of

OF DRAMA 🙂

HUBERT HEFFNER
Indiana University

AN INTRODUCTION TO LITERATURE
*by Herbert Barrows, Hubert Heffner,
John Ciardi, and Wallace Douglas*

HOUGHTON MIFFLIN COMPANY
Boston · The Riverside Press Cambridge

PREFATORY NOTE

(To the Complete Edition)

There are many volumes designed to introduce college students to literature. What novelty can be claimed for this book comes from its plan. The four skilled and experienced teachers who have served as editors were not limited in their work by any imposed uniformity of treatment. They were asked instead to organize their approaches to fiction and drama, to poetry and prose, exactly as they would their own courses in these kinds of writing.

The result is four highly idiosyncratic presentations, ranging from Mr. Barrows's catholic and persuasive survey of the short story to Mr. Douglas's lively polemic for modern prose, from Mr. Heffner's detached and orderly analysis of drama to an examination of poetry marked by all the brilliance and conviction readers have come to expect from that poet and defender of poetry, Mr. Ciardi. The customary teaching materials are here. The characteristics, the conventions, and the special effects of each kind of writing are set forth, and the necessary critical terms are introduced. But each editor has done this in his own way.

Yet the book does have a deeper unity, which derives from certain assumptions shared by the editors. I recall some twenty years ago being a member of a group of graduate students in English to whom Robert Frost offered this advice: "Don't work. Worry!" This was his counsel to poets, he said, and he thought it might apply to us as well. One or two of our professors regarded his words as subversive of discipline, but we took them, I am sure correctly, as a clue to the kind of understanding of literature that makes its study really valuable. In like manner the editors of this book see literature as an unending source of delight, not merely as a "subject" to be pursued systematically like any other. They propose formal analysis to the student, not as an end in itself, but as a means of widening his range of comprehension and deepening his enjoyment of the thing comprehended. The beginning student, eager and curious, but largely unread and uninformed, will find them reliable guides to the "extension of life" which literature uniquely offers.

GORDON N. RAY

CONTENTS

CONTENTS

THE

NATURE

OF DRAMA

DRAMA, UNLIKE OTHER KINDS OF LITERATURE, is written not primarily to be read by an individual reader but to be presented on a stage by actors for the entertainment of an audience, and hence to attract mass responses. This objective conditions its nature and structure. The major aim of drama, like that of the other arts, is aesthetic in that it attempts to move people emotionally, to arouse their interests, and to satisfy those interests. The interests and the satisfactions may be on a relatively low aesthetic level, and a play may be merely the temporary amusement of an idle hour; or the interests satisfied, and hence the play, may be on a level as high as that attained by any art. On the highest level drama is a primal means of ordering human existence, of interpreting life, and of giving it meaning. It is one of the chief instruments through which man has attempted to explore and explain his own nature. Its history from the time of the Greeks to the present is a record of the changing conceptions of human nature. It provides us with no less than a universal picture of the nature of man, individual man and social man, ludicrous man and noble man, good man and evil man. The average individual in a single lifetime, even with the widest possible acquaintance, can come to know intimately relatively few human beings, and directly from this experience it is not possible to understand the vast complexities of human nature and the wide potentials of human conduct. An intimate knowledge of dramatic literature gives an additional dimension of experience in knowing man and his capacities for feeling, thought, and action. Drama is an ideal means to this understanding, for it has something of the universal appeal that music has: in one or another of its forms, everyone can enjoy and appreciate it. And in performance, drama can be in some degree experienced by even those who do not comprehend its words. To see how drama gives us insight into man and his conduct, it is necessary to examine in some detail the chief aspects of its nature and structure.

Drama, like other kinds of literature, renders a human action, but unlike other kinds, it allows the agents in that action to represent directly their characters, emotions, and deeds. Drama resembles lyric poetry in its concern for sensations, feelings, emotions, moods, thoughts—in short, the inner life of characters who are the agents in dramatic action. It differs from the lyric in that it is concerned with these inner states not as ends in themselves but as motivations toward actions. It more closely resembles narrative literature—the epic, novel, short story, and tale—by the fact that it is organized in terms of a story. Through characters in action, that is through incidents, episodes, complications, and resolutions, drama, like the epic and the novel, renders a complete story from a beginning to a dramatically logical conclusion. As in all other literature, the chief means of drama is the meaningful combination of words into discourse. It differs from epic and novel in that the discourse of drama is the direct discourse of the agents of its story; hence their movements, gestures, intonation of voice, facial changes—their vocal and pantomimic expression, the dramatic manner—are requisite to the rendering of a drama. In order to attain its fullest effectiveness drama employs two other means, the rhythm and melody of speech and occasionally of song, along with discourse; hence practically the whole range of poetic and stylistic devices is available to the dramatist.

The story which a drama tells is not merely a random series of incidents and episodes such as may make up a travel narrative or a tale of adventures. In such stories the agent who undergoes or experiences the succession of events may in no sense cause them. In drama what happens to its agents is partly caused by what those agents are, by their characters; hence character in drama, as in novel and epic, is a basic determinant of action. What happens in a play, what characters say and will and do, is made to seem in large measure the outcome of what they are. On the other hand, character in drama is shaped by action in that the kind of action which the playwright chooses will determine the formulation of the characters he creates to perform that action and make it probable. For purposes of emphasis, this reciprocal relationship of character and action may be stated thus: Character in drama is formally determined by the whole action, whereas action has characters as its material cause. A dramatic action is one which would probably or necessarily result from the kind of characters who are the agents in it. Because of this intricate relationship of character and action, and because plays are written to be performed by actors on a stage before audiences, the structure of drama is complex indeed.

Since plays are written to be performed, that is to "happen" in a place and time in which the reader or spectator imaginatively participates as though he were actually present as the events take place, the action of drama has always the illusion of being present action. Even though the action of the play ostensibly occurs in the past and in a distant place, the spectator in viewing it imagines himself to be "there." The action of an epic or a novel, on the other hand, always gives the sensation of being past action, even though the novel may be about contemporary events and characters. Its action is narrated by an omniscient author, by one of the agents, or by an observer who is not an agent in the plot. Hence, even though he purports to be telling about contemporary events as they occur, obviously for him to be able to narrate them they have already occurred. Thus the novel always presents a past action leading toward the present, whereas the drama always presents present action leading toward the future. It is, perhaps, this immediacy of drama, even more than the fact that the individual spectator is part of a mass audience participating in mass responses, that accounts for the powerful effect which may be realized not only by seeing a play in the theatre, but by the trained reader reading a play.

There is one further important difference between the drama and the novel. The art of drama is an art of intensification, while the art of the novel is in general an art of extension. Intensity is a characteristic of dramatic effect. As a result, major characters in drama, and especially in serious drama, are depicted under the stress of relatively high tensions. Except for brief moments of contrast, the placidity and calm of ordinary daily living finds little place in a play. By its nature drama renders life at its highest pitch and represents those periods in human character and action that are decisive and final. This necessary concentration upon the climactic moments in human conduct makes the span of action in drama relatively brief. It does not allow that slow and gradual development of character, that inclusion of many minor episodes and incidents, nor that slow and almost imperceptible growth of character into action, which are possible in the novel. This intensity in drama is true not merely of the action and the agents, but also of the dialogue. Intensity, along with an accompanying momentousness, is one of the chief characteristics of the dramatic as the term is popularly used. Occasionally dramatists have sought to attain something of the extensiveness available to the novelist but have usually found such an attempt dangerous to dramatic effect.

All these things taken together account for yet another aspect of drama, the constant pull inherent in it toward the realistic. Performance on the stage requires that living actors as suitable embodiments of the characters shall appear in the roles of the agents and shall speak the

words and do the deeds called for in the action. Whatever exploit the
plot may require of them must be physically and convincingly enacted
before an audience. An actual Peter Pan must be seen to fly through the
air; a satisfactory embodiment of Ariel must appear, move, and speak; a
convincing Ghost of King Hamlet must stalk the night. The drama,
therefore, presents problems of probability not exactly the same as those
of the short story, the novel, or the epic.

UNITY AND PROBABILITY

To be fully effective as a work of art, drama must have *unity*. Like fine
lyrics, great plays have a unity of mood and effect, though in such plays
divergent and various moods and effects are often combined to create this
greater harmony. Style, too, must be either strictly unified or unified by
harmonious combination. Shakespeare's plays frequently attain unity of
effect, mood, and style through the harmonious combination of such
discordant elements as highly lyrical or tragic scenes with comic ones. In
the plays of Racine, on the other hand, there are few if any such discords. Mood, style, and the harmonious combination of discords are
technical devices which, rightly used, contribute to the one unity
absolutely essential to drama—the unity of action. Without unity of action, a play cannot be an entity; it falls apart. Unity of action is attained
by so ordering and arranging the plot that the beginning initiates and
sets in motion forces and complications which, through their working out
and resolution, lead to the ending. In the beginning of a dramatic action human affairs, the affairs of the characters involved, have reached a
state of relative equilibrium, a state of quiet or rest. However much tension, turmoil, and strife have preceded the beginning, at that moment
things are relatively quiet. Then some character or some force sets in motion the tensions and complications already potentially existing among the
group of characters or within one of them. The working out and expression of the initiating tension produces further and perhaps wider complications, which lead to yet others, until the forces originally set in
motion, gathering momentum as they move along, somehow work to a
conclusion. At the end, the process of change has been completed and
the exciting forces exhausted, so that equilibrium exists once more, but
a quite different equilibrium. Thus the end of a play is the consequence
of the beginning, and the beginning is the initiating cause of the end.

This kind of unified action is attained through a variety of devices
which contribute to the *probability* of the action. One of the chief devices of probability in plot is the arrangement of the incidents in terms of
antecedents and consequences. There are, of course, incidents in plays
which have neither antecedents nor consequences, but they are not in
the main stream of the action. There are also incidents whose antecedents are to be found in character rather than in previous incidents.
Antecedents of either character or action serve to make happenings
probable. As used in dramatic criticism probability is a poetic term, a

technical critical term. It does not mean mathematical or statistical probability, nor natural probability, nor the probability of common sense. It means believable within the assumptions of the life-frame imagined by the dramatist. The action of a play may be imagined as occurring in a space ship in outer space, or in the year three thousand and fifty; and yet it may be made dramatically probable and wholly convincing. The fairies in *A Midsummer Night's Dream*, and Ariel and Caliban in *The Tempest*, are just as probable artistically as are any of the other characters in those plays. Probability is the creation of the dramatic poet and is accomplished through the art with which he uses the various devices of plot, characterization, dialogue, and spectacle. There may even be devices of thought and of music (the music of speech, at least) which make a given incident, character, or speech seem probable. Often a playwright gains credibility for his plot and his characters by making them seem as nearly like the people and events of daily life as possible; that is, he makes them seem real in the same way that conventionally and commonly known persons and actions appear real. Such an endeavor leads to realism in style. But a playwright's vision of action and character may not be on the realistic plane and therefore the kind of credibility he is seeking may require another and a different style of rendering. Thus in drama probability is a determinant of style.

Every well-formulated play is a unity or a whole; that is, it is complete as a play. This unity is attained chiefly through the unification of the action, though other devices of various kinds may contribute to the effect. Action means change; hence all plays are about changes in people and human affairs. Such a change may be unified in three different ways. First, it may be unified in terms of action, in terms of the beginning initiating the end and the end completing the beginning. One of the chief devices of plot for this kind of unification is the arrangement of events into antecedents and consequences, discussed above. A second way in which change may be given unity is by making the beginning initiate a chain of events that inevitably or probably leads to the ending; hence probability itself is a device of unification. A plot may be unified in two other ways: in terms of a completed change in character, or in terms of a completed change in thought. King Lear in the play that bears his name represents a completed change in character; so does Othello. Both plays are likewise unified in terms of action, and *King Lear* contains a completed change in thought. Great plays are often unified in all three of these ways, but certain modern didactic plays may be largely or wholly unified only in terms of thought. Bertolt Brecht's *The Private Life of The Master Race*, which consists of a series of disjointed scenes, is so unified, as are some of Shaw's plays, especially *Misalliance*.

FORM AND STYLE IN DRAMA

Art is the formulation or organization of a special vision of nature or of some aspect of human life. Form is the ordering or organizing of this

specific vision of nature or life as the artist sees it at the time. The dramatist formulates an action in which human characters are the agents. In
terms of these human agents, an action may move between two extremes, as from happiness to unhappiness or from unhappiness to happiness. A change toward unhappiness tends to become serious for the
agents involved in the action. The change may be trivial and temporary,
or it may be significant and permanent. In order for the seriousness of the
action to be significant and enduring, the characters involved must have
stature. They can gain stature in terms of themselves—of what they
intrinsically are and what they do—and in terms of what they stand for
or signify. Thus the common man may be given stature to the extent that
he is made to represent a whole class or type. Moreover, the characters
in an action may swing between two extremes, the good and the evil.
Good characters in a struggle against unhappiness win sympathy and
admiration; evil characters excite antipathy, though certain evil characters, such as Macbeth, Iago, and Milton's Satan, may also elicit a degree
of admiration. Nobility of character, then, is essentially moral. Place and
position alone will not make a character noble, though they may give
wider scope and dimension to his actions, and may serve as signs of his
nobility. A serious action involving characters significant enough to win
our sympathy and admiration as they suffer and act against threats to
their happiness will arouse in us fear for the outcome of their predica-
ments and pity for their misfortunes. These powers, fear and pity, are the
distinctive powers of the dramatic form known as tragedy.

The dramatist may conceive the action he is organizing and the
characters he is creating as normal or a-normal. In so far as characters or
actions deviate from an accepted norm, thus far are they potentially
ludicrous or ridiculous. The a-normality of character or action may be
very slight. Viola's a-normality in *Twelfth Night* is nothing more than
the assumption of boy's clothing—with all the implications of that action. But from that one ludicrous attribute flow all of the comic predica-
ments in which she becomes involved. On the other hand, the a-normality
may be as morally significant as that of Volpone or Tartuffe. Such significant a-normalities call forth something more than mere laughter. They
arouse ridicule, even biting satire, resulting from moral indignation. This
way of formulating action and character results in comedy, which, like
tragedy, has two powers as a form, though two different ones—not pity
and fear, but laughter and ridicule. The change which takes place in the
action of comedy is from relative unhappiness or entanglement to happiness or a satisfying resolution. Though there are numerous types of
comedy, ranging from farce to the most sophisticated comedy of manners,
there are two broad categories which arise from differences in the playwright's vision of his characters and action. There is the kind of comedy,
which Shakespeare wrote, in which the author seems to say "Lord,
what fools *we* mortals be—some of the time." And there is the kind, which
Ben Jonson wrote, that seems to say "Lord, what fools *those* mortals be—

most of the time." The first kind emphasizes laughter, though ridicule is certainly present; the second emphasizes ridicule but must also employ laughter. This second kind has been called corrective, punitive, or judicial comedy. In a sense, however, all comedy is corrective in that it exposes the a-normal in character and action. Normality in both human character and human actions is conceived in terms of a particular culture and a specific society; hence comedy always tends to be social in nature.

The creation of a play requires the ordering and organization of all the parts of its structure. The action must be shaped into a plot; the agents or characters must be given those attributes which will make their speech and action probable; the dialogue must be instilled with meaning and significance; and the visual happenings must be rightly arranged. Thus the form in which the playwright conceives his play will influence each element and part of it. Though we may speak generally about these two broad categories of form—tragedy and comedy—actually every play has its own distinct form and its own specific powers. Two plays may bear a resemblance to each other as definite types of tragedy or comedy, but no two plays are exactly alike in form.

There is a third category of dramatic form that has been variously called tragicomedy, dramatic romance, *drame*, and melodrama. In this form the action is temporarily or seemingly threatening but ends happily for the sympathetic characters. The powers of this form are that it arouses, and purges, fear and hate. The audience feels hate for an antagonist or villain who in the end reaps a merited punishment. This form of drama requires a double ending, happiness for the sympathetic characters and unhappiness for the antipathetic. Because, among other reasons, hate is highly compatible with ridicule, comic situations are freely interspersed with serious actions in plays of this kind. The comic is also used to relieve tension and to give assurance of an ultimately satisfactory outcome. This third form resembles tragedy in making use of a temporarily serious action and in raising one of the tragic powers, fear. It resembles comedy by employing comic situations and characters and by an ending that resembles that of comedy. However serious the threats to the sympathetic characters may seem to be, those threats must be alleviated or eliminated in the end. Consequently this is a highly popular form in the theatre and is the usual form in motion pictures which attempt any degree of seriousness. Like tragedy and comedy, this form of drama embraces a wide variety of types.

Tragedy, since it is serious throughout and there is never any doubt that it is so, is an exploration of the meaning of life. It is an attempt to examine or assess the nature of good and evil. Tragedy is an assertion that life has worth and meaning, and that man has dignity and nobility. Even such a nihilistic tragedy as Eugene O'Neill's *The Iceman Cometh* has to assume some scheme of ultimate values, for without such values tragedy is impossible. Moreover, tragedy represents human life at its highest intensity, at the climax of those moments when human beings come face to face with reality. Tragedy is the supreme art of meaningful man in action. It is, therefore, an exploration of the meaning of life and the nature of man.

Comedy likewise has its significance in its exploration of social man. It aids the human being to see what is ludicrous or ridiculous in character and action. It exposes and corrects the deviations of human nature and conduct, and is thus an upholder of the normative and the sane. The norm which it supports may be an ideal norm or a cultural and social one. Comedy is an instrument of cohesion in societies and of sanity in man. It restrains excesses and exposes deficiencies in human nature and conduct. By displaying the ludicrous both in character and action, comedy depicts man as less than a great figure of tragic nobility engaged in some enduring, significant action; yet in some of their embroilments, certain comic characters are brought very close to the borderline of the truly serious. Comedy should not be considered the antithesis of tragedy; it is, on the contrary, the complement of tragedy. Both are essential for a whole and rounded portrayal of the nature of man and a revelation of the potentialities and range of his actions.

We shall see shortly that it is useful to think of a play as composed of six qualitative elements or parts. Just as all these parts are involved in its organization and formulation, so are they all in turn affected by the style in which the play is written. Style in drama is therefore a complex matter and difficult to define simply. Technically, style is the way in which the means of rendering are joined to the manner. In other terms, style is the product of the age, the author's view of life, and the way he chooses to tell his story. Since plays are written to be performed on a stage, and not merely to be read, the characteristics of the theatre and of stage production influence style. Thus we can distinguish the style of Greek tragedy and comedy from the style of the Elizabethan or the modern. Style is likewise determined by the particular vision of the playwright, his view of life and his conception of its meaning. Hence we can distinguish the style of Shakespeare from that of his contemporary Ben Jonson. The author's vision likewise helps to determine the kind or level of probability which he will create; hence style is also a sign of probability. In modern drama the realistic and naturalistic style has been dominant since the mid-nineteenth century, though the romantic and the so-called expressionistic schools have played no inconsiderable part. Realism as applied to art is a nineteenth-century term coined by the French to designate an author's approach to and vision of life and the way in which he renders that vision. Realism as a method is always relative to the conventionally accepted view of reality and to the artist's outlook. Hence the realism of Euripides is not the same as the realism of Shakespeare, the realism of Shakespeare not the same as that of Jonson, and the realism of Jonson is distinctly different from that of Ibsen. In general the realist sees the tangible world of man and things, the commonly apprehensible world, as the ultimate reality, whereas the romanticist is apt to find reality in a less mundane, more intangible world of poetry and imagination. Even when the romantic employs the commonly known elements of the ordinary world as these are generally experienced, he sees through them to the ideal, the colorful, and the imaginative. The realist, on the other hand, concentrates upon the perceptible details of man and his environment as seen through the eyes of the normal, average observer. Yet again, the expressionist and his fellow artists (the symbolists and impressionists in France, the school of the grotesque in Italy) insist that these surface details which the realists strive so earnestly to reproduce are at best merely a sign of a reality that lies behind and beyond tangible and observable phenomena. Life and man are far more complex, these dramatists maintain, than outward appearance shows; hence the expressionist resorts to distortion and symbol in his attempt to render the meaning he sees behind appearance. In four of the plays included in this book we shall see four different exemplifications of realism; in a fifth (*The Wild Duck*) we shall see a realist moving towards and employing symbolism; and in the sixth (*Six Characters in Search of An Author*) we shall explore an example of the Italian school of the grotesque, akin to the expressionistic method. In every play style, or mode of presentation, influences the playwright's depiction of man and of his actions.

THE PARTS OF A PLAY

A play as a whole, as a unit, is made up of various parts or elements, and the way in which these are blended together will be a final determinant of its form. To put this idea in other words, in giving form to a play the playwright must create and put these elements together in some right—that is, effective—order. The parts of a play may be thought of in several ways. In terms of quantity the parts of a modern play are the acts and scenes into which it is divided. From the standpoint of form these quantitative parts are not unimportant, but far more important are the qualitative elements. These may be variously described, but the designation and arrangement used by Aristotle in the *Poetics* almost twenty-five hundred years ago is still the most complete and adequate. According to that analysis a play as a poetic composition (not as a stage performance) has six constituent parts, named here in the order of their importance: *Plot, character, thought, diction, music,* and *spectacle.*

Of these, plot is the over-all organizing principle of drama. In terms of structure it is the end toward which the other parts are ordered as means. It formally determines the five other parts, and these may be considered materials out of which plots are made. In its simplest terms plot may be conceived as the arrangement of the incidents in a story or action. The incidents are those things which the agents do (and say, for a speech may be a dramatic action) because they are or have the kinds of characters they have. On the other hand, they have the kinds of characters they have because they must perform certain actions in the plot; hence plot formally controls characterization, and character is the primary material out of which plot is constructed. A fully formed plot, since it is the arrangement of the incidents, is the organization of all the qualitative parts into a whole.

Now, plot itself can be analyzed into component elements or parts. Its material parts are three. The first of these is the inner experience of the characters, what goes on within them as individuals—their sensations, emotions, sufferings, tensions, and deliberations. This inner experience, rightly organized and ordered, leads to discoveries, the second material part of plot. Every plot is composed of discoveries—a succession of revelations to the audience of events, feelings, states of mind, and relationships among the persons involved in the plot. These discoveries may in part be simple and incidental, or they may be more important, relating to things on which the whole movement of the action hinges. Discoveries, in turn, when rightly organized, lead to the third material part of the plot—reversals, which represent complete changes in the drift or direction of the action. Discovery is action in that it is a change from ignorance to knowledge; reversal is a more highly formal action in that it is a complete change in the direction of the action. A plot may be based largely upon inner experience leading to limited discoveries, as in *The Cherry Orchard;* or it may be based upon discoveries and reversal, as in *Candida.* Discoveries result in climaxes, high points of interest. Reversals result from crises, or turning points in the action.

Plot also has two formal parts, complication and resolution. Every well constructed play is arranged in terms of a complicating or involving action, leading to a crisis or turning point, and resulting in a disentanglement, unwinding, or resolution. This whole plot, in turn, is composed of episodes which reflect the same structure in smaller compass; that is, each episode also has a complication, a crisis, and a resolution. In that part of the play which precedes the conclusion, each episode, through its own internal development and conclusion, sets in motion further involvements which lead to yet further episodes. It is largely these involvements that arouse suspense, and it is principally their conclusions that create surprise.

So much, then, for the importance of plot. Character, the second of Aristotle's six "parts" of a play, is (technically) the differentiation of one agent from another. The playwright achieves this differentiation by assigning traits to the agents, ranging from the most obvious externals to extremely subtle differences of temperament and make-up. A simple but basic kind of differentiation is biological: the man-agent vs. the woman-agent. On the next level, the physical, come such differentiations as tall man-agent vs. short man-agent, or blond woman vs. brunette. All visual features, such as posture, facial expression, gesture, dress, and other distinguishing physical traits are of this kind. The next important means of differentiating characters is through their bent or attitude.

Bent is that disposition of a personality with which he was endowed, as we say, at birth. Iago was born evil; Falstaff inherited a humorous disposition. Attitude is similar to disposition but is usually thought of as acquired through association and status. The old maid or the pedagog (the absent-minded professor) are stock comic characters because they have acquired an a-normal attitude that amounts to a bent or disposition of character. Hamlet's attitude is that of a thoughtful, just, young prince. On still a fourth level, characters may be differentiated in terms of emotions (*e*-motion: *e* = the Latin *ex*, out of, from within). Emotional traits account to a large extent for the tensions, desires, and drives of a character. Bent and disposition lead to habitual actions; emotion may lead to surprising ones. Emotions and desires, when not immediately gratified by action, lead to deliberation, and the kind of deliberation of which an agent is capable does a great deal toward characterizing him. Deliberation may be either expedient—that is about ways and means—or it may be moral, about ethical considerations. When a character is moved to moral deliberation, he becomes a serious agent. Thus deliberation provides a high level of character differentiation between the ludicrous and the serious. The end and purpose of deliberation is decision, the very highest kind of character differentiation. Decision is an act of the will which may lead to a deed, a speech, or a change within the character. Often it results in these three things together. Hence it is apparent that moral decision represents the highest formal differentiation of character in terms of change. To represent or analyze character as we have just done is to conceive of it in terms of action. A character deciding is a character acting, however his decision may be expressed.

And so we come to thought. This element in drama can be revealed by what the characters say and do. A gesture, a shrug of the shoulders, a facial expression, or an elaborate piece of pantomimic action may convey the thought of a character quite as forcibly as a speech, perhaps even more so. It is apparent, then, that thought in drama includes sensations, feelings, and emotions, as well as deliberation. Since the action of a drama is made up of the actions and reactions of the characters in it, in a well-organized play the thought is cumulative. Feelings and emotions in one character generate feelings and emotions in others, and culminate in deeds, which in turn produce other feelings and emotions that motivate further deeds. In a sense, then, a play is built like an argument, except that feelings, emotions, deliberations, and deeds take the place of facts and logic in a rhetorical argument. Considered as an argument, it may be said that a play culminates in a statement or conclusion about human nature and human conduct, a philosophic statement about a particular vision of life. In this sense, finally, the play as a whole is the rendering of a thought. Thought in the sense used earlier is the basic material out of which playwrights construct characters; thought as the argument of the whole play is an element of the plot structure.

Diction is simply the dialogue of the play, the combination of words into speeches. Formally, it is controlled by the thought of the characters; that is, what the characters say and how they say it are determined by what they feel and think. Diction, in turn, is the primary material out of which they construct and render their thoughts. It is the central means of drama and, since drama is in a major sense an art of language, it is a significant part of the play as a whole. It is, however, subordinate to and dependent upon plot, character, and thought. The first requisite of dramatic diction is clearness. The second is that it be not flat and commonplace, but arresting, colorful, exciting, memorable—in short, rich and beautiful.

A spoken word is a single sound or a combination of sounds. When a series of words is skillfully patterned into a speech and properly spoken by an actor, it will have a rhythm and a melody which aids in conveying its feeling and thought. This is the "music" of dramatic diction. The diction may be in realistic and colloquial prose, or at the other extreme it may be so highly formalized in rhythm and melody that it is best rendered in song. The experienced actor knows that the simplest prose speech may be altered through the music of speech melody to convey a variety of meanings. Take such a simple speech as "Close the door." Speak it as a stern command; then speak it as a simple request to a friend; then speak it as a question; finally, speak it as an exclamation of startled surprise. In all these utterances the diction remains the same, while the changing music—or melody—gives a variety of meanings and effects. Music is a means through which diction serves thought. In a great dramatic speech the music becomes highly complex and subtle. Whole scenes, as well as single speeches, have their variations of rhythm and melody. Indeed, a play as a whole may be considered as a tonal composition, and some directors are keenly aware of the fine effects to be gained through rhythm and melody in the staging of certain plays.

Spectacle, the last and least of Aristotle's six qualitative parts of a play as a poetic composition, includes the total visual production. Setting, costumes, and lighting are obvious aspects of spectacle. Equally or even more important are the pantomimic actions of the characters. Off-stage sounds, though not literally a part of spectacle, are closely related and may be substitutes for spectacle. An automobile coming to a screeching stop on the pavement outside, and perhaps the sound of its horn, may be a substitute for a view of its arrival. To say that spectacle is the last of the six qualitative parts in the composition of a play is not to say that it is insignificant in the staging of the play. When a play is staged through visual and tonal means, spectacle becomes a major part of its presentation. Hence we may say that music and spectacle become the means of joining the art of dramatic composition to the art of stage presentation.

DRAMA AS A MEANINGFUL ART

While it is possible for the trained reader to experience fully the effects of a play by reading it, plays are nonetheless written to be performed upon a stage by actors before an audience. For most people plays are actualized and their full potential is realized only in performance. Drama is, however, a separate art from stage production, though of course the two are conjoined.

Drama as art is designed to produce an aesthetic experience in the reader or spectator. The effect it produces is basically emotional and is analogous to the effect of a musical composition or a painting. Such an aesthetic emotional experience enlarges an individual's awareness of himself and his understanding of his fellow men. Drama, however, is in a sense more meaningful than such arts as music and painting, sculpture and architecture, because drama has language as its central means. Language adds a cognitive element to drama which music and painting do not possess. Drama not only moves us emotionally in a way analogous to that of music, but through its diction and spectacle it also makes statements of thought which affect us intellectually. A play, as we have tried to show, is an ordered and organized rendering of a certain vision of human life. In so far as that vision is significant and the resultant rendering is effective, the play, like a great action in life itself, will arouse numerous thoughts, deductions, and conclusions. *Hamlet*, for example, as a profound insight into man and his fate, has been interpreted and reinterpreted down through the three and a half centuries since it was written. When the playwright-poet writes such a play, or any significant play, he creates an ordered universe, and the order of that universe is dominantly a moral order. Even in comedy, which treats social man in his deviations, if one traces those deviations back to their logical bases, they rest upon moral distinctions. Drama, then, is an exploration of the moral order of life and a revelation of the nature of man—moral man, social man, typical man, a-typical man, individual man, ludicrous man, evil man, man in all of his multiform aspects.

In our modern world, because physics and other sciences have undermined the very bases of the formerly accepted metaphysics, and because no new and satisfying philosophy of life and the nature of man has as yet been developed and propounded, there is considerable confusion about man and his world—not his physical universe but the moral order of that universe which exists within the spirit of man. In consequence our modern world is one of warring ideologies and international clashes. This turmoil is reflected in modern art, and nowhere more completely than in the drama. Modern dramatists are attempting to explore and redefine the nature of man and to find meaning in his life. Thus far, the modern spirit has not been very hospitable to a settled vision of the nobility of man and the significance of his life; hence, modern drama has not given us any outstanding body of great tragedies. That spirit has been more hospitable to comedy, tragicomedy, and forms closely allied to these. Hence the selections in this section include no examples of great tragedy.

THE WILD DUCK

Henrik Ibsen

Henrik Johan Ibsen (1828–1906) son of an impoverished but formerly substantial bourgeois family, was born in Skein, Norway. Shortly before his sixteenth birthday he was taken from school and apprenticed to an apothecary in the provincial town of Grimstad. Here as a poverty-stricken apprentice without means even to buy adequate clothing, and something of a social outcast, the boy turned to writing and eventually determined to acquire a university education. In 1850, he went to a cramming school in Christiania (Oslo) to prepare himself for the entrance examinations, on which he was conditioned when he attempted them. In that year his first play, *Cataline*, was published through the generosity of a friend and his short play, *The Warrior's Barrow*, was given three performances at the Royal Theatre. In November of 1851, he was appointed theatre poet to the newly established theatre in Bergen, a position which required him to stage a repertory of plays and to write annually an original play in celebration of founder's day. He remained in Bergen for five years, gaining experience in the theatre and as a playwright. After his return to Christiania in 1857 as theatre poet and director of a theatre, he married Susannah Thoresen in 1858. Plagued by constant failures at the theatre and by growing dissensions with his audience, as well as by his failure to receive proper recognition in the form of a pension, he left Norway in 1864, aided financially by his friend and fellow playwright Bjornstjerne Bjornson. His self-imposed exile, during which he lived in Germany and in Italy, lasted until 1891, when he was welcomed back to Norway as a national hero and her most famous son. He died in Christiania on 23 May 1906, already recognized as the greatest of modern dramatists.

Ibsen wrote and published or had produced twenty-five plays; as follows: *Cateline* (1850), *The Warrior's Barrow* (1850), *St. John's Night* (1853), *Lady Inger of Ostraat* (1855), *The Feast at Solhaug* (1856), *Olaf Liljekrans* (1857), *The Vikings at Helgeland* (1857), *Love's Comedy* (1862), *The Pretenders* (1863), *Brand* (1866), *Peer Gynt* (1867), *The League of Youth* (1869), *Emperor and Galilean* (1873), *Pillars of Society* (1877), *A Doll's House* (1879), *Ghosts* (1881), *An Enemy of The People* (1882), *The Wild Duck* (1884), *Rosmersholm* (1886), *The Lady from The Sea* (1888), *Hedda Gabler* (1890), *The Master Builder* (1892), *Little Eyolf* (1894), *John Gabriel Borkman* (1896), *When We Dead Awaken* (1899).

Ibsen's work is conventionally divided into three periods: The early period of romantic saga plays and plays based upon folk materials, cul-

FROM the book *The Doll's House, The Wild Duck, and The Lady from the Sea*, by Henrik Ibsen, translated by R. Farquharson Sharp. Everyman's Library edition published by E. P. Dutton & Co., Inc. Reprinted by permission of the publishers.

minating with *Peer Gynt;* a middle period of realistic social problem plays, culminating with *An Enemy of the People* but also including the later *Hedda Gabler;* and a final period of symbolic plays, beginning with *The Wild Duck* and culminating with his last play, *When We Dead Awaken.* In this scheme *The Wild Duck* is a transitional play, treating realistically a domestic situation with large social implications, but attempting to extend its significance beyond realistically revealed meanings by employing the symbol of the wild duck. The wild duck is a tangible object in the play which is analogically applied, especially by Gregers, to indicate an attitude of human personality under certain conditions of life. It thereby becomes a symbol with a variety of meanings, which can be applied to several characters and circumstances in the action.

In Ibsen's earlier realistic problem plays, especially *A Doll's House* and *Ghosts,* he had insisted that human beings must be truthful, self-determining agents; that the blind following of conventional mores could lead to disaster; and that marriage must be based upon complete understanding without concealment of any kind, and mutual respect between man and wife. To the militant young Ibsenites developing throughout Europe at the time of *The Wild Duck,* Ibsen was the upholder of the ideal. Their crusading spirit, and their complete lack of tolerance and understanding, undoubtedly disgusted Ibsen. Gregers Werle, the antipathetic character of *The Wild Duck,* is his representation of these crusaders. In this play, Ibsen asserts and examines a conception that was destined to occupy a large place in later literature, including drama: The necessity for illusion—or as Relling calls it, the life-lie—among human beings.

Apparently Ibsen believed that normal, natural, sane, and balanced people, such as Gina, even though relatively ignorant, could live without it. So can a highly intelligent man such as Dr. Relling, the *raisonneur* of the play. But weak creatures, such as Hjalmar and Molvik, and sick-souled people, such as Gregers, are incapable of living without illusions. Hjalmar is one of the most ludicrous figures among Ibsen's characters, and Gregers one of the most satirically portrayed. The normative Gina and the adolescent Hedvig are among his most charming. But Ibsen's vision of the terrible mess which sick-souled reformers can make of people's lives is too serious for straight satiric comedy, nor in his view are these people great enough for sustained tragedy. Hence, he adopts the form of tragicomedy for this play.

WERLE, a merchant and manufacturer

GREGERS WERLE, his son

OLD EKDAL

HJALMAR EKDAL, his son, a photographer

GINA EKDAL, Hjalmar's wife

HEDVIG, their daughter, aged fourteen

MRS. SÖRBY, the elder Werle's housekeeper

RELLING, a doctor

MOLVIK, an ex-student of theology

GRAABERG, a bookkeeper in Werle's office

PETTERSEN, Werle's servant

JENSEN, a hired waiter

A Flabby Guest

A Thin-haired Guest

A Short-sighted Guest

Six other Guests at Werle's dinner-party

Several hired Servants

(*The first Act takes place in the elder Werle's house; the other four at Hjalmar Ekdal's*)

ACT I

(SCENE.—*A handsomely and comfortably furnished study in* WERLE'S *house. Bookcases and upholstered furniture; a desk, covered with papers and documents, in the middle of the floor; the lamps are lit and have green shades, producing a soft light in the room. At the back are folding doors which have been thrown open and the portière drawn back. Through these is visible a large and well-appointed room, brightly lit with lamps and branch candlesticks. A small private door, on the righthand side of the study, leads to the office. On the left is a fireplace, with a cheerful fire, and beyond it folding doors leading to the dining-room.*

WERLE'S *servant* PETTERSEN, *in livery, and the hired waiter* JENSEN, *in black, are setting the study in order. In the large room at the back two or three other waiters are moving about, tidying the room and lighting more candles. From within the dining-room the noise of the guests' talking and laughing can be heard; someone raps on a glass with a knife, silence follows and a toast is proposed; applause follows and the hum of conversation begins again.*)

PETTERSEN (*lighting a lamp on the mantelpiece and putting a shade over it*).   Hark at 'em, Jensen; the old man's up now, making a long speech to propose Mrs. Sörby's health.

JENSEN (*moving a chair forward*).   Do you think what people say about those two is true, that there's something between them?

PETTERSEN.   Goodness knows.

JENSEN.   He's been a gay old dog in his time, hasn't he?

PETTERSEN.   Maybe.

JENSEN.   They say this dinner-party is in honour of his son.

PETTERSEN. Yes, he came home yesterday.

JENSEN. I never knew old Werle had a son.

PETTERSEN. Oh yes, he has a son, but he sticks up at the works at Höidal; he hasn't once been in the town all the years I have been in service here.

A WAITER (*in the doorway to the other room*). Pettersen, there is an old chap here who—

PETTERSEN (*muttering*). Devil take him, what is anyone coming now for!

(*Old* EKDAL *appears from the inner room. He is dressed in a weather-worn greatcoat with a high collar, carries a stick and a fur cap in his hands, and a paper parcel under his arm. He wears a dirty reddish-brown wig and a small grey moustache.*)

PETTERSEN (*going towards him*). Good Lord!—what do you want in here?

EKDAL (*in the doorway*). I want so badly to get into the office, Pettersen.

PETTERSEN. The office was closed an hour ago, and—

EKDAL. They told me that at the door, old man. But Graaberg is still there. Be a good chap, Pettersen, and let me slip in that way. (*Points to the private door.*) I've been that way before.

PETTERSEN. All right, you can go in. (*Opens the door.*) But, whatever you do, don't forget to go out the proper way, because we have got guests here.

EKDAL. Yes, yes—I know. Thanks, dear old Pettersen! My good old friend! Thanks! (*Under his breath.*) Old codfish! (*Goes into the office.* PETTERSEN *shuts the door after him.*)

JENSEN. Is that fellow one of the clerks?

PETTERSEN. No, he only does odd jobs of copying when there is any wanted. But I can tell you old Ekdal was a fine fellow in his day.

JENSEN. He looks as if he had seen better times.

PETTERSEN. That he has. He was a lieutenant, though you wouldn't think it.

JENSEN. The deuce he was!

PETTERSEN. True as I'm alive. But he took to the timber trade, or something. They say he played old Werle a remarkably dirty trick once. The two of them were in partnership up at Höidal at that time. Oh, I know all about old Ekdal, I do. Many's the glass of bitters or bottle of beer we've drunk together at Mother Eriksen's.

JENSEN. I shouldn't have thought he had much to stand treat with.

PETTERSEN. Good Lord, Jensen, it's me that's stood the treat! Besides, I think one ought to be a bit civil to gentry that have come down in the world.

JENSEN. Did he go bankrupt, then?

PETTERSEN. No, it was a deal worse than that. He went to gaol.

JENSEN. To gaol!

PETTERSEN. Or perhaps it was the penitentiary—. (*Listens.*) Sh! they are getting up from table now.

(*The dining-room doors are thrown open by a couple of servants. Mrs. SÖRBY comes out, talking to two of the guests. The others follow her by degrees, with the elder WERLE amongst them. HJALMAR EKDAL and GREGERS WERLE come last.*)

MRS. SÖRBY (*to the* SERVANT, *in passing*). We will take coffee in the music-room, Pettersen.

PETTERSEN. Very good, ma'am.

(*Mrs. SÖRBY and the two gentlemen go into the inner room and out to the right of it.* PETTERSEN *and* JENSEN *follow them.*)

THE FLABBY GUEST (*to the* THIN-HAIRED GUEST). Whew!—it's hard work eating through a dinner like that!

THE THIN-HAIRED GUEST. Oh, with a little good-will, it's amazing what you can get through in three hours.

THE FLABBY GUEST. Yes, but afterwards, my dear sir, afterwards!

ANOTHER GUEST. I believe the coffee and liqueurs are to be served in the music-room.

THE FLABBY GUEST. Good! Then perhaps Mrs. Sörby will play us something.

THE THIN-HAIRED GUEST (*in a low voice*). So long as she doesn't make us dance to a tune we don't like.

THE FLABBY GUEST. Not a bit of it; Bertha would never go back on her old friends. (*They laugh and go into the inner room.*)

WERLE (*in a low and depressed voice*). I don't think anybody noticed it, Gregers.

GREGERS (*looking at him*). What?

WERLE. Didn't you notice it either?

GREGERS. What was there to notice?

WERLE. We were thirteen at table.

GREGERS. Really? Were we?

WERLE (*with a look towards* HJALMAR EKDAL). We are always accustomed to sit down twelve. (*Turns to the other guests.*) Come along in here, gentlemen. (*He leads the way out through the inner room, and is followed by all the others except* HJALMAR *and* GREGERS.)

HJALMAR (*who has heard what they were saying*). You shouldn't have invited me, Gregers.

GREGERS. What? This party is supposed to be in my honour. Why should I not invite my best and only friend?

HJALMAR. But I don't believe your father likes it. I never come to the house.

GREGERS. So I understand. But I wanted to see you and talk to you, because I expect to be going away again directly.—Well, we two old schoolfellows have drifted a long way apart from each other, haven't we? We have not met for sixteen or seventeen years.

HJALMAR. Is it so long?

GREGERS. It is indeed. And how is the world treating you? You look well. You have almost become corpulent!

HJALMAR. Well, I should hardly call it corpulent; but probably I look more of a man than I did then.

GREGERS. That you do; there is certainly more of your outer man.

HJALMAR (*sadly*). But the inner man, Gregers! Believe me, there is a vast difference there. You know what a disastrous blow has fallen on me and mine, since we two last met.

GREGERS (*lowering his voice*). How is your father getting on now?

HJALMAR. My dear fellow, don't let us talk about it. My poor unfortunate father lives at home with me, of course. He has not another creature in the world to cling to. But you can understand what torture it is to me to speak about it. Tell me, rather, how you have been getting on up there at the works.

GREGERS. It has been splendidly lonely. I have had a fine opportunity to ruminate over all sorts of things. Come here, let us make ourselves more comfortable. (*He sits down in an armchair by the fire and pushes* HJALMAR *into another beside him.*)

HJALMAR (*with feeling*). Anyway, Gregers, I am grateful to you for asking me here; it shows that you no longer bear me any grudge.

GREGERS (*astonished*). What should make you think I had any grudge against you?

HJALMAR. Just at first you certainly had.

GREGERS. When?

HJALMAR. After that miserable affair happened. And it was perfectly natural that you should, seeing that your own father was within a hair's breadth of being drawn into this—this terrible business.

GREGERS. Was that any reason for my bearing you a grudge? Who put that idea into your head?

HJALMAR. I know you did, Gregers; your father himself told me so.

GREGERS (*with a start*). My father! Did he, indeed? Ah!—And so that's why you never let me hear from you—not a single word?

HJALMAR. Yes.

GREGERS. Not even when you went and turned yourself into a photographer?

HJALMAR. Your father said I had better not write to you about anything at all.

GREGERS (*looking straight in front of him*). Well, perhaps he was right. But tell me now, Hjalmar, are you tolerably content with your present position?

HJALMAR (*with a slight sigh*). Oh yes, oh yes; I may say so, certainly. It was a bit difficult for me at first, as you can understand. It was such an entirely new life to take up. But then the old life could never have been the same any more. My father's hopeless disaster—the shame and disgrace, Gregers—

GREGERS (*feelingly*). Yes, yes—of course, of course.

HJALMAR. It was impossible to think of going on with my studies; we hadn't a shilling left—worse than that, there were debts, most of them owed to your father, I believe—

GREGERS. Hm!—

HJALMAR. So that it seemed to me the best thing was to drop the old life and all its associations, once and for all. It was chiefly due to your father's advice that I did so; and as he was so kind in helping me—

GREGERS. My father was?

HJALMAR. Surely you know he was? Where do you suppose I could find the money to learn photography and set myself up in a studio? That costs a bit, I can tell you.

GREGERS. And did my father pay for all this?

HJALMAR. Yes, my dear fellow, didn't you know that? I understood that he had written to you about it.

GREGERS. He never said a word about its being his doing. He must have forgotten. We have never written anything but business letters to each other. So it was really my father—!

HJALMAR. Yes, that it was, indeed. He has never wanted anyone to know anything about it, but it was he. And it was thanks to him, too, that I was able to marry. But perhaps that is news to you too?

GREGERS. I knew nothing whatever about it. (*Takes him by the arm.*) I can't tell you, my dear Hjalmar, how glad all this makes me—and how it pains me at the same time. I may have been unjust to my father after all, in some things. It shows at any rate that he has a heart. There is evidence of a conscience about it—

HJALMAR. Of a conscience—?

GREGERS. Well, call it what you like. I can't tell you how glad I am to hear this about my father.—And so you are a married man, Hjalmar. It will be a long time before I shall be able to say that of myself. Well, I hope you are happy in your marriage.

HJALMAR. Very happy. I have as pretty and as capable a wife as a man could wish, and she is by no means without education either.

GREGERS (*slightly surprised*). I should hope not!

HJALMAR. Well, life is an education, you see. Her daily companionship with me—and we see a few clever people now and then. I can assure you, you would hardly know it was the same Gina.

GREGERS. Gina?

HJALMAR. Yes, don't you remember her name was Gina?

GREGERS. What Gina? I don't know—

HJALMAR. Have you forgotten that she had a place in this house once?

GREGERS (*glancing at him*). Is it Gina Hansen?

HJALMAR. Of course it is Gina Hansen.

GREGERS. Who kept house for us that last year when my mother was ill?

HJALMAR. Certainly. But I thought, my dear fellow, that your father had written to you about my marriage.

GREGERS (*rising*). Yes, he did; but not that it was—. (*Walks up and down.*) Yes, wait a bit. I expect he did, now that I think of it. My father always writes me such brief letters. (*Sits down on the arm of* HJALMAR's *chair.*) Tell me, Hjalmar—it's curious—how did you come to make Gina's —your wife's acquaintance?

HJALMAR. It was quite simple. Gina was not here any longer. Everything was upside down in the house then with your mother's illness; Gina could not put up with it, so she took herself off. That was the year before your mother died—or I daresay it was the same year.

GREGERS. It was the same year. I was up at the works then. And after that?

HJALMAR. Well, Gina went home to her mother, a very active and hard-working woman, who kept a small restaurant. And she had a room to let, a very nice, comfortable room—

GREGERS. And you were fortunate enough to get it, I suppose?

HJALMAR. Yes, and in fact it was your father who put the idea into my head. And that, you see, was the way I came to know Gina.

GREGERS. And it ended in your falling in love?

HJALMAR. Yes. Young people don't take long to fall in love, you know.

GREGERS (*rises again and walks about*). Tell me, was it when you were engaged that my father induced you—I mean, was it then that you began to think of taking up photography?

HJALMAR. Certainly. I was so anxious to get some settled occupation, and both your father and I thought photography offered the best chances. And Gina thought so too. Yes, and there was another reason, I must tell you; it turned out that, fortunately, Gina had taken some lessons in retouching photography.

GREGERS. It was extraordinarily lucky altogether.

HJALMAR (*in a pleased voice as he rises*). Yes, wasn't it! Don't you think everything happened wonderfully luckily for me?

GREGERS. I do, indeed. It looks as if my father had been a sort of providence to you.

HJALMAR (*heartily*). He did not forsake his old friend's son in the day of trouble. He has a heart, you see.

MRS. SÖRBY (*coming in on the elder* WERLE's *arm*). Don't be obstinate, dear Mr. Werle. You must not stay in there any longer staring at all those lights. It is bad for your eyes.

WERLE (*slips his arm out of hers and passes his hand over his eyes*). Well, I really believe you are right.

MRS. SÖRBY (*to the guests, who are in the other room*). If anyone would like a glass of punch, he must come in here and get it.

THE FAT GUEST (*coming up to her*). Is it really true that you are determined to deprive us of the sacred right of smoking?

MRS. SÖRBY. Yes, it's forbidden in here, in Mr. Werle's sanctum.

THE THIN-HAIRED GUEST. When did you enact this cruel law about tobacco, Mrs. Sörby?

MRS. SÖRBY. After our last dinner, when certain persons allowed themselves to overstep the mark altogether.

THE THIN-HAIRED GUEST. Mayn't we overstep it just a wee bit?—not the least bit?

MRS. SÖRBY. Not the least bit in any direction, Mr. Balle.

(*Most of the* GUESTS *have come in by this time. The* SERVANTS *hand round the punch.*)

WERLE (*to* HJALMAR, *who is standing apart by a table*). What are you looking at there, Ekdal?

HJALMAR. I was just looking at an album, Mr. Werle.

THE THIN-HAIRED GUEST (*who is wandering about the room*). Ah, photographs! They must interest you, of course.

THE FAT GUEST (*who has settled himself in an armchair*). Haven't you brought any of your own with you?

HJALMAR. No, I haven't.

THE FAT GUEST. You should have; it's an excellent thing for the digestion to sit and look at pictures.

THE THIN-HAIRED GUEST. And it contributes to the general entertainment, you know.

THE SHORT-SIGHTED GUEST. And all contributions are thankfully received.

MRS. SÖRBY. They think that when one is asked out to dinner one ought to do something to earn it, Mr. Ekdal.

THE FAT GUEST. Which is a real pleasure when one gets a good dinner for it.

THE THIN-HAIRED GUEST. And when it is a case of a struggle for existence, then—

MRS. SÖRBY. You are right there! (*They go on laughing and joking.*)

GREGERS (*aside, to* HJALMAR). You must join in, Hjalmar.

HJALMAR (*wincing*). How on earth am I to join in?

THE FAT GUEST. Don't you think, Mr. Werle, that Tokay may be considered a comparatively wholesome drink?

WERLE (*standing by the fire*). I can vouch for the Tokay you had today, anyway; it is of one of the very finest years. But I have no doubt you noticed that.

THE FAT GUEST. Yes, it had a wonderfully delicate flavour.

HJALMAR (*hesitatingly*). Is there a difference between the years then?

THE FAT GUEST (*laughing*). Well, that's good!

WERLE (*with a smile*). It's evidently waste of money to give him a fine wine.

THE THIN-HAIRED GUEST. Tokay grapes are like photographs, Mr. Ekdal; they need sunshine. Isn't that so?

HJALMAR. Yes, the light is a great point, certainly.

MRS. SÖRBY. Then it is just the same with all you gentlemen in official positions; you all like to bask in the sunshine of Court favour.

THE THIN-HAIRED GUEST. Come, come!—that's a very ancient joke!

THE SHORT-SIGHTED GUEST.   Mrs. Sörby is coming out!

THE FAT GUEST.   And at our expense. (*Wags his finger.*) Madam Bertha! Madam Bertha!

MRS. SÖRBY.   Another thing that is true of you, too, is that different years' vintages may differ vastly. The old vintages are the best.

THE SHORT-SIGHTED GUEST.   Do you reckon me among the old ones?

MRS. SORBY.   Far from it.

THE THIN-HAIRED GUEST.   Listen to that! But what about me, dear Mrs. Sörby?

THE FAT GUEST.   Yes, and me! What vintage do you consider us?

MRS. SÖRBY.   Very sweet years, both of you! (*She puts a glass of punch to her lips; the* GUESTS *continue laughing and joking with her.*)

WERLE.   Mrs. Sörby can always get neatly out of a difficult position, if she likes. Don't put your glasses down; Pettersen, fill them up!—Gregers, come and have a glass with me. (GREGERS *does not move.*) Won't you join us, Ekdal? I had no opportunity of drinking with you at dinner.

(GRAABERG, *the bookkeeper, peeps into the room through the private door.*)

GRAABERG.   I beg your pardon, sir, but I can't get out.

WERLE.   Have you got locked in again?

GRAABERG.   Yes, and Flagstad has gone off with the keys.

WERLE.   All right, come out this way.

GRAABERG.   But I have someone with me—

WERLE.   Come along, come along, both of you. Don't mind us.

(GRAABERG *and old* EKDAL *come out of the office.* WERLE *gives an involuntary exclamation of disgust; the laughing and joking stops suddenly.* HJALMAR *starts at the sight of his father, puts down his glass and turns towards the fireplace.*)

EKDAL (*keeping his eyes on the ground and bowing awkwardly from side to side as he goes out, mumbling*).   Excuse me! Come the wrong way—door's locked—door's locked—Excuse me!

[*Exit at the back, with* GRAABERG.

WERLE (*between his teeth*).   Confound that Graaberg!

GREGERS (*with mouth hanging open and eyes staring, to* HJALMAR).   Surely that was never—!

THE FAT GUEST.   What is it? Who was that?

GREGERS.   Nothing; only the bookkeeper and another man.

THE THIN-HAIRED GUEST (*to* HJALMAR).   Was he a friend of yours?

HJALMAR.   I don't know—I didn't notice—

THE FAT GUEST (*rising*).   What the deuce is all this about? (*He joins some of the others, who are talking below their breath.*)

MRS. SÖRBY (*whispers to the* SERVANT).   Give him something to take away with him—something good.

PETTERSEN (*nodding*).   I will.   [*Exit.*

GREGERS (*in a low and shaking voice, to* HJALMAR).   So it was really he?

HJALMAR.   Yes.

GREGERS. And yet you stood there and said you didn't know him!

HJALMAR (*in a loud whisper*). How could I—

GREGERS. Acknowledge your own father?

HJALMAR (*bitterly*). If you were in my place, you would—

(*The* GUESTS, *who have been talking in low tones, now raise their voices with an obvious effort.*)

THE THIN-HAIRED GUEST (*coming up genially to* HJALMAR *and* GREGERS). Well, I suppose you two are talking over old times at College, eh? Won't you smoke, Mr. Ekdal? Shall I give you a light? Ah, I forgot, we mustn't smoke.

HJALMAR. Thank you, I don't care to.

THE FAT GUEST. Can't you recite some charming little poem to us, Mr. Ekdal? You used to have a great talent for that.

HJALMAR. I am sorry I cannot remember anything.

THE FAT GUEST. What a pity. Well, what shall we do, Balle? (*The two* GUESTS *go together into the other room.*)

HJALMAR (*sadly*). Gregers, I must go away. When Fate has dealt a man such a blow as it has done to me, you know—. Say good-night to your father from me.

GREGERS. Yes, yes. Are you going straight home?

HJALMAR. Yes. Why?

GREGERS. Well, perhaps I may come along and see you presently.

HJALMAR. No, you mustn't do that. Don't come to my house. Mine is a sad home, Gregers—especially after a splendid entertainment like this. We can always find some place in the town to meet.

MRS. SÖRBY (*coming up to them, and speaking low*). Are you going, Mr. Ekdal?

HJALMAR. Yes.

MRS. SÖRBY. Remember me to Gina.

HJALMAR. Thank you.

MRS. SÖRBY. And tell her I shall be up to see her some day soon.

HJALMAR. Yes, thanks. (*To* GREGERS.) Stay here. I will slip out unobserved. (*He goes out through the other room.*)

MRS. SÖRBY (*to the* SERVANT *who has come back*). Well, did you give the old man something to take with him?

PETTERSEN. Yes, ma'am; I gave him a bottle of brandy.

MRS. SÖRBY. Oh, you might have found something better than that to give him.

PETTERSEN. No, indeed, ma'am. Brandy is what he likes best, I know.

THE FAT GUEST (*standing in the doorway with a piece of music in his hand*). Shall we play a duet, Mrs. Sörby?

MRS. SÖRBY. Certainly.

THE GUESTS. Bravo! Bravo! (*They and all the* GUESTS *go out of the room.* GREGERS *remains standing by the fire. His father is looking for something on the writing-table and seems anxious for* GREGERS *to go; as* GREGERS *does not move,* WERLE *goes towards the door.*)

GREGERS. Father, will you wait a moment?

WERLE (*stopping*). What is it?

GREGERS. I want a word with you.

WERLE. Can't it wait till we are alone?

GREGERS. No, it can't. Perhaps we shall never find ourselves alone.

WERLE (*coming nearer him*). What do you mean by that?

(*During the following conversation the sound of the piano is heard faintly from the other room.*)

GREGERS. How could you let that family come so miserably to grief?

WERLE. You mean the Ekdals, I presume.

GREGERS. Yes, I mean the Ekdals. Lieutenant Ekdal and you were once so intimate.

WERLE. A great deal too intimate, unfortunately, and I have been paying for it these many years. It is him I have to thank for the fact that my good name and reputation have suffered to some extent too.

GREGERS (*in a low voice*). Was he really the only one guilty?

WERLE. Who else, if you please!

GREGERS. He and you were in partnership over that big purchase of timber—

WERLE. But you know that it was Ekdal who made the map of the ground—that misleading map. He was responsible for the illegal felling of timber on Government property. In fact, he was responsible for the whole business. I had no knowledge of what Lieutenant Ekdal was undertaking.

GREGERS. Lieutenant Ekdal seems to have had no knowledge himself of what he was undertaking.

WERLE. Maybe. But the fact remains that he was found guilty and I was acquitted.

GREGERS. Yes, I am quite aware there were no proofs.

WERLE. An acquittal is an acquittal. Why are you raking up these horrible old stories, which have whitened my hair before its time? Is this what your mind has been brooding upon up there all these years? I can assure you, Gregors, that here in town the whole story has been forgotten long ago, as far as I am concerned.

GREGERS. But what about that wretched family?

WERLE. What could you have expected me to do for them? When Ekdal regained his freedom he was a broken man, absolutely past help. There are some men who go under entirely if Fate hits them ever so little, and never come to the surface again. Believe me, Gregers, I could have done no more than I have, without exposing myself to all sorts of suspicion and gossip—

GREGERS. Suspicion—? Quite so.

WERLE. I got Ekdal copying to do at the office, and I pay him a great deal more for his work than it is worth.

GREGERS (*without looking at him*). I have no doubt of that.

WERLE. You smile? Perhaps you don't believe it is true? I am quite aware it doesn't appear in my accounts; I never enter such payments as that.

GREGERS (*with a cold smile*). I quite agree that there are certain expenses it is better not to enter in one's accounts.

WERLE (*with a start*). What do you mean?

GREGERS (*in a more confident tone*). Have you entered in your accounts what it cost you to have Hjalmar Ekdal taught photography?

WERLE. I? Why should I have entered that?

GREGERS. I know now that it was you who paid for it. And I know, too, that it was you who made it possible for him to settle down as he has done.

WERLE. And, after all that, you say I have done nothing for the Ekdals! I can assure you that family has caused me enough expense, in all conscience.

GREGERS. Have you entered any one item of it in your accounts?

WERLE. Why do you ask that?

GREGERS. I have my reasons. Tell me this—didn't your great solicitude for your old friend's son begin just at the time he was contemplating getting married?

WERLE. Good Lord!—after all these years, how can I—?

GREGERS. You wrote to me at the time—a business letter, naturally—and in a postscript, in just one or two words, you told me Hjalmar Ekdal had married a Miss Hansen.

WERLE. Well, that was true; that was her name.

GREGERS. But you never mentioned the fact that this Miss Hansen was Gina Hansen, our former housekeeper.

WERLE (*laughs ironically, but in a constrained manner*). No, I didn't suppose you were so specially interested in our former housekeeper.

GREGERS. Nor was I. But (*lowering his voice*) there was someone else in this house who *was* specially interested in her.

WERLE. What do you mean? (*In an angry voice.*) You don't mean that you refer to me?

GREGERS (*in a low voice, but firmly*). Yes, I refer to you.

WERLE. And you dare—! You have the audacity to—! And as for this ungrateful photographer fellow—how dare he presume to come here and make such accusations!

GREGERS. Hjalmar has never said a single word of the kind. I don't believe that he has even a suspicion of anything of the sort.

WERLE. Then where have you got it from? Who could have told you such a thing?

GREGERS. My poor unhappy mother told me, the last time I saw her.

WERLE. Your mother! I might have thought as much! She and you were always together in everything. It was she from the very first who drew you apart from me.

GREGERS. No, it was the suffering and humiliation she had to undergo, till at last it broke her down and drove her to such a miserable end.

WERLE. She had not the least suffering or humiliation to undergo—not more than many others, anyway! But there is no dealing with sickly and hysterical folk. I have good reason to know that. And so you have been brooding over such a suspicion as this!—you have been raking up all sorts of ancient rumours and slanders about your own father!—Let me tell you, Gregers, I really think at your age you might find something more useful to do.

GREGERS. Yes, I think it is quite time I did.

WERLE. And perhaps, if you did, you would be easier in your mind than you appear to be at present. What possible point is there in your drudging away at the works, year in and year out, like the merest clerk, and refusing to accept a shilling more than the ordinary wages? It is simply folly on your part.

GREGERS. Ah, if only I were as certain of that as you are!

WERLE. I think I understand. You want to be independent, not to be under the slightest obligation to me. Well, now there happens to be an opportunity for you to become independent, to be your own master entirely.

GREGERS. Indeed? and what may that be?

WERLE. When I wrote to you that I had urgent reasons for asking you to come to town at once—well—

GREGERS. Well, what is it exactly that you want? I have been waiting all day for you to tell me.

WERLE. I propose to offer you a partnership in the firm.

GREGERS. I!—a partner in your firm?

WERLE. Yes. It need not necessitate our always being together. You might manage the business here in town, and I would go up to the works.

GREGERS. You?

WERLE. Yes. You see, I am no longer as fit for my work as I used to be. I am obliged to be careful of my eyes, Gregers; they have begun to get a bit weak.

GREGERS. They were always that.

WERLE. Not as weak as they are now. And, besides that, circumstances might make it desirable for me to live up there, at any rate for a while.

GREGERS. Such an idea has never entered into my mind.

WERLE. Listen, Gregers; we seem to stand apart from each other in very many ways, but after all we are father and son. It seems to me we ought to be able to come to some kind of an understanding with one another.

GREGERS. To outward appearance, I suppose you mean?

WERLE. Well, at any rate that would be something. Think over it, Gregers. Doesn't it appear to you as a possibility? Eh?

GREGERS (looking at him coldly). There is something at the bottom of all this.

WERLE. What do you mean?

GREGERS. You probably intend to make use of me in some way.

WERLE. Two people as closely connected as we are can always be of use to one another.

GREGERS. Possibly.

WERLE. I want you to stay at home with me for a bit. I am a lonely man, Gregers; I have always felt lonely, all my life, and I feel it more than ever now that I am no longer young. I need some companionship.

GREGERS. You have Mrs. Sörby.

WERLE. Yes, that is true; and she has, to tell you the truth, become almost indispensable to me. She is clever and easygoing, and livens up the house—and I need that sort of thing badly.

GREGERS. Quite so; you seem to me to have just what you want.

WERLE. Yes, but I am afraid it can't last. Under such circumstances a woman is easily put into a false position in the eyes of the world. Indeed, one might almost say that the man is not much safer.

GREGERS. Oh, when a man gives such good dinners as you do, he can take considerable liberties with public opinion.

WERLE. Yes, but what about her, Gregers? I am so afraid she won't put up with it any longer. And even if she did—if out of attachment to me she were to disregard gossip and scandal, and so on—? You have a very strong sense of justice, Gregers; doesn't it seem to you that—

GREGERS (*interrupting him*). Tell me this, without beating about the bush; are you thinking of marrying her?

WERLE. And if I were, what then?

GREGERS. Exactly. What then?

WERLE. Would it be a thing you would find it impossible to countenance?

GREGERS. Not in the least. Not by any means.

WERLE. Well, I was not sure whether perhaps, out of respect for your mother's memory, you—

GREGERS. I am not sentimental.

WERLE. Well, whether you are or not, you have at any rate lifted a heavy weight off my mind. It is an immense pleasure to me that I can count on your sympathy in this matter.

GREGERS (*looking intently at him*). Now I understand how it is you want to make use of me.

WERLE. Make use of you? What an expression!

GREGERS. Oh, don't let us be so nice in our choice of words—at any rate when we are alone. (*With a short laugh.*) I see! This was the reason why it was absolutely necessary for me to come to town—to help you to make a pretence of family life here for Mrs. Sörby's edification!—a touching tableau, father and son! That would be something new.

WERLE. How dare you take that tone with me!

GREGERS. When was there any family life here? Never, as long as I can remember. But now, if you please, a little of that sort of thing is desirable. It would undeniably have a splendid effect if it could get about that the son has hastened home, on the wings of filial piety, to attend his old father's wedding. What becomes then of all the rumours of what his poor dead mother had suffered and endured? They are absolutely silenced; her son's action would do that.

WERLE. Gregers—I don't believe there is anyone living towards whom you feel as bitterly as you do to me.

GREGERS (*in a low voice*). I have seen you at too close quarters.

WERLE. You have seen me through your mother's eyes. (*Lowering his voice a little.*) But you ought to remember that her eyes were—were—clouded now and then.

GREGERS (*trembling*). I understand what you mean. But who is to blame for my mother's unfortunate weakness? You, and all your—! The last of them was this woman that was foisted upon Hjalmar Ekdal when you were tired of her. Faugh!

WERLE (*shrugging his shoulders*). Just the way your mother used to talk.

GREGERS (*without paying any attention to him*). And there he is now, like a big unsuspecting child, in the middle of all this deceit; living under the same roof with a woman like that, without the slightest idea that what he calls his home is built on a lie. (*Taking a step nearer his father.*) When I look back on all you have done, it is like looking at a battle-field strewn on every side with ruined lives.

WERLE. I am beginning to think the gulf between us two is too wide to be bridged.

GREGERS (*controls himself and bows*). I agree with you; and therefore I will take my hat and go.

WERLE. Go? Out of the house?

GREGERS. Yes, I see at last some object to live for.

WERLE. What may that be?

GREGERS. You would only laugh, if I told you.

WERLE. A lonely man doesn't laugh so readily, Gregers.

GREGERS (*pointing to the back of the room*). Look, father—Mrs. Sörby is playing blind man's buff with your guests. Good-night, and good-bye. (*He goes out. The* GUESTS *are heard merrily laughing as they come into the other room.*)

WERLE (*muttering scornfully after* GREGERS). Ha! Ha! Poor chap—and he says he is not sentimental!

ACT II

(SCENE.—HJALMAR EKDAL'S *studio, a fairly large attic room. On the right, a sloping roof with large glass windows, half covered by a blue curtain. The door leading into the room is in the right-hand corner, and further forward on the same side is a door leading to a sitting-room. In the left-hand wall are two doors, with a stove between them. In the back wall are wide double doors, arranged so as to slide back on either side.*)

The studio is simply but comfortably furnished. Between the doors on the right, near the wall, stands a sofa with a table and some chairs; on the table a shaded lamp is lit. An old armchair is drawn up by the stove. Photographic apparatus and instruments are scattered here and there about the room. Against the back wall, to the left of the double doors, is a bookcase, containing some books, boxes, bottles of chemicals, and a variety of instruments and tools. On the table are lying photographs, paintbrushes, paper, and so forth. GINA EKDAL *is sitting on a chair by the table, sewing.* HEDVIG *is on the sofa reading a book, with her thumbs in her ears and her hands shading her eyes.*)

GINA (*who has glanced several times at* HEDVIG *with restrained anxiety, calls to her*). Hedvig! (HEDVIG *does not hear her.*)

GINA (*louder*). Hedvig!

HEDVIG (*puts her hands down and looks up*). Yes, mother?

GINA. Hedvig, you must be good and not sit there reading any longer.

HEDVIG. Mayn't I read a little more, mother? Just a little?

GINA. No, no, you must put your book away. Your father doesn't like it; he don't ever read in the evening himself.

HEDVIG (*shutting her book*). No, father doesn't care so much about reading.

GINA (*puts down her sewing and takes up a pencil and a little note-book*). Do you remember how much we paid for the butter to-day?

HEDVIG. One and ninepence.

GINA. That's right. (*Writes it down.*) It's frightful, the amount of butter we get through in this house. And then there was the smoked sausage and the cheese—let me see—(*writes*)—and then there was the ham—(*adds up*)—there, that lot alone comes to—

HEDVIG. And then there's the beer.

GINA. Yes, of course. (*Puts it down.*) It soon mounts up, but it can't be helped.

HEDVIG. But then you and I didn't need anything hot for dinner, as father was out.

GINA. No, that was lucky. And, what's more, I have taken eight and sixpence for photographs.

HEDVIG. As much as that!

GINA. Yes, eight and sixpence exactly.

(*Silence.* GINA *resumes her sewing.* HEDVIG *takes a piece of paper and a pencil and begins drawing, shading her eyes with her left hand.*)

HEDVIG. Isn't it funny to think of father at a big dinner-party at Mr. Werle's?

GINA. He is not, strictly speaking, Mr. Werle's guest, it was the son who invited him. (*After a pause.*) We have nothing to do with Mr. Werle.

HEDVIG. I wish most awfully he would come home. He promised to ask Mrs. Sörby for something nice to bring back to me.

GINA. Ah, there's plenty of good things going in that house, I can tell you.

HEDVIG (*resuming her drawing*). And I believe I am a bit hungry too. (*Old* EKDAL *comes in, a roll of papers under his arm and a parcel sticking out of his pocket.*)

GINA. How late you are to-night, grandfather—

EKDAL. They had locked up the office. I had to wait for Graaberg; and then I was obliged to go through—hm!

HEDVIG. Did they give you some more copying, grandfather?

EKDAL. All this lot. Just look!

GINA. That's splendid.

HEDVIG. And you have got a parcel in your pocket, too.

EKDAL. Have I? Oh, that's nothing, that's nothing. (*Puts down his stick in a corner of the room.*) This will keep me busy for a long time, Gina. (*Pulls one of the sliding doors at the back a little open.*) Hush! (*He looks in through the door for a moment and then shuts it again carefully.*) Ha, ha! They are all asleep together in there. And she has gone into the basket of her own accord. Ha, ha!

HEDVIG. Are you quite sure she isn't cold in the basket, grandfather?

EKDAL. What an idea! Cold? In all that straw? (*Goes to the farther door on the left.*) Are there matches here?

GINA. There's some on the chest of drawers. (EKDAL *goes into his room.*)

HEDVIG. Isn't it nice that grandfather has got all this fresh copying to do!

GINA. Yes, poor old grandfather; he will be able to make a little pocket-money.

HEDVIG. And won't be able to sit all the morning at that horrid restaurant of Mrs. Eriksen's over there.

GINA. Yes, that's another thing.

HEDVIG (*after a short pause*). Do you think they are still at dinner?

GINA. Goodness knows. Very likely they are.

HEDVIG. Just think what a lovely dinner father must be having. I know he will be in such a good temper when he comes home. Don't you think so, mother?

GINA. Yes, but just think how nice it would be if we could tell him we had let the room.

HEDVIG. We don't need that to-night.

GINA. Oh, every little helps. And the room is standing empty.

HEDVIG. I mean that we don't need to be able to tell him that to-night. He will be in good spirits anyway. We shall be all the better of the news about the room for another time.

GINA (*looking at her*). Do you like having some good news to tell your father when he comes home of an evening?

HEDVIG. Yes, because things seem to go pleasanter then.

GINA (*thoughtfully*). There's something in that, certainly.

(*Old* EKDAL *comes in again, and is going out by the nearer door on the left.*)

GINA (*turning in her chair*). Do you want something in the kitchen, grandfather?

EKDAL. Yes, I do. Don't get up. [*Exit.*

GINA. I hope he is not poking the fire, in there. (*After a short pause.*) Hedvig, do see what he is up to.

(EKDAL *returns with a little jug of hot water.*)

HEDVIG. Have you been getting some hot water, grandfather?

EKDAL. Yes, I have. I want it for something—I have got some writing to do, and my ink is all dried up as thick as porridge—hm!

GINA. But you ought to have your supper first. It is all laid in there.

EKDAL. I can't bother about supper, Gina. I'm dreadfully busy, I tell you. I won't have anyone coming into my room, not anyone—hm! (*Goes into his room.* GINA *and* HEDVIG *exchange glances.*)

GINA (*in a low voice*). Can you imagine where he has got the money from?

HEDVIG. I expect he has got it from Graaberg.

GINA. Not a bit of it. Graaberg always sends his pay to me.

HEDVIG. Then he must have got a bottle on credit somewhere.

GINA. Poor grandfather, no one would give him credit.

(*Enter* HJALMAR EKDAL, *wearing an overcoat and a grey felt hat.*)

GINA (*throws down her sewing and gets up*). Back already, Hjalmar?

HEDVIG (*at the same time, jumping up*). Fancy your coming now, father!

HJALMAR (*taking off his hat*). Oh, most of the guests were leaving.

HEDVIG. So early?

HJALMAR. Yes, it was a dinner-party, you know. (*Begins taking off his coat.*)

GINA. Let me help you.

HEDVIG. And me too. (*They take off his coat, Gina hangs it on the wall.*) Were there many there, father?

HJALMAR. Oh no, not many. We were just twelve or fourteen at table.

GINA. And you had a chat with all of them?

HJALMAR. A little, yes; but Gregers practically monopolised me.

GINA. Is Gregers as ugly as ever?

HJALMAR. Well, he's not particularly handsome. Isn't the old man in yet?

HEDVIG. Yes, grandfather is busy writing.

HJALMAR. Did he say anything?

GINA. No, what about?

HJALMAR. Didn't he say anything about—? I fancied I heard he had been to Graaberg. I will go in and see him for a moment.

GINA. No, no, it's not worth while.

HJALMAR. Why not? Did he say he didn't want me to go in?

GINA. He doesn't want anyone to go in to-night.

HEDVIG (*making signs to her*). Hm—hm!

GINA (*taking no notice*). He came in and fetched himself some hot water.

HJALMAR. Then I suppose he is—?

GINA. Yes, that's it.

HJALMAR. Good heavens—my poor old grey-haired father! Well, anyway, let him have what little pleasure he can. (*Old* EKDAL *comes out of his room wearing a dressing-gown and smoking a pipe.*)

EKDAL. Ah, you are back. I thought I heard your voice.

HJALMAR. I have just come in.

EKDAL. You didn't see me, then?

HJALMAR. No, but they told me you had gone through—and so I thought I would come after you.

EKDAL. Nice of you, Hjalmar—hm! What were all those people?

HJALMAR. Oh, all sorts. Flor was there, and Balle, and Kaspersen, and what's-his-name—I don't remember—all of them men about the Court, you know.

EKDAL (*nodding*). Do you hear that, Gina? All of 'em men about the Court!

GINA. Yes, they are very fine in that house now.

HEDVIG. Did any of them sing, father—or recite?

HJALMAR. No, they only talked nonsense. They wanted me to recite to them, but I wasn't going to do that.

EKDAL. You weren't going to do that, eh?

GINA. I think you might have done that.

HJALMAR. No, I don't think one ought to be at everybody's beck and call. (*Walking up and down.*) Anyway, I am not going to be.

EKDAL. No, no, Hjalmar's not that sort.

HJALMAR. I fail to see why I should be expected to amuse others if I happen to go out for once. Let the others exert themselves a little. These fellows go from one house to another, eating and drinking, every day of their lives. I think they should take the trouble to do something in return for all the excellent meals they get.

GINA. But you didn't tell them that?

HJALMAR (*humming*). Hm—hm—hm; they heard something that astonished them, I can tell you.

EKDAL. And all of 'em men about the Court!

HJALMAR. That didn't save them. (*Casually.*) And then we had a little argument about Tokay.

EKDAL. Tokay, did you say? That's a grand wine, if you like!

HJALMAR. It *can* be a grand wine. But of course, you know, all vintages are not of the same quality; it entirely depends how much sunshine the vines have had.

GINA. There isn't anything you don't know, Hjalmar.

EKDAL. And did they want to argue about that?

HJALMAR. They tried to; but they were informed that it was just the same with Court officials. All years are not equally good in their case either, they were told.

GINA. I don't know how you think of such things!

EKDAL. Ha—ha! They had to put that in their pipes and smoke it?

HJALMAR. We let them have it straight between the eyes.

EKDAL. Do you hear that, Gina? Straight between the eyes!—and men about the Court too!

GINA. Fancy that, straight between the eyes!

HJALMAR. Yes, but I don't want you to talk about it. One doesn't repeat such things as that. The whole thing passed off quite amicably, of course. They were very genial, pleasant fellows. Why should I want to hurt their feelings? Not I.

EKDAL. But straight between the eyes—

HEDVIG (*coaxingly*). How funny it is to see you in dress clothes. You look very nice in dress clothes, father.

HJALMAR. Yes, don't you think so? And this really fits me beautifully. It looks almost as if it had been made for me—a little tight in the armholes, perhaps—help me, Hedvig. (*Takes off the coat.*) I would rather put on my jacket. Where have you put my jacket, Gina?

GINA. Here it is. (*Brings the jacket and helps him on with it.*)

HJALMAR. That's better! Be sure you don't forget to let Molvik have the suit back to-morrow morning.

GINA (*folding it up*). I will see to it.

HJALMAR (*stretching himself*). Ah, that's more comfortable. And I rather fancy a loose, easy coat like this suits my style better. Don't you think so, Hedvig?

HEDVIG. Yes, father.

HJALMAR. Especially if I tie my cravat with flowing ends, like this—what do you think?

HEDVIG. Yes, it goes so well with your beard and your thick curly hair.

HJALMAR. I don't know that I should call it curly; I should think "wavy" was a better word.

HEDVIG. Yes, it has beautiful waves in it.

HJALMAR. That's it—wavy.

HEDVIG (*after a little pause, pulling his coat*). Father!

HJALMAR. Well, what is it?

HEDVIG. You know quite well.

HJALMAR. No, indeed I don't.

HEDVIG (*half laughing and half crying*). Father, you mustn't tease me any longer.

HJALMAR. But what is it?

HEDVIG (*shaking him*). Don't pretend! Out with them, father—the good things you promised to bring home to me.

HJALMAR. There, just fancy my having forgotten all about it!

HEDVIG. No, you are only making fun of me, Father! It's too bad. Where have you hidden it?

HJALMAR. Upon my word, I forgot all about it! But wait a bit, Hedvig, I have got something else for you. (*Rises, and hunts in the pockets of the dress coat.*)

HEDVIG (*jumping and clapping her hands*). Oh, mother! mother!

GINA. You see, if you only give him time—

HJALMAR (*holding out a bit of paper*). Look, here it is.

HEDVIG. That! It is only a piece of paper.

HJALMAR. It is the bill of fare, my dear—the whole bill of fare. Here is "Menu" at the top, that means the bill of fare.

HEDVIG. Is that all you have got?

HJALMAR. I forgot to bring anything else, I tell you. But I can tell you all these good things were a great treat. Sit down at the table now and read the list, and I will describe the taste of all the dishes to you. Look, Hedvig.

HEDVIG (*gulping down her tears*). Thank you. (*She sits down, but does not read it.* GINA *makes signs to her, and* HJALMAR *notices it.*)

HJALMAR (*walking up and down*). It is incredible what the father of a family is expected to be able to think about; and if he forgets the slightest little thing, he is sure to see glum faces at once. Well, one gets accustomed even to that. (*Stands by the stove beside his father.*) Have you taken a peep in there this evening, father?

EKDAL. Of course I have. She has gone into the basket.

HJALMAR. Has she gone into the basket? She is beginning to get accustomed to it, then.

EKDAL. Yes, I told you she would. But, you know, there are some little matters—

HJALMAR. Little improvements, eh?

EKDAL. Yes, but we must see to them.

HJALMAR. Very well, let us talk over these improvements, father. Come and sit on the sofa.

EKDAL. Quite so. But I think I will just attend to my pipe first—it wants cleaning. Hm! (*Goes into his room.*)

GINA (*smiling at* HJALMAR). Clean his pipe!

HJALMAR. Come, come, Gina—let him be. Poor, broken-down old fellow. Yes, these improvements—we had better get them off our hands to-morrow.

GINA. You won't have time to-morrow, Ekdal.

HEDVIG (*interrupting*). Oh yes, he will, mother!

GINA. Remember those prints that have got to be retouched. They have asked for them over and over again.

HJALMAR. Bless my soul, those prints again! I'll finish those off easily enough. Are there any new orders?

GINA. No, worse luck. There are only the two appointments you booked for to-morrow.

HJALMAR. Nothing else? Well, of course, if people won't exert themselves—

GINA. But what am I to do? I am sure I advertise as much as I can.

HJALMAR. Yes, you advertise!—and you see how much good it does. I suppose nobody has been to look at the room either?

GINA. Not yet.

HJALMAR. What else could you expect? If people won't keep their wits about them—. You really must pull yourself together, Gina.

HEDVIG (*coming forward*). Shall I get you your flute, father?

HJALMAR. No, no; I have no room for pleasures in my life. (*Walking about.*) Work, work—I will show you what work means to-morrow, you may be sure of that. I shall go on working as long as my strength holds out—

GINA. My dear Hjalmar, I didn't mean you to take me up that way.

HEDVIG. Wouldn't you like me to bring you a bottle of beer, father?

HJALMAR. Certainly not, I don't want anything. (*Stops suddenly.*) Beer?—did you say beer?

HEDVIG (*briskly*). Yes, father; lovely cool beer.

HJALMAR. Well, if you insist on it, I don't mind if you bring me a bottle.

GINA. Yes, do, Hedvig; then we shall feel cosy.

(HEDVIG *runs towards the kitchen.* HJALMAR, *who is standing by the stove, stops her, looks at her, and draws her towards him.*)

HJALMAR. My little Hedvig!

HEDVIG (*with tears of joy in her eyes*). Dear, kind father!

HJALMAR. No, you mustn't call me that. There was I, sitting at the rich man's table, enjoying myself, sitting there filling myself with all his good things—. I might at least have remembered—!

GINA (*sitting down at the table*). Don't be absurd, Hjalmar.

HJALMAR. It's true. But you mustn't think too much of that. You know, anyway, how much I love you.

HEDVIG (*throwing her arms round him*). And we love you so awfully, father!

HJALMAR. And if sometimes I am unreasonable with you, you will remember—won't you—that I am a man beset by a host of cares. There, there! (*Wipes his eyes.*) No beer at such a moment as this. Give me my flute. (HEDVIG *runs to the bookcase and gets it for him.*) Thank you. That's better. With my flute in my hand, and you two beside me—! (HEDVIG *sits down at the table beside* GINA. HJALMAR *walks up and down, then resolutely begins playing a Bohemian country-dance, but in very slow time and very sentimentally. He soon stops, stretches out his left hand to* GINA *and says in a voice full of emotion.*) No matter if we have to live poorly and frugally, Gina—this is our home; and I will say this, that it is good to be at home again. (*He resumes his playing; shortly afterwards a knock is heard at the door.*)

GINA (*getting up*). Hush, Hjalmar—I think there is some one at the door.

HJALMAR (*laying down his flute*).   Of course!

(GINA *goes and opens the door.*)

GREGERS WERLE (*speaking outside the door*).   I beg your pardon—

GINA (*retreating a little*).   Ah!

GREGERS (*outside*).   Is this where Mr. Ekdal the photographer lives?

GINA.   Yes, it is.

HJALMAR (*going to the door*).   Gregers! Is it you after all? Come in, come in.

GREGERS (*coming in*).   I told you I would come up and see you.

HJALMAR.   But to-night—? Have you left all your guests?

GREGERS.   I have left my guests and my home. Good evening, Mrs. Ekdal. I don't suppose you recognise me?

GINA.   Of course I do; you are not so difficult to recognise, Mr. Werle.

GREGERS.   I suppose not; I am like my mother, and no doubt you remember her a little.

HJALMAR.   Did you say that you had left your home?

GREGERS.   Yes, I have gone to an hotel.

HJALMAR.   Indeed? Well, as you are here, take off your things and sit down.

GREGERS.   Thank you. (*He takes off his coat. He has changed his clothes, and is dressed in a plain grey suit of provincial cut.*)

HJALMAR.   Sit down here on the sofa. Make yourself at home.

(GREGERS *sits on the sofa and* HJALMAR *on the chair by the table.*)

GREGERS (*looking round him*).   So this is where you live, Hjalmar. Do you work here too?

HJALMAR.   This is the studio, as you can see—

GINA.   It is our largest room, and so we prefer sitting in here.

HJALMAR.   We used to live in better quarters, but these have one great advantage, there is such a splendid amount of space—

GINA.   And we have a room on the other side of the passage, which we can let.

GREGERS (*to* HJALMAR).   Ah!—have you any lodgers?

HJALMAR.   No, not yet. It is not so easy, you know; one has to make an effort to get them. (*To* HEDVIG.) What about that beer? (HEDVIG *nods and goes into the kitchen.*)

GREGERS.   Is that your daughter?

HJALMAR.   Yes, that is Hedvig.

GREGERS.   Your only child?

HJALMAR.   Our only child, yes. She is the source of our greatest happiness and—(*lowering his voice*) also of our keenest sorrow.

GREGERS.   What do you mean?

HJALMAR.   She is dangerously threatened with the loss of her sight.

GREGERS.   Going blind!

HJALMAR.   Yes. There are only the first symptoms of it at present, and all may go well for some time yet. But the doctor has warned us. It is inevitable.

GREGERS. What a terrible misfortune! What is the cause of it?

HJALMAR (*sighing*). It is hereditary, apparently.

GREGERS (*starting*). Hereditary?

GINA. Hjalmar's mother had weak eyes too.

HJALMAR. Yes, so my father tells me; I can't remember her, you know.

GREGERS. Poor child! And how does she take it?

HJALMAR. Oh well, you will understand that we have not had the heart to tell her anything about it. She suspects nothing. She is as happy and careless as a bird, singing about the house, and so she is flitting through her life into the blackness that awaits her. (*Despairingly.*) It is terribly hard for me, Gregers.

(HEDVIG *comes in, bringing a tray with beer and glasses, and sets it down on the table.*)

HJALMAR (*stroking her hair*). Thank you, dear, thank you. (HEDVIG *puts her arms round his neck and whispers in his ear.*) No—no bread and butter, thanks—unless perhaps you would take some, Gregers?

GREGERS (*shaking his head*). No, thanks.

HJALMAR (*still speaking in a melancholy tone*). Well, you may as well bring in a little, all the same. If you have a crusty piece, I should prefer it—and be sure to see that there is enough butter on it. (HEDVIG *nods happily and goes into the kitchen again.*)

GREGERS (*who has followed her with his eyes*). She seems well and strong in other respects.

GINA. Yes, thank heaven, she is quite well in every other way.

GREGERS. She looks as if she will be like you when she grows up, Mrs. Ekdal. How old is she now?

GINA. Hedvig is just fourteen; her birthday is the day after to-morrow.

GREGERS. She is tall for her age.

GINA. Yes, she has grown a lot this last year.

GREGERS. These young people growing up make us realise our own age. How long have you been married now?

GINA. We have been married—let me see—just fifteen years.

GREGERS. Can it be so long as that!

GINA (*looks at him watchfully*). It is indeed.

HJALMAR. Yes, that it is. Fifteen years all but a few months. (*Changes the subject.*) They must have seemed long years to you up at the works, Gregers.

GREGERS. They did seem so while I was getting through them; but now, looking back on them, I can scarcely believe it is all that time.

(Old EKDAL *comes in from his room, without his pipe, and wearing his old military cap. He walks a little unsteadily.*)

EKDAL. Now then, Hjalmar, we can sit down and talk over those—hm! What is it—what is it?

HJALMAR (*going towards him*). Father, some one is here—Gregers Werle. I don't know whether you remember him?

EKDAL (*looking at* GREGERS, *who has risen*). Werle? Do you mean the son? What does he want with me?

HJALMAR. Nothing; it is me he has come to see.

EKDAL. Oh, then there is nothing the matter?

HJALMAR. No, of course not.

EKDAL (*swinging his arms*). I don't mind, you know; I am not afraid, but—

GREGERS (*going up to him*). I only want to bring you a greeting from your old hunting-ground, Lieutenant Ekdal.

EKDAL. My hunting-ground?

GREGERS. Yes, from up there round the Höidal works.

EKDAL. Ah, up there. I was well known up there once.

GREGERS. You were a mighty hunter in those days.

EKDAL. Ah, that I was, I believe you. You are looking at my cap. I need ask no one's leave to wear it here indoors. So long as I don't go into the streets with it on—

(HEDVIG *brings in a plate of bread and butter, and puts it on the table.*)

HJALMAR. Sit down, father, and have a glass of beer. Help yourself, Gregers.

(EKDAL *totters over to the sofa, mumbling.* GREGERS *sits down on a chair beside him.* HJALMAR *sits on the other side of* GREGERS. GINA *sits a little way from the table and sews;* HEDVIG *stands beside her* FATHER.)

GREGERS. Do you remember, Lieutenant Ekdal, how Hjalmar and I used to come up and see you in the summer-time and at Christmas?

EKDAL. Did you? No—no—I don't remember that. But I can tell you I was a fine sportsman in those days. I have shot bears, too—nine of 'em, I have shot.

GREGERS (*looking at him sympathetically*). And now you get no more shooting.

EKDAL. Oh, I don't know about that. I get some sport still now and then. Not that sort of sport, of course. In the forests, you know—the forests, the forests—! (*Drinks.*) Are the forests looking fine up there now?

GREGERS. Not so fine as in your day. A lot of them have been cut down.

EKDAL (*lowering his voice, as if afraid*). That's a dangerous thing to do. That brings trouble. The forests avenge themselves.

HJALMAR (*filling his* FATHER's *glass*). Now, father—a little more.

GREGERS. How can a man like you, who were always accustomed to be in the open, live in a stuffy town, boxed in by four walls like this?

EKDAL (*looking at* HJALMAR *with a quiet smile*). Oh, it is not so bad here, not at all so bad.

GREGERS. But think of all you were always accustomed to—the cool, refreshing breezes, the free life in the woods and on the moors, among the beasts and birds—

EKDAL (*smiling*). Hjalmar, shall we show it to him?

HJALMAR (*hastily and with some embarrassment*). No, no, father—not to-night.

GREGERS. What does he want to show me?

HJALMAR. Oh, it is only a sort of—. You can see it some other time.

GREGERS (*continues talking to* EKDAL). What I had in my mind, Lieutenant Ekdal, was that you should come back up to the works with me; I am going back there very soon. You could easily get some copying to do up there too; and here you haven't a single thing to give you pleasure or to amuse you.

EKDAL (*staring at him in amazement*). I haven't a single thing to—!

GREGERS. Well, of course, you have Hjalmar; but then he has his own family ties. But a man like you, who has always felt so strongly the call of a free, unfettered life—

EKDAL (*striking the table*). Hjalmar, he *shall* see it!

HJALMAR. But, father, is it worth while now? It is dark, you know.

EKDAL. Nonsense, there is moonlight. (*Gets up.*) He *shall* see it, I say. Let me pass—and you come and help me, Hjalmar.

HEDVIG. Yes, do, father!

HJALMAR. (*getting up*). Very well.

GREGERS (*to* GINA). What does he want me to see?

GINA. Oh, you mustn't expect to see anything very wonderful.

(EKDAL *and* HJALMAR *have gone to the back of the stage, and each of them pushes back one side of the sliding doors.* HEDVIG *helps the old man;* GREGERS *remains standing by the sofa;* GINA *sits quietly sewing. The open doors disclose a large, irregularly-shaped attic, full of recesses and with two stove-pipes running up through it. Through the little roof-windows the bright moonlight is pouring in upon certain spots in the attic; the rest of it is in deep shadow.*)

EKDAL (*to* GREGERS). Come close and have a look.

GREGERS (*going to him.*) What is there for me to see?

EKDAL. Come and take a good look. Hm!

HJALMAR (*in a slightly constrained tone*). This is all my father's, you know.

GREGERS (*comes to the door and looks into the attic*). You keep poultry then, Lieutenant Ekdal!

EKDAL. I should think we did keep poultry. They are roosting now; but you should just see them in the daytime!

HEDVIG. And we have got a—

EKDAL. Hush! Hush! Don't say anything yet.

GREGERS. You have got pigeons too, I see.

EKDAL. Yes, I shouldn't wonder if we had got pigeons too! They have nesting-boxes up there under the eaves, you see; pigeons like to roost well above ground, you know.

GREGERS. They are not common pigeons, though.

EKDAL. Common pigeons! No, I should think not! We have got

tumblers, and a pair of pouters too. But come and look here! Can you see that hutch over there against the wall?

GREGERS.   Yes, what is it for?

EKDAL.   That's where the rabbits sleep at night.

GREGERS.   What, have you got rabbits too?

EKDAL.   Yes, you bet we have rabbits! He is asking if we have got rabbits, Hjalmar! Hm! But now I will show you the great sight! Now you shall see it! Get out of the way, Hedvig. Just stand here; that's it; now look in there. Don't you see a basket with straw in it?

GREGERS.   Yes. And I see a bird lying in the basket.

EKDAL.   Hm!—a bird!

GREGERS.   Isn't it a duck?

HJALMAR.   But what kind of a duck, should you say?

HEDVIG.   It isn't an ordinary duck.

EKDAL.   Sh!

GREGERS.   It isn't a foreign bird either.

EKDAL.   No, Mr.—Werle, that is no foreign bird, because it is a wild duck.

GREGERS.   No! is it really? A wild duck?

EKDAL.   Yes, that it is. The "bird," as you call it, is a wild duck. That's our wild duck.

HEDVIG.   My wild duck. It belongs to me.

GREGERS.   Is it possible it can live up here in the attic? Does it do well?

EKDAL.   Of course it has a trough of water to splash about in.

HJALMAR.   And gets fresh water every other day.

GINA (*turning to* HJALMAR).   Hjalmar, dear, it is getting icy cold in here, you know.

EKDAL.   Hm! we will shut it up then. We mustn't disturb their night's rest. Catch hold, Hedvig. (HJALMAR *and* HEDVIG *push the doors together.*) Some other time you shall see it properly. (*Sits down in the arm-chair by the stove.*) They are most remarkable birds, wild ducks, I can tell you.

GREGERS.   But how did you manage to capture it?

EKDAL.   I didn't capture it. It is a certain person in the town here, that we have to thank for it.

GREGERS (*with a slight start*).   I suppose that man is not my father, by any chance?

EKDAL.   You have hit it. Your father and no one else. Hm!

HJALMAR.   It is funny you should guess that, Gregers.

GREGERS.   You told me you were indebted to my father for so many different things; so I thought very likely—

GINA.   But we didn't get the duck from Mr. Werle himself—

EKDAL.   It is Haakon Werle we have to thank for it all the same, Gina. (*To* GREGERS.) He was out in a boat, you see, and shot it. But your father's sight isn't good, you know, and it was only wounded.

GREGERS.   I see, it was only slightly hit.

HJALMAR.   Yes, only in two or three places.

HEDVIG.   It was hit in the wing, so it couldn't fly.

GREGERS.   I see; then I suppose it dived down to the bottom?

EKDAL (*sleepily in a thick voice*).   Naturally. Wild duck always do that. They stick down at the bottom—as deep as they can get—bite fast hold of the weed and wrack and all the rubbish that is down there. And so they never come up again.

GREGERS.   But, Lieutenant Ekdal, your wild duck came up again.

EKDAL.   He had an extraordinarily clever dog, your father. And the dog—it dived after it and hauled it up again.

GREGERS (*turning to* HJALMAR).   And then you got it?

HJALMAR.   Not directly. It was brought to your father's house first, but it didn't thrive there; so Pettersen asked leave to kill it—

EKDAL (*half asleep*).   Hm!—Pettersen—yes—old codfish!—

HJALMAR (*lowering his voice*).   That was how we got it, you see. Father knows Pettersen a little, and heard this about the wild duck, and managed to get it handed over to him.

GREGERS.   And now it thrives quite well in the attic there?

HJALMAR.   Yes, perfectly well. It has grown fat. It has been so long in there now that it has forgotten all about its own wild life; and that was all that was necessary.

GREGERS.   You are right there, Hjalmar. Only, never let it see the sky and the water.—But I mustn't stay any longer. I think your father has gone to sleep.

HJALMAR.   Oh, don't go on that account.

GREGERS.   But, by the way—you said you had a room to let, a room you don't use?

HJALMAR.   Yes—why? Do you happen to know any one—?

GREGERS.   Can I have the room?

HJALMAR.   You?

GINA.   What, you, Mr. Werle?

GREGERS.   Can I have the room? If so, I will move in early to-morrow morning.

HJALMAR.   Certainly, by all means—

GINA.   But, Mr. Werle, it really isn't the sort of room to suit you.

HJALMAR.   Gina, how can you say that!

GINA.   Well, it isn't big enough or light enough, and—

GREGERS.   That doesn't matter at all, Mrs. Ekdal.

HJALMAR.   I should call it a very nice room, and not so badly furnished either.

GINA.   But remember the couple that are lodging underneath.

GREGERS.   Who are they?

GINA.   One of them used to be a private tutor—

HJALMAR.   Mr. Molvik—he has taken a degree—

GINA.   And the other is a doctor of the name of Relling.

GREGERS. Relling? I know him a little; he used to practise up at Höidal at one time.

GINA. They are a regular pair of good-for-nothings. They are often out on the spree in the evening, and they come home late at night and not always quite—

GREGERS. I should easily get accustomed to that. I hope I shall settle down like the wild duck.

GINA. Well, I think you ought to sleep over it first, anyway.

GREGERS. You don't seem to like the idea of having me in the house, Mrs. Ekdal.

GINA. Gracious me! what makes you think that?

HJALMAR. I must say it is extremely odd of you, Gina. (*To* GREGERS.) Tell me, do you propose remaining here in town for the present?

GREGERS (*putting on his overcoat*). Yes, now I propose to remain here.

HJALMAR. But not at home with your father? What do you intend to do with yourself?

GREGERS. Ah, if only I knew that, it would be all plain sailing. But when one has had the misfortune to be christened "Gregers"—"Gregers," and "Werle" to follow—did you ever hear anything so hideous?—

HJALMAR. It doesn't sound so to me.

GREGERS (*shuddering*). I should feel inclined to spit on any fellow with a name like that. Once a man has had the misfortune to find himself saddled with the name of Gregers Werle, as I have—

HJALMAR (*laughing*). Ha, ha! Well, but if you weren't Gregers Werle, what would you like to be?

GREGERS. If I could choose, I would rather be a clever dog than anything else.

GINA. A dog!

HEDVIG (*involuntarily*). Oh no!

GREGERS. Yes, an extraordinarily clever dog; the sort of dog that would go down to the bottom after wild duck, when they dive down and bite fast hold of the weed and wrack in the mud.

HJALMAR. I will tell you what it is, Gregers—I don't understand a word of all this.

GREGERS. No, and I daresay the meaning is not very pretty either. Well, then, early to-morrow morning I will move in. (*To* GINA.) I shan't give you any trouble; I do everything for myself. (*To* HJALMAR.) We will finish our chat to-morrow. Good-night, Mrs. Ekdal. (*Nods to* HEDVEG.) Good-night.

GINA. Good-night, Mr. Werle.

HEDVIG. Good-night.

HJALMAR (*who has lit a candle*). Wait a moment, I must give you a light; it is sure to be dark on the stair. (GREGERS *and* HJALMAR *go out by the outer door*.)

GINA (*staring in front of her, with her sewing lying on her lap*). A funny idea, to want to be a dog!

HEDVIG. Do you know, mother—I believe he meant something quite different by that.

GINA. What else could he mean?

HEDVIG. I don't know; but I thought he seemed to mean something quite different from what he said—all the time.

GINA. Do you think so? It certainly was queer.

HJALMAR (*coming back*). The lamp was still lit. (*Puts out the candle and lays it down.*) Now, at last one can get a chance of something to eat. (*Begins to eat the bread and butter.*) Well, you see, Gina—if only you keep your wits about you—

GINA. How do you mean, keep your wits about you?

HJALMAR. Well, anyway we have had a bit of luck, to succeed in letting the room at last. And, besides, to a man like Gregers—a dear old friend.

GINA. Well, I really don't know what to say about it.

HEDVIG. Oh mother, you will see it will be lovely.

HJALMAR. You certainly are very odd. A little while ago you were so bent on letting the room, and now you don't like it.

GINA. Oh, I do, Hjalmar—if only it had been to some one else. What do you suppose his father will say?

HJALMAR. Old Werle? It is no business of his.

GINA. But you may be sure things have gone wrong between them again, as the young man is leaving his father's house. You know the sort of terms those two are on.

HJALMAR. That may be all very true, but—

GINA. And it is quite likely his father may think that you are at the bottom of it all.

HJALMAR. Let him think what he likes! Mr. Werle has done a wonderful lot for me; I am the last to want to deny it. But that is no reason why I should think myself bound to consult him in everything all my life.

GINA. But, Hjalmar dear, it might end in grandfather's suffering for it; he might lose the little bit of money he gets from Graaberg.

HJALMAR. I feel almost inclined to say I wish he might! Don't you suppose it is a humiliating thing for a man like me, to see his grey-haired old father treated like an outcast? But I think that sort of thing is nearly at an end. (*Takes another piece of bread and butter.*) I have a mission in life, and I shall fulfil it!

HEDVIG. Oh yes, father, do!

GINA. Sh! Don't wake him up.

HJALMAR (*lowering his voice*). I *shall* fulfil it, I say. The day will come when—when—. And that is why it is a good thing we got the room let; it puts me in a more independent position. And a man who has a mission in life must be independent of others. (*Stands by his father's chair and speaks with emotion.*) Poor old white-haired father! You may depend on your Hjalmar! He has broad shoulders—strong shoulders, at any rate. Some fine day you shall wake up, and—. (*To GINA.*) Don't you believe it?

GINA (*getting up*). Of course I do; but the first thing is to see about getting him to bed.

HJALMAR. Yes, come along then. (*They lift the old man carefully.*)

ACT III

(SCENE.—HJALMAR EKDAL'S *studio, the following morning. The sun is shining in through the big window in the sloping roof, where the curtain has been drawn back.* HJALMAR *is sitting at the table busy retouching a photograph. Various other portraits are lying in front of him. After a few moments* GINA *comes in by the outer door, in hat and cloak, and carrying a covered basket.*)

HJALMAR. Back already, Gina?

GINA. Yes, I've no time to waste. (*She puts the basket down on a chair and takes her things off.*)

HJALMAR. Did you look in on Gregers?

GINA. Yes, that I did; and a nice sight too! He had made the room in a pretty state as soon as he arrived.

HJALMAR. How?

GINA. He said he wanted to do everything for himself, you know. So he tried to set the stove going; and what must he do but shut the register, so that the whole room was filled with smoke. Ouf!—there was a stink like—

HJALMAR. You don't mean it!

GINA. But that's not the best of it. He wanted to put the fire out then, so he emptied his ewer into the stove, and flooded the whole floor with a filthy mess.

HJALMAR. What a nuisance!

GINA. I have just got the porter's wife to clean up after him, the pig; but the room won't be fit to go into till the afternoon.

HJALMAR. What is he doing with himself in the meantime?

GINA. He said he would go out for a bit.

HJALMAR. I went to see him, too, for a minute, after you went out.

GINA. So he told me. You have asked him to lunch.

HJALMAR. Just for a snack of lunch, you know. The first day he is here —we could hardly do less. You are sure to have something in the house.

GINA. I will go and see what I can find.

HJALMAR. Don't be too scrimpy, though; because I fancy Relling and Molvik are coming up too. I happened to meet Relling on the stair, you see, and so I had to—

GINA. Are we to have those two as well?

HJALMAR. Bless my soul!—a little bit more or less can't make much difference.

(*Old* EKDAL *opens his door and looks in.*)

EKDAL. Look here, Hjalmar— (*Seeing* GINA.) Oh!

GINA.   Do you want something, grandfather?

EKDAL.   No, no—it doesn't matter. Hm! (*Goes into his room again.*)

GINA (*taking up her basket*).   Keep your eye on him, and see he doesn't go out.

HJALMAR.   Yes, yes, I will. Look here, Gina—a little herring salad would be rather nice; I rather fancy Relling and Molvik were making a night of it last night.

GINA.   So long as they don't come before I am ready—

HJALMAR.   They won't do that. Take your time.

GINA.   Very well, and you can get a little work done in the meantime.

HJALMAR.   Don't you see I *am* working? I am working as hard as I can.

GINA.   You will be able to get those off your hands, you see. (*Takes her basket into the kitchen.* HJALMAR *resumes his work on the photographs with evident reluctance.*)

EKDAL (*peeps in, and, after looking round the studio, says in a low voice*).   Have you finished that work?

HJALMAR.   I am working away at these portraits—

EKDAL.   Well, well, it doesn't matter—if you are so busy— Hm! (*Goes in again, but leaves his door open.* HJALMAR *goes on working for a little in silence; then lays down his brush and goes to the door.*)

HJALMAR.   Are you busy, father?

EKDAL (*from within, in an aggrieved voice*).   If you are busy, I'm busy too. Hm!

HJALMAR.   Quite so, quite so. (*Returns to his work. After a few moments* EKDAL *comes out of his room again.*)

EKDAL.   Hm! Look here, Hjalmar, I am not so busy as all that.

HJALMAR.   I thought you were doing your copying.

EKDAL.   Deuce take Graaberg! Can't he wait a day or two? It's not a matter of life and death, I suppose.

HJALMAR.   No; and you are not his slave, anyway.

EKDAL.   And there is that other matter in there—

HJALMAR.   Quite so. Do you want to go in? Shall I open the doors for you?

EKDAL.   I don't think it would be a bad idea.

HJALMAR (*rising*).   And then we shall have got *that* off our hands.

EKDAL.   Just so, yes. It must be ready by to-morrow morning early. We did say to-morrow, didn't we? Eh?

HJALMAR.   Yes, to-morrow.

(HJALMAR *and* EKDAL *each pull back a division of the sliding-door. The morning sun is shining in through the top-lights of the attic; some of the pigeons are flying about, others sitting cooing on the rafters; from time to time the sound of hens cackling is heard from the recesses of the attic.*)

HJALMAR.   There—now you can start, father.

EKDAL (*going in*).   Aren't you coming, too?

HJALMAR. Well, I don't know—I think I—. (*Seeing* GINA *at the kitchen door.*) No, I haven't time; I must work. But we must use our patent arrangement. (*He pulls a cord and lowers a curtain, of which the bottom part is made out of a strip of old sailcloth, while the upper part is a fisherman's net stretched out. When it is down, the floor of the attic is no longer visible.*) That's it. Now I can sit down in peace for a little.

GINA. Is he rummaging about in there again?

HJALMAR. Would you rather he had gone straight to the wine-shop? (*Sitting down.*) Is there anything you want? You look so—

GINA. I only wanted to ask if you thought we could have lunch in here?

HJALMAR. Yes; I suppose we have no sitters coming as early as that?

GINA. No, I don't expect anyone except the engaged couple who want to be taken together.

HJALMAR. Why the devil can't they be taken together some other day!

GINA. It is all right, Hjalmar dear; I arranged to take them in the afternoon, when you are having your nap.

HJALMAR. That's capital! Yes, then, we will have lunch in here.

GINA. Very well, but there is no hurry about laying the lunch; you can have the table for a good while yet.

HJALMAR. Can't you see that I am taking every opportunity that I can to use the table!

GINA. Then you will be free afterwards, you see. (*Goes into the kitchen again. Short pause.*)

EKDAL (*standing in the attic doorway, behind the net*). Hjalmar!

HJALMAR. Well?

EKDAL. I am afraid we shall be obliged to move the water-trough after all.

HJALMAR. Exactly what I have said all along.

EKDAL. Hm—hm—hm! (*Moves away from the door.*)

(HJALMAR *goes on with his work for a little, then glances at the attic, and is just getting up when* HEDVIG *comes in from the kitchen; thereupon he sits down again promptly.*)

HJALMAR. What do you want?

HEDVIG. Only to come in to you, father.

HJALMAR (*after a moment's pause*). You seem to be very inquisitive. Were you sent to watch me?

HEDVIG. Of course not.

HJALMAR. What is your mother doing in there now?

HEDVIG. She's busy making a herring salad. (*Goes up to the table.*) Isn't there any little thing I could help you with, father?

HJALMAR. No, no. It is right that I should be the one to work away at it all—as long as my strength holds out. There is no fear of my wanting help, Hedvig—at any rate so long as my health doesn't give way.

HEDVIG. Oh, father—don't say such horrid things! (*She wanders about the room, then stands in the attic doorway and looks in.*)

HJALMAR. What is he about in there?

HEDVIG.   I fancy he is making a new path to the water-trough.

HJALMAR.   He will never be able to manage that by himself. What a nuisance it is that I am obliged to sit here and—

HEDVIG (*going to him*).   Let me have the brush, father; I can do it, you know.

HJALMAR.   Nonsense, you would only hurt your eyes.

HEDVIG.   Not a bit of it. Give me the brush.

HJALMAR (*getting up*).   Well, certainly it wouldn't take me more than a minute or two.

HEDVIG.   Pooh! What harm can it do me? (*Takes the brush from him.*) Now then. (*Sits down.*) I have got one here as a model, you know.

HJALMAR.   But don't hurt your eyes! Do you hear? I won't be responsible; you must take the responsibility yourself, understand that.

HEDVIG (*going on with the work*). Yes, yes, I will.

HJALMAR. Clever little girl! Just for a minute or two, you understand. (*He stoops under the net and goes into the attic. HEDVIG sits still, working. HJALMAR's voice and his FATHER's are heard discussing something.*)

HJALMAR (*coming to the net*).   Hedvig, just give me the pincers; they are on the shelf. And the chisel. (*Looks back into the attic.*) Now you will see, father. Just let me show you first what I mean. (HEDVIG *has fetched the tools, and gives them to him.*) Thanks. I think it was a good thing I came, you know. (*Goes into the attic. Sounds of carpentering and talking are heard from within. HEDVIG stands looking after him. A moment later a knock is heard at the outer door, but she does not notice it.*)

GREGERS WERLE (*who is bareheaded and without an overcoat, comes in and stands for a moment in the doorway*).   Ahem!

HEDVIG (*turns round and goes to him*).   Oh, good-morning! Won't you come in?

GREGERS.   Thanks. (*Glances towards the attic.*) You seem to have workmen in the house.

HEDVIG.   No, it's only father and grandfather. I will go and tell them.

GREGERS.   No, no, don't do that; I would rather wait a little. (*Sits down on the sofa.*)

HEDVIG.   It's so untidy here— (*Begins to collect the photographs.*)

GREGERS.   Oh, let them be. Are they portraits that want finishing?

HEDVIG.   Yes, just a little job I was helping father with.

GREGERS.   Anyway, don't let me disturb you.

HEDVIG.   Oh, you don't. (*She draws the things to her again and sits down to her work. GREGERS watches her for a time without speaking.*)

GREGERS.   Has the wild duck had a good night?

HEDVIG.   Yes, thanks, I think it had.

GREGERS (*turning towards the attic*).   In the daylight it looks quite a different place from what it did in moonlight.

HEDVIG.   Yes, it has such a different look at different times. In the morning it looks quite different from in the evening, and when it rains you wouldn't think it was the same place as on a fine day.

GREGERS. Ah, have you noticed that?

HEDVIG. You couldn't help noticing it.

GREGERS. Are you fond of being in there with the wild duck, too?

HEDVIG. Yes, when I can—

GREGERS. But I expect you haven't much time for that. I suppose you go to school?

HEDVIG. No, I don't go to school any more. Father is afraid of my hurting my eyes.

GREGERS. I see; I suppose he reads with you himself, then?

HEDVIG. He has promised to read with me, but he hasn't had time so far.

GREGERS. But isn't there anyone else to give you a little help?

HEDVIG. Yes, there is Mr. Molvik, but he isn't always exactly—quite—that is to say—

GREGERS. Not quite sober?

HEDVIG. That's it.

GREGERS. I see; then you have a good deal of time to yourself. And, in there, I suppose, it is like a little world of its own, isn't it?

HEDVIG. Yes, exactly. And there are such lots of wonderful things in there.

GREGERS. Are there?

HEDVIG. Yes, there are great cupboards full of books, and in lots of the books there are pictures.

GREGERS. I see.

HEDVIG. And then there is an old desk with drawers and flaps in it, and a great clock with figures that ought to come out when it strikes. But the clock isn't going any longer.

GREGERS. So time has ceased to exist in there—besides the wild duck.

HEDVIG. Yes. And there is an old paint-box and things—and all the books.

GREGERS. And you like reading the books?

HEDVIG. Yes, when I can manage it. But the most of them are in English, and I can't read that; so then I look at the pictures. There is a great big book called *Harrison's History of London;* it is quite a hundred years old, and there's a tremendous lot of pictures in it. At the beginning there's a picture of Death, with an hour-glass, and a girl. I don't like that. But there are all the other pictures of churches, and castles, and streets, and big ships sailing on the sea.

GREGERS. But, tell me, where did you get all these wonderful things from?

HEDVIG. Oh, an old sea-captain lived here once, and he used to bring them home with him. They called him the Flying Dutchman; it was a funny thing to call him, because he wasn't a Dutchman at all.

GREGERS. Wasn't he?

HEDVIG. No. But one day he never came back, and all these things were left here.

GREGERS. Tell me this—when you are sitting in there looking at the pictures, don't you want to get away out into the big world and see it for yourself?

HEDVIG. Not I! I want to stay at home here always and help father and mother.

GREGERS. To finish photographs?

HEDVIG. No, not only that. What I should like best of all would be to learn to engrave pictures like those in the English books.

GREGERS. Hm! what does your father say to that?

HEDVIG. I don't think father likes it; he is so funny about that. Just fancy, he wants me to learn such absurd things as basket-making and straw-plaiting! I don't see any good in my doing that.

GREGERS. Nor do I.

HEDVIG. But father is right so far, that if I had learnt to make baskets, I could have made the new basket for the wild duck.

GREGERS. Yes, so you could; and it was your business to see it was comfortable, wasn't it?

HEDVIG. Yes, because it is my wild duck.

GREGERS. Of course it is.

HEDVIG. Yes, it's my very own. But I lend it to father and grandfather as long as they like.

GREGERS. I see, but what do they want with it?

HEDVIG. Oh, they look after it, and build places for it, and all that sort of thing.

GREGERS. I see; it is the most important person in there.

HEDVIG. That it is, because it is a real, true wild duck. Poor thing, it hasn't anyone to make friends with; isn't it a pity!

GREGERS. It has no brothers and sisters, as the rabbits have.

HEDVIG. No. The hens have got lots of others there, that they were chickens with; but it has come right away from all its friends, poor thing. It is all so mysterious about the wild duck. It has got no friends—and no one knows where it came from, either.

GREGERS. And then it has been down to the ocean's depths.

HEDVIG (*looks quickly at him, half smiles and asks*). Why do you say "the ocean's depths"?

GREGERS. What else should I say?

HEDVIG. You might have said "the bottom of the sea."

GREGERS. Isn't it just the same if I say "the ocean's depths"?

HEDVIG. It sounds so funny to me to hear anyone else say "the ocean's depths."

GREGERS. Why? Tell me why.

HEDVIG. No, I won't; it's only foolishness.

GREGERS. It isn't. Tell me why you smiled.

HEDVIG. It is because whenever I happen to think all at once—all in a moment—of what is in there, the whole room and all that is in it make me think of "the ocean's depths." But that's all nonsense.

GREGERS. No, don't say that.

HEDVIG. Well, it's nothing but an attic.

GREGERS (*looking earnestly at her*). Are you so sure of that?

HEDVIG (*astonished*). Sure that it's an attic?

GREGERS. Yes; are you so sure of that?

(HEDVIG *is silent and looks at him open-mouthed.* GINA *comes in from the kitchen to lay the table.*)

GREGERS (*rising*). I am afraid I have come too early.

GINA. Oh, well, you have got to be somewhere; and we shall very soon be ready. Clear up the table, Hedvig. (HEDVIG *gathers up the things; she and* GINA *lay the table during the following dialogue.* GREGERS *sits down in the armchair and turns over the pages of an album.*)

GREGERS. I hear you can retouch photos, Mrs. Ekdal.

GINA (*glancing at him*). Mhm! I can.

GREGERS. That must have come in very handy.

GINA. How do you mean?

GREGERS. As Hjalmar has taken to photography, I mean.

HEDVIG. Mother can take photographs too.

GINA. Oh, yes, of course I got taught to do that.

GREGERS. I suppose it is you who run the business, then?

GINA. Well, when Hjalmar hasn't time himself, I—

GREGERS. His old father takes up a great deal of his time, I suppose?

GINA. Yes, and it isn't the sort of work for a man like Hjalmar to go taking rubbishin' portraits all day long.

GREGERS. Quite so; but still, when he had once gone in for the thing—

GINA. I will ask you to understand, Mr. Werle, that Hjalmar is not an ordinary photographer.

GREGERS. Just so, just so; but— (*A shot is fired within the attic.* GREGERS *starts up.*) What's that!

GINA. Bah! now they are at their firing again.

GREGERS. Do they use guns in there too?

HEDVIG. They go out shooting.

GREGERS. What on earth—? (*Goes to the attic door.*) Have you gone out shooting, Hjalmar?

HJALMAR (*inside the net*). Oh, are you there? I didn't know. I was so busy— (*To* HEDVIG.) To think of your not telling us! (*Comes into the studio.*)

GREGERS. Do you go shooting in there in the attic?

HJALMAR (*showing a double-barrelled pistol*). Oh, only with this old thing.

GINA. Yes, you and grandfather will do yourselves a mischief some day with that there gun.

HJALMAR (*angrily*). I think I have mentioned that a firearm of this kind is called a pistol.

GINA. Well, that doesn't make it much better, that I can see.

GREGERS. So you have become a sportsman too, Hjalmar?

HJALMAR.   Oh, we only go after a rabbit or two now and then. It is principally to please my father, you know.

GINA.   Men are funny creatures, they must always have something to bemuse them.

HJALMAR (*irritably*).   Quite so, quite so; men must always have something to amuse them.

GINA.   Well, that's exactly what I said.

HJALMAR.   Well,—ahem! (*To* GREGERS.) It happens very fortunately, you see, that the attic is so situated that no one can hear us shooting. (*Lays down the pistol on the top shelf of the bookcase.*) Don't touch the pistol, Hedvig; one barrel is loaded, remember.

GREGERS (*looking through the net*).   You have got a sporting gun too, I see.

HJALMAR.   That is father's old gun. It won't shoot any longer, there is something gone wrong with the lock. But it is rather fun to have it there all the same; we can take it to pieces now and then and clean it, and grease it, and put it together again. Of course it's my father's toy, really.

HEDVIG (*going to* GREGERS).   Now you can see the wild duck properly.

GREGERS.   I was just looking at it. It seems to me to trail one wing a little.

HJALMAR.   Well, no wonder; it was wounded.

GREGERS.   And it drags one foot a little—isn't that so?

HJALMAR.   Perhaps just a tiny bit.

HEDVIG.   Yes, that was the foot the dog fixed its teeth into.

HJALMAR.   But otherwise it hasn't the slightest blemish; and that is really remarkable when you consider that it has had a charge of shot in its wing and has been between a dog's teeth—

GREGERS (*glancing at* HEDVIG).   And has been down so long in the ocean's depths.

HEDVIG (*with a smile*).   Yes.

GINA (*standing by the table*).   That blessed wild duck! The whole place is turned upside down for it.

HJALMAR.   Ahem!—shall you soon have finished laying the table?

GINA.   Yes, very soon. Come and help me, Hedvig. (*She and* HEDVIG *go into the kitchen.*)

HJALMAR (*in an undertone*).   I think perhaps you had better not stand there watching my father; he doesn't like it. (GREGERS *comes away from the attic door.*) And I had better shut the doors, before the others arrive. Sh! Sh! Get in with you! (*He hoists up the netting and pulls the doors together.*) That contrivance is my own invention. It is really quite an amusement to have things to contrive and to repair when they go wrong. Besides, it is an absolute necessity, you see, because Gina wouldn't like to have rabbits and fowls wandering about the studio.

GREGERS.   Of course not, and I suppose the studio is really your wife's domain?

HJALMAR.   I hand over the ordinary business as much as possible to her, for that enables me to shut myself up in the sitting-room and give my mind to more important matters.

GREGERS. What are they, Hjalmar?

HJALMAR. I wonder you haven't asked that before. But perhaps you haven't heard anyone speak of the invention?

GREGERS. The invention? No.

HJALMAR. Really? You haven't heard of it? Oh well, of course, up there in those outlandish parts—

GREGERS. Then you have made an invention?

HJALMAR. Not exactly made it yet, but I am working hard at it. You can surely understand that when I decided to take up photography, it was not with the idea of merely taking ordinary portraits.

GREGERS. No, that is what your wife was saying to me just now.

HJALMAR. I vowed to myself that, if I devoted my powers to this trade, I would so dignify it, that it should become both an art and a science. And so I decided to make this remarkable invention.

GREGERS. And what is the nature of the invention? What is the idea?

HJALMAR. My dear fellow, you mustn't ask me for details yet. It takes time, you know. And you mustn't suppose it is vanity that impels me. I assure you I don't work for my own sake. No, no; it is the object of my life that is in my thoughts night and day.

GREGERS. What object is that?

HJALMAR. Do you forget that poor old white-haired man?

GREGERS. Your poor father? Yes, but what exactly can you do for him?

HJALMAR. I can revive his dead self-respect by restoring the name of Ekdal to honour and dignity.

GREGERS. So that is the object of your life.

HJALMAR. Yes. I mean to rescue that poor shipwrecked being; for shipwrecked he was, when the storm broke over him. As soon as those horrible investigations were begun, he was no longer himself. That very pistol there—the same that we use to shoot rabbits with—has played its part in the tragedy of the Ekdals.

GREGERS. That pistol! Indeed?

HJALMAR. When the sentence of imprisonment was pronounced, he had his pistol in his hand—

GREGERS. Did he mean to—?

HJALMAR. Yes, but he did not dare. He was a coward; so dazed and so broken in spirit was he by that time. Can you conceive it? He, a soldier, a man who had shot nine bears and was the descendant of two lieutenant-colonels—one after the other, of course—. Can you conceive it, Gregers?

GREGERS. Yes, I can conceive it very well.

HJALMAR. I can't. And I will tell you how the pistol a second time played a part in the history of our house. When they had dressed him in prison clothes and put him under lock and key—that was a terrible time for me, my friend. I kept the blinds down on both my windows. When I peeped out, I saw the sun shining as usual. I could not understand it.

I saw people going along the street, laughing and talking about casual matters. I could not understand that. It seemed to me as if the whole universe must be standing still as if it were eclipsed.

GREGERS. I felt exactly that when my mother died.

HJALMAR. It was at one of those moments that Hjalmar Ekdal pointed the pistol at his own heart.

GREGERS. Then you too meant to—?

HJALMAR. Yes.

GREGERS. But you didn't shoot?

HJALMAR. No. At that critical moment I gained the victory over myself. I went on living. But I can tell you it makes a call upon a man's courage to choose life under such conditions.

GREGERS. Well, that depends how you look at it.

HJALMAR. No, there is no question about it. But it was best so, for now I shall soon have completed my invention; and Relling thinks, and so do I, that my father will be allowed to wear his uniform again. I shall claim that as my only reward.

GREGERS. It is the matter of the uniform, then, that he—

HJALMAR. Yes, that is what he covets and yearns for most of all. You can't imagine how it cuts me to the heart. Every time we keep any little anniversary—such as our wedding-day, or anything of that sort—the old man comes in dressed in the uniform he used to wear in his happier days. But if he hears so much as a knock at the door, he hurries into his room again as fast as his poor old legs will carry him—because, you see, he daren't show himself like that to strangers. It is enough to break a son's heart to see it, I can tell you!

GREGERS. And about when do you suppose the invention will be ready?

HJALMAR. Oh, bless my soul!—you can't expect me to tell you to a day! A man who has the inventive genius can't control it exactly as he wishes. Its working depends in great measure on inspiration—on a momentary suggestion—and it is almost impossible to tell beforehand at what moment it will come.

GREGERS. But I suppose it is making good progress?

HJALMAR. Certainly it is making progress. Not a day passes without my turning it over in my mind. It possesses me entirely. Every afternoon, after I have had my lunch, I lock myself in the sitting-room where I can ruminate in peace. But it is no use trying to hurry me! that can do no good—Relling says so, too.

GREGERS. But don't you think all those arrangements in the attic there, distract you and divert your attention too much?

HJALMAR. Not a bit, not a bit; quite the contrary. You mustn't say that. It is impossible for me to be perpetually poring over the same exhausting train of ideas. I must have something as a secondary occupation, to fill in the blank hours when I am waiting for inspiration. Nothing that I am doing can prevent the flash of inspiration coming when it has to come.

GREGERS.   My dear Hjalmar, I am beginning to think you have something of the wild duck in you.

HJALMAR.   Something of the wild duck? How do you mean?

GREGERS.   You have dived down and bitten yourself fast in the weeds.

HJALMAR.   I suppose you refer to that well-nigh fatal blow that
crippled my father, and me as well?

GREGERS.   Not exactly that. I won't say that you have been wounded,
like the duck; but you have got into a poisonous marsh, Hjalmar; you have
contracted an insidious disease and have dived down to the bottom to die
in the dark.

HJALMAR.   I? Die in the dark? Look here, Gregers, you really must
stop talking such nonsense.

GREGERS.   Make your mind easy, I shall find a way to get you up to
the surface again. I have got an object in life too, now; I discovered it
yesterday.

HJALMAR.   Maybe, but you will have the goodness to leave me out of
it. I can assure you that—apart, of course, from my very natural melancholy—I feel as well as any man could wish to be.

GREGERS.   That very fact is a result of the poison.

HJALMAR.   Now, my dear Gregers, be good enough not to talk any more
nonsense about diseases and poisons. I am not accustomed to conversation
of that sort; in my house no one ever speaks to me about ugly things.

GREGERS.   I can well believe it.

HJALMAR.   Yes, that sort of thing doesn't suit me at all. And there *are*
no marsh poisons, as you call them, here. The photographer's home is a
humble one—that I know; and my means are small. But I am an inventor,
let me tell you, and the breadwinner of a family. That raises me up above
my humble circumstances.—Ah, here they come with the lunch!

(GINA *and* HEDVIG *bring in bottles of beer, a decanter of brandy,
glasses, and so forth. At the same time* RELLING *and* MOLVIK *come in
from the passage. They neither of them have hats or overcoats on;*
MOLVIK *is dressed in black.*)

GINA (*arranging the table*).   Ah, you have just come at the right
moment.

RELLING.   Molvik thought he could smell herring-salad, and then there
was no holding him. Good-morning again, Ekdal.

HJALMAR.   Gregers, let me introduce Mr. Molvik, and Doctor—ah, of
course you know Relling?

GREGERS.   Slightly, yes.

RELLING.   Mr. Werle junior, isn't it? Yes, we have had one or two
passages-at-arms up at the Höidal works. Have you just moved in?

GREGERS.   I only moved in this morning.

RELLING.   Molvik and I live just below you; so you haven't far to go
for a doctor or a parson, if you should need them!

GREGERS.   Thanks, it is quite possible I may; because yesterday we
were thirteen at table.

HJALMAR.   Oh, come—don't get on to ugly topics again!

RELLING.   You may make your mind easy, Ekdal; it isn't you that events point to.

HJALMAR.   I hope not, for my family's sake. But now let us sit down, and eat, drink, and be merry.

GREGERS.   Shall we not wait for your father?

HJALMAR.   No, he likes to have his lunch in his own room, later. Come along!

(*The men sit down at table, and eat and drink.* GINA *and* HEDVIG *move about, waiting on them.*)

RELLING.   Molvik was disgracefully drunk again yesterday, Mrs. Ekdal.

GINA.   What? Yesterday again?

RELLING.   Didn't you hear him when I came home with him last night?

GINA.   No, I can't say I did.

RELLING.   It is just as well; Molvik was disgusting last night.

GINA.   Is that true, Mr. Molvik?

MOLVIK.   Let us draw a veil over last night's doings. Such things have no connection with my better self.

RELLING (*to* GREGERS).   It comes over him like a spell; and then I have to go out on the spree with him. Mr. Molvik is a demoniac, you see.

GREGERS.   A demoniac?

RELLING.   Molvik is a demoniac, yes.

GREGERS.   Hm!

RELLING.   And demoniacs are not capable of keeping to a perfectly straight line through life; they have to stray a little bit now and then.— Well, and so you can still stand it up at those disgustingly dirty works?

GREGERS.   I have stood it till now.

RELLING.   And has your "demand," that you used to go about presenting, been met?

GREGERS.   My demand? (*Understanding him.*) Oh, I see.

HJALMAR.   What is this demand of yours, Gregers?

GREGERS.   He is talking nonsense.

RELLING.   It is perfectly true. He used to go round to all the cottagers' houses presenting what he called "the demand of the ideal."

GREGERS.   I was young then.

RELLING.   You are quite right, you were very young. And as for the "demand of the ideal," I never heard of your getting anyone to meet it while I was up there.

GREGERS.   Nor since, either.

RELLING.   Ah, I expect you have learnt enough to make you reduce the amount of your demand.

GREGERS.   Never when I am dealing with a man who *is* a man.

HJALMAR.   That seems to me very reasonable. A little butter, Gina.

RELLING.   And a piece of pork for Molvik.

MOLVIK.   Ugh! not pork!

(*Knocking is heard at the attic door.*)

HJALMAR.   Open the door, Hedvig; father wants to come out.

(HEDVIG *opens the door a little. Old* EKDAL *comes in, holding a fresh rabbit-skin. He shuts the door after him.*)

EKDAL.   Good-morning, gentlemen. I have had good sport; shot a big one.

HJALMAR.   And you have skinned it without me—!

EKDAL.   Yes, and salted it too. Nice, tender meat, rabbit's meat; and sweet, too; tastes like sugar. I hope you will enjoy your lunch, gentlemen! (*Goes into his room.*)

MOLVIK (*getting up*).   Excuse me—I can't—I must go downstairs at once—

RELLING.   Have some soda-water, you duffer!

MOLVIK (*hurrying away*).   Ugh!—Ugh! (*Goes out by the outer door.*)

RELLING (*to* HJALMAR).   Let us drink to the old sportsman's health.

HJALMAR (*clinking glasses with him*).   To the old sportsman on the brink of the grave!—yes.

RELLING.   To the grey-haired—(*drinks*)—tell me, is it grey hair he has got, or white?

HJALMAR.   As a matter of fact, it is between the two; but, as far as that goes, he hasn't much hair of any kind left.

RELLING.   Oh, well—a wig will take a man through the world. You are really very fortunate, you know, Ekdal. You have got a splendid object in life to strive after—

HJALMAR.   And you may be sure I *do* strive after it.

RELLING.   And you have got your clever wife, paddling about in her felt slippers, with that comfortable waddle of hers, making everything easy and cosy for you.

HJALMAR.   Yes, Gina—(*nodding—to her*) you are an excellent companion to go through life with, my dear.

GINA.   Oh, don't sit there making fun of me.

RELLING.   And then your little Hedvig, Ekdal!

HJALMAR (*with emotion*).   My child, yes! My child first and foremost. Come to me, Hedvig. (*Stroking her hair.*) What day is to-morrow?

HEDVIG (*shaking him*).   No, you mustn't say anything about it, father.

HJALMAR.   It makes my heart bleed to think what a meagre affair it will be—just a little festive gathering in the attic there—

HEDVIG.   But that will be just lovely, father!

RELLING.   Only wait till the great invention is finished, Hedvig!

HJALMAR.   Yes, indeed—then you will see! Hedvig, I am determined to make your future safe. You shall live in comfort all your life. I shall demand something for you—something or other; and that shall be the poor inventor's only reward.

HEDVIG (*throwing her arms round his neck*).   Dear, dear father!

RELLING (*to* GREGERS).   Well, don't you find it very pleasant, for a change, to sit at a well-furnished table in the midst of a happy family circle?

GREGERS.   As far as I am concerned, I don't thrive in a poisonous atmosphere.

RELLING.   A poisonous atmosphere?

HJALMAR.   Oh, don't begin that nonsense again!

GINA.   Goodness knows there's no poisonous atmosphere here, Mr. Werle; I air the place thoroughly every mortal day.

GREGERS (*rising from table*).   No airing will drive away the foulness I refer to.

HJALMAR.   Foulness!

GINA.   What do you think of that, Hjalmar!

RELLING.   Excuse me, but isn't it more likely that you yourself have brought the foulness with you from the mines up there?

GREGERS.   It is just like you to suggest that what I bring to a house is foulness.

RELLING (*going up to him*).   Listen to me, Mr. Werle junior. I have a strong suspicion that you are going about still with the original un-abridged "demand of the ideal" in your pocket.

GREGERS.   I carry it in my heart.

RELLING.   Carry the damned thing where you like; but I advise you not to play at presenting demand notes here, as long as I am in the house.

GREGERS.   And suppose I do, nevertheless?

RELLING.   Then you will go downstairs head first. Now you know.

HJALMAR (*rising*).   Really, Relling!

GREGERS.   Well, throw me out, then—

GINA (*interposing*).   You mustn't do any such thing, Mr. Relling. But this I will say, Mr. Werle; it doesn't come well from you, who made all that filthy mess with your stove, to come in here and talk about foulness. (*A knock is heard at the outer door.*)

HEDVIG.   Somebody is knocking, mother.

HJALMAR.   There now, I suppose we are going to be pestered with people!

GINA.   Let me go and see. (*She goes to the door and opens it, starts, shudders and draws back.*) Oh, my goodness!

(*The elder* WERLE, *wearing a fur coat, steps into the doorway.*)

WERLE.   Pardon me, but I fancy my son is living in this house.

GINA (*breathlessly*).   Yes.

HJALMAR (*coming up to them*).   Mr. Werle, won't you be so good as to—

WERLE.   Thanks. I only want to speak to my son.

GREGERS.   What do you want? Here I am.

WERLE.   I want to speak to you in your own room.

GREGERS.   In my own room—very well. (*Turns to go.*)

GINA.   No, goodness knows it is not in a state for you to—

WERLE.   Well, outside in the passage, then. I want to see you alone.

HJALMAR.   You can do so here, Mr. Werle. Come into the sitting-room, Relling.

(HJALMAR *and* RELLING *go out to the right.* GINA *takes* HEDVIG *with
her into the kitchen.*)

GREGERS (*after a short pause*).   Well, here we are, alone now.

WERLE.   You made use of certain expressions last night—and, seeing
that now you have taken up your abode with the Ekdals, I am driven to
suppose that you are meditating some scheme or other against me.

GREGERS.   I am meditating opening Hjalmar Ekdal's eyes. He shall see
his position as it really is; that is all.

WERLE.   Is this the object in life that you spoke of yesterday?

GREGERS.   Yes. You have left me no other.

WERLE.   Is it I that have upset your mind, Gregers?

GREGERS.   You have upset my whole life. I am not thinking of what
we said about my mother—but it is you I have to thank for the fact that
I am harried and tortured by a guilt-laden conscience.

WERLE.   Oh, it's your conscience that you are crazy about, is it?

GREGERS.   I ought to have taken a stand against you long ago, when
the trap was laid for Lieutenant Ekdal. I ought to have warned him, for
I suspected then what the outcome of it would be.

WERLE.   Yes, you should have spoken then.

GREGERS.   I had not the courage to; I was so cowed and so scared of
you. I can't tell you how afraid I was of you, both then and long after.

WERLE.   You are not afraid of me now, apparently.

GREGERS.   No, fortunately. The wrong that both I and—others have
done to old Ekdal can never be undone; but I can set Hjalmar free from
the falsehood and dissimulation that are dragging him down.

WERLE.   Do you imagine you will do any good by that?

GREGERS.   I am confident of it.

WERLE.   Do you really think Hjalmar Ekdal is the sort of man to thank
you for such a service?

GREGERS.   Certainly.

WERLE.   Hm!—we shall see.

GREGERS.   And, besides, if I am to go on living, I must do something to
cure my sick conscience.

WERLE.   You will never cure it. Your conscience has been sickly from
childhood. It is an inheritance from your mother, Gregers—the only thing
she did leave you.

GREGERS (*with a bitter smile*).   Haven't you managed yet to get over
your mistaken calculation in thinking a fortune was coming to you with
her?

WERLE.   Don't let us talk about irrelevant matters. Are you determined
on this course?—to set Hjalmar Ekdal on what you suppose to be the
right scent?

GREGERS.   Yes, quite determined.

WERLE.   Well, in that case, I might have spared myself the trouble of
coming here; because I suppose it isn't any use asking you to come home
again.

GREGERS.   No.

WERLE.   And you won't come into the firm, either?

GREGERS.   No.

WERLE.   So be it. But now that I propose to make a new marriage, the estate will be divided between us.

GREGERS (*quickly*).   No, I won't have that.

WERLE.   You won't have it?

GREGERS.   No, I won't have it. My conscience forbids it.

WERLE (*after a short pause*).   Shall you go up to the works again?

GREGERS.   No. I don't consider myself in your service any longer.

WERLE.   But what are you going to do?

GREGERS.   Only attain the object of my life; nothing else.

WERLE.   Yes—but afterwards? What will you live on?

GREGERS.   I have saved a little out of my pay.

WERLE.   That won't last you long.

GREGERS.   I think it will last out my time.

WERLE.   What do you mean?

GREGERS.   I shall answer no more questions.

WERLE.   Good-bye, then, Gregers.

GREGERS.   Good-bye. (WERLE *goes out.*)

HJALMAR (*peeping in*).   Has he gone?

GREGERS.   Yes. (HJALMAR *and* RELLING *come in; at the same time* GINA *and* HEDVIG *come from the kitchen.*)

RELLING.   That lunch was a failure.

GREGERS.   Get your things on, Hjalmar; you must come for a long walk with me.

HJALMAR.   With pleasure. What did your father want? Was it anything to do with me?

GREGERS.   Come along out; we must have a little talk. I will go and get my coat. (*Goes out.*)

GINA.   You oughtn't to go out with him, Hjalmar.

RELLING.   No, don't. Stay where you are.

HJALMAR (*taking his hat and coat*).   What do you mean! When an old friend feels impelled to open his mind to me in private—?

RELLING.   But, devil take it, can't you see the fellow is mad, crazy, out of his senses!

GINA.   It is quite true. His mother had fits of that kind from time to time.

HJALMAR.   Then he has all the more need of a friend's watchful eye. (*To* GINA.) Be sure and see that dinner is ready in good time. Good-bye just now. (*Goes out by the outer door.*)

RELLING.   It's a great pity the fellow didn't go to hell in one of the mines at Höidal.

GINA.   Good lord!—what makes you say that?

RELLING (*muttering*).   Oh, I have my own reasons.

GINA.   Do you think he is really mad?

RELLING. No, unfortunately. He is not madder than most people. But he has got a disease in his system, right enough.

GINA. What is the matter with him?

RELLING. I will tell you, Mrs. Ekdal. He is suffering from acute rectitudinal fever.

GINA. Rectitudinal fever?

HEDVIG. Is that a kind of disease?

RELLING. Indeed it is; it is a national disease; but it only crops up sporadically. (*Nods to* GINA.) Thanks for my lunch. (*Goes out by the outer door.*)

GINA (*walking about uneasily*). Ugh!—that Gregers Werle—he was always a horrid creature.

HEDVIG (*standing at the table and looking searchingly at her*). It all seems to me very odd.

ACT IV

(THE SAME SCENE.—*A photograph has just been taken; the camera, with a cloth thrown over it, a stand, a couple of chairs and a small table are in the middle of the floor. Afternoon light; the sun is on the point of setting; a little later it begins to grow dark.* GINA *is standing at the open door, with a small box and a wet glass plate in her hands, speaking to someone outside.*)

GINA. Yes, without fail. If I promise a thing, I keep my word. The first dozen shall be ready by Monday. Good-morning! (*Steps are heard going down the stair.* GINA *shuts the door, puts the plate in the box and replaces the whole in the camera.* HEDVIG *comes in from the kitchen.*)

HEDVIG. Are they gone?

GINA (*tidying the room*). Yes, thank goodness I have finished with them at last.

HEDVIG. Can you imagine why father hasn't come home yet?

GINA. Are you sure he is not downstairs with Relling?

HEDVIG. No, he isn't. I went down the back-stair just now to see.

GINA. And there is the dinner standing and getting cold for him.

HEDVIG. Think of father being so late! He is always so particular to come home in time for dinner.

GINA. Oh, he will come directly, no doubt.

HEDVIG. I wish he would; it seems so odd here to-day, somehow.

GINA (*calls out*). Here he is! (HJALMAR *comes in from the passage.*)

HEDVIG (*going to him*). Father, we have been waiting such a time for you!

GINA (*glancing at him*). What a long time you have been out, Hjalmar.

HJALMAR (*without looking at her*). I was rather long, yes. (*He takes off his overcoat.* GINA *and* HEDVIG *offer to help him, but he waves them aside.*)

GINA. Perhaps you have had your dinner with Mr. Werle.

HJALMAR (*hanging up his coat*). No.

GINA (*going towards the kitchen*). I will bring it in for you, then.

HJALMAR. No, let it be. I don't want anything to eat now.

HEDVIG (*going up to him*). Aren't you well, father?

HJALMAR. Well? Oh, yes, well enough. Gregers and I had a very exhausting walk.

GINA. You shouldn't have done that, Hjalmar; you are not accustomed to it.

HJALMAR. Ah!—one has to get accustomed to a great many things in this world. (*Walks up and down.*) Has anyone been here while I was out?

GINA. No one but the engaged couple.

HJALMAR. No new orders?

GINA. No, not to-day.

HEDVIG. Someone is sure to come to-morrow, father, you will see.

HJALMAR. Let us hope so. To-morrow I intend to set to work as hard as I can.

HEDVIG. To-morrow! But—have you forgotten what day to-morrow is?

HJALMAR. Ah, that is true. Well, the day after to-morrow then. For the future I mean to do everything myself; I don't wish anyone to help me in the work at all.

GINA. But what's the good of that, Hjalmar? It will only make your life miserable. I can do the photographing all right, and you can give your time to the invention.

HEDVIG. And to the wild duck, father—and all the hens and rabbits.

HJALMAR. Don't talk such nonsense! from to-morrow I am never going to set foot in the attic again.

HEDVIG. But, father, you know you promised me that to-morrow we should have a little festivity—

HJALMAR. That's true. Well, from the day after to-morrow, then. As for that confounded wild duck, I should have great pleasure in wringing its neck!

HEDVIG (*with a scream*). The wild duck!

GINA. Did you ever hear such a thing!

HEDVIG (*pulling him by the arm*). Yes, but, father, it is my wild duck!

HJALMAR. That is why I won't do it. I haven't the heart—haven't the heart to do it, for your sake, Hedvig. But I feel in the bottom of my heart that I ought to do it. I ought not to tolerate under my roof a single creature that has been in that man's hands.

GINA. But, good heavens, as it was from that ass Pettersen that grandfather got it—

HJALMAR (*walking up and down*). But there are certain claims—what shall I call them?—let us say claims of the ideal—absolute demands on a man, that he cannot set aside without injuring his soul.

HEDVIG (*following him about*). But think, father, the wild duck—the poor wild duck!

HJALMAR (*standing still*). Listen. I will spare it—for your sake. I will not hurt a hair of its head—well, as I said, I will spare it. There are greater difficulties than that to be tackled. Now you must go out for a little, as usual, Hedvig; it is dark enough now for you.

HEDVIG. No, I don't want to go out now.

HJALMAR. Yes, you must go out. Your eyes seem to me to be watering. All these vapours in here are not good for you. There is a bad atmosphere in this house.

HEDVIG. All right; I will run down the back-stair and go for a little stroll. My cloak and hat—? Oh, they are in my room. Father—promise you won't do the wild duck any harm while I am out.

HJALMAR. It shall not lose a feather of its head. (*Drawing her to him.*) You and I, Hedvig—we two!—now run along, dear. (HEDVIG *nods to her parents and goes out through the kitchen.* HJALMAR *walks up and down without raising his eyes.*) Gina!

GINA. Yes?

HJALMAR. From to-morrow—or let us say from the day after to-morrow—I should prefer to keep the household books myself.

GINA. You want to keep the household books too!

HJALMAR. Yes, or at any rate to keep account of what our income is.

GINA. Bless the man—that's simple enough!

HJALMAR. I am not sure; you seem to me to make what I give you go an astonishingly long way. (*Stands still and looks at her.*) How do you manage it?

GINA. Because Hedvig and I need so little.

HJALMAR. Is it true that father is so liberally paid for the copying he does for old Mr. Werle?

GINA. I don't know about its being so liberal. I don't know what is usually paid for that kind of work.

HJALMAR. Well, roughly speaking, what does he make? Tell me.

GINA. It varies; roughly speaking, I should say it is about what he costs us and a little pocket-money over.

HJALMAR. What he costs us! And you have never told me that before?

GINA. No, I couldn't. You seemed so pleased to think that he had everything from you.

HJALMAR. And in reality he had it from old Werle!

GINA. Oh, well, Mr. Werle has got plenty to spare.

HJALMAR. Light the lamp for me, please.

GINA (*lighting it*). Besides, we don't really know if it is Mr. Werle himself; it might be Graaberg—

HJALMAR. Why do you want to shift it on to Graaberg?

GINA. I know nothing about it; I only thought—

HJALMAR. Hm!

GINA. It wasn't me that got the copying for grandfather, remember that. It was Bertha, when she came to the house.

HJALMAR. Your voice seems to me to be unsteady.

GINA (*putting the shade on the lamp*). Does it?

HJALMAR. And your hands are shaking, aren't they?

GINA (*firmly*). Tell me straight, Hjalmar, what nonsense has he been telling you about me?

HJALMAR. Is it true—can it possibly be true—that there was anything between you and old Mr. Werle when you were in service there?

GINA. It's not true. Not then. Mr. Werle was always after me, true enough. And his wife thought there was something in it; and then there was the devil's own fuss. Not a moment's peace did she give me, that woman—and so I threw up my place.

HJALMAR. But afterwards?

GINA. Well, then I went home. And my mother—she wasn't what you thought her, Hjalmar; she talked a heap of nonsense to me about this, that and the other. Mr. Werle was a widower by that time, you know.

HJALMAR. Well, and then?

GINA. It's best you should know it. He never let me alone, till he had had his way.

HJALMAR (*clasping his hands.*) And this is the mother of my child! How could you conceal such a thing from me?

GINA. It was wrong of me, I know. I ought to have told you about it long ago.

HJALMAR. You ought to have told me at the first,—then I should have known what sort of a woman you were.

GINA. But would you have married me, all the same?

HJALMAR. How can you suppose such a thing!

GINA. No; and that's why I didn't dare to tell you anything then. I had got to love you so dearly, as you know. And I couldn't make myself utterly wretched—

HJALMAR (*walking about*). And this is my Hedvig's mother! And to know that I owe everything I see here—(*kicks at a chair*)—my whole home—to a favoured predecessor! Ah, that seducer, Werle!

GINA. Do you regret the fourteen—the fifteen years we have lived together?

HJALMAR (*standing in front of her*). Tell me this. Haven't you regretted every day—every hour—this web of lies you have enmeshed me in? Answer me! Haven't you really suffered agonies of regret and remorse?

GINA. My dear Hjalmar, I have had plenty to do thinking about the housekeeping and all the work there was to do every day—

HJALMAR. Then you never wasted a thought on what your past had been!

GINA. No—God knows I had almost forgotten all about that old trouble.

HJALMAR. Oh, this callous, insensate content! There is something so shocking about it, to me. Just think of it!—not a moment's regret.

GINA. But you tell me this, Hjalmar—what would have become of you if you hadn't found a wife like me?

HJALMAR.   A wife like you!

GINA.   Yes; I have always been a better business man than you, so to speak. Of course, it is true I am a year or two older than you.

HJALMAR.   What would have become of me?

GINA.   Yes, you had got into all sorts of bad ways when you first met me; you can't deny that.

HJALMAR.   You talk about bad ways? You can't understand how a man feels when he is overcome with grief and despair—especially a man of my ardent temperament.

GINA.   No, very likely not. And I oughtn't to say much about it anyway, because you made a real good husband as soon as you had a home of your own. And here we had got such a comfortable, cosy home, and Hedvig and I were just beginning to be able to spend a little bit on ourselves for food and clothes—

HJALMAR.   In a swamp of deceit, yes.

GINA.   If only that hateful fellow hadn't poked his nose in here!

HJALMAR.   I used to think, too, that I had a happy home. It was a delusion. Where am I to look now for the necessary incentive to bring my invention into existence? Perhaps it will die with me; and then it will be your past, Gina, that has killed it.

GINA (*on the brink of tears*).   Don't talk about such things, Hjalmar. I, that have all along only wanted what was best for you!

HJALMAR.   I ask you—what has become of the dream of the breadwinner now? When I lay in there on the sofa, thinking over my invention, I used to have a presentiment that it would use up all my powers. I used to feel that when the great day came when I should hold my patent in my hands, that day would be the day of my—departure. And it was my dream, too, that you would be left as the well-to-do widow of the departed inventor.

GINA (*wiping away her tears*).   You mustn't talk such nonsense, Hjalmar. I pray God I never may live to see the day when I am left a widow!

HJALMAR.   Well, it is of no consequence now. It is all over now, anyway—all over now!

(GREGERS WERLE *opens the outer door cautiously and looks in.*)

GREGERS.   May I come in?

HJALMAR.   Yes, come in.

GREGERS (*advances with a beaming, happy face, and stretches out his hand to them*).   Well, you dear people—! (*Looks alternately at one and the other and whispers to* HJALMAR.) Haven't you done it yet?

HJALMAR (*aloud*).   It is done.

GREGERS.   It is?

HJALMAR.   I have passed through the bitterest moment of my life.

GREGERS.   But the most elevating too, I expect.

HJALMAR.   Well, we have got it off our hands for the present, anyway.

GINA.   God forgive you, Mr. Werle.

GREGERS (*greatly surprised*).   But, I don't understand.

HJALMAR.   What don't you understand?

GREGERS.   After such a momentous enlightenment—an enlightenment that is to be the starting-point of a completely new existence—a real companionship, founded on truth and purged of all falsehood—

HJALMAR.   Yes, I know; I know.

GREGERS.   I certainly expected, when I came in, to be met by the light of transfiguration in the faces of you both. And yet I see nothing but gloomy, dull, miserable—

GINA (*taking off the lampshade*).   Quite so.

GREGERS.   I daresay you won't understand me, Mrs. Ekdal. Well, well —you will in time. But you, Hjalmar? You must feel consecrated afresh by this great enlightenment?

HJALMAR.   Yes, of course I do. This is to say—in a sort of way.

GREGERS.   Because there is surely nothing in the world that can compare with the happiness of forgiveness and of lifting up a guilty sinner in the arms of love.

HJALMAR.   Do you think it is so easy for a man to drink the bitter cup that I have just drained?

GREGERS.   No, not for an ordinary man, I daresay. But for a man like you—!

HJALMAR.   Good heavens, I know that well enough. But you mustn't rush me, Gregers. It takes time, you know.

GREGERS.   You have a lot of the wild duck in you, Hjalmar.

(RELLING *has come in by the outer door.*)

RELLING.   Hullo! are you talking about the old wild duck again?

HJALMAR.   Yes, the one old Mr. Werle winged.

RELLING.   Old Mr. Werle—? Is it him you are talking about?

HJALMAR.   Him and—the rest of us.

RELLING (*half aloud, to* GREGERS).   I wish the devil would fly away with you!

HJALMAR.   What are you saying?

RELLING.   I was breathing an earnest wish that this quack doctor would take himself off home. If he stays here he is capable of being the death of both of you.

GREGERS.   No harm is coming to these two, Mr. Relling. I won't speak about Hjalmar; we know him. And as for his wife, I have little doubt that she, too, has the springs of trustworthiness and sincerity deep down in her heart.

GINA (*nearly crying*).   Then you ought to have let me be as I was.

RELLING (*to* GREGERS).   Would it be indiscreet to ask precisely what you think you are doing here?

GREGERS.   I am trying to lay the foundation of a true marriage.

RELLING.   Then you don't think Ekdal's marriage is good enough as it is?

GREGERS.   Oh, it is as good a marriage as many others, I daresay. But a true marriage it has never yet been.

HJALMAR. You have never had your eyes opened to the demands of the ideal, Relling.

RELLING. Rubbish, my dear chap!—But, excuse me, Mr. Werle, how many "true marriages," roughly speaking, have you seen in your life?

GREGERS. I scarcely think I have seen a single one.

RELLING. Nor I either.

GREGERS. But I have seen such hundreds of marriages of the opposite kind, and I have had the opportunity of watching at close quarters the mischief such a marriage may do to both parties.

HJALMAR. A man's moral character may be completely sapped; that is the dreadful part of it.

RELLING. Well, I have never exactly been married, so I can't lay down the law on the matter. But this I do know, that the child is part of the marriage too—and you must leave the child in peace.

HJALMAR. Ah—Hedvig! My poor little Hedvig!

RELLING. Yes, you will have the goodness to keep Hedvig out of the matter. You two are grown people; goodness knows, you may play ducks and drakes with your happiness, for all I care. But you must walk warily with Hedvig, believe me; otherwise it may end in your doing her a great mischief.

HJALMAR. A great mischief?

RELLING. Yes, or it may end in her doing a great mischief to herself— and perhaps to others too.

GINA. But how can you know anything about it, Mr. Relling?

HJALMAR. There is no imminent danger for her eyes, is there?

RELLING. What I mean has nothing to do with her eyes at all. But Hedvig is at a critical age. She may take all sorts of strange fancies into her head.

GINA. There!—and to be sure she is doing that already! She has begun to be very fond of meddling with the fire, out in the kitchen. She calls it playing at houses-on-fire. Often and often I have been afraid she *would* set the house on fire.

RELLING. There you are. I knew it.

GREGERS (*to* RELLING). But how do you explain such a thing?

RELLING (*sulkily*). She is becoming a woman, my friend.

HJALMAR. So long as the child has me—! So long as my life lasts—! (*A knock is heard at the door.*)

GINA. Hush, Hjalmar; there is someone outside. (*Calls out.*) Come in! (MRS. SÖRBY, *dressed in outdoor clothes, comes in.*)

MRS. SÖRBY. Good-evening!

GINA (*going to her*). Bertha!—is it you!

MRS. SÖRBY. Certainly it's me! But perhaps I have come at an inconvenient time?

HJALMAR. Not at all; a messenger from *that* house—

MRS. SÖRBY (*to* GINA.) To tell you the truth, I rather hoped I shouldn't find your men-folk at home just now; I just ran up to have a little chat with you and say good-bye.

GINA. Oh? Are you going away?

MRS. SÖRBY. Early to-morrow morning, yes—up to Höidal. Mr. Werle went this afternoon. (*Meaningly, to* GREGERS.) He asked to be remembered to you.

GINA. Just fancy—!

HJALMAR. So Mr. Werle has gone away?—and now you are going to join him?

MRS. SÖRBY. Yes, what do you say to that, Mr. Ekdal?

HJALMAR. Be careful what you are doing, I say.

GREGERS. I can explain. My father and Mrs. Sörby are going to be married!

HJALMAR. Going to be married!

GINA. Oh, Bertha! Has it come to that?

RELLING (*his voice faltering a little*). Is this really true?

MRS. SÖRBY. Yes, my dear Relling, it is perfectly true.

RELLING. Are you going to marry again?

MRS. SÖRBY. Yes, that's what it has come to. Mr. Werle has got a special licence, and we are going to get married very quietly up at the works.

GREGERS. Then I suppose I must wish you happiness, like a good stepson.

MRS. SÖRBY. Many thanks—if you mean it. And I am sure I hope it will mean happiness, both for Mr. Werle and for me.

RELLING. You can confidently hope that. Mr. Werle never gets drunk —so far as I know; and I don't imagine he is in the habit of ill-treating his wives, either, as the late lamented horse-doctor used to do.

MRS. SÖRBY. Sörby is dead; let him alone. And even he had his good points.

RELLING. Mr. Werle has points that are better, I expect.

MRS. SÖRBY. At any rate he hasn't wasted all that was best in him. A man who does that must take the consequences.

RELLING. To-night I shall go out with Molvik.

MRS. SÖRBY. That is wrong of you. Don't do that—for my sake, don't.

RELLING. There is nothing else for it. (*To* HJALMAR.) You can come too, if you like.

GINA. No, thank you. Hjalmar is not going with you to places of *that* kind.

HJALMAR (*half aloud in an irritated voice*). Oh, do hold your tongue!

RELLING. Good-bye, Mrs.—Werle. (*Goes out at the outer door.*)

GREGERS (*to* Mrs. SÖRBY). You and Doctor Relling seem to know each other pretty well.

MRS. SÖRBY. Yes, we have known each other many years. At one time it looked as if our friendship were going to ripen into something warmer.

GREGERS. But, luckily for you, I suppose, it didn't.

MRS. SÖRBY. You may well say so. But I have always been chary of giving way to impulse. A woman mustn't absolutely throw herself away, either.

GREGERS. Are you not in the least afraid of my letting my father get a hint of this old acquaintance?

MRS. SÖRBY. Of course I have told him about it myself.

GREGERS. Indeed?

MRS. SÖRBY. You father knows every single thing with a grain of truth in it that anyone could find to tell him about me. I have told him absolutely everything; it was the first thing I did when he made it evident what his intentions were.

GREGERS. Then you have been more frank than is usually the case, I expect.

MRS. SÖRBY. I always have been frank. It is the best way for us women.

HJALMAR. What do you say to that, Gina?

GINA. Oh, women are all so different. Some are built that way; some aren't.

MRS. SÖRBY. Well, Gina, I believe now that the wisest line to take is the one I have taken. And Mr. Werle hasn't concealed anything on his side, either. It is that, you see, that knits us so closely together. Now he can sit and talk to me as fearlessly as a child. That is a thing he has never had a chance of doing yet. All his young days, and for the best years of his life, when he was a healthy and vigorous man, he had to sit and listen to nothing but sermons on his sins. And very often the point of the sermons turned on the most imaginary offences—at least, so it seems to me.

GINA. Yes, it's quite certain that's true.

GREGERS. If you ladies are going into those subjects, I had better take my leave.

MRS. SÖRBY. Oh, you can stay, for that matter. I won't say a word more. But I wanted you to understand that I have done nothing deceitful or in the least degree underhand. Very likely you think I am coming in for a great slice of luck; and so I am, in a way. But, all the same, I don't believe I shall be taking more than I shall be giving. At any rate I shall never forsake him; and what I *can* do is to look after him and care for him as no one else can, now that he will soon be helpless.

HJALMAR. Soon be helpless?

GREGERS (*to* Mrs. SÖRBY). Don't speak of that here.

MRS. SÖRBY. There is no use concealing it any longer, however much he would like to. He is going blind.

HJALMAR (*with a start*). Going blind? That is extraordinary. Is he going blind too?

GINA. A great many people do.

MRS. SÖRBY. And one can well imagine what that means to a business man. Well, I shall try to use my eyes for him as well as I can. But I mustn't stay any longer; I am frightfully busy just now.—Oh, I was to tell you this, Mr. Ekdal, that if there were anything in which Mr. Werle could be of service to you, you were just to go to Graaberg about it.

GREGERS. A message that I should think Hjalmar Ekdal would be *very* grateful for!

MRS. SÖRBY. Really? I rather think there was a time when—

GINA. He's quite right, Bertha. Hjalmar doesn't need to take anything from Mr. Werle now.

HJALMAR (*slowly and weightily*). Will you give my kind regards to your future husband, and say that I mean as soon as possible to call on Graaberg—

GREGERS. What! Do you really mean to do that?

HJALMAR. To call on Graaberg, I say, and ask for an account of the sum I owe his employer. I will pay that debt of honour—ha! ha! debt of honour is a good name for it!—but enough of that. I will pay the whole sum, with five per cent. interest.

GINA. But, my dear Hjalmar, we have no money to do that with, Heaven knows!

HJALMAR. Will you tell your *fiancé* that I am working busily at my invention. Will you tell him that what keeps up my strength for this exhausting task is the desire to be quit of a painful burden of debt. That is why I am working at this invention. The whole proceeds of it shall be devoted to freeing myself from the obligation under which your future husband's pecuniary advances have laid me.

MRS. SÖRBY. Something or other has happened in this house.

HJALMAR. You are right.

MRS. SÖRBY. Well—good-bye, then. I had something I wanted to talk over with you, Gina; but that must wait till another time. Good-bye! (HJALMAR *and* GREGERS *bow silently;* GINA *follows her to the door.*)

HJALMAR. Not farther than the door, Gina! (MRS. SÖRBY *goes out;* GINA *shuts the door after her.*) There, Gregers. Now I have got that load of debt off my hands.

GREGERS. Soon you will, any way.

HJALMAR. I think my attitude may be called correct.

GREGERS. You are the man I always took you for.

HJALMAR. In certain cases it is impossible to overlook the claim of the ideal. As breadwinner of the family, I have to writhe and smart under this. I can tell you it is by no means a joke for a man, who is not well off, to get free from a debt of many years' standing, over which the dust of oblivion, so to speak, has collected. But that makes no difference; the manhood in me demands its rights too.

GREGERS (*putting his hands on his shoulders*). Dear Hjalmar, wasn't it a good thing I came?

HJALMAR. Yes.

GREGERS. Hasn't it been a good thing that you have got a clear knowledge of the whole situation?

HJALMAR (*a little impatiently*). Of course it's a good thing. But there is one thing that goes against my sense of what is right.

GREGERS. What is that?

HJALMAR. Old Mr. Werle writes to Hedvig that her old grandfather need not bother himself with copying work any longer, but that for the future he will be entitled to five pounds a month paid from the office—

GREGERS. Aha!

HEDVIG. Five pounds, mother!—I read that.

GINA. How nice for grandfather!

HJALMAR. Five pounds a month, as long as he needs it; that means, naturally, till his death.

GINA. Well, then, he is provided for, poor old man.

HJALMAR. But that is not all. You didn't read the rest, Hedvig. Afterwards the gift is to be transferred to you.

HEDVIG. To me! All that?

HJALMAR. You are assured the same amount for the whole of your life, it says. Do you hear that, Gina?

GINA. Yes, yes, I hear.

HEDVIG. Just think of it—I am to get all that money. (*Shakes him.*) Father, father, aren't you glad?

HJALMAR (*moving away from her*). Glad! (*Walks up and down.*) What a future—what a picture it calls up to my eyes! It is Hedvig for whom he provides so liberally—Hedvig!

GINA. Yes, it's Hedvig's birthday—

HEDVIG. You shall have it all the same, father! Of course I shall give all the money to you and mother.

HJALMAR. To your mother, yes!—that's just the point.

GREGERS. Hjalmar, this is a trap he is laying for you.

HJALMAR. Do you think this is another trap?

GREGERS. When he was here this morning, he said: "Hjalmar Ekdal is not the man you imagine he is."

HJALMAR. Not the man—!

GREGERS. "You will see," he said.

HJALMAR. You will see whether I allow myself to be put off with a bribe—

HEDVIG. Mother, what does it all mean?

GINA. Go away and take your things off. (HEDVIG *goes out by the kitchen door, half in tears.*)

GREGERS. Yes, Hjalmar—now we shall see who is right, he or I.

HJALMAR (*tears the paper slowly across, and lays the two pieces on the table*). That is my answer.

GREGERS. That is what I expected.

HJALMAR (*goes over to* GINA, *who is standing by the stove, and speaks to her in a low voice*). No more lies, now. If everything was over between you and him when you—when you began to love me, as you call it, why was it that he put us in a position to marry?

GINA. I suppose he thought he would get a footing in the house.

HJALMAR. Only that? Wasn't he afraid of a certain possibility?

GINA. I don't understand what you mean.

HJALMAR. I want to know, whether—whether your child has the right to live under my roof.

GINA (*drawing herself up, with eyes flashing*). Can you ask that!

HJALMAR. You shall answer this question. Does Hedvig belong to me —or to—? Well?

GINA (*looking at him with cold bravado*). I don't know.

HJALMAR (*in a trembling voice*). You don't know?

GINA. How should I know? A woman like me—

HJALMAR (*quietly, as he turns away from her*). Then I have no longer any part in this house.

GREGERS. Think well what you are doing, Hjalmar!

HJALMAR (*putting on his overcoat*). There is nothing here for a man like me to think about.

GREGERS. Indeed there is a tremendous lot here for you to think about. You three must be together, if you are going to reach the goal of self-sacrificing forgiveness.

HJALMAR. I have no desire for that. Never! Never! My hat! (*Takes his hat.*) My home has fallen into ruins round me. (*Bursts into tears.*) Gregers, I have no child now!

HEDVIG (*who has opened the kitchen door*). What are you saying! (*Goes to him.*) Father! Father!

GINA. Now, what's to happen!

HJALMAR. Don't come near me, Hedvig! Go away—go away! I can't bear to see you. Ah—the eyes! Good-bye. (*Goes towards the door.*)

HEDVIG (*clings to him, screaming*). No, no! Don't turn away from me.

GINA (*crying out*). Look at the child, Hjalmar! Look at the child!

HJALMAR. I won't! I can't! I must get out of here—away from all this! (*He tears himself away from* HEDVIG *and goes out by the outer door.*)

HEDVIG (*with despair in her eyes*). He is going away from us, mother! He is going away! He will never come back!

GINA. Don't cry, Hedvig. Father will come back.

HEDVIG (*throws herself on the sofa, sobbing*). No, no,—he will never come back any more.

GREGERS. Will you believe that I meant all for the best, Mrs. Ekdal?

GINA. I almost believe you did; but, God forgive you, all the same.

HEDVIG (*lying on the sofa*). I think this will kill me! What have I done to him? Mother, you *must* get him home again!

GINA. Yes, yes; only be quiet, and I will go out and look for him. (*Puts on her coat.*) Perhaps he has gone down to Relling. But, if I go, you mustn't lie there crying. Will you promise me that?

HEDVIG (*sobbing convulsively*). Yes, I won't cry—if only father comes back.

GREGERS (*to* GINA, *as she goes out*). Would it not be better, anyway, to let him first fight his bitter fight to the end?

GINA. He can do that afterwards. First and foremost we must get the child quiet. (*Goes out.*)

HEDVIG (*sitting upright and wiping away her tears*). Now you must tell me what is the matter. Why won't father have anything to do with me any more?

GREGERS. You mustn't ask that until you are a big girl and grown up.

HEDVIG (*gulping down her tears*). But I can't go on being so wretchedly miserable till I am a big girl and grown up. I believe I know what it is—perhaps I am not really father's child.

GREGERS (*uneasily*). How on earth could that be?

HEDVIG. Mother might have found me. And now perhaps father has found that out; I have read of such things.

GREGERS. Well, even if it were so—

HEDVIG. Yes, it seems to me he might love me just as much in spite of that—even more. We had the wild duck sent us as a present, too, but all the same I love it very dearly.

GREGERS (*to divert her thoughts*). The wild duck—that's true! Let's talk about the wild duck a little, Hedvig.

HEDVIG. The poor wild duck!—he can't bear to look at it any more, either. Just fancy, he wanted to wring its neck.

GREGERS. Oh, he won't do that.

HEDVIG. No, but he said so. And I think it was so unkind of him to say so, because I say a prayer every night for the wild duck, and pray that it may be preserved from death and anything that will harm it.

GREGERS (*looking at her*). Do you say your prayers at night?

HEDVIG. Of course.

GREGERS. Who taught you?

HEDVIG. I taught myself. It was once when father was very ill and had leeches on his neck, and said he was at the point of death.

GREGERS. Really?

HEDVIG. So I said a prayer for him when I had got into bed—and since then I have gone on doing it.

GREGERS. And now you pray for the wild duck too?

HEDVIG. I thought it would be best to put the wild duck in the prayer too, because it was so sickly at first.

GREGERS. Do you say prayers in the morning, too?

HEDVIG. No, of course I don't.

GREGERS. Why don't you say them in the morning as well?

HEDVIG. Because in the morning it is light, and there is nothing more to be afraid of.

GREGERS. And your father wanted to wring the neck of the wild duck that you love so dearly?

HEDVIG. No, he said it would be a great pleasure to him to do it, but that he would spare it for my sake; and I think that was very nice of father.

GREGERS (*coming nearer to her*). But now, suppose you sacrificed the wild duck, of your own free will, for his sake?

HEDVIG (*getting up*). The wild duck?

GREGERS. Suppose now you gave up for him, as a free-will offering, the dearest possession you have in the world?

HEDVIG. Do you think it would help?

GREGERS. Try it, Hedvig.

HEDVIG (*gently, with glistening eyes*). Yes, I will try it.

GREGERS. Have you really the strength of mind to do it, do you think?

HEDVIG. I will ask grandfather to shoot the wild duck for me.

GREGERS. Yes, do. But not a word about anything of the kind to your mother.

HEDVIG. Why not?

GREGERS. She doesn't understand us.

HEDVIG. The wild duck! I will try it the first thing to-morrow morning. (GINA *comes in by the outer door.* HEDVIG *goes to her.*) Did you find him, mother?

GINA. No, but I heard he had gone out and taken Relling with him.

GREGERS. Are you certain?

GINA. Yes, the porter's wife said so. Molvik has gone with them too, she said.

GREGERS. And this, when his mind is so sorely in need of fighting in solitude—!

GINA (*taking off her things*). Oh, you never know what men are going to do. Heaven knows where Relling has taken him off to! I ran over to Mrs. Eriksen's, but they weren't there.

HEDVIG (*struggling with her tears*). Oh, suppose he never comes back any more!

GREGERS. He'll come back. I have a message to give him in the morning, and you will see how he will come home. You may go to sleep quite hopefully about that, Hedvig. Good-night. (*Goes out.*)

HEDVIG (*throws herself into* GINA's *arms, sobbing*). Mother! Mother!

GINA (*patting her on the back and sighing*). Yes, yes,—Relling was right. This is what happens when mad folk come presenting these demands that no one can make head or tail of.

ACT V

(THE SAME SCENE.—*The cold grey light of morning is shining in; wet snow is lying on the large panes of the skylight.* GINA *comes in from the kitchen wearing a high apron and carrying a broom and a duster, and goes towards the sitting-room door. At the same moment* HEDVIG *comes hurriedly in from the passage.*)

GINA (*stopping*). Well?

HEDVIG. Mother, I rather think he is downstairs with Relling—

GINA. Look at that, now!

HEDVIG. Because the porter's wife said she heard two people come in with Relling when he came home last night.

GINA.   That's just what I thought.

HEDVIG.   But that is no good if he won't come up to us.

GINA.   At any rate I shall be able to go down and have a talk with him. (*Old* EKDAL *comes in from his room, in dressing-gown and slippers and smoking his pipe.*)

EKDAL.   Look here, Hjalmar—. Isn't Hjalmar at home?

GINA.   No, he has gone out.

EKDAL.   So early? and in such a heavy snowstorm? Well, well; that's his affair. I can take my morning stroll by myself. (*He opens the attic door;* HEDVIG *helps him. He goes in, and she shuts the door after him.*)

HEDVIG (*in an undertone*).   Just think, mother—when poor grandfather hears that father wants to go away from us!

GINA.   Nonsense—grandfather mustn't hear anything about it. It's God's mercy he wasn't here yesterday when all that rumpus was going on.

HEDVIG.   Yes, but—

(GREGERS *comes in by the outer door.*)

GREGERS.   Well? Have you any trace of him yet?

GINA.   He is most likely downstairs with Relling, I am told.

GREGERS.   With Relling! Can he really have been out with that fellow?

GINA.   That he has, evidently.

GREGERS.   Yes, but he—who so urgently needed solitude to pull himself seriously together—!

GINA.   You may well say so.

(RELLING *comes in from the passage.*)

HEDVIG (*going up to him*).   Is father in your rooms?

GINA (*at the same time*).   Is he there?

RELLING.   Certainly he is.

HEDVIG.   And you never told us!

RELLING.   Yes, I know I'm a beast. But first of all I had the other beast to keep in order—our demoniac gentleman, I mean—and after that I fell so dead asleep that—

GINA.   What does Hjalmar say to-day?

RELLING.   He doesn't say anything at all.

HEDVIG.   Hasn't he talked to you at all?

RELLING.   Not a blessed word.

GREGERS.   Of course not; I can understand that very well.

GINA.   But what is he doing with himself, then?

RELLING.   He is lying on the sofa, snoring.

GINA.   Is he? Hjalmar's a fine hand at snoring.

HEDVIG.   Is he asleep? Can he sleep?

RELLING.   Well, it looks like it.

GREGERS.   It is easy to understand that; after the conflict of soul that has torn him—

GINA.   Besides, he has never been accustomed to rambling out at night.

HEDVIG.   I daresay it is a good thing he is getting some sleep, mother.

GINA. I think so, too; and it would be a pity to wake him up too soon. Many thanks, Mr. Relling. Now first of all I must get the house cleaned up and tidied a bit, and then—. Come and help me, Hedvig. (*She goes with* HEDVIG *into the sitting-room.*)

GREGERS (*turning to* RELLING). What do you think of the spiritual upheaval that is going on in Hjalmar Ekdal?

RELLING. As far as I am concerned, I haven't noticed any spiritual upheaval going on in him at all.

GREGERS. What! After such a crisis, when the whole of his life has been shifted on to a new basis? How can you suppose that a personality like Hjalmar's—

RELLING. Personality!—he? Even if he ever had any tendency to any such abnormality as you call "personality," it has been absolutely rooted out of him and destroyed when he was a boy. I can assure you of that.

GREGERS. It would certainly be very strange if that were true, in the case of a man brought up with such loving care as he was.

RELLING. By those two crazy hysterical maiden aunts of his, do you mean?

GREGERS. Let me tell you that they were women who were never oblivious to the demands of the ideal—but if I say that, you will only begin making fun of me again.

RELLING. No, I am in no humour for that. Besides, I know all about them. He has delivered himself to me of any amount of rhetoric about these two "soul-mothers" of his. But I don't think he has much to thank them for. Ekdal's misfortune is that all his life he has been looked upon as a shining light in his own circle—

GREGERS. And is he not that?—in profundity of mind, I mean?

RELLING. I have never noticed anything of the sort. His father believed it, I daresay; the poor old lieutenant has been a simpleton all his days.

GREGERS. He has been a man with a childlike mind all his days; that is a thing you can't understand.

RELLING. All right! But when our dear sweet Hjalmar became a student of sorts, he was at once accepted amongst his fellow-students as the great light of the future. Good-looking he was, too, the nincompoop— pink and white—just what common girls like for a lover; and with his susceptible disposition and that sympathetic voice of his, and the facility with which he declaimed other people's verses and other people's thoughts—

GREGERS (*indignantly*). Is it Hjalmar Ekdal that you are speaking of like this?

RELLING. Yes, by your leave; for that is the real man, instead of the idol you have been falling on your knees to.

GREGERS. I venture to think I was not so blind as all that.

RELLING. Well, it's not far from the truth, anyway. You are a sick man too, you see.

GREGERS. You are right there.

RELLING. Quite so. You are suffering from a complicated complaint. First of all there is that debilitating rectitudinal fever of yours; and then, what's worse, you are always in a raving delirium of hero-worship—you must always have some object of admiration that you really have no concern with.

GREGERS. I certainly can only find that by looking outside of my own concerns.

RELLING. But you are so monstrously mistaken as to these miraculous beings you think you find around you. This is just another case of your coming to a workman's cottage to present your "demands of the ideal"; but the people in this house are all insolvent.

GREGERS. If you haven't any higher opinion of Hjalmar Ekdal than that, how can you find any pleasure in being always hand-in-glove with him?

RELLING. Bless your heart—I am supposed to be a kind of doctor, though you mightn't think it; and it is only my duty to pay some attention to the poor invalids I live in the house with.

GREGERS. Really! Is Hjalmar Ekdal a sick man too, then?

RELLING. All the world is sick, pretty nearly—that's the worst of it.

GREGERS. And what treatment are you using for Hjalmar?

RELLING. My usual one. I am trying to keep up the make-believe of life in him.

GREGERS. The make-believe? I don't think I heard you aright?

RELLING. Yes, I said make-believe. That is the stimulating principle of life, you know.

GREGERS. May I ask what sort of a make-believe enters into the scheme of Hjalmar's life?

RELLING. No, you mayn't. I never disclose secrets like that to quacks. You were making an even worse mess of his case than I. My method has stood the test of trial. I have applied it in Molvik's case too. I have made a "demoniac" of him. That is the blister I have put on *his* neck.

GREGERS. Isn't he a demoniac, then?

RELLING. What in heaven's name do you mean by "being a demoniac"? That is only a bit of make-believe I invented to keep the life in him. If I hadn't done that, the poor honest wretch would have given way to self-contempt and despair years ago. And the same with the old lieutenant there! But he has happened to hit upon the cure by himself.

GREGERS. Lieutenant Ekdal? what of him?

RELLING. Well, what do you make of an old bear-stalker, like him, going into that dark attic there to shoot rabbits? There isn't a happier sportsman in the world than that poor old man playing about in there in that scrap-heap. The four or five withered Christmas trees that he has kept are the same to him as the great tall live trees in the Höidal forests; the cocks and hens are the wild-fowl in the tree-tops; and the rabbits, that lop about all over the attic floor, are the big game this famous back-woodsman used to pit himself against.

GREGERS.   Poor old man! Yes, he has indeed had to endure the quenching of all his youthful ideals.

RELLING.   And, while I think of it, Mr. Werle junior—don't use that outlandish word "ideals." There is a good homegrown word—"falsehoods."

GREGERS.   Do you really think the two things are the same?

RELLING.   Just as nearly as typhus and putrid fever are.

GREGERS.   Doctor Relling, I won't give in till I have rescued Hjalmar from your clutches.

RELLING.   So much the worse for him. If you take away make-believe from the average man, you take away his happiness as well. (*To* HEDVIG, *who has come in from the sitting-room.*) Well, little wild-duck mother, I am going down now to see whether your daddy is still lying pondering over the wonderful invention. (*Goes out by the outer door.*)

GREGERS (*going up to* HEDVIG).   I can see by your face that the deed isn't done yet.

HEDVIG.   What deed? Oh, the wild duck. No.

GREGERS.   Your courage failed you when the time came to do it, I suppose?

HEDVIG.   No, it's not that. But when I woke up early this morning and remembered all we said, it all seemed so strange to me.

GREGERS.   Strange?

HEDVIG.   Yes, I don't know—. Last night, when we were talking about it, it seemed such a splendid idea; but, after my sleep, when I remembered it again, it all seemed different.

GREGERS.   I see; I suppose it was impossible for you to grow up here without something being injured in you.

HEDVIG.   I don't care anything about that; if only father would come up, then—

GREGERS.   Ah, if only your eyes had been opened to what makes life worth living—if you possessed the true, happy, courageous spirit of self-sacrifice—you would see how you would be able to bring him up to you. But I have faith in you still, Hedvig. (*Goes out by the outer door.* HEDVIG *walks up and down; she is just going into the kitchen, but at the same moment a knock is heard on the attic door; she goes and opens it a little, and old* EKDAL *comes out, after which she shuts the door again.*)

EKDAL.   Hm! There's not much pleasure in taking one's morning walk alone.

HEDVIG.   Haven't you felt inclined for any shooting, grandfather?

EKDAL.   It isn't the weather for shooting to-day. Too dark in there, you can hardly see a hand's length.

HEDVIG.   Have you never felt inclined to shoot anything else but the rabbits?

EKDAL.   Why? Aren't the rabbits good enough sport?

HEDVIG.   Yes, but the wild duck?

EKDAL.   Ho! ho!—are you afraid I shall shoot your wild duck for you? Never in the world: I would never do that.

HEDVIG. No, I suppose you couldn't; wild duck must be very hard to shoot.

EKDAL. Couldn't! I should rather think I could.

HEDVIG. How would you manage it, grandfather?—not my wild duck, I mean, but with others?

EKDAL. I would see that I shot them in the breast, you know, because that is the surest place. And you must shoot against the lie of the feathers, do you understand—not with the lie of the feathers.

HEDVIG. Do they die then, grandfather?

EKDAL. Certainly they do, if you shoot properly. Well, I must go in and make myself tidy. Hm!—you understand—hm! (*Goes into his room.* HEDVIG *waits a little; glances at the door, then goes to the bookcase, stands on tiptoe, and takes the pistol down from the shelf and looks at it.* GINA *comes in from the sitting-room, with her broom and duster.* HEDVIG *hastily puts down the pistol unnoticed.*)

GINA. Don't go rummaging among your father's things, Hedvig.

HEDVIG (*moving away from the bookcase*). I only wanted to put things straight a little.

GINA. You had much better go into the kitchen and see if the coffee is keeping hot; I will take his tray with me, when I go down to him.

(HEDVIG *goes out.* GINA *begins to sweep and clean the studio. After a while the outer door is opened slowly, and* HJALMAR *looks in. He is wearing his overcoat, but is without his hat; he is unwashed and his hair is ruffled and untidy; his eyes are dull and heavy.* GINA *stands still with the broom in her hand and looks at him.*)

GINA. Well there, Hjalmar!—have you come after all?

HJALMAR (*walks in and answers in a dull voice*). I have come—but only to go away again directly.

GINA. Yes, yes—I suppose so. But, mercy me, what a sight you are!

HJALMAR. What a sight?

GINA. And your good overcoat too! It *has* had a doing!

HEDVIG (*from the kitchen doorway*). Mother, shall I—? (*Sees* HJAL-MAR, *screams with joy and runs to him.*) Father! father!

HJALMAR (*turning away and waving her back*). Go away, go away! (*To* GINA.) Make her go away from me, I tell you!

GINA (*in an undertone*). Go into the sitting-room, Hedvig. (HEDVIG *goes in silently.*)

HJALMAR (*pulling out the table-drawer, with a show of being busy.*) I must have my books with me. Where are my books?

GINA. What books?

HJALMAR. My scientific works, of course—the technical journals I use for my invention.

GINA (*looking in the bookcase*). Are they these unbound ones?

HJALMAR. Of course they are.

GINA (*laying a pile of magazines on the table*). Shan't I get Hedvig to cut them for you?

HJALMAR. I don't need to have them cut. (*Short silence.*)

GINA. Is it settled that you leave us, then, Hjalmar?

HJALMAR (*rummaging among the books*). I should think that was evident.

GINA. Yes, yes.

HJALMAR (*vehemently*). I can't come here and get a knife into my heart every hour of the day!

GINA. God forgive you, for saying such hard things of me.

HJALMAR. Prove to me—

GINA. I think it is you should prove to me.

HJALMAR. After a past like yours? There are certain demands—one might almost call them demands of the ideal—

GINA. But what about grandfather? What is to become of him, poor old man?

HJALMAR. I know my duty; the helpless old man will go with me. I shall go into the town and make my arrangements.—Hm—(*hestitatingly*)—has anyone found my hat on the stairs?

GINA. No. Have you lost your hat?

HJALMAR. Of course I must have had it when I came in last night, there's no doubt of that; but this morning I couldn't find it.

GINA. Good Lord!—wherever did you go with those two scamps?

HJALMAR. Don't ask silly questions. Do you suppose I am in a condition to remember details?

GINA. I only hope you haven't caught cold, Hjalmar. (*Goes into the kitchen.*)

HJALMAR (*talks to himself in an angry undertone while he empties the table drawer*). You are a scoundrel, Relling! You are a blackguard!—a shameless seducer!—I should like to murder you! (*He puts some old letters on one side, comes upon the torn paper of the day before, takes it up and looks at the pieces, but puts it down hastily as* GINA *comes in.*)

GINA (*putting down a breakfast tray on the table*). Here is a drop of something hot, if you could fancy it. And some bread and butter and a little salt meat with it.

HJALMAR (*glancing at the tray*). Salt meat? Never under this roof!— It is true I haven't tasted a bit of food for four-and-twenty hours, but that makes no difference.—My notes! The beginning of my memoirs! Where on earth are my diary and my important papers? (*Opens the sitting-room door, but draws back.*) There she is again!

GINA. Good gracious, the child must be somewhere!

HJALMAR. Come out. (*Stands aside, and* HEDVIG *comes out into the studio, looking frightened.* HJALMAR *stands with his hand on the doorhandle.*) In these last moments I am spending in my former home, I wish to be protected from those who have no business here. (*Goes into the room.*)

HEDVIG (*goes with a bound towards her mother and speaks in a low trembling voice*). Does he mean me?

GINA. Stay in the kitchen, Hedvig; or, no—better go into your own room. (*Talks to* HJALMAR, *as she goes in to him.*) Wait a minute, Hjalmar; don't turn all the drawers upside down; I know where all the things are.

HEDVIG (*stands motionless for a moment frightened and irresolute, biting her lips to keep back the tears. Then she clenches her hands convulsively and says softly.*) The wild duck! (*She creeps over and takes the pistol from the shelf, opens the attic door a little, slips in and shuts the door after her.* HJALMAR *and* GINA *are heard wrangling in the sitting-room.* HJALMAR *comes out carrying some note-books and old loose papers which he lays on the table.*)

HJALMAR. That portmanteau won't nearly hold them! There are a hundred and one things I must take with me.

GINA (*following him with the portmanteau*). Well, let the rest wait. Just take a shirt and a pair of drawers with you.

HJALMAR. Poof!—these exhausting preparations—! (*Takes off his overcoat and throws it on the sofa.*)

GINA. And there is the coffee getting all cold, too.

HJALMAR. Hm! (*Drinks a mouthful absently and then another.*)

GINA (*dusting the backs of the chairs*). You will have a job to find another big attic like this for the rabbits.

HJALMAR. What! Have I got to take all the rabbits with me too?

GINA. Yes, grandfather can't live without his rabbits, I am sure.

HJALMAR. He will have to get accustomed to it. I have got to renounce what is of a deal more vital importance than rabbits.

GINA (*dusting the bookcase*). Shall I put your flute in the portmanteau for you?

HJALMAR. No. No flute for me. But give me the pistol.

GINA. Are you going to take that there gun with you?

HJALMAR. Yes. My loaded pistol.

GINA (*looking for it*). It isn't here. He must have taken it in with him.

HJALMAR. Is he in the attic?

GINA. No doubt he is.

HJALMAR. Hm—poor lonely old fellow. (*Takes a piece of bread and butter, eats it and drinks up his cup of coffee.*)

GINA. If only we hadn't let our other room, you might have moved in there.

HJALMAR. I should be living under the same roof with—! Never—never!

GINA. But couldn't you put up for a day or two in the sitting-room? You should have it all to yourself.

HJALMAR. Never within these walls.

GINA. Well, then, downstairs, with Relling and Molvik?

HJALMAR. Don't mention those fellows' names! The very thought of them almost takes my appetite away. No, no—I must go out into the storm and snow—go from house to house seeking shelter for my father and myself.

GINA. But you have no hat, Hjalmar! You know you have lost your hat.

HJALMAR. Oh, those scum of the earth, steeped in every vice!—I must get a hat as I go. (*Takes another piece of bread and butter.*) I must make the necessary arrangements. I am not going to endanger my life. (*Searches for something on the tray.*)

GINA. What are you looking for?

HJALMAR. Butter.

GINA. I will get some in a moment. (*Goes into the kitchen.*)

HJALMAR (*calling after her*). Oh, it's of no consequence. Dry bread will do just as well for me.

GINA (*bringing in a butter-dish*). See, this is fresh churned.

(*She pours out another cup of coffee for him; he sits down on the sofa, puts more butter on his bread, and eats and drinks for a little while in silence.*)

HJALMAR. If I decided to do so, could I—without being exposed to intrusion on anyone's part—put up for a day or two in the sitting-room there?

GINA. Of course you could, if only you would.

HJALMAR. Because I don't see there is any possibility of getting all father's things out in a moment.

GINA. And, besides that, you have got to tell him first that you don't mean to live here with us any longer.

HJALMAR (*pushing his cup away*). Yes, that's another thing; I have got to open up all this complicated question again—I must consider the situation; I must have time to breathe; I cannot sustain all these burdens in a single day.

GINA. No, and in such vile weather as it is, too.

HJALMAR (*turning over Mr. WERLE's letter*). I see this paper is still lying here.

GINA. Yes, I haven't touched it.

HJALMAR. The rubbish is no concern of mine—

GINA. Well, I am sure *I* had no idea of doing anything with it.

HJALMAR. But it might be as well not to let it get out of sight altogether. In all the upset of my moving, it might so easily—

GINA. I'll take care of it, Hjalmar.

HJALMAR. The deed of gift, after all, belongs first and foremost to my father, and it is his affair whether he chooses to make any use of it.

GINA (*sighing*). Yes, poor old father.

HJALMAR. Just for the sake of safety—where can I find some paste?

GINA (*going to the book-shelf*). Here is the paste-pot.

HJALMAR. And a brush.

GINA. Here is a brush too. (*Brings them to him.*)

HJALMAR (*taking up a pair of scissors*). Just a strip of paper along the back—. (*Cuts and pastes.*) Far be it from me to want to do anything amiss with other people's property—least of all with what belongs to a poor old man—and, indeed, to someone else as well. There we are! Let it lie there for a little. And when it is dry, take it away. I don't wish ever to set eyes on the paper again. Never!

(GREGERS WERLE *comes in from the passage.*)

GREGERS (*slightly astonished*). What—are you sitting here, Hjalmar?

HJALMAR (*getting up hurriedly*). I had sunk down from exhaustion.

GREGERS. You have been having some breakfast, I see.

HJALMAR. The body makes its claims felt sometimes, too.

GREGERS. What have you decided to do?

HJALMAR. For a man like me, there is only one thing to be done, I am just engaged in putting my most important things together. But it takes time, as you may suppose.

GINA (*a little impatiently*). Well, am I to get the room ready for you, or pack your portmanteau?

HJALMAR (*with a glance of irritation towards* GREGERS). Pack—and get the room ready as well!

GREGERS (*after a short pause*). I should never have thought this would be the end of it. Is there really any necessity for you to leave house and home?

HJALMAR (*walking about uneasily*). What do you want me to do, then?—I am not fit to stand unhappiness, Gregers. I need a sense of security and peace about me.

GREGERS. But can't you have that here? Just make the trial. It seems to me that now you have firm ground to build upon—and to begin afresh. Remember, too, you have your invention to live for.

HJALMAR. Oh, don't talk to me about my invention. I shouldn't wonder if that were a very long way off.

GREGERS. Really?

HJALMAR. Good heavens! Yes. Just tell me what you suppose I am going to invent? Other people have invented most things already. It becomes harder every day—

GREGERS. But you, who have worked so hard at it—

HJALMAR. It was that scoundrel Relling who set me on to it.

GREGERS. Relling?

HJALMAR. Yes, it was he that first called my attention to my talent for making some remarkable discovery in photography.

GREGERS. Aha!—it was Relling!

HJALMAR. I got so much happiness out of it, Gregers. Not so much for the sake of the invention itself, as because Hedvig believed in it—believed in it with a child's wholehearted enthusiasm. Perhaps I should say that I have been fool enough to go and fancy she believed in it.

GREGERS. Can you really suppose that Hedvig has not been genuine about it?

HJALMAR. I can suppose anything now. It is Hedvig that stands in my way. She has taken all the sunshine out of my life.

GREGERS. Hedvig? Can you say that of Hedvig? How can she have done anything of the sort?

HJALMAR (*without answering him*).   How unspeakably I have loved that child! How unspeakably happy I have felt every time I came home into my poor room, and she ran to meet me with her sweet little half-closed eyes!—Credulous fool! I loved her so unspeakably, that I deluded myself with the dream that she loved me just as much.

GREGERS.   Do you say that was a delusion?

HJALMAR.   How can I tell? I can get nothing whatever out of Gina, and she is so utterly lacking in any sense of the ideal side of all these complications. But to you I feel forced to open my mind, Gregers. There is that terrible doubt—perhaps Hedvig has never really honestly loved me.

GREGERS.   It is possible you may have proof of that. (*Listens.*) What is that? I thought I heard the wild duck cry.

HJALMAR.   It is the wild duck quacking. Father is in the attic.

GREGERS.   Is he? (*A look of happiness lights up his face.*) I tell you, you may have proof yet that your poor misunderstood Hedvig loves you.

HJALMAR.   What proof can she give me? I daren't believe in any assurances from that quarter.

GREGERS.   There is not an atom of deceitfulness in Hedvig.

HJALMAR.   Ah, Gregers, that is just what I am not so certain about. Who knows what Gina and that Mrs. Sörby may have sat here whispering and gossiping about? And Hedvig is generally all ears, I can tell you. Perhaps the deed of gift did not come so unexpectedly, after all. Indeed, I thought I noticed something.

GREGERS.   What sort of spirit is this that has taken hold of you?

HJALMAR.   I have had my eyes opened. Just you wait. You will see the deed of gift is only a beginning. Mrs. Sörby has all along been very thick with Hedvig, and now she has it in her power to do whatever she pleases for the child. They can take her from me whenever they like.

GREGERS.   Hedvig will never leave you.

HJALMAR.   Don't be so sure of that. If they come beckoning to her with their hands full of gifts—. And I have loved her so unspeakably! I, who would have thought it my greatest joy to take her carefully by the hand and lead her through life—just as one leads a child, who is frightened of the dark, through a great empty room! Now I feel such a gnawing certainty that the poor photographer, up in his garret here, has never really and truly been anything to her. She has only been cunningly careful to keep on a good footing with me till the time came.

GREGERS.   You don't really believe that, Hjalmar?

HJALMAR.   That is just the cruellest part of it—that I don't know what to believe—and that I never shall know. But can you really doubt that it is as I say? Ha! ha! You rely far too much on your "demands of the ideal," my good Gregers! If the others were to come, with their hands full, and call to the child: "Come away from him: you will learn what life is with us—"

GREGERS (*hastily*).   Well, what then, do you suppose?

HJALMAR.   If I asked her then: "Hedvig, are you willing to give up

this life they offer you, for my sake?" (*Laughs derisively.*) Thank you!—
you would just hear what answer I should get.

(*A pistol shot is heard from within the attic.*)

GREGERS (*with a happy shout*). Hjalmar!

HJALMAR. Listen to that. He must needs go shooting too.

GINA (*coming in*). Hjalmar, I think grandfather is blundering about in the attic by himself.

HJALMAR. I will look in—

GREGERS (*quickly and with emotion*). Wait a moment! Do you know what that was?

HJALMAR. Of course I know.

GREGERS. No, but you don't. I know. That was the proof you wanted!

HJALMAR. What proof?

GREGERS. That was a child's act of sacrifice. She has got your father to shoot the wild duck.

HJALMAR. Shoot the wild duck!

GINA. Fancy that, now!

HJALMAR. What for?

GREGERS. She wanted to sacrifice, for your sake, what she prized most in the world; because she believed it would make you love her again.

HJALMAR. (*tenderly with emotion*). Poor child!

GINA. What things she thinks of!

GREGERS. She only wanted your love again, Hjalmar; she did not feel as if she could live without it.

GINA (*struggling with her tears*). There you are, Hjalmar!

HJALMAR. Gina, where is she?

GINA (*sniffing*). Poor thing, she is sitting out in the kitchen, I expect.

HJALMAR (*crosses the room and opens the kitchen door*). Hedvig—come! Come here to me! (*Looks round.*) No, she is not there.

GINA. Then she must be in her own little room.

HJALMAR (*who has gone out to look*). No, she is not here either. (*Comes in.*) She must have gone out.

GINA. Yes, you wouldn't have her anywhere in the house.

HJALMAR. If only she would come home soon, so that I could let her know—. Everything will go well now, Gregers; now I believe we can begin life over again.

GREGERS (*quietly*). I knew it was through the child that reparation would be made.

(*Old EKDAL comes to the door of his room; he is in full uniform, and is occupied in trying to buckle on his sword.*)

HJALMAR (*in astonishment*). Father! are you there!

GINA. Was it in your own room that you fired?

EKDAL (*indignantly as he approaches*). So you go shooting alone, do you, Hjalmar?

HJALMAR (*anxious and perplexed*). Wasn't it you, then, that was shooting in the attic?

EKDAL. I shooting? Hm!

GREGERS (*calls to* HJALMAR). She has shot the wild duck herself, don't you see?

HJALMAR. What can it mean! (*Hurries to the attic door, tears it aside, looks in, and gives a loud scream.*) Hedvig!

GINA (*running to the door*). Heavens! what is it?

HJALMAR (*going in*). She is lying on the floor!

GREGERS. Hedvig on the floor! (*Goes in to* HJALMAR.)

GINA (*at the same time*). Hedvig! (*From within the garret.*) Oh, no! no! no!

EKDAL. Ho! ho! does she go out shooting too!

(HJALMAR, GINA *and* GREGERS *carry* HEDVIG *into the studio; the pistol is clasped tight in the fingers of her right hand, which is hanging down.*)

HJALMAR (*distractedly*). The pistol has gone off—and she has been shot. Call for help! Help!

GINA (*runs into the passage and calls out*). Relling! Relling! Doctor Relling! come up as quickly as ever you can! (HJALMAR *and* GREGERS *lay* HEDVIG *on the sofa.*)

EKDAL (*quietly*). The forests avenge themselves.

HJALMAR (*on his knees beside* HEDVIG). She is coming to now. She is coming to—yes, yes, yes.

GINA (*who has come in again*). Where has she been shot? I can't see anything. (RELLING *comes in hurriedly with* MOLVIK *at his heels; the latter is without waistcoat or necktie, and with his coat flying open.*)

RELLING. What is the matter?

GINA. They say Hedvig has shot herself.

HJALMAR. Come here and help!

RELLING. Shot herself! (*Pushes the table aside and begins to examine her.*)

HJALMAR (*looking anxiously up at him*). It can't be dangerous, Relling? What? She hardly bleeds at all. It can't be dangerous?

RELLING. How did it happen?

HJALMAR. I can't imagine—!

GINA. She wanted to shoot the wild duck.

RELLING. The wild duck?

HJALMAR. The pistol must have gone off.

RELLING. Hm! Quite so.

EKDAL. The forests avenge themselves. But I am not afraid, anyway. (*Goes into the attic and shuts the door after him.*)

HJALMAR. Well, Relling—why don't you say something?

RELLING. The ball has entered the breast.

HJALMAR. Yes—but she's coming to!

GINA (*bursting into tears*). My child, my child!

GREGERS (*in a choked voice*). In the ocean's depths—

HJALMAR (*springing up*). Yes, yes, she *must* live! Oh, for God's sake,

Relling—just for a moment—just long enough for me to let her know how unspeakably I have loved her all the time!

RELLING. The heart has been hit. Internal hæmorrhage. She died on the spot.

HJALMAR. And I hunted her away from me! And she crept like a frightened animal into the attic and died for love of me. (*Sobbing.*) I can never make it right now! I can never tell her—! (*Clenches his fists and cries up to heaven.*) Thou who art there above us—if indeed Thou *art* there! Why hast Thou done this to me!

GINA. Hush, hush! you mustn't take on in that terrible way. We had no right to keep her, I suppose.

MOLVIK. The child is not dead, but sleepeth.

RELLING. Rubbish!

HJALMAR (*goes more calmly over to the sofa and, folding his arms, looks down at* HEDVIG). There she lies, so stiff and still.

RELLING (*trying to take the pistol from her fingers*). She holds so tight, so tight.

GINA. No, no, Relling, don't hurt her fingers; let the thing alone.

HJALMAR. She shall take it with her.

GINA. Yes, let her. But the child mustn't lie out here for a show. She shall go into her own little room, she shall. Carry her with me, Hjalmar. (*She and* HJALMAR *take her up.*)

HJALMAR (*as they carry her out*). Oh, Gina, Gina—can you ever get over this?

GINA. We must help one another. Now, I think, we each have a share in her.

MOLVIK (*stretches out his arms and babbles*). Blessed be the Lord! Earth to earth, dust to dust—

RELLING (*whispering*). Shut up, you fool—you're drunk.

(HJALMAR *and* GINA *carry the body out through the kitchen.* RELLING *stands looking after them.* MOLVIK *sneaks out into the passage.*)

RELLING (*going over to* GREGERS). No one will ever persuade me this was an accident.

GREGERS (*who has stood terror-stricken, his face twitching convulsively*). No one can say how the dreadful thing happened.

RELLING. The flame has scorched her dress. She must have held the pistol to her breast and fired.

GREGERS. Hedvig has not died in vain. You saw how his grief called out all the best that was in him.

RELLING. Most people show their best side in the presence of death. But how long do you suppose this turn for the better will last in his case?

GREGERS. Surely it will last and increase as long as he lives!

RELLING. In eight or nine months little Hedvig will be no more to him than a beautiful theme to declaim upon.

GREGERS. Do you dare to say that of Hjalmar Ekdal?

RELLING. We will talk of it again as soon as the grass has grown over her grave. Then you will hear him pumping up his fine phrases about "the child torn prematurely from her father's loving heart"; you will see him wallowing in emotional fits of self-admiration and self-compassion. Just you wait and see!

GREGERS. If you are right, and I am wrong, life is no longer worth living.

RELLING. Oh, life would be all right if we could only be rid of these infernal fools who come to poor people's doors presenting their "demands of the ideal."

GREGERS (*looking in front of him*). If that is so, I am glad my destiny is what it is.

RELLING. Excuse me, but—what *is* your destiny?

GREGERS (*turning to go*). To be the thirteenth at table.

RELLING. So I should imagine!

QUESTIONS

1. The Wild Duck begins at a leisurely pace and seems at first to be almost a comedy of manners. When in the first act does the major complication of the plot begin? What antecedent actions of the first act result in consequences in later acts? What devices are used to produce comic effects in the first part of the play? How does Ibsen shift to a more serious mood before the act is over? What question or questions are raised and left unanswered at the end of Act One? Are there any other devices or means of raising interest in this first act?

2. Trace and list the sequence of major complications and resolutions which constitute the main story line or central plot. Choose a major complication in the sequence, show how it is initiated, developed to a crisis, and resolved or concluded.

3. List the chief plot discoveries (those which have an important bearing upon the course and/or outcome of the action). Take as an example of major plot discovery Hjalmar's discovery of the parentage of Hedvig. Trace in full the ways in which this discovery is effectuated. To what extent does its manipulation involve reasoning, memory, and a sign or signs (a sign is any kind of acquired or inherited mark or device—a birthmark, for example—which serves to reveal identity)? What characters become involved in the process of the discovery? What effects does the discovery have on each? Are there any self discoveries in the play? To what extent do the discoveries produce changes in the characters and in their lives?

4. Which of the characters are definitely or obviously ludicrous or comic and which are dominantly normal human beings? Among the normal characters, which have at least some slight element of ludicrousness? What traits make each of the comic characters comic? Are any of the comic traits bases for or motivations to action? Among the ludicrous characters, which excite some element of sympathy and which are largely antipathetic?

5. In what ways do the various characterizations of the agents illustrate, support, or exemplify the argument for the necessity of illusion (the life-lie) in man? What incidents support this argument? In what ways, if any, is the symbol of the wild duck related to the argument? Are there any other ideas about the nature of man in the play? Are these related to the central idea of man as a creature of illusions?

6. The wild duck is constantly alluded to in the play. How is the term extended to mean more than the physical object which it first designates? What are its various meanings?

7. If you were a director of an acting company interpreting this play for a contemporary audience what specific effects would you expect the play to produce upon that audience?

THE IMPORTANCE OF
BEING EARNEST

Oscar Wilde

Oscar Fingal O'Flahertie Wills Wilde (1854–1900) was born in Dublin and educated at Trinity College there and at Magdalen College, Oxford. He began his career as a writer during his student days and published his first volume, *Poems*, in 1881. If not the founder, he was the most prominent member of an aesthetic cult characteristic of the *fin-de-siecle* spirit in its emphasis upon "art for art's sake." As a leader of this cult, Wilde was caricatured in the role of Reginald Bunthorne, a fleshly poet, in Gilbert and Sullivan's *Patience* (1881), a bit of notoriety which he relished. Wilde lectured in England and America, wrote rather extensively for the journals of his day, and published several works of fiction, the best of which is *The Portrait of Dorian Gray* (1891). He was sentenced to prison in 1895 on a charge growing out of moral misconduct. In prison he wrote his famous poem, *Ballad of Reading Gaol*, published in 1898, and probably began an autobiographical confession, *De Profundis*, first published after his death in 1905.

Wilde's first plays were melodramas, and even his later witty comedies borrow elements and devices from that school. His plays are as follows: *Vera, or, The Nihilists* (1883), *The Duchess of Padua* (1891), *Salome* (1892), *Lady Windermere's Fan* (1892), *A Woman of No Importance* (1893), *An Ideal Husband* (1895), *The Importance of Being Earnest* (1895). Of these latter four comedies, *The Importance of Being Earnest* is the best and is one of the most brilliant and witty farces written in England during the nineteenth century.

In some of its devices and contrivances, *The Importance of Being Earnest* is reminiscent of melodrama, especially in the resolution. But the play is in form a farcical comedy which delightfully exposes the pretentiousness of certain social modes and conventions. The exposure is accomplished through the resolution of the action by the unexpected establishment of Jack's parentage, by episodes and contrivances in the situation, such as the arrangement of the engagement between Cecily and Algernon and by numerous ludicrous incidents, such as Jack's appearance in mourning for the death of his fictitious brother. It is accomplished in characterization by contrasting Jack as the man-about-town with the grave and serious Jack of the country, Algernon as the frivolous gourmet with Algernon going Bunburying, and especially the social necessity that makes such subterfuges prudent, if not essential. It comes to the fore in the characters of Gwendolen and of Cecily who in the getting of husbands follow some highly unconventional procedures. In terms of character, it is tellingly exposed in the role of Lady Bracknell, the *grande dame* of the piece.

The exposure is most obviously and pleasingly apparent in the witty, paradoxical diction of the play. The conversation is exactly suited to the characters. In this sparkling, witty dialogue, paradox serves its basic function of turning topsy-turvy the conventional clichés of polite conversation and of scores upon scores of popular novels and plays, and of showing these ideas and sentiments to be contrary to actuality. In accomplishing this function, the dialogue at the same time becomes the chief means of comic effect. *The Importance of Being Earnest* is essentially a comedy of wit, rather than a comedy of characters; yet it makes its effective comic commentary upon the nature of man in a conventional social order.

CHARACTERS

JOHN WORTHING, J.P.	LADY BRACKNELL
ALGERNON MONCRIEFF	HON. GWENDOLEN FAIRFAX
REV. CANON CHASUBLE, D.D.	CECILY CARDEW
MERRIMAN (*Butler*)	MISS PRISM (*Governess*)
LANE (*Manservant*)	

THE SCENES OF THE PLAY

ACT   I.   Algernon Moncrieff's Flat in Half-Moon Street, W.
ACT II.   The Garden at the Manor House, Woolton.
ACT III.   Drawing-Room of the Manor House, Woolton.
          Time—The Present.
          Place—London.

ACT I

SCENE.—*Morning-room in* ALGERNON's *flat in Half-Moon Street. The room is luxuriously and artistically furnished. The sound of a piano is heard in the adjoining room.*

  (LANE *is arranging afternoon tea on the table, and after the music has ceased,* ALGERNON *enters.*)

ALGERNON.   Did you hear what I was playing, Lane?
LANE.   I didn't think it polite to listen, sir.
ALGERNON.   I'm sorry for that, for your sake. I don't play accurately—anyone can play accurately—but I play with wonderful expression. As far as the piano is concerned, sentiment is my forte. I keep science for Life.
LANE.   Yes, sir.
ALGERNON.   And, speaking of the science of Life, have you got the cucumber sandwiches cut for Lady Bracknell?
LANE.   Yes, sir. (*Hands them on a salver.*)

ALGERNON (*inspects them, takes two, and sits down on the sofa*). Oh! . . . by the way, Lane, I see from your book that on Thursday night, when Lord Shoreman and Mr. Worthing were dining with me, eight bottles of champagne are entered as having been consumed.

LANE. Yes, sir; eight bottles and a pint.

ALGERNON. Why is it that at a bachelor's establishment the servants invariably drink the champagne? I ask merely for information.

LANE. I attribute it to the superior quality of the wine, sir. I have often observed that in married households the champagne is rarely of a first-rate brand.

ALGERNON. Good Heavens! Is marriage so demoralizing as that?

LANE. I believe it *is* a very pleasant state, sir. I have had very little experience of it myself up to the present. I have only been married once. That was in consequence of a misunderstanding between myself and a young woman.

ALGERNON (*languidly*). I don't know that I am much interested in your family life, Lane.

LANE. No, sir; it is not a very interesting subject. I never think of it myself.

ALGERNON. Very natural, I am sure. That will do, Lane, thank you.

LANE. Thank you, sir. (LANE *goes out.*)

ALGERNON. Lane's views on marriage seem somewhat lax. Really, if the lower orders don't set us a good example, what on earth is the use of them? They seem, as a class, to have absolutely no sense of moral responsibility.

(*Enter* LANE.)

LANE. Mr. Ernest Worthing.

(*Enter* JACK. LANE *goes out.*)

ALGERNON. How are you, my dear Ernest? What brings you up to town?

JACK. Oh, pleasure, pleasure! What else should bring one anywhere? Eating as usual, I see, Algy!

ALGERNON (*stiffly*). I believe it is customary in good society to take some slight refreshment at five o'clock. Where have you been since last Thursday?

JACK (*sitting down on the sofa*). In the country.

ALGERNON. What on earth do you do there?

JACK (*pulling off his gloves*). When one is in town one amuses oneself. When one is in the country one amuses other people. It is excessively boring.

ALGERNON. And who are the people you amuse?

JACK (*airily*). Oh, neighbours, neighbours.

ALGERNON. Got nice neighbours in your part of Shropshire?

JACK. Perfectly horrid! Never speak to one of them.

ALGERNON. How immensely you must amuse them! (*Goes over and takes sandwich.*) By the way, Shropshire is your county, is it not?

The Importance of Being Earnest

JACK. Eh? Shropshire? Yes, of course. Hallo! Why all these cups? Why cucumber sandwiches? Why such reckless extravagance in one so young? Who is coming to tea?

ALGERNON. Oh! merely Aunt Augusta and Gwendolen.

JACK. How perfectly delightful!

ALGERNON. Yes, that is all very well; but I am afraid Aunt Augusta won't quite approve of your being here.

JACK. May I ask why?

ALGERNON. My dear fellow, the way you flirt with Gwendolen is perfectly disgraceful. It is almost as bad as the way Gwendolen flirts with you.

JACK. I am in love with Gwendolen. I have come up to town expressly to propose to her.

ALGERNON. I thought you had come up for pleasure? . . . I call that business.

JACK. How utterly unromantic you are!

ALGERNON. I really don't see anything romantic in proposing. It is very romantic to be in love. But there is nothing romantic about a definite proposal. Why, one may be accepted. One usually is, I believe. Then the excitement is all over. The very essence of romance is uncertainty. If ever I get married, I'll certainly try to forget the fact.

JACK. I have no doubt about that, dear Algy. The Divorce Court was specially invented for people whose memories are so curiously constituted.

ALGERNON. Oh! there is no use speculating on that subject. Divorces are made in Heaven—— (JACK *puts out his hand to take a sandwich.* ALGERNON *at once interferes.*) Please don't touch the cucumber sandwiches. They are ordered specially for Aunt Augusta. (*Takes one and eats it.*)

JACK. Well, you have been eating them all the time.

ALGERNON. That is quite a different matter. She is my aunt. (*Takes plate from below.*) Have some bread and butter. The bread and butter is for Gwendolen. Gwendolen is devoted to bread and butter.

JACK (*advancing to table and helping himself*). And very good bread and butter it is, too.

ALGERNON. Well, my dear fellow, you need not eat as if you were going to eat it all. You behave as if you were married to her already. You are not married to her already, and I don't think you ever will be.

JACK. Why on earth do you say that?

ALGERNON. Well, in the first place girls never marry the men they flirt with. Girls don't think it right.

JACK. Oh, that is nonsense!

ALGERNON. It isn't. It is a great truth. It accounts for the extraordinary number of bachelors that one sees all over the place. In the second place, I don't give my consent.

JACK. Your consent!

ALGERNON. My dear fellow, Gwendolen is my first cousin. And before

I allow you to marry her, you will have to clear up the whole question of Cecily. (*Rings bell.*)

JACK.   Cecily! What on earth do you mean? What do you mean, Algy, by Cecily? I don't know anyone of the name of Cecily.

(*Enter* LANE.)

ALGERNON.   Bring me that cigarette case Mr. Worthing left in the smoking-room the last time he dined here.

LANE.   Yes, sir. (LANE *goes out.*)

JACK.   Do you mean to say you have had my cigarette case all this time? I wish to goodness you had let me know. I have been writing frantic letters to Scotland Yard about it. I was very nearly offering a large reward.

ALGERNON.   Well, I wish you would offer one. I happen to be more than usually hard up.

JACK.   There is no good offering a large reward now that the thing is found.

(*Enter* LANE *with the cigarette case on a salver.* ALGERNON *takes it at once.* LANE *goes out.*)

ALGERNON.   I think that is rather mean of you, Ernest, I must say. (*Opens case and examines it.*) However, it makes no matter, for, now that I look at the inscription, I find that the thing isn't yours after all.

JACK.   Of course it's mine. (*Moving to him.*) You have seen me with it a hundred times, and you have no right whatsoever to read what is written inside. It is a very ungentlemanly thing to read a private cigarette case.

ALGERNON.   Oh! it is absurd to have a hard-and-fast rule about what one should read and what one shouldn't. More than half of modern culture depends on what one shouldn't read.

JACK.   I am quite aware of the fact, and I don't propose to discuss modern culture. It isn't the sort of thing one should talk of in private. I simply want my cigarette case back.

ALGERNON.   Yes; but this isn't your cigarette case. This cigarette case is a present from someone of the name of Cecily, and you said you didn't know anyone of that name.

JACK.   Well, if you want to know, Cecily happens to be my aunt.

ALGERNON.   Your aunt!

JACK.   Yes. Charming old lady she is, too. Lives at Tunbridge Wells. Just give it back to me, Algy.

ALGERNON (*retreating to back of sofa*).   But why does she call herself little Cecily if she is your aunt and lives at Tunbridge Wells? (*Reading.*) "From little Cecily with her fondest love."

JACK (*moving to sofa and kneeling upon it*).   My dear fellow, what on earth is there in that? Some aunts are tall, some aunts are not tall. That is a matter that surely an aunt may be allowed to decide for herself. You seem to think that every aunt should be exactly like your aunt! That is absurd! For Heaven's sake give me back my cigarette case. (*Follows* ALGERNON *round the room.*)

ALGERNON. Yes. But why does your aunt call you her uncle? "From little Cecily, with her fondest love to her dear Uncle Jack." There is no objection, I admit, to an aunt being a small aunt, but why an aunt, no matter what her size may be, should call her own nephew her uncle, I can't quite make out. Besides, your name isn't Jack at all; it is Ernest.

JACK. It isn't Ernest; it's Jack.

ALGERNON. You have always told me it was Ernest. I have introduced you to everyone as Ernest. You answer to the name of Ernest. You look as if your name was Ernest. You are the most earnest looking person I ever saw in my life. It is perfectly absurd your saying that your name isn't Ernest. It's on your cards. Here is one of them. (*Taking it from case.*) "Mr. Ernest Worthing, B 4, The Albany." I'll keep this as a proof your name is Ernest if ever you attempt to deny it to me, or to Gwendolen, or to anyone else. (*Puts the card in his pocket.*)

JACK. Well, my name is Ernest in town and Jack in the country, and the cigarette case was given to me in the country.

ALGERNON. Yes, but that does not account for the fact that your small Aunt Cecily, who lives at Tunbridge Wells, calls you her dear uncle. Come, old boy, you had much better have the thing out at once.

JACK. My dear Algy, you talk exactly as if you were a dentist. It is very vulgar to talk like a dentist when one isn't a dentist. It produces a false impression.

ALGERNON. Well, that is exactly what dentists always do. Now, go on! Tell me the whole thing. I may mention that I have always suspected you of being a confirmed and secret Bunburyist; and I am quite sure of it now.

JACK. Bunburyist? What on earth do you mean by a Bunburyist?

ALGERNON. I'll reveal to you the meaning of that incomparable expression as soon as you are kind enough to inform me why you are Ernest in town and Jack in the country.

JACK. Well, produce my cigarette case first.

ALGERNON. Here it is. (*Hands cigarette case.*) Now produce your explanation, and pray make it improbable. (*Sits on sofa.*)

JACK. My dear fellow, there is nothing improbable about my explanation at all. In fact it's perfectly ordinary. Old Mr. Thomas Cardew, who adopted me when I was a little boy, made me in his will guardian to his grand-daughter, Miss Cecily Cardew. Cecily, who addresses me as her uncle from motives of respect that you could not possibly appreciate, lives at my place in the country under the charge of her admirable governess, Miss Prism.

ALGERNON. Where is that place in the country, by the way?

JACK. That is nothing to you, dear boy. You are not going to be invited. . . . I may tell you candidly that the place is not in Shropshire.

ALGERNON. I suspected that, my dear fellow! I have Bunburyed all over Shropshire on two separate occasions. Now, go on. Why are you Ernest in town and Jack in the country?

JACK. My dear Algy, I don't know whether you will be able to understand my real motives. You are hardly serious enough. When one is placed in the position of guardian, one has to adopt a very high moral tone on all subjects. It's one's duty to do so. And as a high moral tone can hardly be said to conduce very much to either one's health or one's happiness, in order to get up to town I have always pretended to have a younger brother of the name of Ernest, who lives in the Albany, and gets into the most dreadful scrapes. That, my dear Algy, is the whole truth pure and simple.

ALGERNON.   The truth is rarely pure and never simple. Modern life would be very tedious if it were either, and modern literature a complete impossibility!

JACK.   That wouldn't be at all a bad thing.

ALGERNON.   Literary criticism is not your forte, my dear fellow. Don't try it. You should leave that to people who haven't been at a University. They do it so well in the daily papers. What you really are is a Bunburyist. I was quite right in saying you were a Bunburyist. You are one of the most advanced Bunburyists I know.

JACK.   What on earth do you mean?

ALGERNON.   You have invented a very useful younger brother called Ernest, in order that you may be able to come up to town as often as you like. I have invented an invaluable permanent invalid called Bunbury, in order that I may be able to go down into the country whenever I choose. Bunbury is perfectly invaluable. If it wasn't for Bunbury's extraordinary bad health, for instance, I wouldn't be able to dine with you at Willis's to-night, for I have been really engaged to Aunt Augusta for more than a week.

JACK.   I haven't asked you to dine with me anywhere to-night.

ALGERNON.   I know. You are absolutely careless about sending out invitations. It is very foolish of you. Nothing annoys people so much as not receiving invitations.

JACK.   You had much better dine with your Aunt Augusta.

ALGERNON.   I haven't the smallest intention of doing anything of the kind. To begin with, I dined there on Monday, and once a week is quite enough to dine with one's own relatives. In the second place, whenever I do dine there I am always treated as a member of the family, and sent down with either no woman at all, or two. In the third place, I know perfectly well whom she will place me next to, to-night. She will place me next Mary Farquhar, who always flirts with her own husband across the dinner-table. That is not very pleasant. Indeed, it is not even decent . . . and that sort of thing is enormously on the increase. The amount of women in London who flirt with their own husbands is perfectly scandalous. It looks so bad. It is simply washing one's clean linen in public. Besides, now that I know you to be a confirmed Bunburyist I naturally want to talk to you about Bunburying. I want to tell you the rules.

JACK.   I'm not a Bunburyist at all. If Gwendolen accepts me, I am going to kill my brother, indeed I think I'll kill him in any case. Cecily is a little too much interested in him. It is rather a bore. So I am going to get rid of Ernest. And I strongly advise you to do the same with Mr. . . . with your invalid friend who has the absurd name.

ALGERNON. Nothing will induce me to part with Bunbury, and if you ever get married, which seems to me extremely problematic, you will be very glad to know Bunbury. A man who marries without knowing Bunbury has a very tedious time of it.

JACK. That is nonsense. If I marry a charming girl like Gwendolen, and she is the only girl I ever saw in my life that I would marry, I certainly won't want to know Bunbury.

ALGERNON. Then your wife will. You don't seem to realize, that in married life three is company and two is none.

JACK (*sentensiously*). That, my dear young friend, is the theory that the corrupt French Drama has been propounding for the last fifty years.

ALGERNON. Yes; and that the happy English home has proved in half the time.

JACK. For heaven's sake, don't try to be cynical. It's perfectly easy to be cynical.

ALGERNON. My dear fellow, it isn't easy to be anything now-a-days. There's such a lot of beastly competition about. (*The sound of an electric bell is heard.*) Ah! that must be Aunt Augusta. Only relatives, or creditors, ever ring in that Wagnerian manner. Now, if I get her out of the way for ten minutes, so that you can have an opportunity for proposing to Gwendolen, may I dine with you to-night at Willis's?

JACK. I suppose so, if you want to.

ALGERNON. Yes, but you must be serious about it. I hate people who are not serious about meals. It is so shallow of them.

(*Enter* LANE.)

LANE. Lady Bracknell and Miss Fairfax. (ALGERNON *goes forward to meet them. Enter* LADY BRACKNELL *and* GWENDOLEN.)

LADY BRACKNELL. Good afternoon, dear Algernon, I hope you are behaving very well.

ALGERNON. I'm feeling very well, Aunt Augusta.

LADY BRACKNELL. That's not quite the same thing. In fact the two things rarely go together. (*Sees* JACK *and bows to him with icy coldness.*)

ALGERNON (*to* GWENDOLEN). Dear me, you are smart!

GWENDOLEN. I am always smart! Aren't I, Mr. Worthing?

JACK. You're quite perfect, Miss Fairfax.

GWENDOLEN. Oh! I hope I am not that. It would leave no room for developments, and I intend to develop in *many directions*. (GWENDOLEN *and* JACK *sit down together in the corner.*)

LADY BRACKNELL. I'm sorry if we are a little late, Algernon, but I was obliged to call on dear Lady Harbury. I hadn't been there since her poor husband's death. I never saw a woman so altered; she looks quite twenty years younger. And now I'll have a cup of tea, and one of those nice cucumber sandwiches you promised me.

ALGERNON. Certainly, Aunt Augusta. (*Goes over to tea-table.*)

LADY BRACKNELL. Won't you come and sit here, Gwendolen?

GWENDOLEN. Thanks, mamma, I'm quite comfortable where I am.

ALGERNON (*picking up empty plate in horror*). Good heavens! Lane! Why are there no cucumber sandwiches? I ordered them specially.

LANE (*gravely*). There were no cucumbers in the market this morning, sir. I went down twice.

ALGERNON. No cucumbers!

LANE. No, sir. Not even for ready money.

ALGERNON. That will do, Lane, thank you.

LANE. Thank you, sir. (*Goes out.*)

ALGERNON. I am greatly distressed, Aunt Augusta, about there being no cucumbers, not even for ready money.

LADY BRACKNELL. It really makes no matter, Algernon. I had some crumpets with Lady Harbury, who seems to me to be living entirely for pleasure now.

ALGERNON. I hear her hair has turned quite gold from grief.

LADY BRACKNELL. It certainly has changed its colour. From what cause I, of course, cannot say. (ALGERNON *crosses and hands tea.*) Thank you. I've quite a treat for you to-night, Algernon. I am going to send you down with Mary Farquhar. She is such a nice woman, and so attentive to her husband. It's delightful to watch them.

ALGERNON. I am afraid, Aunt Augusta, I shall have to give up the pleasure of dining with you to-night after all.

LADY BRACKNELL (*frowning*). I hope not, Algernon. It would put my table completely out. Your uncle would have to dine upstairs. Fortunately he is accustomed to that.

ALGERNON. It is a great bore, and, I need hardly say, a terrible disappointment to me, but the fact is I have just had a telegram to say that my poor friend Bunbury is very ill again. (*Exchanges glances with* JACK.) They seem to think I should be with him.

LADY BRACKNELL. It is very strange. This Mr. Bunbury seems to suffer from curiously bad health.

ALGERNON. Yes; poor Bunbury is a dreadful invalid.

LADY BRACKNELL. Well, I must say, Algernon, that I think it is high time that Mr. Bunbury made up his mind whether he was going to live or to die. This shilly-shallying with the question is absurd. Nor do I in any way approve of the modern sympathy with invalids. I consider it morbid. Illness of any kind is hardly a thing to be encouraged in others. Health is the primary duty of life. I am always telling that to your poor uncle, but he never seems to take much notice . . . as far as any improvement in his ailments goes. I should be much obliged if you would ask Mr. Bunbury, from me, to be kind enough not to have a relapse on Saturday, for I rely on you to arrange my music for me. It is my last reception and one wants something that will encourage conversation, particularly at the end of the season when everyone has practically said whatever they had to say, which, in most cases, was probably not much.

ALGERNON.   I'll speak to Bunbury, Aunt Augusta, if he is still conscious, and I think I can promise you he'll be all right by Saturday. You see, if one plays good music, people don't listen, and if one plays bad music, people don't talk. But I'll run over the programme I've drawn out, if you will kindly come into the next room for a moment.

LADY BRACKNELL.   Thank you, Algernon. It is very thoughtful of you. (*Rising, and following* ALGERNON.) I'm sure the programme will be delightful, after a few expurgations. French songs I cannot possibly allow. People always seem to think that they are improper, and either look shocked, which is vulgar, or laugh, which is worse. But German sounds a thoroughly respectable language, and indeed, I believe is so. Gwendolen, you will accompany me.

GWENDOLEN.   Certainly, mamma. (LADY BRACKNELL *and* ALGERNON *go into the music-room,* GWENDOLEN *remains behind.*)

JACK.   Charming day it has been, Miss Fairfax.

GWENDOLEN.   Pray don't talk to me about the weather, Mr. Worthing. Whenever people talk to me about the weather, I always feel quite certain that they mean something else. And that makes me so nervous.

JACK.   I do mean something else.

GWENDOLEN.   I thought so. In fact, I am never wrong.

JACK.   And I would like to be allowed to take advantage of Lady Bracknell's temporary absence . . .

GWENDOLEN.   I would certainly advise you to do so. Mamma has a way of coming back suddenly into a room that I have often had to speak to her about.

JACK (*nervously*).   Miss Fairfax, ever since I met you I have admired you more than any girl . . . I have ever met since . . . I met you.

GWENDOLEN.   Yes, I am quite aware of the fact. And I often wish that in public, at any rate, you had been more demonstrative. For me you have always had an irresistible fascination. Even before I met you I was far from indifferent to you. (JACK *looks at her in amazement.*) We live, as I hope you know, Mr. Worthing, in an age of ideals. The fact is constantly mentioned in the more expensive monthly magazines, and has reached the provincial pulpits I am told: and my ideal has always been to love some one of the name of Ernest. There is something in that name that inspires absolute confidence. The moment Algernon first mentioned to me that he had a friend called Ernest, I knew I was destined to love you.

JACK.   You really love me, Gwendolen.

GWENDOLEN.   Passionately!

JACK.   Darling! You don't know how happy you've made me.

GWENDOLEN.   My own Ernest!

JACK.   But you don't really mean to say that you couldn't love me if my name wasn't Ernest?

GWENDOLEN.   But your name is Ernest.

JACK.   Yes, I know it is. But supposing it was something else? Do you mean to say you couldn't love me then?

GWENDOLEN (*glibly*). Ah! that is clearly a metaphysical speculation, and like most metaphysical speculations has very little reference at all to the actual facts of real life, as we know them.

JACK. Personally, darling, to speak quite candidly, I don't much care about the name of Ernest . . . I don't think that name suits me at all.

GWENDOLEN. It suits you perfectly. It is a divine name. It has a music of its own. It produces vibrations.

JACK. Well, really, Gwendolen, I must say that I think there are lots of other much nicer names. I think, Jack, for instance, a charming name.

GWENDOLEN. Jack? . . . No, there is very little music in the name Jack, if any at all, indeed. It does not thrill. It produces absolutely no vibrations. . . . I have known several Jacks, and they all, without exception, were more than usually plain. Besides, Jack is a notorious domesticity for John! And I pity any woman who is married to a man called John. She would probably never be allowed to know the entrancing pleasure of a single moment's solitude. The only really safe name is Ernest.

JACK. Gwendolen, I must get christened at once—I mean we must get married at once. There is no time to be lost.

GWENDOLEN. Married, Mr. Worthing?

JACK (*astounded*). Well . . . surely. You know that I love you, and you led me to believe, Miss Fairfax, that you were not absolutely indifferent to me.

GWENDOLEN. I adore you. But you haven't proposed to me yet. Nothing has been said at all about marriage. The subject has not even been touched on.

JACK. Well . . . may I propose to you now?

GWENDOLEN. I think it would be an admirable opportunity. And to spare you any possible disappointment, Mr. Worthing, I think it only fair to tell you quite frankly beforehand that I am fully determined to accept you.

JACK. Gwendolen!

GWENDOLEN. Yes, Mr. Worthing, what have you got to say to me?

JACK. You know what I have got to say to you.

GWENDOLEN. Yes, but you don't say it.

JACK. Gwendolen, will you marry me? (*Goes on his knees.*)

GWENDOLEN. Of course I will, darling. How long you have been about it! I am afraid you have had very little experience in how to propose.

JACK. My own one, I have never loved anyone in the world but you.

GWENDOLEN. Yes, but men often propose for practice. I know my brother Gerald does. All my girl-friends tell me so. What wonderfully blue eyes you have, Ernest! They are quite, quite blue. I hope you will always look at me just like that, especially when there are other people present.

(*Enter* LADY BRACKNELL.)

LADY BRACKNELL. Mr. Worthing! Rise, sir, from this semi-recumbent posture. It is most indecorous.

GWENDOLEN. Mamma! (*He tries to rise; she restrains him.*) I must beg you to retire. This is no place for you. Besides, Mr. Worthing has not quite finished yet.

LADY BRACKNELL. Finished what, may I ask?

GWENDOLEN. I am engaged to Mr. Worthing, mamma. (*They rise together.*)

LADY BRACKNELL. Pardon me, you are not engaged to anyone. When you do become engaged to some one, I, or your father, should his health permit him, will inform you of the fact. An engagement should come on a young girl as a surprise, pleasant or unpleasant, as the case may be. It is hardly a matter that she could be allowed to arrange for herself. . . . And now I have a few questions to put to you, Mr. Worthing. While I am making these inquiries, you, Gwendolen, will wait for me below in the carriage.

GWENDOLEN (*reproachfully*). Mamma!

LADY BRACKNELL. In the carriage, Gwendolen! (GWENDOLEN *goes to the door. She and* JACK *blow kisses to each other behind* LADY BRACK-NELL's *back.* LADY BRACKNELL *looks vaguely about as if she could not understand what the noise was. Finally turns round.*) Gwendolen, the carriage!

GWENDOLEN. Yes, mamma. (*Goes out, looking back at* JACK.)

LADY BRACKNELL (*sitting down*). You can take a seat, Mr. Worthing. (*Looks in her pocket for note-book and pencil.*)

JACK. Thank you, Lady Bracknell, I prefer standing.

LADY BRACKNELL (*pencil and note-book in hand*). I feel bound to tell you that you are not down on my list of eligible young men, although I have the same list as the dear Duchess of Bolton has. We work together, in fact. However, I am quite ready to enter your name, should your answers be what a really affectionate mother requires. Do you smoke?

JACK. Well, yes, I must admit I smoke.

LADY BRACKNELL. I am glad to hear it. A man should always have an occupation of some kind. There are far too many idle men in London as it is. How old are you?

JACK. Twenty-nine.

LADY BRACKNELL. A very good age to be married at. I have always been of opinion that a man who desires to get married should know either everything or nothing. Which do you know?

JACK (*after some hesitation*). I know nothing, Lady Bracknell.

LADY BRACKNELL. I am pleased to hear it. I do not approve of anything that tampers with natural ignorance. Ignorance is like a delicate exotic fruit; touch it and the bloom is gone. The whole theory of modern education is radically unsound. Fortunately in England, at any rate, education produces no effect whatsoever. If it did, it would prove a serious danger to the upper classes, and probably lead to acts of violence in Grosvenor Square. What is your income?

JACK. Between seven and eight thousand a year.

LADY BRACKNELL (*makes a note in her book*).   In land, or in investments?

JACK.   In investments, chiefly.

LADY BRACKNELL.   That is satisfactory. What between the duties expected of one during one's life-time, and the duties exacted from one after one's death, land has ceased to be either a profit or a pleasure. It gives one position, and prevents one from keeping it up. That's all that can be said about land.

JACK.   I have a country house with some land, of course, attached to it, about fifteen hundred acres, I believe; but I don't depend on that for my real income. In fact, as far as I can make out, the poachers are the only people who make anything out of it.

LADY BRACKNELL.   A country house! How many bedrooms? Well, that point can be cleared up afterwards. You have a town house, I hope? A girl with a simple, unspoiled nature, like Gwendolen, could hardly be expected to reside in the country.

JACK.   Well, I own a house in Belgrave Square, but it is let by the year to Lady Bloxham. Of course, I can get it back whenever I like, at six months' notice.

LADY BRACKNELL.   Lady Bloxham? I don't know her.

JACK.   Oh, she goes about very little. She is a lady considerably advanced in years.

LADY BRACKNELL.   Ah, now-a-days that is no guarantee of respectability of character. What number in Belgrave Square?

JACK.   149.

LADY BRACKNELL (*shaking her head*).   The unfashionable side. I thought there was something. However, that could easily be altered.

JACK.   Do you mean the fashion, or the side?

LADY BRACKNELL (*sternly*).   Both, if necessary, I presume. What are your politics?

JACK.   Well, I am afraid I really have none. I am a Liberal Unionist.

LADY BRACKNELL.   Oh, they count as Tories. They dine with us. Or come in the evening, at any rate. Now to minor matters. Are your parents living?

JACK.   I have lost both my parents.

LADY BRACKNELL.   Both? . . . That seems like carelessness. Who was your father? He was evidently a man of some wealth. Was he born in what the Radical papers call the purple of commerce, or did he rise from the ranks of the aristocracy?

JACK.   I am afraid I really don't know. The fact is, Lady Bracknell, I said I had lost my parents. It would be nearer the truth to say that my parents seem to have lost me . . . I don't actually know who I am by birth. I was . . . well, I was found.

LADY BRACKNELL.   Found!

JACK.   The late Mr. Thomas Cardew, an old gentleman of a very charitable and kindly disposition, found me, and gave me the name of

Worthing, because he happened to have a first-class ticket for Worthing in his pocket at the time. Worthing is a place in Sussex. It is a seaside resort.

LADY BRACKNELL. Where did the charitable gentleman who had a first-class ticket for this seaside resort find you?

JACK (*gravely*). In a hand-bag.

LADY BRACKNELL. A hand-bag?

JACK (*very seriously*). Yes, Lady Bracknell. I was in a hand-bag—a somewhat large, black leather hand-bag, with handles to it—an ordinary hand-bag in fact.

LADY BRACKNELL. In what locality did this Mr. James or Thomas, Cardew come across this ordinary hand-bag?

JACK. In the cloak-room at Victoria Station. It was given to him in mistake for his own.

LADY BRACKNELL. The cloak-room at Victoria Station?

JACK. Yes. The Brighton line.

LADY BRACKNELL. The line is immaterial. Mr. Worthing, I confess I feel somewhat bewildered by what you have just told me. To be born, or at any rate bred, in a hand-bag, whether it had handles or not, seems to me to display a contempt for the ordinary decencies of family life that remind one of the worst excesses of the French Revolution. And I presume you know what that unfortunate movement led to? As for the particular locality in which the hand-bag was found, a cloak-room at a railway station might serve to conceal a social indiscretion—has probably, indeed, been used for that purpose before now—but it could hardly be regarded as an assured basis for a recognized position in good society.

JACK. May I ask you then what you would advise me to do? I need hardly say I would do anything in the world to ensure Gwendolen's happiness.

LADY BRACKNELL. I would strongly advise you, Mr. Worthing, to try and acquire some relations as soon as possible, and to make a definite effort to produce at any rate one parent, of either sex, before the season is quite over.

JACK. Well, I don't see how I could possibly manage to do that. I can produce the hand-bag at any moment. It is in my dressing-room at home. I really think that should satisfy you, Lady Bracknell.

LADY BRACKNELL. Me, sir! What has it to do with me? You can hardly imagine that I and Lord Bracknell would dream of allowing our only daughter—a girl brought up with the utmost care to marry into a cloak-room, and form an alliance with a parcel? Good morning, Mr. Worthing!
(LADY BRACKNELL *sweeps out in majestic indignation.*)

JACK. Good morning! (ALGERNON, *from the other room, strikes up the Wedding March.* JACK *looks perfectly furious, and goes to the door.*) For goodness' sake don't play that ghastly tune, Algy! How idiotic you are! (*The music stops, and* ALGERNON *enters cheerily.*)

ALGERNON. Didn't it go off all right, old boy? You don't mean to say

Gwendolen refused you? I know it is a way she has. She is always refusing people. I think it is most ill-natured of her.

JACK.   Oh, Gwendolen is as right as a trivet. As far as she is concerned, we are engaged. Her mother is perfectly unbearable. Never met such a Gorgon . . . I don't really know what a Gorgon is like, but I am quite sure that Lady Bracknell is one. In any case, she is a monster, without being a myth, which is rather unfair. . . . I beg your pardon, Algy, I suppose I shouldn't talk about your own aunt in that way before you.

ALGERNON.   My dear boy, I love hearing my relations abused. It is the only thing that makes me put up with them at all. Relations are simply a tedious pack of people, who haven't got the remotest knowledge of how to live, nor the smallest instinct about when to die.

JACK.   Oh, that is nonsense!

ALGERNON.   It isn't!

JACK.   Well, I won't argue about the matter. You always want to argue about things.

ALGERNON.   That is exactly what things were originally made for.

JACK.   Upon my word, if I thought that, I'd shoot myself . . . (*A pause.*) You don't think there is any chance of Gwendolen becoming like her mother in about a hundred and fifty years, do you, Algy?

ALGERNON.   All women become like their mothers. That is their tragedy. No man does. That's his.

JACK.   Is that clever?

ALGERNON.   It is perfectly phrased! and quite as true as any observation in civilized life should be.

JACK.   I am sick to death of cleverness. Everybody is clever now-a-days. You can't go anywhere without meeting clever people. The thing has become an absolute public nuisance. I wish to goodness we had a few fools left.

ALGERNON.   We have.

JACK.   I should extremely like to meet them. What do they talk about?

ALGERNON.   The fools? Oh! about the clever people, of course.

JACK.   What fools!

ALGERNON.   By the way, did you tell Gwendolen the truth about your being Ernest in town, and Jack in the country?

JACK (*in a very patronizing manner*).   My dear fellow, the truth isn't quite the sort of thing one tells to a nice, sweet, refined girl. What extraordinary ideas you have about the way to behave to a woman!

ALGERNON.   The only way to behave to a woman is to make love to her, if she is pretty, and to someone else if she is plain.

JACK.   Oh, that is nonsense.

ALGERNON.   What about your brother? What about the profligate Ernest?

JACK.   Oh, before the end of the week I shall have got rid of him. I'll say he died in Paris of apoplexy. Lots of people die of apoplexy, quite suddenly, don't they?

ALGERNON. Yes, but it's hereditary, my dear fellow. It's a sort of thing that runs in families. You had much better say a severe chill.

JACK. You are sure a severe chill isn't hereditary, or anything of that kind?

ALGERNON. Of course it isn't!

JACK. Very well, then. My poor brother Ernest is carried off suddenly in Paris, by a severe chill. That gets rid of him.

ALGERNON. But I thought you said that . . . Miss Cardew was a little too much interested in your poor brother Ernest? Won't she feel his loss a good deal?

JACK. Oh, that is all right. Cecily is not a silly, romantic girl, I am glad to say. She has got a capital appetite, goes for long walks, and pays no attention at all to her lessons.

ALGERNON. I would rather like to see Cecily.

JACK. I will take very good care you never do. She is excessively pretty, and she is only just eighteen.

ALGERNON. Have you told Gwendolen yet that you have an excessively pretty ward who is only just eighteen?

JACK. Oh! one doesn't blurt these things out to people. Cecily and Gwendolen are perfectly certain to be extremely great friends. I'll bet you anything you like that half an hour after they have met, they will be calling each other sister.

ALGERNON. Women only do that when they have called each other a lot of other things first. Now, my dear boy, if we want to get a good table at Willis's, we really must go and dress. Do you know it is nearly seven?

JACK (*irritably*). Oh! it always is nearly seven.

ALGERNON. Well, I'm hungry.

JACK. I never knew you when you weren't. . . .

ALGERNON. What shall we do after dinner? Go to a theatre?

JACK. Oh, no! I loathe listening.

ALGERNON. Well, let us go to the Club?

JACK. Oh, no! I hate talking.

ALGERNON. Well, we might trot around to the Empire at ten?

JACK. Oh, no! I can't bear looking at things. It is so silly.

ALGERNON. Well, what shall we do?

JACK. Nothing!

ALGERNON. It is awfully hard work doing nothing. However, I don't mind hard work where there is no definite object of any kind.

(*Enter* LANE.)

LANE. Miss Fairfax.

(*Enter* GWENDOLEN. LANE *goes out*.)

ALGERNON. Gwendolen, upon my word!

GWENDOLEN. Algy, kindly turn your back. I have something very particular to say to Mr. Worthing.

ALGERNON. Really, Gwendolen, I don't think I can allow this at all.

GWENDOLEN. Algy, you always adopt a strictly immoral attitude towards life. You are not quite old enough to do that. (ALGERNON *retires to the fireplace.*)

JACK.   My own darling!

GWENDOLEN.   Ernest, we may never be married. From the expression on mamma's face I fear we never shall. Few parents now-a-days pay any regard to what their children say to them. The old-fashioned respect for the young is fast dying out. Whatever influence I ever had over mamma, I lost at the age of three. But although she may prevent us from becoming man and wife, and I may marry someone else, and marry often, nothing that she can possibly do can alter my eternal devotion to you.

JACK.   Dear Gwendolen.

GWENDOLEN.   The story of your romantic origin, as related to me by mamma, with unpleasing comments, has naturally stirred the deeper fibres of my nature. Your Christian name has an irresistible fascination. The simplicity of your character makes you exquisitely incomprehensible to me. Your town address at the Albany I have. What is your address in the country?

JACK.   The Manor House, Woolton, Hertfordshire. (ALGERNON, *who has been carefully listening, smiles to himself, and writes the address on his shirt-cuff. Then picks up the Railway Guide.*)

GWENDOLEN.   There is a good postal service, I suppose? It may be necessary to do something desperate. That, of course, will require serious consideration. I will communicate with you daily.

JACK.   My own one!

GWENDOLEN.   How long do you remain in town?

JACK.   Till Monday.

GWENDOLEN.   Good! Algy, you may turn round now.

ALGERNON.   Thanks, I've turned round already.

GWENDOLEN.   You may also ring the bell.

JACK.   You will let me see you to your carriage, my own darling?

GWENDOLEN.   Certainly.

JACK (*to* LANE, *who now enters*).   I will see Miss Fairfax out.

LANE.   Yes, sir. (JACK *and* GWENDOLEN *go off.* LANE *presents several letters on a salver to* ALGERNON. *It is to be surmised that they are bills, as* ALGERNON, *after looking at the envelopes, tears them up.*)

ALGERNON.   A glass of sherry, Lane.

LANE.   Yes, sir.

ALGERNON.   To-morrow, Lane, I'm going Bunburying.

LANE.   Yes, sir.

ALGERNON.   I shall probably not be back till Monday. You can put up my dress clothes, my smoking jacket, and all the Bunbury suits . . .

LANE.   Yes, sir. (*Handing sherry.*)

ALGERNON.   I hope to-morrow will be a fine day, Lane.

LANE.   It never is, sir.

ALGERNON.   Lane, you're a perfect pessimist.

LANE.   I do my best to give satisfaction, sir.

(*Enter* JACK. LANE *goes off*.)

JACK.   There's a sensible, intellectual girl! the only girl I ever cared for in my life. (ALGERNON *is laughing immoderately*.) What on earth are you so amused at?

ALGERNON.   Oh, I'm a little anxious about poor Bunbury, that's all.

JACK.   If you don't take care, your friend Bunbury will get you into a serious scrape some day.

ALGERNON.   I love scrapes. They are the only things that are never serious.

JACK.   Oh, that's nonsense, Algy. You never talk anything but nonsense.

ALGERNON.   Nobody ever does. (JACK *looks indignantly at him, and leaves the room.* ALGERNON *lights a cigarette, reads his shirt-cuff and smiles.*)

ACT II

SCENE.—*Garden at the Manor House. A flight of gray stone steps leads up to the house. The garden, an old-fashioned one, full of roses. Time of year, July. Basket chairs, and a table covered with books, are set under a large yew tree.*

(MISS PRISM *discovered seated at the table.* CECILY *is at the back watering flowers.*)

MISS PRISM (*calling*).   Cecily, Cecily! Surely such a utilitarian occupation as the watering of flowers is rather Moulton's duty than yours? Especially at a moment when intellectual pleasures await you. Your German grammar is on the table. Pray open it at page fifteen. We will repeat yesterday's lesson.

CECILY (*coming over very slowly*).   But I don't like German. It isn't at all a becoming language. I know perfectly well that I look quite plain after my German lesson.

MISS PRISM.   Child, you know how anxious your guardian is that you should improve yourself in every way. He laid particular stress on your German, as he was leaving for town yesterday. Indeed, he always lays stress on your German when he is leaving for town.

CECILY.   Dear Uncle Jack is so very serious! Sometimes he is so serious that I think he cannot be quite well.

MISS PRISM (*drawing herself up*).   Your guardian enjoys the best of health, and his gravity of demeanour is especially to be commended in one so comparatively young as he is. I know no one who has a higher sense of duty and responsibility.

CECILY.   I suppose that is why he often looks a little bored when we three are together.

MISS PRISM.   Cecily! I am surprised at you. Mr. Worthing has many troubles in his life. Idle merriment and triviality would be out of place in

his conversation. You must remember his constant anxiety about that unfortunate young man, his brother.

CECILY.   I wish Uncle Jack would allow that unfortunate young man,
his brother, to come down here sometimes. We might have a good influence over him, Miss Prism. I am sure you certainly would. You know German, and geology, and things of that kind influence a man very much.
(CECILY *begins to write in her diary.*)

MISS PRISM (*shaking her head*).   I do not think that even I could produce any effect on a character that, according to his own brother's admission, is irretrievably weak and vacillating. Indeed, I am not sure that I
would desire to reclaim him. I am not in favour of this modern mania for
turning bad people into good people at a moment's notice. As a man sows
so let him reap. You must put away your diary, Cecily. I really don't see
why you should keep a diary at all.

CECILY.   I keep a diary in order to enter the wonderful secrets of my
life. If I didn't write them down I should probably forget all about them.

MISS PRISM.   Memory, my dear Cecily, is the diary that we all carry
about with us.

CECILY.   Yes, but it usually chronicles the things that have never happened, and couldn't possibly have happened. I believe that Memory is responsible for nearly all the three-volume novels that Mudie sends us.

MISS PRISM.   Do not speak slightingly of the three-volume novel,
Cecily. I wrote one myself in earlier days.

CECILY.   Did you really, Miss Prism? How wonderfully clever you are!
I hope it did not end happily? I don't like novels that end happily. They
depress me so much.

MISS PRISM.   The good ended happily, and the bad unhappily. That is
what Fiction means.

CECILY.   I suppose so. But it seems very unfair. And was your novel
ever published?

MISS PRISM.   Alas! no. The manuscript unfortunately was abandoned.
I use the word in the sense of lost or mislaid. To your work, child, these
speculations are profitless.

CECILY (*smiling*).   But I see dear Dr. Chasuble coming up through the
garden.

MISS PRISM (*rising and advancing*).   Dr. Chasuble! This is indeed a
pleasure.

(*Enter* CANON CHASUBLE.)

CHASUBLE.   And how are we this morning? Miss Prism, you are, I trust,
well?

CECILY.   Miss Prism has just been complaining of a slight headache.
I think it would do her so much good to have a short stroll with you in the
park, Dr. Chasuble.

MISS PRISM.   Cecily, I have not mentioned anything about a headache.

CECILY.   No, dear Miss Prism, I know that, but I felt instinctively that you had a headache. Indeed I was thinking about that, and not about my German lesson, when the Rector came in.

CHASUBLE. I hope, Cecily, you are not inattentive.

CECILY. Oh, I am afraid I am.

CHASUBLE. That is strange. Were I fortunate enough to be Miss Prism's pupil, I would hang upon her lips. (MISS PRISM *glares.*) I spoke metaphorically.—My metaphor was drawn from bees. Ahem! Mr. Worthing, I suppose, has not returned from town yet?

MISS PRISM. We do not expect him till Monday afternoon.

CHASUBLE. Ah yes, he usually likes to spend his Sunday in London. He is not one of those whose sole aim is enjoyment, as, by all accounts, that unfortunate young man, his brother, seems to be. But I must not disturb Egeria and her pupil any longer.

MISS PRISM. Egeria? My name is Lætitia, Doctor.

CHASUBLE (*bowing*). A classical allusion merely, drawn from the Pagan authors. I shall see you both no doubt at Evensong.

MISS PRISM. I think, dear Doctor, I will have a stroll with you. I find I have a headache after all, and a walk might do it good.

CHASUBLE. With pleasure, Miss Prism, with pleasure. We might go as far as the schools and back.

MISS PRISM. That would be delightful. Cecily, you will read your Political Economy in my absence. The chapter on the Fall of the Rupee you may omit. It is somewhat too sensational. Even these metallic problems have their melodramatic side. (*Goes down the garden with Dr. Chasuble.*)

CECILY (*picks up books and throws them back on table.*)   Horrid Political Economy! Horrid Geography! Horrid, horrid German!

(*Enter MERRIMAN with a card on a salver.*)

MERRIMAN. Mr. Ernest Worthing has just driven over from the station. He has brought his luggage with him.

CECILY (*takes the card and reads it*). "Mr. Ernest Worthing, B 4 The Albany, W." Uncle Jack's brother! Did you tell him Mr. Worthing was in town?

MERRIMAN. Yes, Miss. He seemed very much disappointed. I mentioned that you and Miss Prism were in the garden. He said he was anxious to speak to you privately for a moment.

CECILY. Ask Mr. Ernest Worthing to come here. I suppose you had better talk to the housekeeper about a room for him.

MERRIMAN. Yes, Miss. (MERRIMAN *goes off.*)

CECILY. I have never met any really wicked person before. I feel rather frightened. I am so afraid he will look just like everyone else.

(*Enter ALGERNON, very gay and debonair.*)

He does!

ALGERNON (*raising his hat*). You are my little cousin Cecily, I'm sure.

CECILY. You are under some strange mistake. I am not little. In fact, I am more than usually tall for my age. (ALGERNON *is rather taken aback.*)

But I am your cousin Cecily. You, I see from your card, are Uncle Jack's brother, my cousin Ernest, my wicked cousin Ernest.

ALGERNON.   Oh! I am not really wicked at all, cousin Cecily. You mustn't think that I am wicked.

CECILY.   If you are not, then you have certainly been deceiving us all in a very inexcusable manner. I hope you have not been leading a double life, pretending to be wicked and being really good all the time. That would be hypocrisy.

ALGERNON (*looks at her in amazement*).   Oh! of course I have been rather reckless.

CECILY.   I am glad to hear it.

ALGERNON.   In fact, now you mention the subject, I have been very bad in my own small way.

CECILY.   I don't think you should be so proud of that, though I am sure it must have been very pleasant.

ALGERNON.   It is much pleasanter being here with you.

CECILY.   I can't understand how you are here at all. Uncle Jack won't be back till Monday afternoon.

ALGERNON.   That is a great disappointment. I am obliged to go up by the first train on Monday morning. I have a business appointment that I am anxious . . . to miss.

CECILY.   Couldn't you miss it anywhere but in London?

ALGERNON.   No; the appointment is in London.

CECILY.   Well, I know, of course, how important it is not to keep a business engagement, if one wants to retain any sense of the beauty of life, but still I think you had better wait till Uncle Jack arrives. I know he wants to speak to you about your emigrating.

ALGERNON.   About my what?

CECILY.   Your emigrating. He has gone up to buy your outfit.

ALGERNON.   I certainly wouldn't let Jack buy my outfit. He has no taste in neckties at all.

CECILY.   I don't think you will require neckties. Uncle Jack is sending you to Australia.

ALGERNON.   Australia! I'd sooner die.

CECILY.   Well, he said at dinner on Wednesday night, that you would have to choose between this world, the next world, and Australia.

ALGERNON.   Oh, well! The accounts I have received of Australia and the next world, are not particularly encouraging. This world is good enough for me, cousin Cecily.

CECILY.   Yes, but are you good enough for it?

ALGERNON.   I'm afraid I'm not that. That is why I want you to reform me. You might make that your mission, if you don't mind, cousin Cecily.

CECILY.   I'm afraid I've not time, this afternoon.

ALGERNON.   Well, would you mind my reforming myself this afternoon?

CECILY.   That is rather Quixotic of you. But I think you should try.

ALGERNON. I will. I feel better already.

CECILY. You are looking a little worse.

ALGERNON. That is because I am hungry.

CECILY. How thoughtless of me. I should have remembered that when one is going to lead an entirely new life, one requires regular and wholesome meals. Won't you come in?

ALGERNON. Thank you. Might I have a button-hole first? I never have any appetite unless I have a button-hole first.

CECILY. A Maréchal Niel? (*Picks up scissors.*)

ALGERNON. No, I'd sooner have a pink rose.

CECILY. Why? (*Cuts a flower.*)

ALGERNON. Because you are like a pink rose, cousin Cecily.

CECILY. I don't think it can be right for you to talk to me like that. Miss Prism never says such things to me.

ALGERNON. Then Miss Prism is a short-sighted old lady. (CECILY *puts the rose in his button-hole.*) You are the prettiest girl I ever saw.

CECILY. Miss Prism says that all good looks are a snare.

ALGERNON. They are a snare that every sensible man would like to be caught in.

CECILY. Oh! I don't think I would care to catch a sensible man. I shouldn't know what to talk to him about.

(*They pass into the house.* MISS PRISM *and* DR. CHASUBLE *return.*)

MISS PRISM. You are too much alone, dear Dr. Chasuble. You should get married. A misanthrope I can understand—a womanthrope, never!

CHASUBLE (*with a scholar's shudder*). Believe me, I do not deserve so neologistic a phrase. The precept as well as the practice of the Primitive Church was distinctly against matrimony.

MISS PRISM (*sententiously*). That is obviously the reason why the Primitive Church has not lasted up to the present day. And you do not seem to realize, dear Doctor, that by persistently remaining single, a man converts himself into a permanent public temptation. Men should be careful; this very celibacy leads weaker vessels astray.

CHASUBLE. But is a man not equally attractive when married?

MISS PRISM. No married man is ever attractive except to his wife.

CHASUBLE. And often, I've been told, not even to her.

MISS PRISM. That depends on the intellectual sympathies of the woman. Maturity can always be depended on. Ripeness can be trusted. Young women are green. (DR. CHASUBLE *starts.*) I spoke horticulturally. My metaphor was drawn from fruits. But where is Cecily?

CHASUBLE. Perhaps she followed us to the schools.

(*Enter* JACK *slowly from the back of the garden. He is dressed in the deepest mourning, with crape hat-band and black gloves.*)

MISS PRISM. Mr. Worthing!

CHASUBLE. Mr. Worthing?

MISS PRISM. This is indeed a surprise. We did not look for you till Monday afternoon.

JACK (*shakes* MISS PRISM'S *hand in a tragic manner*).   I have returned sooner than I expected. Dr. Chasuble, I hope you are well?

CHASUBLE.   Dear Mr. Worthing, I trust this garb of woe does not betoken some terrible calamity?

JACK.   My brother.

MISS PRISM.   More shameful debts and extravagance?

CHASUBLE.   Still leading his life of pleasure?

JACK (*shaking his head*).   Dead!

CHASUBLE.   Your brother Ernest dead?

JACK.   Quite dead.

MISS PRISM.   What a lesson for him! I trust he will profit by it.

CHASUBLE.   Mr. Worthing, I offer you my sincere condolence. You have at least the consolation of knowing that you were always the most generous and forgiving of brothers.

JACK.   Poor Ernest! He had many faults, but it is a sad, sad blow.

CHASUBLE.   Very sad indeed. Were you with him at the end?

JACK.   No. He died abroad; in Paris, in fact. I had a telegram last night from the manager of the Grand Hotel.

CHASUBLE.   Was the cause of death mentioned?

JACK.   A severe chill, it seems.

MISS PRISM.   As a man sows, so shall he reap.

CHASUBLE (*raising his hand*).   Charity, dear Miss Prism, charity! None of us are perfect. I myself am peculiarly susceptible to draughts. Will the interment take place here?

JACK.   No. He seems to have expressed a desire to be buried in Paris.

CHASUBLE.   In Paris! (*Shakes his head.*) I fear that hardly points to any very serious state of mind at the last. You would no doubt wish me to make some slight allusion to this tragic domestic affliction next Sunday. (JACK *presses his hand convulsively.*) My sermon on the meaning of the manna in the wilderness can be adapted to almost any occasion, joyful, or, as in the present case, distressing. (*All sigh.*) I have preached it at harvest celebrations, christenings, confirmations, on days of humiliation and festal days. The last time I delivered it was in the Cathedral, as a charity sermon on behalf of the Society for the Prevention of Discontentment among the Upper Orders. The Bishop, who was present, was much struck by some of the analogies I drew.

JACK.   Ah, that reminds me, you mentioned christenings I think, Dr. Chasuble? I suppose you know how to christen all right? (DR. CHASUBLE *looks astounded.*) I mean, of course, you are continually christening, aren't you?

MISS PRISM.   It is, I regret to say, one of the Rector's most constant duties in this parish. I have often spoken to the poorer classes on the subject. But they don't seem to know what thrift is.

CHASUBLE.   But is there any particular infant in whom you are interested, Mr. Worthing? Your brother was, I believe, unmarried, was he not?

JACK. Oh, yes.

MISS PRISM (*bitterly*). People who live entirely for pleasure usually are.

JACK. But it is not for any child, dear Doctor. I am very fond of children. No! the fact is, I would like to be christened myself, this afternoon, if you have nothing better to do.

CHASUBLE. But surely, Mr. Worthing, you have been christened already?

JACK. I don't remember anything about it.

CHASUBLE. But have you any grave doubts on the subject?

JACK. I certainly intend to have. Of course, I don't know if the thing would bother you in any way, or if you think I am a little too old now.

CHASUBLE. Not at all. The sprinkling, and, indeed, the immersion of adults is a perfectly canonical practice.

JACK. Immersion!

CHASUBLE. You need have no apprehensions. Sprinkling is all that is necessary, or indeed I think advisable. Our weather is so changeable. At what hour would you wish the ceremony performed?

JACK. Oh, I might trot around about five if that would suit you.

CHASUBLE. Perfectly, perfectly! In fact I have two similar ceremonies to perform at that time. A case of twins that occurred recently in one of the outlying cottages on your own estate. Poor Jenkins the carter, a most hard-working man.

JACK. Oh! I don't see much fun in being christened along with other babies. It would be childish. Would half-past five do?

CHASUBLE. Admirably! Admirably! (*Takes out watch.*) And now, dear Mr. Worthing, I will not intrude any longer into a house of sorrow. I would merely beg you not to be too much bowed down by grief. What seem to us bitter trials at the moment are often blessings in disguise.

MISS PRISM. This seems to me a blessing of an extremely obvious kind.

(*Enter* CECILY *from the house.*)

CECILY. Uncle Jack! Oh, I am pleased to see you back. But what horrid clothes you have on! Do go and change them.

MISS PRISM. Cecily!

CHASUBLE. My child! my child! (CECILY *goes towards* JACK; *he kisses her brow in a melancholy manner.*)

CECILY. What is the matter, Uncle Jack? Do look happy! You look as if you had a toothache and I have such a surprise for you. Who do you think is in the dining-room? Your brother!

JACK. Who?

CECILY. Your brother Ernest. He arrived about half an hour ago.

JACK. What nonsense! I haven't got a brother.

CECILY. Oh, don't say that. However badly he may have behaved to you in the past he is still your brother. You couldn't be so heartless as to disown him. I'll tell him to come out. And you will shake hands with him, won't you, Uncle Jack? (*Runs back into the house.*) . . .

CHASUBLE. These are very joyful tidings.

MISS PRISM. After we had all been resigned to his loss, his sudden return seems to me peculiarly distressing.

JACK. My brother is in the dining-room? I don't know what it all means. I think it is perfectly absurd.

(*Enter* ALGERNON *and* CECILY *hand in hand. They come slowly up to* JACK.)

JACK. Good heavens! (*Motions* ALGERNON *away.*)

ALGERNON. Brother John, I have come down from town to tell you that I am very sorry for all the trouble I have given you, and that I intend to lead a better life in the future. (JACK *glares at him and does not take his hand.*)

CECILY. Uncle Jack, you are not going to refuse your own brother's hand?

JACK. Nothing will induce me to take his hand. I think his coming down here disgraceful. He knows perfectly well why.

CECILY. Uncle Jack, do be nice. There is some good in everyone. Ernest has just been telling me about his poor invalid friend, Mr. Bunbury, whom he goes to visit so often. And surely there must be much good in one who is kind to an invalid, and leaves the pleasures of London to sit by a bed of pain.

JACK. Oh, he has been talking about Bunbury, has he?

CECILY. Yes, he has told me all about poor Mr. Bunbury, and his terrible state of health.

JACK. Bunbury! Well, I won't have him talk to you about Bunbury or about anything else. It is enough to drive one perfectly frantic.

ALGERNON. Of course I admit that the faults were all on my side. But I must say that I think that Brother John's coldness to me is peculiarly painful. I expected a more enthusiastic welcome, especially considering it is the first time I have come here.

CECILY. Uncle Jack, if you don't shake hands with Ernest I will never forgive you.

JACK. Never forgive me?

CECILY. Never, never, never!

JACK. Well, this is the last time I shall ever do it. (*Shakes hands with* ALGERNON *and glares.*)

CHASUBLE. It's pleasant, is it not, to see so perfect a reconciliation? I think we might leave the two brothers together.

MISS PRISM. Cecily, you will come with us.

CECILY. Certainly, Miss Prism. My little task of reconciliation is over.

CHASUBLE. You have done a beautiful action to-day, dear child.

MISS PRISM. We must not be premature in our judgments.

CECILY. I feel very happy. (*They all go off.*)

JACK. You young scoundrel, Algy, you must get out of this place as soon as possible. I don't allow any Bunburying here.

(*Enter* MERRIMAN.)

MERRIMAN. I have put Mr. Ernest's things in the room next to yours, sir. I suppose that is all right?

JACK. What?

MERRIMAN. Mr. Ernest's luggage, sir. I have unpacked it and put it in the room next to your own.

JACK. His luggage?

MERRIMAN. Yes, sir. Three portmanteaus, a dressing-case, two hat-boxes, and a large luncheon-basket.

ALGERNON. I am afraid I can't stay more than a week this time.

JACK. Merriman, order the dog-cart at once. Mr. Ernest has been suddenly called back to town.

MERRIMAN. Yes, sir. (*Goes back into the house.*)

ALGERNON. What a fearful liar you are, Jack. I have not been called back to town at all.

JACK. Yes, you have.

ALGERNON. I haven't heard anyone call me.

JACK. Your duty as a gentleman calls you back.

ALGERNON. My duty as a gentleman has never interfered with my pleasures in the smallest degree.

JACK. I can quite understand that.

ALGERNON. Well, Cecily is a darling.

JACK. You are not to talk of Miss Cardew like that. I don't like it.

ALGERNON. Well, I don't like your clothes. You look perfectly ridiculous in them. Why on earth don't you go up and change? It is perfectly childish to be in deep mourning for a man who is actually staying for a whole week with you in your house as a guest. I call it grotesque.

JACK. You are certainly not staying with me for a whole week as a guest or anything else. You have got to leave . . . by the four-five train.

ALGERNON. I certainly won't leave you so long as you are in mourning. It would be most unfriendly. If I were in mourning you would stay with me, I suppose. I should think it very unkind if you didn't.

JACK. Well, will you go if I change my clothes?

ALGERNON. Yes, if you are not too long. I never saw anybody take so long to dress, and with such little result.

JACK. Well, at any rate, that is better than being always over-dressed as you are.

ALGERNON. If I am occasionally a little over-dressed, I make up for it by being always immensely over-educated.

JACK. Your vanity is ridiculous, your conduct an outrage, and your presence in my garden utterly absurd. However, you have got to catch the four-five, and I hope you will have a pleasant journey back to town. This Bunburying, as you call it, has not been a great success for you. (*Goes into the house.*)

ALGERNON. I think it has been a great success. I'm in love with Cecily, and that is everything. (*Enter CECILY at the back of the garden. She picks up the can and begins to water the flowers.*) But I must see her before I go, and make arrangements for another Bunbury. Ah, there she is.

CECILY.   Oh, I merely came back to water the roses. I thought you were with Uncle Jack.

ALGERNON.   He's gone to order the dog-cart for me.

CECILY.   Oh, is he going to take you for a nice drive?

ALGERNON.   He's going to send me away.

CECILY.   Then have we got to part?

ALGERNON.   I am afraid so. It's a very painful parting.

CECILY.   It is always painful to part from people whom one has known for a very brief space of time. The absence of old friends one can endure with equanimity. But even a momentary separation from anyone to whom one has just been introduced is almost unbearable.

ALGERNON.   Thank you.

(*Enter* MERRIMAN.)

MERRIMAN.   The dog-cart is at the door, sir. (ALGERNON *looks appealingly at* CECILY.)

CECILY.   It can wait, Merriman . . . for . . . five minutes.

MERRIMAN.   Yes, miss. (*Exit* MERRIMAN.)

ALGERNON.   I hope, Cecily, I shall not offend you if I state quite frankly and openly that you seem to me to be in every way the visible personification of absolute perfection.

CECILY.   I think your frankness does you great credit, Ernest. If you will allow me I will copy your remarks into my diary. (*Goes over to table and begins writing in diary.*)

ALGERNON.   Do you really keep a diary? I'd give anything to look at it. May I?

CECILY.   Oh, no. (*Puts her hand over it.*) You see, it is simply a very young girl's record of her own thoughts and impressions, and consequently meant for publication. When it appears in volume form I hope you will order a copy. But pray, Ernest, don't stop. I delight in taking down from dictation. I have reached "absolute perfection." You can go on. I am quite ready for more.

ALGERNON (*somewhat taken aback*).   Ahem! Ahem!

CECILY.   Oh, don't cough, Ernest. When one is dictating one should speak fluently and not cough. Besides, I don't know how to spell a cough. (*Writes as* ALGERNON *speaks.*)

ALGERNON (*speaking very rapidly*).   Cecily, ever since I first looked upon your wonderful and incomparable beauty, I have dared to love you wildly, passionately, devotedly, hopelessly.

CECILY.   I don't think that you should tell me that you love me wildly, passionately, devotedly, hopelessly. Hopelessly doesn't seem to make much sense, does it?

ALGERNON.   Cecily!

(*Enter* MERRIMAN.)

MERRIMAN.   The dog-cart is waiting, sir.

ALGERNON.   Tell it to come round next week, at the same hour.

MERRIMAN (*looks at* CECILY, *who makes no sign*).   Yes, sir. (MERRI-MAN *retires.*)

CECILY.   Uncle Jack would be very much annoyed if he knew you were staying on till next week, at the same hour.

ALGERNON.   Oh, I don't care about Jack. I don't care for anybody in the whole world but you. I love you, Cecily. You will marry me, won't you?

CECILY.   You silly you! Of course. Why, we have been engaged for the last three months.

ALGERNON.   For the last three months?

CECILY.   Yes, it will be exactly three months on Thursday.

ALGERNON.   But how did we become engaged?

CECILY.   Well, ever since dear Uncle Jack first confessed to us that he had a younger brother who was very wicked and bad, you of course have formed the chief topic of conversation between myself and Miss Prism. And of course a man who is much talked about is always very attractive. One feels there must be something in him after all. I daresay it was foolish of me, but I fell in love with you, Ernest.

ALGERNON.   Darling! And when was the engagement actually settled?

CECILY.   On the 4th of February last. Worn out by your entire ignorance of my existence, I determined to end the matter one way or the other, and after a long struggle with myself I accepted you under this dear old tree here. The next day I bought this little ring in your name, and this is the little bangle with the true lovers' knot I promised you always to wear.

ALGERNON.   Did I give you this? It's very pretty, isn't it?

CECILY.   Yes, you've wonderfully good taste, Ernest. It's the excuse I've always given for your leading such a bad life. And this is the box in which I keep all your dear letters. (*Kneels at table, opens box, and produces letters tied up with blue ribbon.*)

ALGERNON.   My letters! But my own sweet Cecily, I have never written you any letters.

CECILY.   You need hardly remind me of that, Ernest. I remember only too well that I was forced to write your letters for you. I wrote always three times a week, and sometimes oftener.

ALGERNON.   Oh, do let me read them, Cecily?

CECILY.   Oh, I couldn't possibly. They would make you far too conceited. (*Replaces box.*) The three you wrote me after I had broken off the engagement are so beautiful, and so badly spelled, that even now I can hardly read them without crying a little.

ALGERNON.   But was our engagement ever broken off?

CECILY.   Of course it was. On the 22nd of last March. You can see the entry if you like. (*Shows diary.*) "To-day I broke off my engagement with Ernest. I feel it is better to do so. The weather still continues charming."

ALGERNON.   But why on earth did you break it off? What had I done?

I had done nothing at all. Cecily, I am very much hurt indeed to hear you broke it off. Particularly when the weather was so charming.

CECILY.   It would hardly have been a really serious engagement if it hadn't been broken off at least once. But I forgave you before the week was out.

ALGERNON (*crossing to her, and kneeling*).   What a perfect angel you are, Cecily.

CECILY.   You dear romantic boy. (*He kisses her, she puts her fingers through his hair.*) I hope your hair curls naturally, does it?

ALGERNON.   Yes, darling, with a little help from others.

CECILY.   I am so glad.

ALGERNON.   You'll never break off our engagement again, Cecily?

CECILY.   I don't think I could break it off now that I have actually met you. Besides, of course, there is the question of your name.

ALGERNON.   Yes, of course. (*Nervously.*)

CECILY.   You must not laugh at me, darling, but it had always been a girlish dream of mine to love some one whose name was Ernest. (ALGERNON *rises*, CECILY *also.*) There is something in that name that seems to inspire absolute confidence. I pity any poor married woman whose husband is not called Ernest.

ALGERNON.   But, my dear child, do you mean to say you could not love me if I had some other name?

CECILY.   But what name?

ALGERNON.   Oh, any name you like—Algernon, for instance. . . .

CECILY.   But I don't like the name of Algernon.

ALGERNON.   Well, my own dear, sweet, loving little darling, I really can't see why you should object to the name of Algernon. It is not at all a bad name. In fact, it is rather an aristocratic name. Half of the chaps who get into the Bankruptcy Court are called Algernon. But seriously, Cecily . . . (*moving to her*) . . . if my name was Algy, couldn't you love me?

CECILY (*rising*).   I might respect you, Ernest, I might admire your character, but I fear that I should not be able to give you my undivided attention.

ALGERNON.   Ahem! Cecily! (*Picking up hat.*) Your Rector here is, I suppose, thoroughly experienced in the practice of all the rites and ceremonials of the church?

CECILY.   Oh, yes. Dr. Chasuble is a most learned man. He has never written a single book, so you can imagine how much he knows.

ALGERNON.   I must see him at once on a most important christening— I mean on most important business.

CECILY.   Oh!

ALGERNON.   I sha'n't be away more than half an hour.

CECILY.   Considering that we have been engaged since February the 14th, and that I only met you to-day for the first time, I think it is rather hard that you should leave me for so long a period as half an hour. Couldn't you make it twenty minutes?

ALGERNON. I'll be back in no time. (*Kisses her and rushes down the garden.*)

CECILY. What an impetuous boy he is. I like his hair so much. I must enter his proposal in my diary.

(*Enter* MERRIMAN.)

MERRIMAN. A Miss Fairfax has just called to see Mr. Worthing. On very important business, Miss Fairfax states.

CECILY. Isn't Mr. Worthing in his library?

MERRIMAN. Mr. Worthing went over in the direction of the Rectory some time ago.

CECILY. Pray ask the lady to come out here; Mr. Worthing is sure to be back soon. And you can bring tea.

MERRIMAN. Yes, miss. (*Goes out.*)

CECILY. Miss Fairfax! I suppose one of the many good elderly women who are associated with Uncle Jack in some of his philanthropic work in London. I don't quite like women who are interested in philanthropic work. I think it is so forward of them.

(*Enter* MERRIMAN.)

MERRIMAN. Miss Fairfax.

(*Enter* GWENDOLEN.)   (*Exit* MERRIMAN.)

CECILY (*advancing to meet her*). Pray let me introduce myself to you. My name is Cecily Cardew.

GWENDOLEN. Cecily Cardew? (*Moving to her and shaking hands.*) What a very sweet name! Something tells me that we are going to be great friends. I like you already more than I can say. My first impressions of people are never wrong.

CECILY. How nice of you to like me so much after we have known each other such a comparatively short time. Pray sit down.

GWENDOLEN (*still standing up*). I may call you Cecily, may I not?

CECILY. With pleasure!

GWENDOLEN. And you will always call me Gwendolen, won't you?

CECILY. If you wish.

GWENDOLEN. Then that is all quite settled, is it not?

CECILY. I hope so. (*A pause. They both sit down together.*)

GWENDOLEN. Perhaps this might be a favorable opportunity for my mentioning who I am. My father is Lord Bracknell. You have never heard of papa, I suppose?

CECILY. I don't think so.

GWENDOLEN. Outside the family circle, papa, I am glad to say, is entirely unknown. I think that is quite as it should be. The home seems to me to be the proper sphere for the man. And certainly once a man begins to neglect his domestic duties he becomes painfully effeminate, does he not? And I don't like that. It makes men so very attractive. Cecily, mamma, whose views on education are remarkably strict, has brought me up to be extremely short-sighted; it is part of her system; so do you mind my looking at you through my glasses?

CECILY. Oh, not at all, Gwendolen. I am very fond of being looked at.

GWENDOLEN (*after examining* CECILY *carefully through a lorgnette*). You are here on a short visit, I suppose.

CECILY. Oh, no, I live here.

GWENDOLEN (*severely*). Really? Your mother, no doubt, or some female relative of advanced years, resides here also?

CECILY. Oh, no. I have no mother, nor, in fact, any relations.

GWENDOLEN. Indeed?

CECILY. My dear guardian, with the assistance of Miss Prism, has the arduous task of looking after me.

GWENDOLEN. Your guardian?

CECILY. Yes, I am Mr. Worthing's ward.

GWENDOLEN. Oh! It is strange he never mentioned to me that he had a ward. How secretive of him! He grows more interesting hourly. I am not sure, however, that the news inspires me with feelings of unmixed delight. (*Rising and going to her.*) I am very fond of you, Cecily; I have liked you ever since I met you. But I am bound to state that now that I know that you are Mr. Worthing's ward, I cannot help expressing a wish you were— well, just a little older than you seem to be—and not quite so very alluring in appearance. In fact, if I may speak candidly——

CECILY. Pray do! I think that whenever one has anything unpleasant to say, one should always be quite candid.

GWENDOLEN. Well, to speak with perfect candour, Cecily, I wish that you were fully forty-two, and more than usually plain for your age. Ernest has a strong upright nature. He is the very soul of truth and honour. Disloyalty would be as impossible to him as deception. But even men of the noblest possible moral character are extremely susceptible to the influence of the physical charms of others. Modern, no less than Ancient History supplies us with many most painful examples of what I refer to. If it were not so, indeed, History would be quite unreadable.

CECILY. I beg your pardon, Gwendolen, did you say Ernest?

GWENDOLEN. Yes.

CECILY. Oh, but it is not Mr. Ernest Worthing who is my guardian. It is his brother—his elder brother.

GWENDOLEN (*sitting down again*). Ernest never mentioned to me that he had a brother.

CECILY. I am sorry to say they have not been on good terms for a long time.

GWENDOLEN. Ah! that accounts for it. And now that I think of it I have never heard any man mention his brother. The subject seems distasteful to most men. Cecily, you have lifted a load from my mind. I was growing almost anxious. It would have been terrible if any cloud had come across a friendship like ours, would it not? Of course you are quite, quite sure that it is not Mr. Ernest Worthing who is your guardian?

CECILY. Quite sure. (*A pause.*) In fact, I am going to be his.

GWENDOLEN (*enquiringly*). I beg your pardon?

CECILY (*rather shy and confidingly*).   Dearest Gwendolen, there is no reason why I should make a secret of it to you. Our little county newspaper is sure to chronicle the fact next week. Mr. Ernest Worthing and I are engaged to be married.

GWENDOLEN (*quite politely, rising*).   My darling Cecily, I think there must be some slight error. Mr. Ernest Worthing is engaged to me. The announcement will appear in the *Morning Post* on Saturday at the latest.

CECILY (*very politely, rising*).   I am afraid you must be under some misconception. Ernest proposed to me exactly ten minutes ago. (*Shows diary.*)

GWENDOLEN (*examines diary through her lorgnette carefully*).   It is certainly very curious, for he asked me to be his wife yesterday afternoon at 5.30. If you would care to verify the incident, pray do so. (*Produces diary of her own.*) I never travel without my diary. One should always have something sensational to read in the train. I am so sorry, dear Cecily, if it is any disappointment to you, but I am afraid *I* have the prior claim.

CECILY.   It would distress me more than I can tell you, dear Gwendolen, if it caused you any mental or physical anguish, but I feel bound to point out that since Ernest proposed to you he clearly has changed his mind.

GWENDOLEN (*meditatively*).   If the poor fellow has been entrapped into any foolish promise I shall consider it my duty to rescue him at once, and with a firm hand.

CECILY (*thoughtfully and sadly*).   Whatever unfortunate entanglement my dear boy may have got into, I will never reproach him with it after we are married.

GWENDOLEN.   Do you allude to me, Miss Cardew, as an entanglement? You are presumptuous. On an occasion of this kind it becomes more than a moral duty to speak one's mind. It becomes a pleasure.

CECILY.   Do you suggest, Miss Fairfax, that I entrapped Ernest into an engagement? How dare you? This is no time for wearing the shallow mask of manners. When I see a spade I call it a spade.

GWENDOLEN (*satirically*).   I am glad to say that I have never seen a spade. It is obvious that our social spheres have been widely different.

(*Enter MERRIMAN, followed by the footman. He carries a salver, tablecloth, and plate-stand. CECILY is about to retort. The presence of the servants exercises a restraining influence, under which both girls chafe.*)

MERRIMAN.   Shall I lay tea here as usual, miss?

CECILY (*sternly, in a calm voice*).   Yes, as usual. (*MERRIMAN begins to clear and lay cloth. A long pause. CECILY and GWENDOLEN glare at each other.*)

GWENDOLEN.   Are there many interesting walks in the vicinity, Miss Cardew?

CECILY.   Oh, yes, a great many. From the top of one of the hills quite close one can see five counties.

GWENDOLEN.   Five counties! I don't think I should like that. I hate crowds.

CECILY (*sweetly*).   I suppose that is why you live in town? (GWENDOLEN *bites her lip, and beats her foot nervously with her parasol.*)

GWENDOLEN (*looking round*).   Quite a well-kept garden this is, Miss Cardew.

CECILY.   So glad you like it, Miss Fairfax.

GWENDOLEN.   I had no idea there were any flowers in the country.

CECILY.   Oh, flowers are as common here, Miss Fairfax, as people are in London.

GWENDOLEN.   Personally I cannot understand how anybody manages to exist in the country, if anybody who is anybody does. The country always bores me to death.

CECILY.   Ah! This is what the newspapers call agricultural depression, is it not? I believe the aristocracy are suffering very much from it just at present. It is almost an epidemic amongst them, I have been told. May I offer you some tea, Miss Fairfax?

GWENDOLEN (*with elaborate politeness*).   Thank you. (*Aside.*) Detestable girl! But I require tea!

CECILY (*sweetly*).   Sugar?

GWENDOLEN (*superciliously*).   No, thank you. Sugar is not fashionable any more. (CECILY *looks angrily at her, takes up the tongs and puts four lumps of sugar into the cup.*)

CECILY (*severely*).   Cake or bread and butter?

GWENDOLEN (*in a bored manner*).   Bread and butter, please. Cake is rarely seen at the best houses nowadays.

CECILY (*cuts a very large slice of cake, and puts it on the tray*). Hand that to Miss Fairfax. (MERRIMAN *does so, and goes out with footman.* GWENDOLEN *drinks the tea and makes a grimace. Puts down cup at once, reaches out her hand to the bread and butter, looks at it, and finds it is cake. Rises in indignation.*)

GWENDOLEN.   You have filled my tea with lumps of sugar, and though I asked most distinctly for bread and butter, you have given me cake. I am known for the gentleness of my disposition, and the extraordinary sweetness of my nature, but I warn you, Miss Cardew, you may go too far.

CECILY (*rising*).   To save my poor, innocent, trusting boy from the machinations of any other girl there are no lengths to which I would not go.

GWENDOLEN.   From the moment I saw you I distrusted you. I felt that you were false and deceitful. I am never deceived in such matters. My first impressions of people are invariably right.

CECILY.   It seems to me, Miss Fairfax, that I am trespassing on your valuable time. No doubt you have many other calls of a similar character to make in the neighbourhood.

(*Enter* JACK.)

GWENDOLEN (*catching sight of him*).   Ernest! My own Ernest!

JACK. Gwendolen! Darling! (*Offers to kiss her.*)

GWENDOLEN (*drawing back*). A moment! May I ask if you are engaged to be married to this young lady? (*Points to* CECILY.)

JACK (*laughing*). To dear little Cecily! Of course not! What could have put such an idea into your pretty little head?

GWENDOLEN. Thank you. You may. (*Offers her cheek.*)

CECILY (*very sweetly*). I knew there must be some misunderstanding, Miss Fairfax. The gentleman whose arm is at present around your waist is my dear guardian, Mr. John Worthing.

GWENDOLEN. I beg your pardon?

CECILY. This is Uncle Jack.

GWENDOLEN (*receding*). Jack! Oh!

(*Enter* ALGERNON.)

CECILY. Here is Ernest.

ALGERNON (*goes straight over to* CECILY *without noticing anyone else.*) My own love! (*Offers to kiss her.*)

CECILY (*drawing back*). A moment, Ernest! May I ask you—are you engaged to be married to this young lady?

ALGERNON (*looking round*). To what young lady? Good heavens! Gwendolen!

CECILY. Yes, to good heavens, Gwendolen, I mean to Gwendolen.

ALGERNON (*laughing*). Of course not! What could have put such an idea into your pretty little head?

CECILY. Thank you. (*Presenting her cheek to be kissed.*) You may. (ALGERNON *kisses her.*)

GWENDOLEN. I felt there was some slight error, Miss Cardew. The gentleman who is now embracing you is my cousin, Mr. Algernon Moncrieff.

CECILY (*breaking away from* ALGERNON). Algernon Moncrieff! Oh! (*The two girls move towards each other and put their arms round each other's waists as if for protection.*)

CECILY. Are you called Algernon?

ALGERNON. I cannot deny it.

CECILY. Oh!

GWENDOLEN. Is your name really John?

JACK (*standing rather proudly*). I could deny it if I liked. I could deny anything if I liked. But my name certainly is John. It has been John for years.

CECILY (*to* GWENDOLEN). A gross deception has been practised on both of us.

GWENDOLEN. My poor wounded Cecily!

CECILY. My sweet, wronged Gwendolen!

GWENDOLEN (*slowly and seriously*). You will call me sister, will you not? (*They embrace.* JACK *and* ALGERNON *groan and walk up and down.*)

CECILY (*rather brightly*). There is just one question I would like to be allowed to ask my guardian.

GWENDOLEN. An admirable idea! Mr. Worthing, there is just one question I would like to be permitted to put to you. Where is your brother Ernest? We are both engaged to be married to your brother Ernest, so it is a matter of some importance to us to know where your brother Ernest is at present.

JACK (*slowly and hesitatingly*). Gwendolen—Cecily—it is very painful for me to be forced to speak the truth. It is the first time in my life that I have ever been reduced to such a painful position, and I am really quite inexperienced in doing anything of the kind. However I will tell you quite frankly that I have no brother Ernest. I have no brother at all. I never had a brother in my life, and I certainly have not the smallest intention of ever having one in the future.

CECILY (*surprised*). No brother at all?

JACK (*cheerily*). None!

GWENDOLEN (*severely*). Had you never a brother of any kind?

JACK (*pleasantly*). Never. Not even of any kind.

GWENDOLEN. I am afraid it is quite clear, Cecily, that neither of us is engaged to be married to anyone.

CECILY. It is not a very pleasant position for a young girl suddenly to find herself in. Is it?

GWENDOLEN. Let us go into the house. They will hardly venture to come after us there.

CECILY. No, men are so cowardly, aren't they? (*They retire into the house with scornful looks.*)

JACK. This ghastly state of things is what you call Bunburying, I suppose?

ALGERNON. Yes, and a perfectly wonderful Bunbury it is. The most wonderful Bunbury I have ever had in my life.

JACK. Well, you've no right whatsoever to Bunbury here.

ALGERNON. That is absurd. One has a right to Bunbury anywhere one chooses. Every serious Bunburyist knows that.

JACK. Serious Bunburyist! Good heavens!

ALGERNON. Well, one must be serious about something, if one wants to have any amusement in life. I happen to be serious about Bunburying. What on earth you are serious about I haven't got the remotest idea. About everything, I should fancy. You have such an absolutely trivial nature.

JACK. Well, the only small satisfaction I have in the whole of this wretched business is that your friend Bunbury is quite exploded. You won't be able to run down to the country quite so often as you used to do, dear Algy. And a very good thing, too.

ALGERNON. Your brother is a little off colour, isn't he, dear Jack? You won't be able to disappear to London quite so frequently as your wicked custom was. And not a bad thing, either.

JACK. As for your conduct towards Miss Cardew, I must say that your taking in a sweet, simple, innocent girl like that is quite inexcusable. To say nothing of the fact that she is my ward.

ALGERNON. I can see no possible defence at all for your deceiving a brilliant, clever, thoroughly experienced young lady like Miss Fairfax. To say nothing of the fact that she is my cousin.

JACK. I wanted to be engaged to Gwendolen, that is all. I love her.

ALGERNON. Well, I simply wanted to be engaged to Cecily. I adore her.

JACK. There is certainly no chance of your marrying Miss Cardew.

ALGERNON. I don't think there is much likelihood, Jack, of you and Miss Fairfax being united.

JACK. Well, that is no business of yours.

ALGERNON. If it was my business, I wouldn't talk about it. (*Begins to eat muffins.*) It is very vulgar to talk about one's business. Only people like stock-brokers do that, and then merely at dinner parties.

JACK. How you can sit there, calmly eating muffins, when we are in this horrible trouble. I can't make out. You seem to me to be perfectly heartless.

ALGERNON. Well, I can't eat muffins in an agitated manner. The butter would probably get on my cuffs. One should always eat muffins quite calmly. It is the only way to eat them.

JACK. I say it's perfectly heartless your eating muffins at all, under the circumstances.

ALGERNON. When I am in trouble, eating is the only thing that consoles me. Indeed, when I am in really great trouble, as anyone who knows me intimately will tell you, I refuse everything except food and drink. At the present moment I am eating muffins because I am unhappy. Besides, I am particularly fond of muffins. (*Rising.*)

JACK (*rising*). Well, that is no reason why you should eat them all in that greedy way. (*Takes muffins from* ALGERNON.)

ALGERNON (*offering tea-cake*). I wish you would have tea-cake instead. I don't like tea-cake.

JACK. Good heavens! I suppose a man may eat his own muffins in his own garden.

ALGERNON. But you have just said it was perfectly heartless to eat muffins.

JACK. I said it was perfectly heartless of you, under the circumstances. That is a very different thing.

ALGERNON. That may be. But the muffins are the same. (*He seizes the muffin-dish from* JACK.)

JACK. Algy, I wish to goodness you would go.

ALGERNON. You can't possibly ask me to go without having some dinner. It's absurd. I never go without my dinner. No one ever does, except vegetarians and people like that. Besides I have just made arrangements with Dr. Chasuble to be christened at a quarter to six under the name of Ernest.

JACK. My dear fellow, the sooner you give up that nonsense the better. I made arrangements this morning with Dr. Chasuble to be christened myself at 5.30, and I naturally will take the name of Ernest. Gwendolen would wish it. We can't both be christened Ernest. It's absurd. Besides, I have a perfect right to be christened if I like. There is no evidence at all that I ever have been christened by anybody. I should think it extremely probable I never was, and so does Dr. Chasuble. It is entirely different in your case. You have been christened already.

ALGERNON. Yes, but I have not been christened for years.

JACK. Yes, but you have been christened. That is the important thing.

ALGERNON. Quite so. So I know my constitution can stand it. If you are not quite sure about your ever having been christened, I must say I think it rather dangerous your venturing on it now. It might make you very unwell. You can hardly have forgotten that someone very closely connected with you was very nearly carried off this week in Paris by a severe chill.

JACK. Yes, but you said yourself that a severe chill was not hereditary.

ALGERNON. It usedn't to be, I know—but I daresay it is now. Science is always making wonderful improvements in things.

JACK (*picking up the muffin-dish*). Oh, that is nonsense; you are always talking nonsense.

ALGERNON. Jack, you are at the muffins again! I wish you wouldn't. There are only two left. (*Takes them.*) I told you I was particularly fond of muffins.

JACK. But I hate tea-cake.

ALGERNON. Why on earth then do you allow tea-cake to be served up for your guests? What ideas you have of hospitality!

JACK. Algernon! I have already told you to go. I don't want you here. Why don't you go?

ALGERNON. I haven't quite finished my tea yet, and there is still one muffin left. (JACK *groans, and sinks into a chair.* ALGERNON *still continues eating.*)

CURTAIN

ACT III

SCENE.—*Morning-room at the Manor House.* GWENDOLEN *and* CECILY *are at the window, looking out into the garden.*

GWENDOLEN. The fact that they did not follow us at once into the house, as anyone else would have done, seems to me to show that they have some sense of shame left.

CECILY. They have been eating muffins. That looks like repentance.

GWENDOLEN (*after a pause*). They don't seem to notice us at all. Couldn't you cough?

GWENDOLEN. They're looking at us. What effrontery!

CECILY. They're approaching. That's very forward of them.

GWENDOLEN. Let us preserve a dignified silence.

CECILY.   Certainly. It's the only thing to do now.

(*Enter* JACK, *followed by* ALGERNON. *They whistle some dreadful popular air from a British opera.*)

GWENDOLEN.   This dignified silence seems to produce an unpleasant effect.

CECILY.   A most distasteful one.

GWENDOLEN.   But we will not be the first to speak.

CECILY.   Certainly not.

GWENDOLEN.   Mr. Worthing, I have something very particular to ask you. Much depends on your reply.

CECILY.   Gwendolen, your common sense is invaluable. Mr. Moncrieff, kindly answer me the following question. Why did you pretend to be my guardian's brother?

ALGERNON.   In order that I might have an opportunity of meeting you.

CECILY (*to* GWENDOLEN).   That certainly seems a satisfactory explanation, does it not?

GWENDOLEN.   Yes, dear, if you can believe him.

CECILY.   I don't. But that does not affect the wonderful beauty of his answer.

GWENDOLEN.   True. In matters of grave importance, style, not sincerity, is the vital thing. Mr. Worthing, what explanation can you offer to me for pretending to have a brother? Was it in order that you might have an opportunity of coming up to town to see me as often as possible?

JACK.   Can you doubt it, Miss Fairfax?

GWENDOLEN.   I have the gravest doubts upon the subject. But I intend to crush them. This is not the moment for German scepticism. (*Moving to* CECILY.) Their explanations appear to be quite satisfactory, especially Mr. Worthing's. That seems to me to have the stamp of truth upon it.

CECILY.   I am more than content with what Mr. Moncrieff said. His voice alone inspires one with absolute credulity.

GWENDOLEN.   Then you think we should forgive them?

CECILY.   Yes. I mean no.

GWENDOLEN.   True! I had forgotten. There are principles at stake that one cannot surrender. Which of us should tell them? The task is not a pleasant one.

CECILY.   Could we not both speak at the same time?

GWENDOLEN.   An excellent idea! I nearly always speak at the same time as other people. Will you take the time from me?

CECILY.   Certainly. (GWENDOLEN *beats time with uplifted finger.*)

GWENDOLEN *and* CECILY (*speaking together*).   Your Christian names are still an insuperable barrier. That is all!

JACK *and* ALGERNON (*speaking together*).   Our Christian names! Is that all? But we are going to be christened this afternoon.

GWENDOLEN (*to* JACK).   For my sake you are prepared to do this terrible thing?

JACK. I am.

CECILY (*to* ALGERNON). To please me you are ready to face this fearful ordeal?

ALGERNON. I am!

GWENDOLEN. How absurd to talk of the equality of the sexes! Where questions of self-sacrifice are concerned, men are infinitely beyond us.

JACK. We are. (*Clasps hands with* ALGERNON.)

CECILY. They have moments of physical courage of which we women know absolutely nothing.

GWENDOLEN (*to* JACK). Darling!

ALGERNON (*to* CECILY). Darling! (*They fall into each other's arms.*)

(*Enter* MERRIMAN. *When he enters he coughs loudly, seeing the situation.*)

MERRIMAN. Ahem! Ahem! Lady Bracknell!

JACK. Good heavens!

(*Enter* LADY BRACKNELL. *The couples separate in alarm. Exit* MERRIMAN.)

LADY BRACKNELL. Gwendolen! What does this mean?

GWENDOLEN. Merely that I am engaged to be married to Mr. Worthing, Mamma.

LADY BRACKNELL. Come here. Sit down. Sit down immediately. Hesitation of any kind is a sign of mental decay in the young, of physical weakness in the old. (*Turns to* JACK.) Apprised, sir, of my daughter's sudden flight by her trusty maid, whose confidence I purchased by means of a small coin, I followed her at once by a luggage train. Her unhappy father is, I am glad to say, under the impression that she is attending a more than usually lengthy lecture by the University Extension Scheme on the Influence of a Permanent Income on Thought. I do not propose to undeceive him. Indeed I have never undeceived him on any question. I would consider it wrong. But of course, you will clearly understand that all communication between yourself and my daughter must cease immediately from this moment. On this point, as indeed on all points, I am firm.

JACK. I am engaged to be married to Gwendolen, Lady Bracknell!

LADY BRACKNELL. You are nothing of the kind, sir. And now, as regards Algernon! . . . Algernon!

ALGERNON. Yes, Aunt Augusta.

LADY BRACKNELL. May I ask if it is in this house that your invalid friend Mr. Bunbury resides?

ALGERNON (*stammering*). Oh, no! Bunbury doesn't live here. Bunbury is somewhere else at present. In fact, Bunbury is dead.

LADY BRACKNELL. Dead! When did Mr. Bunbury die? His death must have been extremely sudden.

ALGERNON (*airily*). Oh, I killed Bunbury this afternoon. I mean poor Bunbury died this afternoon.

LADY BRACKNELL. What did he die of?

ALGERNON.   Bunbury? Oh, he was quite exploded.

LADY BRACKNELL.   Exploded! Was he the victim of a revolutionary outrage? I was not aware that Mr. Bunbury was interested in social legislation. If so, he is well punished for his morbidity.

ALGERNON.   My dear Aunt Augusta, I mean he was found out! The doctors found out that Bunbury could not live, that is what I mean—so Bunbury died.

LADY BRACKNELL.   He seems to have had great confidence in the opinion of his physicians. I am glad, however, that he made up his mind at the last to some definite course of action, and acted under proper medical advice. And now that we have finally got rid of this Mr. Bunbury, may I ask, Mr. Worthing, who is that young person whose hand my nephew Algernon is now holding in what seems to me a peculiarly unnecessary manner?

JACK.   That lady is Miss Cecily Cardew, my ward. (LADY BRACKNELL *bows coldly to* CECILY.)

ALGERNON.   I am engaged to be married to Cecily, Aunt Augusta.

LADY BRACKNELL.   I beg your pardon?

CECILY.   Mr. Moncrieff and I are engaged to be married, Lady Bracknell.

LADY BRACKNELL (*with a shiver, crossing to the sofa and sitting down*). I do not know whether there is anything peculiarly exciting in the air of this particular part of Hertfordshire, but the number of engagements that go on seems to me considerably above the proper average that statistics have laid down for our guidance. I think some preliminary enquiry on my part would not be out of place. Mr. Worthing, is Miss Cardew at all connected with any of the larger railway stations in London? I merely desire information. Until yesterday I had no idea that there were any families or persons whose origin was a Terminus. (JACK *looks perfectly furious, but restrains himself.*)

JACK (*in a clear, cold voice*).   Miss Cardew is the granddaughter of the late Mr. Thomas Cardew of 149, Belgrave Square, S.W.; Gervase Park, Dorking, Surrey; and the Sporran, Fifeshire, N.B.

LADY BRACKNELL.   That sounds not unsatisfactory. Three addresses always inspire confidence, even in tradesmen. But what proof have I of their authenticity?

JACK.   I have carefully preserved the Court Guide of the period. They are open to your inspection, Lady Bracknell.

LADY BRACKNELL (*grimly*).   I have known strange errors in that publication.

JACK.   Miss Cardew's family solicitors are Messrs. Markby, Markby, and Markby.

LADY BRACKNELL.   Markby, Markby, and Markby? A firm of the very highest position in their profession. Indeed I am told that one of the Mr. Markbys is occasionally to be seen at dinner parties. So far I am satisfied.

JACK (*very irritably*).   How extremely kind of you, Lady Bracknell!

I have also in my possession, you will be pleased to hear, certificates of Miss Cardew's birth, baptism, whooping cough, registration, vaccination, confirmation, and the measles; both the German and the English variety.

LADY BRACKNELL.   Ah! A life crowded with incident, I see; though perhaps somewhat too exciting for a young girl. I am not myself in favour of premature experiences. (*Rises, looks at her watch.*) Gwendolen! the time approaches for our departure. We have not a moment to lose. As a matter of form, Mr. Worthing, I had better ask you if Miss Cardew has any little fortune?

JACK.   Oh, about a hundred and thirty thousand pounds in the Funds. That is all. Good-bye, Lady Bracknell. So pleased to have seen you.

LADY BRACKNELL (*sitting down again*).   A moment, Mr. Worthing. A hundred and thirty thousand pounds! And in the Funds! Miss Cardew seems to me a most attractive young lady, now that I look at her. Few girls of the present day have any really solid qualities, any of the qualities that last, and improve with time. We live, I regret to say, in an age of surfaces. (*To* CECILY.) Come over here, dear. (CECILY *goes across.*) Pretty child! your dress is sadly simple, and your hair seems almost as Nature might have left it. But we can soon alter all that. A thoroughly experienced French maid produces a really marvellous result in a very brief space of time. I remember recommending one to young Lady Lancing, and after three months her own husband did not know her.

JACK (*aside*).   And after six months nobody knew her.

LADY BRACKNELL (*glares at* JACK *for a few moments. Then bends, with a practised smile, to* CECILY).   Kindly turn round, sweet child. (CECILY *turns completely round.*) No, the side view is what I want. (CECILY *presents her profile.*) Yes, quite as I expected. There are distinct social possibilities in your profile. The two weak points in our age are its want of principle and its want of profile. The chin a little higher, dear. Style largely depends on the way the chin is worn. They are worn very high, just at present. Algernon!

ALGERNON.   Yes, Aunt Augusta!

LADY BRACKNELL.   There are distinct social possibilities in Miss Cardew's profile.

ALGERNON.   Cecily is the sweetest, dearest, prettiest girl in the whole world. And I don't care twopence about social possibilities.

LADY BRACKNELL.   Never speak disrespectfully of society, Algernon. Only people who can't get into it do that. (*To* CECILY.) Dear child, of course you know that Algernon has nothing but his debts to depend upon. But I do not approve of mercenary marriages. When I married Lord Bracknell I had no fortune of any kind. But I never dreamed for a moment of allowing that to stand in my way. Well, I suppose I must give my consent.

ALGERNON.   Thank you, Aunt Augusta.

LADY BRACKNELL.   Cecily, you may kiss me!

CECILY (*kisses her*).   Thank you, Lady Bracknell.

LADY BRACKNELL. You may also address me as Aunt Augusta for the future.

CECILY. Thank you, Aunt Augusta.

LADY BRACKNELL. The marriage, I think, had better take place quite soon.

ALGERNON. Thank you, Aunt Augusta.

CECILY. Thank you, Aunt Augusta.

LADY BRACKNELL. To speak frankly, I am not in favour of long engagements. They give people the opportunity of finding out each other's character before marriage, which I think is never advisable.

JACK. I beg your pardon for interrupting you, Lady Bracknell, but this engagement is quite out of the question. I am Miss Cardew's guardian, and she cannot marry without my consent until she comes of age. That consent I absolutely decline to give.

LADY BRACKNELL. Upon what grounds, may I ask? Algernon is an extremely, I may almost say an ostentatiously, eligible young man. He has nothing, but he looks everything. What more can one desire?

JACK. It pains me very much to have to speak frankly to you, Lady Bracknell, about your nephew, but the fact is that I do not approve at all of his moral character. I suspect him of being untruthful. (ALGERNON *and* CECILY *look at him in indignant amazement.*)

LADY BRACKNELL. Untruthful! My nephew Algernon? Impossible! He is an Oxonian.

JACK. I fear there can be no possible doubt about the matter. This afternoon, during my temporary absence in London on an important question of romance, he obtained admission to my house by means of the false pretence of being my brother. Under an assumed name he drank, I've just been informed by my butler, an entire pint bottle of my Perrier-Jouet, Brut, '89; a wine I was specially reserving for myself. Continuing his disgraceful deception, he succeeded in the course of the afternoon in alienating the affections of my only ward. He subsequently stayed to tea, and devoured every single muffin. And what makes his conduct all the more heartless is, that he was perfectly well aware from the first that I have no brother, that I never had a brother, and that I don't intend to have a brother, not even of any kind. I distinctly told him so myself yesterday afternoon.

LADY BRACKNELL. Ahem! Mr. Worthing, after careful consideration I have decided entirely to overlook my nephew's conduct to you.

JACK. That is very generous of you, Lady Bracknell. My own decision, however, is unalterable. I decline to give my consent.

LADY BRACKNELL (*to* CECILY). Come here, sweet child. (CECILY *goes over.*) How old are you, dear?

CECILY. Well, I am really only eighteen, but I always admit to twenty when I go to evening parties.

LADY BRACKNELL. You are perfectly right in making some slight alteration. Indeed, no woman should ever be quite accurate about her age.

It looks so calculating. . . . (*In meditative manner.*) Eighteen, but admitting to twenty at evening parties. Well, it will not be very long before you are of age and free from the restraints of tutelage. So I don't think your guardian's consent is, after all, a matter of any importance.

JACK.   Pray excuse me, Lady Bracknell, for interrupting you again, but it is only fair to tell you that according to the terms of her grandfather's will Miss Cardew does not come legally of age till she is thirty-five.

LADY BRACKNELL.   That does not seem to me to be a grave objection. Thirty-five is a very attractive age. London society is full of women of the very highest birth who have, of their own free choice, remained thirty-five for years. Lady Dumbleton is an instance in point. To my own knowledge she has been thirty-five ever since she arrived at the age of forty, which was many years ago now. I see no reason why our dear Cecily should not be even still more attractive at the age you mention than she is at present. There will be a large accumulation of property.

CECILY.   Algy, could you wait for me till I was thirty-five?

ALGERNON.   Of course I could, Cecily. You know I could.

CECILY.   Yes, I felt it instinctively, but I couldn't wait all that time. I hate waiting even five minutes for anybody. It always makes me rather cross. I am not punctual myself, I know, but I do like punctuality in others, and waiting, even to be married, is quite out of the question.

ALGERNON.   Then what is to be done, Cecily?

CECILY.   I don't know, Mr. Moncrieff.

LADY BRACKNELL.   My dear Mr. Worthing, as Miss Cardew states positively that she cannot wait till she is thirty-five—a remark which I am bound to say seems to me to show a somewhat impatient nature—I would beg of you to reconsider your decision.

JACK.   But my dear Lady Bracknell, the matter is entirely in your own hands. The moment you consent to my marriage with Gwendolen, I will most gladly allow your nephew to form an alliance with my ward.

LADY BRACKNELL (*rising and drawing herself up*).   You must be quite aware that what you propose is out of the question.

JACK.   Then a passionate celibacy is all that any of us can look forward to.

LADY BRACKNELL.   That is not the destiny I propose for Gwendolen. Algernon, of course, can choose for himself. (*Pulls out her watch.*) Come, dear, (GWENDOLEN *rises*) we have already missed five, if not six, trains. To miss any more might expose us to comment on the platform.

(*Enter* DR. CHASUBLE.)

CHASUBLE.   Everything is quite ready for the christenings.

LADY BRACKNELL.   The christenings, sir! Is not that somewhat premature?

CHASUBLE (*looking rather puzzled, and pointing to* JACK *and* ALGERNON).   Both these gentlemen have expressed a desire for immediate baptism.

LADY BRACKNELL.   At their age? The idea is grotesque and irreligious!

Algernon, I forbid you to be baptised. I will not hear of such excesses. Lord Bracknell would be highly displeased if he learned that that was the way in which you wasted your time and money.

CHASUBLE.   Am I to understand then that there are to be no christenings at all this afternoon?

JACK.   I don't think that, as things are now, it would be of much practical value to either of us, Dr. Chasuble.

CHASUBLE.   I am grieved to hear such sentiments from you, Mr. Worthing. They savour of the heretical views of the Anabaptists, views that I have completely refuted in four of my unpublished sermons. However, as your present mood seems to be one peculiarly secular, I will return to the church at once. Indeed, I have just been informed by the pewopener that for the last hour and a half Miss Prism has been waiting for me in the vestry.

LADY BRACKNELL (*starting*).   Miss Prism! Did I hear you mention a Miss Prism?

CHASUBLE.   Yes, Lady Bracknell. I am on my way to join her.

LADY BRACKNELL.   Pray allow me to detain you for a moment. This matter may prove to be one of vital importance to Lord Bracknell and myself. Is this Miss Prism a female of repellent aspect, remotely connected with education?

CHASUBLE (*somewhat indignantly*).   She is the most cultivated of ladies, and the very picture of respectability.

LADY BRACKNELL.   It is obviously the same person. May I ask what position she holds in your household?

CHASUBLE (*severely*).   I am a celibate, madam.

JACK (*interposing*).   Miss Prism, Lady Bracknell, has been for the last three years Miss Cardew's esteemed governess and valued companion.

LADY BRACKNELL.   In spite of what I hear of her, I must see her at once. Let her be sent for.

CHASUBLE (*looking off*).   She approaches; she is nigh.

(*Enter* MISS PRISM *hurriedly.*)

MISS PRISM.   I was told you expected me in the vestry, dear Canon. I have been waiting for you there for an hour and three-quarters. (*Catches sight of* LADY BRACKNELL, *who has fixed her with a stony glare.* MISS PRISM *grows pale and quails. She looks anxiously round as if desirous to escape.*)

LADY BRACKNELL (*in a severe, judicial voice*).   Prism! (MISS PRISM *bows her head in shame.*) Come here, Prism! (MISS PRISM *approaches in a humble manner.*) Prism! Where is that baby? (*General consternation. The Canon starts back in horror.* ALGERNON *and* JACK *pretend to be anxious to shield* CECILY *and* GWENDOLEN *from hearing the details of a terrible public scandal.*) Twenty-eight years ago, Prism, you left Lord Bracknell's house, Number 104, Upper Grosvenor Street, in charge of a perambulator that contained a baby, of the male sex. You never returned. A few weeks later, through the elaborate investigations of the Metropolitan police, the perambulator was discovered at midnight, standing by itself in a remote corner of Bayswater. It contained the manuscript of a three-volume novel of more than usually revolting sentimentality. (MISS PRISM *starts in involuntary indignation.*) But the baby was not there! (*Everyone looks at* MISS PRISM.) Prism, where is that baby? (*A pause.*)

MISS PRISM.   Lady Bracknell, I admit with shame that I do not know. I only wish I did. The plain facts of the case are these. On the morning of the day you mention, a day that is forever branded on my memory, I prepared as usual to take the baby out in its perambulator. I had also with me a somewhat old but capacious hand-bag in which I had intended to place the manuscript of a work of fiction that I had written during my few unoccupied hours. In a moment of mental abstraction, for which I never can forgive myself, I deposited the manuscript in the bassinette, and placed the baby in the hand-bag.

JACK (*who has been listening attentively*).   But where did you deposit the hand-bag?

MISS PRISM.   Do not ask me, Mr. Worthing.

JACK.   Miss Prism, this is a matter of no small importance to me. I insist on knowing where you deposited the hand-bag that contained that infant.

MISS PRISM.   I left it in the cloak-room of one of the larger railway stations in London.

JACK.   What railway station?

MISS PRISM (*quite crushed*).   Victoria. The Brighton line. (*Sinks into a chair.*)

JACK.   I must retire to my room for a moment. Gwendolen, wait here for me.

GWENDOLEN.   If you are not too long, I will wait here for you all my life. (*Exit* JACK *in great excitement.*)

CHASUBLE.   What do you think this means, Lady Bracknell?

LADY BRACKNELL.   I dare not even suspect, Dr. Chasuble. I need hardly tell you that in families of high position strange coincidences are not supposed to occur. They are hardly considered the thing. (*Noises heard overhead as if someone was throwing trunks about. Everybody looks up.*)

CECILY.   Uncle Jack seems strangely agitated.

CHASUBLE.   Your guardian has a very emotional nature.

LADY BRACKNELL.   This noise is extremely unpleasant. It sounds as if he was having an argument. I dislike arguments of any kind. They are always vulgar, and often convincing.

CHASUBLE (*looking up*).   It has stopped now. (*The noise is redoubled.*)

LADY BRACKNELL.   I wish he would arrive at some conclusion.

GWENDOLEN.   This suspense is terrible. I hope it will last.

(*Enter* JACK *with a hand-bag of black leather in his hand.*)

JACK (*rushing over to* MISS PRISM).   Is this the hand-bag, Miss Prism?

Examine it carefully before you speak. The happiness of more than one life depends on your answer.

MISS PRISM (*calmly*). It seems to be mine. Yes, here is the injury it received through the upsetting of a Gower Street omnibus in younger and happier days. Here is the stain on the lining caused by the explosion of a temperance beverage, an incident that occurred at Leamington. And here, on the lock, are my initials. I had forgotten that in an extravagant mood I had had them placed there. The bag is undoubtedly mine. I am delighted to have it so unexpectedly restored to me. It has been a great inconvenience being without it all these years.

JACK (*in a pathetic voice*). Miss Prism, more is restored to you than this hand-bag. I was the baby you placed in it.

MISS PRISM (*amazed*). You?

JACK (*embracing her*). Yes . . . mother!

MISS PRISM (*recoiling in indignant astonishment*). Mr. Worthing! I am unmarried!

JACK. Unmarried! I do not deny that is a serious blow. But after all, who has the right to cast a stone against one who has suffered? Cannot repentance wipe out an act of folly? Why should there be one law for men and another for women? Mother, I forgive you. (*Tries to embrace her again.*)

MISS PRISM (*still more indignant*). Mr. Worthing, there is some error. (*Pointing to* LADY BRACKNELL.) There is the lady who can tell you who you really are.

JACK (*after a pause*). Lady Bracknell, I hate to seem inquisitive, but would you kindly inform me who I am?

LADY BRACKNELL. I am afraid that the news I have to give you will not altogether please you. You are the son of my poor sister, Mrs. Moncrieff, and consequently Algernon's elder brother.

JACK. Algy's elder brother! Then I have a brother after all. I knew I had a brother! I always said I had a brother! Cecily,—how could you have ever doubted that I had a brother? (*Seizes hold of* ALGERNON.) Dr. Chasuble, my unfortunate brother. Miss Prism, my unfortunate brother. Gwendolen, my unfortunate brother. Algy, you young scoundrel, you will have to treat me with more respect in the future. You have never behaved to me like a brother in all your life.

ALGERNON. Well, not till to-day, old boy, I admit. I did my best, however, though I was out of practice. (*Shakes hands.*)

GWENDOLEN (*to* JACK). My own! But what own are you? What is your Christian name, now that you have become someone else?

JACK. Good heavens! . . . I had quite forgotten that point. Your decision on the subject of my name is irrevocable, I suppose?

GWENDOLEN. I never change, except in my affections.

CECILY. What a noble nature you have, Gwendolen!

JACK. Then the question had better be cleared up at once. Aunt Augusta, a moment. At the time when Miss Prism left me in the hand-bag, had I been christened already?

LADY BRACKNELL. Every luxury that money could buy, including christening, had been lavished on you by your fond and doting parents.

JACK. Then I was christened! That is settled. Now, what name was I given? Let me know the worst.

LADY BRACKNELL. Being the eldest son you were naturally christened after your father.

JACK (*irritably*). Yes, but what was my father's Christian name?

LADY BRACKNELL (*meditatively*). I cannot at the present moment recall what the General's Christian name was. But I have no doubt he had one. He was eccentric, I admit. But only in later years. And that was the result of the Indian climate, and marriage, and indigestion, and other things of that kind.

JACK. Algy! Can't you recollect what our father's Christian name was?

ALGERNON. My dear boy, we were never even on speaking terms. He died before I was a year old.

JACK. His name would appear in the Army Lists of the period, I suppose, Aunt Augusta?

LADY BRACKNELL. The General was essentially a man of peace, except in his domestic life. But I have no doubt his name would appear in any military directory.

JACK. The Army Lists of the last forty years are here. These delightful records should have been my constant study. (*Rushes to bookcase and tears the books out.*) M. Generals . . . Mallam, Maxbohm, Magley, what ghastly names they have—Markby, Migsby, Mobbs, Moncrieff! Lieutenant 1840, Captain, Lieutenant-Colonel, Colonel, General 1869, Christian names, Ernest John. (*Puts book very quietly down and speaks quite calmly.*) I always told you, Gwendolen, my name was Ernest didn't I? Well, it is Ernest after all. I mean it naturally is Ernest.

LADY BRACKNELL. Yes, I remember that the General was called Ernest. I knew I had some particular reason for disliking the name.

GWENDOLEN. Ernest! My own Ernest! I felt from the first that you could have no other name!

JACK. Gwendolen, it is a terrible thing for a man to find out suddenly that all his life he has been speaking nothing but the truth. Can you forgive me?

GWENDOLEN. I can. For I feel that you are sure to change.

JACK. My own one!

CHASUBLE (*to* MISS PRISM). Lætitia! (*Embraces her.*)

MISS PRISM (*enthusiastically*). Frederick! At last!

ALGERNON. Cecily! (*Embraces her.*) At last!

JACK. Gwendolen! (*Embraces her.*) At last!

LADY BRACKNELL. My nephew, you seem to be displaying signs of triviality.

JACK. On the contrary, Aunt Augusta, I've now realized for the first time in my life the vital Importance of Being Earnest.

TABLEAU   CURTAIN

QUESTIONS

1. The opening scene of a play may accomplish a number of things, including: (*a*) the focusing of audiece attention; (*b*) raising audience interest; (*c*) forwarding or building that interest; (*d*) introducing major characters; (*e*) telling the audience how to take or how to respond to the play. Which of these does Oscar Wilde accomplish with the opening scenes between Algernon and Lane and between Algernon and Jack? Just how is each accomplished?

2. The plot of *The Importance of Being Earnest* has two major interwoven complications. The chief one involves Jack and Gwendolen and the subsidary one involves Algernon and Cecily. Each complication has an initiation, a rising involvement, a crisis, and a resolution. Trace these for each. Just how are the two interwoven into a unified whole? Are there other minor complications in the action? What are they?

3. The characterization, as befits a farcical comedy of this type, is relatively slight. Most of the characters are presented in terms of bent, disposition, and attitude. List the exact traits of character by which each is differentiated.

4. A major part of the comic effect of this play is created through diction. How many different devices of comic diction can you discover?

5. Which of the devices or traits of characterization noted in question 3 are ludicrous or comic traits?

6. Certain incidents and certain situations in the play are in themselves ludicrous or comic. List the chief examples.

7. Wilde derives some of his comic effect from ridiculing or satirizing certain attitudes, points of view, and ideas. List and classify these.

8. There are some situations in this play which were widely utilized in nineteenth-century melodrama and melodramatic fiction. Name the chief examples. How are these made to contribute to a comic rather than a melodramatic effect?

9. If you were staging this play and had adequate funds for production, would you prefer to stage it in period costume or in modern dress? Why?

10. Assume that you are the director with an adequate cast and adequate production funds for the staging of this play. Prepare a statement on the style of interpretation which you will present as directions to the designers and the actors.

11. Can you state specifically aspects of the nature of man rendered in Wilde's characterizations which would influence the style of acting in their interpretations?

CANDIDA

George Bernard Shaw

George Bernard Shaw (1856–1950) was born in Dublin and went to London when he was twenty years old. He became associated with a Socialist group, the Fabian Society, almost from its founding in 1884 and wrote a series of tracts on political and economic subjects for it. In the Society and elsewhere, he seized upon every opportunity for public speaking and debate. In 1885 he turned to journalism, writing for the *Pall Mall Gazette* and *The World*. He became the music critic for the *Star* in 1888 and dramatic critic for *The Saturday Review* in 1895. Shaw was an early and outspoken exponent of Ibsen drama, seeing it essentially as a means of social criticism and the discussion of ideas. Between 1879 and 1883, he wrote five novels, none of which attracted serious attention. When Jacob T. Grein organized the Independent Theatre in 1891, he found a staunch supporter in Shaw. Shaw was nearing the age of forty before he wrote his first play, *Widowers' Houses*, begun in collaboration with another Ibsenite, William Archer, and was fifty before he achieved his first success in the theatre. Since then and long before his death at the age of ninety-four he came to be recognized as the greatest modern English playwright. In addition to his plays, he was a prolific writer of extended prefaces and other prose works, including *The Quintessence of Ibsenism* (1891), *The Perfect Wagnerite* (1898), *The Intelligent Woman's Guide to Socialism* (1928), among others.

His plays are as follows: *Widowers' Houses* (1892), *The Philanderer* (1892), *Arms and The Man* (1894), *Candida* (1897), *The Man of Destiny* (1897), *The Devil's Disciple* (1897), *You Never Can Tell* (1900), *Captain Brassbound's Conversion* (1900), *Mrs. Warren's Profession* (1902), *John Bull's Other Island* (1903), *How He Lied to Her Husband* (1904), *Man and Superman* (1905), *Major Barbara* (1905), *Caesar and Cleopatra* (1906), *The Doctor's Dilemma* (1906), *Getting Married* (1908), *Press Cuttings* (1909), *The Shewing-up of Blanco Posnet* (1909), *The Dark Lady of The Sonnets* (1910), *Misalliance* (1910), *Fanny's First Play* (1911), *Androcles and The Lion* (1912), *Overruled* (1912), *Pygmalion* (1913), *The Great Catherine* (1913), *Augustus Does His Bit* (1917), *The Inca of Perusalem* (1917), *O'Flaherty V.C.* (1918), *Annajanska, the Bolshevik Empress* (1918), *Heartbreak House* (1919), *Back to Methuselah* (1921), *Saint Joan* (1923), *The Apple Cart* (1929), *On the Rocks* (1933), *Village Wooing* (1933), *The Simpleton of The Unexpected Isles* (1934), *The Millionairess* (1936), *Geneva* (1938), *In Good King Charles's Golden Days* (1939).

Strongly under the influence of the nineteenth century trends in realistic and naturalistic social drama, Shaw believed that the drama's highest

Reprinted by permission of Dodd, Mead & Company.

function was to change the social, political, and moral climate of a people. Drama in his view should be designed to persuade and to convince; hence drama for Shaw was as much a matter of rhetoric as of poetic. Accordingly he developed and wrote a drama of discussion designed to stimulate, provoke, and shock at the same time that it entertained and amused. For such a purpose, witty and satiric comedy was obviously more effective than tragedy—at least to Shaw, who was by nature a comedian. Among his thirty-five plays only one, *Saint Joan,* might be justifiably classed as tragedy.

Of his comedies, *Candida*—subtitled "A Pleasant Play"—has often been called by critics his best constructed play. By this is meant that it is more obviously organized in terms of a completed action and unified through the principle of action than are many of his other comedies. *Candida* is built about an ancient comic subject, the relations of man and woman in marriage. The relations of the sexes have been from the days of Aristophanes and before a fruitful source of hilarity, for perhaps no other human relationship reveals so many aspects of the ludicrousness of man. In play after play, Shaw exploited for comic effects as well as for serious discussion the subjects of marriage and the relations of man and woman. Out of his studies of science, especially genetics, and of philosophy, he evolved his idea of the Life Force and its natural dominance over human beings. Man in the power of this Force, especially when his codes and conduct run counter to it, can be viewed as superbly ludicrous, as in *Man and Superman.* But the ideas of marriage and the man-woman relationships are by no means the only ideas that are made to contribute to the comic effects of *Candida.* This play, like Shaw's other comedies, may rightly be called a comedy of ideas.

But Shaw the dramatist is working with characters and actions and not merely with ideas. His agents are, as their function requires, to a degree caricatured. Morell, "a great baby, pardonably vain of his powers and unconsciously pleased with himself"; Burgess the vulgarian, "softened into sluggish bumptiousness by overfeeding and commercial success"; Lexy, the vacuous vicar but recently from Oxford; and Prossy, the old maid with the old-maid's complaint, are obvious comic deviates who serve to define Shaw's concept of the normal and contribute tellingly to the comic powers of the piece. But what of Candida for whom the play is named? Is she Shaw's normative character, his ideal woman? Her role is certainly normative in working out the complications. But with all her sanity her femininity traps her, even if temporarily, into the absurdity of an older woman relishing the poetic love of an adolescent Shelley. Like the characters, the incidents and the language are masterfully contrived for comic effects. Though a relatively early work, *Candida* is one of Shaw's best comedies.

CHARACTERS

REVEREND JAMES MAVOR MORELL,
    a Christian Socialist Clergyman
    of the Church of England
MISS PROSERPINE GARNETT
    (PROSSY), his secretary-typist

REVEREND ALEXANDER MILL
    (LEXY), his Curate
MR BURGESS, his father-in-law
CANDIDA, his wife
EUGENE MARCHBANKS, a shy young
    poet and friend of the Morells

TIME: *October, 1894.*
PLACE: *The drawing-room and work-room of St Dominic's Parsonage,*
       the home of the Morells.

ACT I

A *fine morning in October 1894 in the north east quarter of London, a vast district miles away from the London of Mayfair and St. James's, and much less narrow, squalid, fetid and airless in its slums. It is strong in unfashionable middle class life: wide-streeted; myriad-populated; well served with ugly iron urinals, Radical clubs, and tram lines carrying a perpetual stream of yellow cars; enjoying in its main thoroughfares the luxury of grass-grown "front gardens" untrodden by the foot of man save as to the path from the gate to the hall door; blighted by a callously endured monotony of miles and miles of unlovely brick houses, black iron railings, stony pavements, slated roofs, and respectably ill dressed or disreputably worse dressed people, quite accustomed to the place, and mostly plodding uninterestedly about somebody else's work. The little energy and eagerness that crop up shew themselves in cockney cupidity and business "push." Even the policemen and the chapels are not infrequent enough to break the monotony. The sun is shining cheerfully: there is no fog; and though the smoke effectually prevents anything, whether faces and hands or bricks and mortar, from looking fresh and clean, it is not hanging heavily enough to trouble a Londoner.*

    This desert of unattractiveness has its oasis. Near the outer end of the Hackney Road is a park of 217 acres, fenced in, not by railings, but by a wooden paling, and containing plenty of greensward, trees, a lake for bathers, flower beds which are triumphs of the admired cockney art of carpet gardening, and a sandpit, originally imported from the seaside for the delight of children, but speedily deserted on its becoming a natural vermin preserve for all the petty fauna of Kingsland, Hackney, and Hoxton. A bandstand, an unfurnished forum for religious, anti-religious, and political orators, cricket pitches, a gymnasium, and an old fashioned stone kiosk are among its attractions. Wherever the prospect is bounded by trees or rising green grounds, it is a pleasant place. Where the ground stretches flat to the grey palings, with bricks and mortar, sky signs, crowded chimneys and smoke beyond, the prospect makes it desolate and sordid.

*The best view of Victoria Park is commanded by the front window of
St Dominic's Parsonage, from which not a brick is visible. The parsonage
is semi-detached, with a front garden and a porch. Visitors go up the flight
of steps to the porch: tradespeople and members of the family go down
by a door under the steps to the basement, with a breakfast room, used for
all meals, in front, and the kitchen at the back. Upstairs, on the level of
the hall door, is the drawing room, with its large plate glass window looking out on the park. In this, the only sitting room that can be spared from
the children and the family meals, the parson, the* REVEREND JAMES MAVOR
MORELL, *does his work. He is sitting in a strong round backed revolving
chair at the end of a long table, which stands across the window, so that
he can cheer himself with a view of the park over his left shoulder. At the
opposite end of the table, adjoining it, is a little table only half as wide
as the other, with a typewriter on it. His typist is sitting at this machine,
with her back to the window. The large table is littered with pamphlets,
journals, letters, nests of drawers, an office diary, postage scales and the
like. A spare chair for visitors having business with the parson is in the
middle, turned to his end. Within reach of his hand is a stationery case,
and a photograph in a frame. The wall behind him is fitted with bookshelves, on which an adept eye can measure the parson's casuistry and
divinity by Maurice's Theological Essays and a complete set of Browning's
poems, and the reformer's politics by a yellow backed Progress and Pov-
erty, Fabian Essays, A Dream of John Ball, Marx's Capital, and half a
dozen other literary landmarks in Socialism. Facing him on the other
side of the room, near the typewriter, is the door. Further down opposite
the fireplace, a bookcase stands on a cellaret, with a sofa near it. There is
a generous fire burning; and the hearth, with a comfortable armchair and
a black japanned flower-painted coal scuttle at one side, a miniature chair
for children on the other, a varnished wooden mantelpiece, with neatly
moulded shelves, tiny bits of mirror let into the panels, a travelling clock
in a leather case (the inevitable wedding present), and on the wall above
a large autotype of the chief figure in Titian's Assumption of the Virgin, is
very inviting. Altogether the room is the room of a good housekeeper, van-
quished, as far as the table is concerned, by an untidy man, but elsewhere mistress of the situation. The furniture, in its ornamental aspect,
betrays the style of the advertized "drawing-room suite" of the pushing
suburban furniture dealer; but there is nothing useless or pretentious in
the room, money being too scarce in the house of an east end parson to
be wasted on snobbish trimmings.*

The REVEREND JAMES MAVOR MORELL *is a Christian Socialist clergyman
of the Church of England, and an active member of the Guild of St. Matthew and the Christian Social Union. A vigorous, genial, popular man of
forty, robust and goodlooking, full of energy, with pleasant, hearty, consid-
erate manners, and a sound unaffected voice, which he used with the clean
athletic articulation of a practised orator, and with a wide range and perfect command of expression. He is a first rate clergyman, able to say what*

he likes to whom he likes, to lecture people without setting himself up against them, to impose his authority on them without humiliating them, and, on occasion, to interfere in their business without impertinence. His well-spring of enthusiasm and sympathetic emotion has never run dry for a moment: he still eats and sleeps heartily enough to win the daily battle between exhaustion and recuperation triumphantly. Withal, a great baby, pardonably vain of his powers and unconsciously pleased with himself. He has a healthy complexion: good forehead, with the brows somewhat blunt, and the eyes bright and eager, mouth resolute but not particularly well cut, and a substantial nose with the mobile spreading nostrils of the dramatic orator, void, like all his features, of subtlety.

The typist, MISS PROSERPINE GARNETT, is a brisk little woman of about 30, of the lower middle class, neatly but cheaply dressed in a black merino skirt and a blouse, notably pert and quick of speech, and not very civil in her manner, but sensitive and affectionate. She is clattering away busily at her machine whilst MORELL opens the last of his morning's letters. He realizes its contents with a comic groan of despair.

PROSERPINE.   Another lecture?

MORELL.   Yes. The Hoxton Freedom Group want me to address them on Sunday morning (*he lays great emphasis on Sunday, this being the unreasonable part of the business*). What are they?

PROSERPINE.   Communist Anarchists, I think.

MORELL.   Just like Anarchists not to know that they cant have a parson on Sunday! Tell them to come to church if they want to hear me: it will do them good. Say I can come on Mondays and Thursdays only. Have you the diary there?

PROSERPINE (*taking up the diary*).   Yes.

MORELL.   Have I any lecture on for next Monday?

PROSERPINE (*referring to the diary*).   Tower Hamlets Radical Club.

MORELL.   Well, Thursday then?

PROSERPINE.   English Land Restoration League.

MORELL.   What next?

PROSERPINE.   Guild of St Matthew on Monday. Independent Labor Party, Greenwich Branch, on Thursday. Monday, Social-Democratic Federation, Mile End Branch. Thursday, first Confirmation class. (*Impatiently.*) Oh, I'd better tell them you cant come. Theyre only half a dozen ignorant and conceited costermongers without five shillings between them.

MORELL (*amused*).   Ah; but you see theyre near relatives of mine.

PROSERPINE (*staring at him*).   Relatives of yours!

MORELL.   Yes: we have the same father—in Heaven.

PROSERPINE (*relieved*).   Oh, is that all?

MORELL (*with a sadness which is a luxury to a man whose voice expresses it so finely*).   Ah, you dont believe it. Everybody says it: nobody believes it: nobody. (*Briskly, getting back to business.*) Well, well!

Come, Miss Proserpine: cant you find a date for the costers? what about the 25th? That was vacant the day before yesterday.

PROSERPINE (*referring to diary*). Engaged. The Fabian Society.

MORELL. Bother the Fabian Society! Is the 28th gone too?

PROSERPINE. City dinner. Youre invited to dine with the Founders' Company.

MORELL. Thatll do: I'll go to the Hoxton Group of Freedom instead. (*She enters the engagement in silence, with implacable disparagement of the Hoxton Anarchists in every line of her face. MORELL bursts open the cover of a copy of The Church Reformer, which has come by post, and glances through Mr. Stewart Headlam's leader and the Guild of St. Matthew news. These proceedings are presently enlivened by the appearance of MORELL's curate, the REVEREND ALEXANDER MILL, a young gentleman gathered by MORELL from the nearest University settlement, whither he had come from Oxford to give the east end of London the benefit of his university training. He is a conceitedly well intentioned, enthusiastic, immature novice, with nothing positively unbearable about him except a habit of speaking with his lips carefully closed a full half inch from each corner for the sake of a finicking articulation and a set of university vowels, this being his chief means so far of bringing his Oxford refinement (as he calls his habits) to bear on Hackney vulgarity. MORELL, whom he has won over by a doglike devotion, looks up indulgently from The Church Reformer, and remarks.*) Well, Lexy? Late again, as usual!

LEXY. I'm afraid so. I wish I could get up in the morning.

MORELL (*exulting in his own energy*). Ha! ha! (*Whimsically.*) Watch and pray, Lexy: watch and pray.

LEXY. I know. (*Rising wittily to the occasion.*) But how can I watch and pray when I am asleep? Isnt that so, Miss Prossy? (*He makes for the warmth of the fire.*)

PROSERPINE (*sharply*). Miss Garnett, if you please.

LEXY. I beg your pardon, Miss Garnett.

PROSERPINE. Youve got to do all the work today.

LEXY (*on the hearth*). Why?

PROSERPINE. Never mind why. It will do you good to earn your supper before you eat it, for once in a way, as I do. Come! dont dawdle. You should have been off on your rounds half an hour ago.

LEXY (*perplexed*). Is she in earnest, Morell?

MORELL (*in the highest spirits: his eyes dancing*). Yes. I am going to dawdle today.

LEXY. You! You don't know how.

MORELL (*rising*). Ha! ha! Don't I? I'm going to have this morning all to myself. My wife's coming back: she's due here at 11.45.

LEXY (*surprised*). Coming back already! with the children? I thought they were to stay to the end of the month.

MORELL. So they are: she's only coming up for two days, to get some flannel things for Jimmy, and to see how we're getting on without her.

LEXY (*anxiously*). But, my dear Morell, if what Jimmy and Fluffy had was scarlatina, do you think it wise—

MORELL. Scarlatina! Rubbish! it was German measles. I brought it into the house myself from the Pycroft Street school. A parson is like a doctor, my boy: he must face infection as a soldier must face bullets. (*He claps* LEXY *manfully on the shoulders.*) Catch the measles if you can, Lexy: she'll nurse you; and what a piece of luck that will be for you! Eh?

LEXY (*smiling uneasily*). It's so hard to understand you about Mrs. Morell—

MORELL (*tenderly*). Ah, my boy, get married: get married to a good woman; and then youll understand. Thats a foretaste of what will be best in the Kingdom of Heaven we are trying to establish on earth. That will cure you of dawdling. An honest man feels that he must pay Heaven for every hour of happiness with a good spell of hard unselfish work to make others happy. We have no more right to consume happiness without producing it than to consume wealth without producing it. Get a wife like my Candida; and youll always be in arrear with your repayment. (*He pats* LEXY *affectionately and moves to leave the room.*)

LEXY. Oh, wait a bit: I forgot. (*Morell halts and turns with the door knob in his hand.*) Your father-in-law is coming round to see you.

(MORELL, *surprised and not pleased, shuts the door again, with a complete change of manner.*)

MORELL. Mr. Burgess?

LEXY. Yes. I passed him in the park, arguing with somebody. He asked me to let you know that he was coming.

MORELL (*half incredulous*). But he hasnt called here for three years. Are you sure, Lexy? Youre not joking, are you?

LEXY (*earnestly*). No sir, really.

MORELL (*thoughtfully*). Hm! Time for him to take another look at Candida before she grows out of his knowledge. (*He resigns himself to the inevitable, and goes out.*)

(LEXY *looks after him with beaming worship.* MISS GARNETT, *not being able to shake* LEXY, *relieves her feelings by worrying the typewriter.*)

LEXY. What a good man! What a thorough loving soul he is! (*He takes* MORELL's *place at the table, making himself very comfortable as he takes out a cigaret.*)

PROSERPINE (*impatiently, pulling the letter she has been working at off the typewriter and folding it*). Oh, a man ought to be able to be fond of his wife without making a fool of himself about her.

LEXY (*shocked*). Oh, Miss Prossy!

PROSERPINE (*snatching at the stationery case for an envelope, in which she encloses the letter as she speaks*). Candida here, and Candida there, and Candida everywhere! (*She licks the envelope.*) It's enough to drive anyone out of their senses (*thumping the envelope to make it stick*) to hear a woman raved about in that absurd manner merely because she's got good hair and a tolerable figure.

LEXY (*with reproachful gravity*). I think her extremely beautiful, Miss Garnett. (*He takes the photograph up; looks at it; and adds, with even greater impressiveness*) extremely beautiful. How fine her eyes are!

PROSERPINE. Her eyes are not a bit better than mine: now! (*He puts down the photograph and stares austerely at her.*) And you know very well you think me dowdy and second rate enough.

LEXY (*rising majestically*). Heaven forbid that I should think of any of God's creatures in such a way! (*He moves stiffly away from her across the room to the neighborhood of the bookcase.*)

PROSERPINE (*sarcastically*). Thank you. That's very nice and comforting.

LEXY (*saddened by her depravity*). I had no idea you had any feeling against Mrs. Morell.

PROSERPINE (*indignantly*). I have no feeling against her. She's very nice, very good-hearted: I'm very fond of her, and can appreciate her real qualities far better than any man can. (*He shakes his head sadly. She rises and comes at him with intense pepperiness.*) You dont believe me? You think I'm jealous? Oh, what a knowledge of the human heart you have, Mr Lexy Mill! How well you know the weaknesses of Woman, dont you? It must be so nice to be a man and have a fine penetrating intellect instead of mere emotions like us, and to know that the reason we dont share your amorous delusions is that we're all jealous of one another! (*She abandons him with a toss of her shoulders, and crosses to the fire to warm her hands.*)

LEXY. Ah, if you women only had the same clue to Man's strength that you have to his weakness, Miss Prossy, there would be no Woman Question.

PROSERPINE (*over her shoulder, as she stoops, holding her hands to the blaze*). Where did you hear Morell say that? You didn't invent it yourself: youre not clever enough.

LEXY. Thats quite true. I am not ashamed of owing him that, as I owe him so many other spiritual truths. He said it at the annual conference of the Women's Liberal Federation. Allow me to add that though they didnt appreciate it, I, a mere man, did. (*He turns to the bookcase again, hoping that this may leave her crushed.*)

PROSERPINE (*putting her hair straight at a panel of mirror in the mantelpiece*). Well, when you talk to me, give me your own ideas, such as they are, and not his. You never cut a poorer figure than when you are trying to imitate him.

LEXY (*stung*). I try to follow his example, not to imitate him.

PROSERPINE (*coming at him again on her way back to her work*). Yes, you do: you imitate him. Why do you tuck your umbrella under your left arm instead of carrying it in your hand like anyone else? Why do you walk with your chin stuck out before you, hurrying along with that eager look in your eyes? you! who never get up before half past nine in the morning. Why do you say "knoaledge" in church, though you always say "knolledge" in private conversation! Bah! do you think I don't know? (*She goes back to the typewriter.*) Here! come and set about your work: weve wasted enough time for one morning. Here's a copy of the diary for today. (*She hands him a memorandum.*)

LEXY (*deeply offended*).   Thank you. (*He takes it and stands at the table with his back to her, reading it. She begins to transcribe her short-hand notes on the typewriter without troubling herself about his feelings.*)

(*The door opens; and* MR BURGESS *enters unannounced. He is a man of sixty, made coarse and sordid by the compulsory selfishness of petty commerce, and later on softened into sluggish bumptiousness by over-feeding and commercial success. A vulgar ignorant guzzling man, offensive and contemptuous to people whose labor is cheap, respectful to wealth and rank, and quite sincere and without rancor or envy in both attitudes. The world has offered him no decently paid work except that of a sweater; and he has become, in consequence, some-what hoggish. But he has no suspicion of this himself, and honestly regards his commercial prosperity as the inevitable and socially wholesome triumph of the ability, industry, shrewdness, and expe-rience in business of a man who in private is easygoing, affectionate, and humorously convivial to a fault. Corporeally he is podgy, with a snoutish nose in the centre of a flat square face, a dust colored beard with a patch of grey in the centre under his chin, and small watery blue eyes with a plaintively sentimental expression, which he trans-fers easily to his voice by his habit of pompously intoning his sentences.*)

BURGESS (*stopping on the threshold, and looking round*).   They told me Mr Morell was here.

PROSERPINE (*rising*).   I'll fetch him for you.

BURGESS (*staring disappointedly at her*).   Youre not the same young lady as hused to typewrite for him?

PROSERPINE.   No.

BURGESS (*grumbling on his way to the hearth-rug*).   No: she was young-er. (MISS GARNETT *stares at him; then goes out, slamming the door.*) Startin on your rounds, Mr Mill?

LEXY (*folding his memorandum and pocketing it*).   Yes; I must be off presently.

BURGESS (*momentously*).   Dont let me detain you, Mr Mill. What I come about is private between me and Mr Morell.

LEXY (*huffily*).   I have no intention of intruding, I am sure, Mr Bur-gess. Good morning.

BURGESS (*patronizingly*).   Oh, good morning to you.

(MORELL *returns as* LEXY *is making for the door.*)

MORELL (*to* LEXY).   Off to work?

LEXY.   Yes, sir.

MORELL.   Take my silk handkerchief and wrap your throat up. Theres a cold wind. Away with you.

(Lexy, *more than consoled for* Burgess's *rudeness, brightens up and goes out.*)

Burgess. Spoilin your korates as usu'l, James. Good mornin. When I pay a man, an' 'is livin depens on me, I keep him in 'is place.

Morell (*rather shortly*). I always keep my curates in their places as my helpers and comrades. If you get as much work out of your clerks and warehousemen as I do out of my curates, you must be getting rich pretty fast. Will you take your old chair?

(*He points with curt authority to the armchair beside the fireplace; then takes the spare chair from the table and sits down at an unfamiliar distance from his visitor.*)

Burgess (*without moving*). Just the same as hever, James!

Morell. When you last called—it was about three years ago, I think —you said the same thing a little more frankly. Your exact words then were "Just as big a fool as ever, James!"

Burgess (*soothingly*). Well, praps I did; but (*with conciliatory cheerfulness*) I meant no hoffence by it. A clorgyman is privileged to be a bit of a fool, you know: it's ony becomin in 'is profession that he should. Anyhow, I come here, not to rake up hold differences, but to let bygones be bygones. (*Suddenly becoming very solemn, and approaching* Morell.) James: three years ago, you done me a hil turn. You done me hout of a contrac; an when I gev you arsh words in my natral disappointment, you turned my daughrter again me. Well, I've come to hact the part of a Kerischin. (*Offering his hand.*) I forgive you, James.

Morell (*starting up*). Confound your impudence!

Burgess (*retreating, with almost lachrymose deprecation of his treatment*). Is that becomin language for a clorgyman, James? And you so particlar, too!

Morell (*hotly*). No, sir: it is not becoming language for a clergyman. I used the wrong word. I should have said damn your impudence: thats what St Paul or any honest priest would have said to you. Do you think I have forgotten that tender of yours for the contract to supply clothing to the workhouse?

Burgess (*in a paroxysm of public spirit*). I hacted in the hinterest of the ratepayers, James. It was the lowest tender: you carnt deny that.

Morell. Yes, the lowest, because you paid worse wages than any other employer—starvation wages—aye, worse than starvation wages—to the women who made the clothing. Your wages would have driven them to the streets to keep body and soul together. (*Getting angrier and angrier.*) Those women were my parishioners. I shamed the Guardians out of accepting your tender: I shamed the ratepayers out of letting them do it: I shamed everybody but you. (*Boiling over.*) How dare you, sir, come here and offer to forgive me, and talk about your daughter, and—

Burgess. Heasy, James! heasy! heasy! Dont git hinto a fluster about nothink. Ive howned I was wrong.

Morell. Have you? I didnt hear you.

BURGESS. Of course I did. I hown it now. Come: I harsk your pardon for the letter I wrote you. Is that enough?

MORELL (*snapping his fingers*). Thats nothing. Have you raised the wages?

BURGESS (*triumphantly*). Yes.

MORELL. What!

BURGESS (*unctuously*). Ive turned a moddle hemployer. I dont hemploy no women now: theyre all sacked; and the work is done by machinery. Not a man 'as less than sixpence a *hour*; and the skilled ands gits the Trade Union rate. (*Proudly.*) What ave you to say to me now?

MORELL (*overwhelmed*). Is it possible! Well, theres more joy in heaven over one sinner that repenteth!—(*Going to* BURGESS *with an explosion of apologetic cordiality.*) My dear Burgess: how splendid of you! I most heartily beg your pardon for my hard thoughts. (*Grasping his hand.*) And now, dont you feel the better for the change? Come! confess! youre happier. You look happier.

BURGESS (*ruefully*). Well, praps I do. I spose I must, since you notice it. At all events, I git my contrax assepted by the County Council. (*Savagely.*) They dussent ave nothink to do with me unless I paid fair wages: curse em for a parcel o meddlin fools!

MORELL (*dropping his hand, utterly discouraged*). So that was why you raised the wages! (*He sits down moodily.*)

BURGESS (*severely, in spreading, mounting tones*). Woy helse should I do it? What does it lead to but drink and huppishness in workin men? (*He seats himself magisterially in the easy chair.*) It's hall very well for you, James: it gits you hinto the papers and makes a great man of you; but you never think of the arm you do, puttin money into the pockets of workin men that they dunno ow to spend, and takin it from people that might be makin a good huse on it.

MORELL (*with a heavy sigh, speaking with cold politeness*). What is your business with me this morning? I shall not pretend to believe that you are here merely out of family sentiment.

BURGESS (*obstinately*). Yes I ham: just family sentiment and nothink helse.

MORELL (*with weary calm*). I dont believe you.

BURGESS (*rising threateningly*). Dont say that to me again, James Mavor Morell.

MORELL (*unmoved*). I'll say it just as often as may be necessary to convince you that it's true. I dont believe you.

BURGESS (*collapsing into an abyss of wounded feeling*). Oh, well, if youre determined to be hunfriendly, I spose I'd better go. (*He moves reluctantly towards the door.* MORELL *makes no sign. He lingers.*) I didn't hexpect to find a hunforgivin spirit in you, James. (MORELL *still not responding, he takes a few more reluctant steps doorwards. Then he comes back, whining.*) We huseter git on well enough, spite of our different hopinions. Woy are you so changed to me? I give you my word I come here in peeorr [pure] frenliness, not wishin to be hon bad terms with my hown daughrter's usban. Come, James: be a Kerischin, and shake ands. (*He puts his hand sentimentally on* MORELL's *shoulder.*)

MORELL (*looking up at him thoughtfully*). Look here, Burgess. Do you want to be as welcome here as you were before you lost that contract?

BURGESS. I do, James. I do—honest.

MORELL. Then why dont you behave as you did then?

BURGESS (*cautiously removing his hand*). Ow d'y'mean?

MORELL. I'll tell you. You thought me a young fool then.

BURGESS (*coaxingly*). No I didnt, James. I—

MORELL (*cutting him short*). Yes, you did. And I thought you an old scoundrel.

BURGESS (*most vehemently deprecating this gross self-accusation on* MORELL's *part*). No you didnt, James. Now you do yourself a hinjustice.

MORELL. Yes I did. Well, that did not prevent our getting on very well together. God made you what I call a scoundrel as He made me what you call a fool. (*The effect of this observation on* BURGESS *is to remove the keystone of his moral arch. He becomes bodily weak, and, with his eyes fixed on* MORELL *in a helpless stare, puts out his hand apprehensively to balance himself, as if the floor had suddenly sloped under him.* MORELL *proceeds, in the same tone of quiet conviction*). It was not for me to quarrel with His handiwork in the one case more than in the other. So long as you come here honestly as a self-respecting, thorough, convinced scoundrel, justifying your scoundrelism and proud of it, you are welcome. But (*and now* MORELL's *tone becomes formidable; and he rises and strikes the back of the chair for greater emphasis*) I wont have you here snivelling about being a model employer and a converted man when youre only an apostate with your coat turned for the sake of a County Council contract. (*He nods at him to enforce the point; then goes to the hearth-rug, where he takes up a comfortably commanding position with his back to the fire, and continues.*) No: I like a man to be true to himself, even in wickedness. Come now: either take your hat and go; or else sit down and give me a good scoundrelly reason for wanting to be friends with me. (*BURGESS, whose emotions have subsided sufficiently to be expressed by a dazed grin, is relieved by this concrete proposition. He ponders it for a moment, and then, slowly and very modestly, sits down in the chair* MORELL *has just left.*) Thats right. Now out with it.

BURGESS (*chuckling in spite of himself*). Well, you orr a queer bird, James, and no mistake. But (*almost enthusiastically*) one carnt elp likin you: besides, as I said afore, of course one dont take hall a clorgyman says seriously, or the world couldnt go on. Could it now? (*He composes himself for graver discourse, and, turning his eyes on* MORELL, *proceeds with dull seriousness.*) Well, I dont mind tellin you, since it's your wish we should be free with one another, that I did think you a bit of a fool once; but I'm beginnin to think that praps I was be'ind the times a bit.

MORELL (*exultant*). Aha! Youre finding that out at last, are you?

BURGESS (*portentously*). Yes: times 'as changed mor'n I could a believed. Five yorr [year] ago, no sensible man would a thought o takin hup with your hideas. I hused to wonder you was let preach at all. Why, I know a clorgyman what 'as bin kep hout of his job for yorrs by the Bishop o London, although the pore feller's not a bit more religious than you are. But today, if hennyone was to horffer to bet me a thousan poun that youll hend by bein a bishop yourself, I dussent take the bet. (*Very impressively.*) You and your crew are gittin hinfluential: I can see that. Theyll ave to give you somethink someday, if it's honly to stop your mouth. You ad the right instinc arter all, James: the line you took is the payin line in the long run for a man o your sort.

MORELL (*offering his hand with thorough decision*). Shake hands, Burgess. Now youre talking honestly. I dont think theyll make me a bishop; but if they do, I'll introduce you to the biggest jobbers I can get to come to my dinner parties.

BURGESS (*who has risen with a sheepish grin and accepted the hand of friendship*). You will ave your joke, James. Our quarrel's made up now, ain it?

A WOMAN'S VOICE. Say yes, James.

(*Startled, they turn quickly and find that* CANDIDA *has just come in, and is looking at them with an amused maternal indulgence which is her characteristic expression. She is a woman of 33, well built, well nourished, likely, one guesses, to become matronly later on, but now quite at her best, with the double charm of youth and motherhood. Her ways are those of a woman who has found that she can always manage people by engaging their affection, and who does so frankly and instinctively without the smallest scruple. So far, she is like any other pretty woman who is just clever enough to make the most of her sexual attractions for trivially selfish ends; but* CANDIDA'S *serene brow, courageous eyes, and well set mouth and chin signify largeness of mind and dignity of character to ennoble her cunning in the affections. A wise-hearted observer, looking at her, would at once guess that whoever had placed the Virgin of the Assumption over her hearth did so because he fancied some spiritual resemblance between them, and yet would not suspect either her husband or herself of any such idea, or indeed of any concern with the art of Titian.*

Just now she is in bonnet and mantle, carrying a strapped rug with her umbrella stuck through it, a hand-bag, and a supply of illustrated papers.)

MORELL (*shocked at his remissness*). Candida! Why—(*he looks at his watch, and is horrified to find it so late*). My darling! (*Hurrying to her and seizing the rug strap, pouring forth his remorseful regrets all the time.*) I intended to meet you at the train. I let the time slip. (*Flinging the rug on the sofa.*) I was so engrossed by—(*returning to her*)—I forgot —oh! (*He embraces her with penitent emotion.*)

BURGESS (*a little shamefaced and doubtful of his reception*). How orr you, Candy? (*She, still in* MORELL's *arms, offers him her cheek, which he kisses.*) James and me is come to an unnerstannin. A honorable unnerstannin. Ain we, James?

MORELL (*impetuously*). Oh bother your understanding! youve kept me late for Candida. (*With compassionate fervor.*) My poor love: how did you manage about the luggage? How—

CANDIDA (*stopping him and disengaging herself*). There! there! there! I wasnt alone. Eugene has been down with us; and we travelled together.

MORELL (*pleased*). Eugene!

CANDIDA. Yes: he's struggling with my luggage, poor boy. Go out, dear, at once; or he'll pay for the cab; and I don't want that. (MORELL *hurries out.* CANDIDA *puts down her hand-bag; then takes off her mantle and bonnet and puts them on the sofa with the rug, chatting meanwhile.*) Well, papa: how are you getting on at home?

BURGESS. The ouse aint worth livin in since you left it, Candy. I wish youd come round and give the gurl a talkin to. Who's this Eugene thats come with you?

CANDIDA. Oh, Eugene's one of James's discoveries. He found him sleeping on the Embankment last June. Havnt you noticed our new picture (*pointing to the Virgin*)? He gave us that.

BURGESS (*incredulously*). Garn! D'you mean to tell me—your hown father!—that cab touts or such like, orf the Embankment, buys pictures like that? (*Severely.*) Dont deceive me, Candy: it's a 'Igh Church picture; and James chose it hisself.

CANDIDA. Guess again. Eugene isnt a cab tout.

BURGESS. Then what is he? (*Sarcastically.*) A nobleman, I spose.

CANDIDA (*nodding delightedly*). Yes. His uncle's a peer! A real live earl.

BURGESS (*not daring to believe such good news*). No!

CANDIDA. Yes. He had a seven day bill for £55 in his pocket when James found him on the Embankment. He thought he couldnt get any money for it until the seven days were up; and he was too shy to ask for credit. Oh, he's a dear boy! We are very fond of him.

BURGESS (*pretending to belittle the aristocracy, but with his eyes gleaming*). Mm! I thort you wouldnt git a hearl's nevvy visitin in Victawriar Pawrk unless he were a bit of a flat. (*Looking again at the picture.*) Of course I dont old with that picture, Candy; but still it's a 'igh class fust rate work of ort: I can see that. Be sure you hintrodooce me to im, Candy. (*He looks at his watch anxiously.*) I can ony stay about two minutes.

(MORELL *comes back with* EUGENE, *whom* BURGESS *contemplates moist-eyed with enthusiasm. He is a strange, shy youth of eighteen, slight, effeminate, with a delicate childish voice, and a hunted tormented expression and shrinking manner that shew the painful sensitiveness of very swift and acute apprehensiveness in youth, before the character has grown to its full strength. Miserably irresolute, he does not know where to stand or what to do. He is afraid of* BURGESS, *and would run away into solitude if he dared; but the very intensity with which he feels a perfectly commonplace position comes from excessive nervous force; and his nostrils, mouth, and eyes betray a fiercely petulant wilfulness, as to the bent of which his brow, already lined with pity, is reassuring. He is so uncommon as to be almost unearthly; and to prosaic people there is something noxious in this unearthliness, just as to poetic people there is something angelic in it. His dress is anarchic. He wears an old blue serge jacket, unbuttoned, over a woolen lawn tennis shirt, with a silk handkerchief for a cravat, trousers matching the jacket, and brown canvas shoes. In these garments he has apparently lain in the heather and waded through the waters; and there is no evidence of his having ever brushed them.*

As he catches sight of a stranger on entering, he stops, and edges along the wall on the opposite side of the room.)

MORELL (*as he enters*). Come along: you can spare us quarter of an hour at all events. This is my father-in-law. Mr Burgess—Mr Marchbanks.

MARCHBANKS (*nervously backing against the bookcase*). Glad to meet you, sir.

BURGESS (*crossing to him with great heartiness, whilst* MORELL *joins* CANDIDA *at the fire*). Glad to meet you, I'm shore, Mr Morchbanks. (*Forcing him to shake hands.*) Ow do you find yoreself this weather? Ope you aint lettin James put no foolish ideas into your ed?

MARCHBANKS. Foolish ideas? Oh, you mean Socialism? No.

BURGESS. Thats right. (*Again looking at his watch.*) Well, I must go now: theres no elp for it. Yore not comin my way, orr you, Mr Morchbanks?

MARCHBANKS. Which way is that?

BURGESS. Victawriar Pawrk Station. Theres a city train at 12.25.

MORELL. Nonsense. Eugene will stay to lunch with us, I expect.

MARCHBANKS (*anxiously excusing himself*). No—I—I—

BURGESS. Well, well, I shornt press you: I bet youd rather lunch with Candy. Some night, I ope, youll come and dine with me at my club, the Freeman Founders in Nortn Folgit. Come: say you will!

MARCHBANKS. Thank you, Mr Burgess. Where is Norton Folgate? Down in Surrey, isnt it?

(BURGESS, *inexpressibly tickled, begins to splutter with laughter.*)

CANDIDA (*coming to the rescue*). Youll lose your train, papa, if you dont go at once. Come back in the afternoon and tell Mr Marchbanks where to find the club.

BURGESS (*roaring with glee*). Down in Surrey! Har, har! thats not a bad one. Well, I never met a man as didnt know Nortn Folgit afore. (*Abashed at his own noisiness.*) Goodbye, Mr Morchbanks: I know yore too 'ighbred to take my pleasantry in bad part. (*He again offers his hand.*)

MARCHBANKS (*taking it with a nervous jerk*). Not at all.

BURGESS. Bye, bye, Candy. I'll look in again later on. So long, James.

MORELL. Must you go?

BURGESS. Dont stir. (*He goes out with unabated heartiness.*)

MORELL. Oh, I'll see you off. (*He follows him.*)

(EUGENE *stares after them apprehensively, holding his breath until* BURGESS *disappears.*)

CANDIDA (*laughing*). Well, Eugene? (*He turns with a start, and comes eagerly towards her, but stops irresolutely as he meets her amused look*). What do you think of my father?

MARCHBANKS. I—I hardly know him yet. He seems to be a very nice old gentleman.

CANDIDA (*with gentle irony*). And youll go to the Freeman Founders to dine with him, wont you?

MARCHBANKS (*miserably, taking it quite seriously*). Yes, if it will please you.

CANDIDA (*touched*). Do you know, you are a very nice boy, Eugene, with all your queerness. If you had laughed at my father I shouldnt have minded; but I like you ever so much better for being nice to him.

MARCHBANKS. Ought I to have laughed? I noticed that he said something funny; but I am so ill at ease with strangers; and I never can see a joke. I'm very sorry. (*He sits down on the sofa, his elbows on his knees and his temples between his fists, with an expression of hopeless suffering.*)

CANDIDA (*bustling him goodnaturedly*). Oh come! You great baby, you! You are worse than usual this morning. Why were you so melancholy as we came along in the cab?

MARCHBANKS. Oh, that was nothing. I was wondering how much I ought to give the cabman. I know it's utterly silly; but you dont know how dreadful such things are to me—how I shrink from having to deal with strange people. (*Quickly and reassuringly.*) But it's all right. He beamed all over and touched his hat when Morell gave him two shillings. I was on the point of offering him ten.

(MORELL *comes back with a few letters and newspapers which have come by the midday post.*)

CANDIDA. Oh, James dear, he was going to give the cabman ten shillings! ten shillings for a three minutes drive! Oh dear!

MORELL (*at the table, glancing through the letters*). Never mind her, Marchbanks. The overpaying instinct is a generous one: better than the underpaying instinct, and not so common.

MARCHBANKS (*relapsing into dejection*). No: cowardice, incompetence. Mrs. Morell's quite right.

CANDIDA. Of course she is. (*She takes up her hand-bag.*) And now I must leave you to James for the present. I suppose you are too much of a poet to know the state a woman finds her house in when she's been away for three weeks. Give me my rug. (EUGENE *takes the strapped rug from the couch, and gives it to her. She takes it in her left hand, having the bag in her right.*) Now hang my cloak across my arm. (*He obeys.*) Now my

hat. (*He puts it into the hand which has the bag.*) Now open the door for
me. (*He hurries before her and opens the door.*) Thanks. (*She goes out;
and* MARCHBANKS *shuts the door.*)

MORELL (*still busy at the table*).   Youll stay to lunch, Marchbanks, of
course.

MARCHBANKS (*scared*).   I mustnt. (*He glances quickly at* MORELL, *but
at once avoids his frank look, and adds, with obvious disingenuousness.*) I
mean I cant.

MORELL.   You mean you wont.

MARCHBANKS (*earnestly*).   No: I should like to, indeed. Thank you
very much. But—but—

MORELL.   But—but—but—but—Bosh! If youd like to stay, stay. If
youre shy, go and take a turn in the park and write poetry until half past
one; and then come in and have a good feed.

MARCHBANKS.   Thank you, I should like that very much. But I really
mustnt. The truth is, Mrs Morell told me not to. She said she didnt think
youd ask me to stay to lunch, but that I was to remember, if you did, that
you didnt really want me to. (*Plaintively.*) She said I'd understand; but
I dont. Please dont tell her I told you.

MORELL (*drolly*).   Oh, is that all? Wont my suggestion that you should
take a turn in the park meet the difficulty?

MARCHBANKS.   How?

MORELL (*exploding good-humoredly*).   Why, you duffer— (*But this
boisterousness jars himself as well as* EUGENE. *He checks himself.*) No: I
wont put it in that way. (*He comes to* EUGENE *with affectionate seriousness.*) My dear lad: in a happy marriage like ours, there is something very
sacred in the return of the wife to her home. (MARCHBANKS *looks quickly
at him, half anticipating his meaning.*) An old friend or a truly noble and
sympathetic soul is not in the way on such occasions; but a chance visitor
is. (*The hunted horror-stricken expression comes out with sudden vivid-
ness in* EUGENE's *face as he understands.* MORELL, *occupied with his own
thoughts, goes on without noticing this.*) Candida thought I would rather
not have you here; but she was wrong. I'm very fond of you, my boy; and
I should like you to see for yourself what a happy thing it is to be married
as I am.

MARCHBANKS.   Happy! Your marriage! You think that! You believe
that!

MORELL (*buoyantly*).   I know it, my lad. Larochefoucauld said that
there are convenient marriages but no delightful ones. You dont know the
comfort of seeing through and through a thundering liar and rotten cynic
like that fellow. Ha! ha! Now, off with you to the park, and write your
poem. Half past one, sharp, mind: we never wait for anybody.

MARCHBANKS (*wildly*).   No: stop: you shant. I'll force it into the light.

MORELL (*puzzled*).   Eh? Force what?

MARCHBANKS.   I must speak to you. There is something that must be
settled between us.

MORELL (*with a whimsical glance at his watch*). Now?

MARCHBANKS (*passionately*). Now. Before you leave this room. (*He retreats a few steps, and stands as if to bar* MORELL'S *way to the door.*)

MORELL (*without moving, and gravely, perceiving now that there is something serious the matter*). I'm not going to leave it my dear boy: I thought you were. (EUGENE, *baffled by his firm tone, turns his back on him, writhing with anger.* MORELL *goes to him and puts his hand on his shoulder strongly and kindly, disregarding his attempt to shake it off.*) Come: sit down quietly; and tell me what it is. And remember: we are friends, and need not fear that either of us will be anything but patient and kind to the other, whatever we may have to say.

MARCHBANKS (*twisting himself round on him*). Oh, I am not forgetting myself: I am only (*covering his face desperately with his hands*) full of horror. (*Then, dropping his hands, and thrusting his face forward fiercely at* MORELL, *he goes on threateningly.*) You shall see whether this is a time for patience and kindness. (MORELL, *firm as a rock, looks indulgently at him.*) Dont look at me in that self-complacent way. You think yourself stronger than I am; but I shall stagger you if you have a heart in your breast.

MORELL (*powerfully confident*). Stagger me, my boy. Out with it.

MARCHBANKS. First—

MORELL. First?

MARCHBANKS. I love your wife.

(MORELL *recoils, and, after staring at him for a moment in utter amazement, bursts into uncontrollable laughter.* EUGENE *is taken aback, but not disconcerted; and he soon becomes indignant and contemptuous.*)

MORELL (*sitting down to have his laugh out*). Why, my dear child, of course you do. Everybody loves her: they cant help it. I like it. But (*looking up jocosely at him*) I say, Eugene: do you think yours is a case to be talked about? Youre under twenty: she's over thirty. Doesnt it look rather too like a case of calf love?

MARCHBANKS (*vehemently*). You dare say that of her! You think that way of the love she inspires! It is an insult to her!

MORELL (*rising quickly, in an altered tone*). To her! Eugene: take care. I have been patient. I hope to remain patient. But there are some things I wont allow. Dont force me to shew you the indulgence I should shew to a child. Be a man.

MARCHBANKS (*with a gesture as if sweeping something behind him*). Oh, let us put aside all that cant. It horrifies me when I think of the doses of it she has had to endure in all the weary years during which you have selfishly and blindly sacrificed her to minister to your self-sufficiency: you! (*turning on him*) who have not one thought—one sense—in common with her.

MORELL (*philosophically*). She seems to bear it pretty well. (*Looking him straight in the face.*) Eugene, my boy: you are making a fool of yourself: a very great fool of yourself. Theres a piece of wholesome plain speaking for you. (*He knocks in the lesson with a nod in his old way, and posts himself on the hearthrug, holding his hands behind him to warm them.*)

MARCHBANKS.   Oh, do you think I dont know all that? Do you think that the things people make fools of themselves about are any less real and true than the things they behave sensibly about? (MORELL's *gaze wavers for the first time. He forgets to warm his hands, and stands listening, startled and thoughtful.*) They are more true: they are the only things that are true. You are very calm and sensible and moderate with me because you can see that I am a fool about your wife; just as no doubt that old man who was here just now is very wise over your Socialism, because he sees that you are a fool about it. (MORELL's *perplexity deepens markedly.* EUGENE *follows up his advantage, plying him fiercely with questions.*) Does that prove you wrong? Does your complacent superiority to me prove that *I* am wrong?

MORELL.   Marchbanks: some devil is putting these words into your mouth. It is easy—terribly easy—to shake a man's faith in himself. To take advantage of that to break a man's spirit is devil's work. Take care of what you are doing. Take care.

MARCHBANKS (*ruthlessly*).   I know. I'm doing it on purpose. I told you I should stagger you.

(*They confront one another threateningly for a moment. Then* MORELL *recovers his dignity.*)

MORELL (*with noble tenderness*).   Eugene: listen to me. Some day, I hope and trust, you will be a happy man like me. (EUGENE *chafes intolerantly, repudiating the worth of his happiness.* MORELL, *deeply insulted, controls himself with fine forbearance, and continues steadily with great artistic beauty of delivery*). You will be married; and you will be working with all your might and valor to make every spot on earth as happy as your own home. You will be one of the makers of the Kingdom of Heaven on earth; and—who knows?—you may be a master builder where I am only a humble journey-man; for dont think, my boy, that I cannot see in you, young as you are, promise of higher powers than I can ever pretend to. I well know that it is in the poet that the holy spirit of man—the god within him—is most godlike. It should make you tremble to think of that— to think that the heavy burthen and great gift of a poet may be laid upon you.

MARCHBANKS (*unimpressed and remorseless, his boyish crudity of assertion telling sharply against* MORELL's *oratory*).   It does not make me tremble. It is the want of it in others that makes me tremble.

MORELL (*redoubling his force of style under the stimulus of his genuine feeling and* EUGENE's *obduracy*).   Then help to kindle it in them—in me —not to extinguish it. In the future, when you are as happy as I am, I will be your true brother in the faith. I will help you to believe that God has given us a world that nothing but our own folly keeps from being a paradise. I will help you to believe that every stroke of your work is sowing happiness for the great harvest that all—even the humblest—shall one day reap. And last, but trust me, not least, I will help you to believe that your wife loves you and is happy in her home. We need such help, Marchbanks: we need it greatly and always. There are so many things to make us doubt, if once we let our understanding be troubled. Even at home, we sit as if in camp, encompassed by a hostile army of doubts. Will you play the traitor and let them in on me?

MARCHBANKS (*looking round wildly*). Is it like this for her here always? A woman, with a great soul, craving for reality, truth, freedom; and being fed on metaphors, sermons, stale perorations, mere rhetoric. Do you think a woman's soul can live on your talent for preaching?

MORELL (*stung*). Marchbanks: you make it hard for me to control myself. My talent is like yours insofar as it has any real worth at all. It is the gift of finding words for divine truth.

MARCHBANKS (*impetuously*). It's the gift of the gab, nothing more and nothing less. What has your knack of fine talking to do with the truth, any more than playing the organ has? Ive never been in your church; but Ive been to your political meetings; and Ive seen you do whats called rousing the meeting to enthusiasm: that is, you excited them until they behaved exactly as if they were drunk. And their wives looked on and saw what fools they were. Oh, it's an old story: youll find it in the Bible. I imagine King David, in his fits of enthusiasm, was very like you. (*Stabbing him with the words.*) "But his wife despised him in her heart."

MORELL (*wrathfully*). Leave my house. Do you hear? (*He advances on him threateningly.*)

MARCHBANKS (*shrinking back against the couch*). Let me alone. Dont touch me. (MORELL *grasps him powerfully by the lapel of his coat: he cowers down on the sofa and screams passionately.*) Stop, Morell: if you strike me, I'll kill myself: I wont bear it. (*Almost in hysterics.*) Let me go. Take your hand away.

MORELL (*with slow emphatic scorn*). You little snivelling cowardly whelp. (*He releases him.*) Go, before you frighten yourself into a fit.

MARCHBANKS (*on the sofa, gasping, but relieved by the withdrawal of* MORELL'S *hand*). I'm not afraid of you: it's you who are afraid of me.

MORELL (*quietly, as he stands over him*). It looks like it, doesnt it?

MARCHBANKS (*with petulant vehemence*). Yes, it does. (MORELL *turns away contemptuously.* EUGENE *scrambles to his feet and follows him.*) You think because I shrink from being brutally handled—because (*with tears in his voice*) I can do nothing but cry with rage when I am met with violence—because I cant lift a heavy trunk down from the top of a cab like you—because I cant fight you for your wife as a drunken navvy would: all that makes you think I'm afraid of you. But youre wrong. If I havnt got what you call British pluck, I havnt British cowardice either: I'm not afraid of a clergyman's ideas. I'll fight your ideas. I'll rescue her from her slavery to them. I'll pit my own ideas against them. You are driving me out of the house because you darent let her choose between your ideas and mine. You are afraid to let me see her again. (MORELL, *angered, turns suddenly on him. He flies to the door in involuntary dread.*) Let me alone, I say. I'm going.

MORELL (*with cold scorn*). Wait a moment: I am not going to touch you: dont be afraid. When my wife comes back she will want to know why you have gone. And when she finds that you are never going to cross our threshold again, she will want to have that explained too. Now I dont wish to distress her by telling her that you have behaved like a blackguard.

MARCHBANKS (*coming back with renewed vehemence*). You shall. You must. If you give any explanation but the true one, you are a liar and a coward. Tell her what I said; and how you were strong and manly, and shook me as a terrier shakes a rat; and how I shrank and was terrified; and how you called me a snivelling little whelp and put me out of the house. If you dont tell her, I will: I'll write it to her.

MORELL (*puzzled*). Why do you want her to know this?

MARCHBANKS (*with lyric rapture*). Because she will understand me, and know that I understand her. If you keep back one word of it from her —if you are not ready to lay the truth at her feet as I am—then you will know to the end of your days that she really belongs to me and not to you. Goodbye. (*Going.*)

MORELL (*terribly disquieted*). Stop: I will not tell her.

MARCHBANKS (*turning near the door*). Either the truth or a lie you must tell her, if I go.

MORELL (*temporizing*). Marchbanks: it is sometimes justifiable—

MARCHBANKS (*cutting him short*). I know: to lie. It will be useless. Goodbye, Mr Clergyman.

(*As he turns to the door, it opens and* CANDIDA *enters in her housekeeping dress.*)

CANDIDA. Are you going, Eugene? (*Looking more observantly at him.*) Well, dear me, just look at you, going out into the street in that state! You are a poet, certainly. Look at him, James! (*She takes him by the coat, and brings him forward, shewing him to* MORELL.) Look at his collar! look at his tie! look at his hair! One would think somebody had been throttling you. (*EUGENE instinctively rises to look round at* MORELL; *but she pulls him back.*) Here! Stand still. (*She buttons his collar; ties his neckerchief in a bow; and arranges his hair.*) There! Now you look so nice that I think youd better stay to lunch after all, though I told you you mustnt. It will be ready in half an hour. (*She puts a final touch to the bow. He kisses her hand.*) Dont be silly.

MARCHBANKS. I want to stay, of course; unless the reverend gentleman your husband has anything to advance to the contrary.

CANDIDA. Shall he stay, James, if he promises to be a good boy and help me to lay the table?

MORELL (*shortly*). Oh yes, certainly: he had better. (*He goes to the table and pretends to busy himself with his papers there.*)

MARCHBANKS (*offering his arm to* CANDIDA). Come and lay the table. (*She takes it. They go to the door together. As they pass out he adds.*) I am the happiest of mortals.

MORELL. So was I—an hour ago.

ACT II

The same day later in the afternoon. The same room. The chair for visitors has been replaced at the table. MARCHBANKS, *alone and idle, is trying to find out how the typewriter works. Hearing someone at the door, he steals guiltily away to the window and pretends to be absorbed in the view.* MISS GARNETT, *carrying the notebook in which she takes down* MORELL's *letters in shorthand from his dictation, sits down at the typewriter and sets to work transcribing them, much too busy to notice* EUGENE. *When she begins the second line she stops and stares at the machine. Something wrong evidently.*

PROSERPINE. Bother! Youve been meddling with my typewriter, Mr. Marchbanks; and theres not the least use in your trying to look as if you hadnt.

MARCHBANKS (*timidly*). I'm very sorry, Miss Garnett. I only tried to make it write. (*Plaintively.*) But it wouldnt.

PROSERPINE. Well, youve altered the spacing.

MARCHBANKS (*earnestly*). I assure you I didnt. I didnt indeed. I only turned a little wheel. It gave a sort of click.

PROSERPINE. Oh, now I understand. (*She restores the spacing, talking volubly all the time.*) I suppose you thought it was a sort of barrel-organ. Nothing to do but turn the handle, and it would write a beautiful love letter for you straight off, eh?

MARCHBANKS (*seriously*). I suppose a machine could be made to write love letters. Theyre all the same, arnt they?

PROSERPINE (*somewhat indignantly: any such discussion, except by way of pleasantry, being outside her code of manners*). How do I know? Why do you ask me?

MARCHBANKS. I beg your pardon. I thought clever people—people who can do business and write letters and that sort of thing—always had to have love affairs to keep them from going mad.

PROSERPINE (*rising, outraged*). Mr. Marchbanks! (*She looks severely at him, and marches majestically to the bookcase.*)

MARCHBANKS (*approaching her humbly*). I hope I havnt offended you. Perhaps I shouldnt have alluded to your love affairs.

PROSERPINE (*plucking a blue book from the shelf and turning sharply on him*). I havnt any love affairs. How dare you say such a thing? The idea! (*She tucks the book under her arm, and is flouncing back to her machine when he addresses her with awakened interest and sympathy.*)

MARCHBANKS. Really! Oh, then you are shy, like me.

PROSERPINE. Certainly I am not shy. What do you mean?

MARCHBANKS (*secretly*). You must be: that is the reason there are so few love affairs in the world. We all go about longing for love: it is the first need of our natures, the first prayer of our hearts; but we dare not utter our longing: we are too shy. (*Very earnestly.*) Oh, Miss Garnett, what would you not give to be without fear, without shame—

PROSERPINE (*scandalized*). Well, upon my word!

MARCHBANKS (*with petulant impatience*). Ah, dont say those stupid things to me: they dont deceive me: what use are they? Why are you afraid to be your real self with me? I am just like you.

PROSERPINE. Like me! Pray are you flattering me or flattering yourself? I dont feel quite sure which. (*She again rises to get back to her work.*)

MARCHBANKS (*stopping her mysteriously*). Hush! I go about in search of love; and I find it in unmeasured stores in the bosoms of others. But when I try to ask for it, this horrible shyness strangles me; and I stand dumb, or worse than dumb, saying meaningless things: foolish lies. And I see the affection I am longing for given to dogs and cats and pet birds, because they come and ask for it. (*Almost whispering.*) It must be asked for: it is like a ghost: it cannot speak unless it is first spoken to. (*At his usual pitch, but with deep melancholy.*) All the love in the world is longing to speak; only it dare not, because it is shy! shy! shy! That is the world's tragedy. (*With a deep sigh he sits in the visitors' chair and buries his face in his hands.*)

PROSERPINE (*amazed, but keeping her wits about her: her point of honor in encounters with strange young men*). Wicked people get over that shyness occasionally, dont they?

MARCHBANKS (*scrambling up almost fiercely*). Wicked people means people who have no love: therefore they have no shame. They have the power to ask love because they dont need it: they have the power to offer it because they have none to give. (*He collapses into his seat, and adds, mournfully.*) But we, who have love, and long to mingle it with the love of others: we cannot utter a word. (*Timidly.*) You find that, dont you?

PROSERPINE. Look here: if you dont stop talking like this, I'll leave the room, Mr. Marchbanks: I really will. It's not proper.

(*She resumes her seat at the typewriter, opening the blue book and preparing to copy a passage from it.*)

MARCHBANKS (*hopelessly*). Nothing thats worth saying is proper. (*He rises, and wanders about the room in his lost way.*) I cant understand you, Miss Garnett. What am I to talk about?

PROSERPINE (*snubbing him*). Talk about indifferent things. Talk about the weather.

MARCHBANKS. Would you talk about indifferent things if a child were by, crying bitterly with hunger?

PROSERPINE. I suppose not.

MARCHBANKS. Well: *I* cant talk about indifferent things with my heart crying out bitterly in its hunger.

PROSERPINE. Then hold your tongue.

MARCHBANKS. Yes: that is what it always comes to. We hold our tongues. Does that stop the cry of your heart? for it does cry: doesnt it? It must, if you have a heart.

PROSERPINE (*suddenly rising with her hand pressed on her heart*). Oh, it's no use trying to work while you talk like that. (*She leaves her little table and sits on the sofa. Her feelings are keenly stirred*). It's no business of yours whether my heart cries or not; but I have a mind to tell you, for all that.

MARCHBANKS. You neednt. I know already that it must.

PROSERPINE. But mind! if you ever say I said so, I'll deny it.

MARCHBANKS (*compassionately*). Yes, I know. And so you havnt the courage to tell him?

PROSERPINE (*bouncing up*). Him! Who?

MARCHBANKS. Whoever he is. The man you love. It might be anybody. The curate, Mr Mill, perhaps.

PROSERPINE (*with disdain*). Mr Mill!!! A fine man to break my heart about, indeed! I'd rather have you than Mr Mill.

MARCHBANKS (*recoiling*). No, really: I'm very sorry; but you mustnt think of that. I—

PROSERPINE (*testily, going to the fire-place and standing at it with her back to him*). Oh, dont be frightened: it's not you. It's not any one particular person.

MARCHBANKS. I know. You feel that you could love anybody that offered—

PROSERPINE (*turning, exasperated*). Anybody that offered! No, I do not. What do you take me for?

MARCHBANKS (*discouraged*). No use. You wont make me real answers: only those things that everybody says. (*He strays to the sofa and sits down disconsolately.*)

PROSERPINE (*nettled at what she takes to be a disparagement of her manners by an aristocrat*). Oh well, if you want original conversation, youd better go and talk to yourself.

MARCHBANKS. That is what all poets do: they talk to themselves out loud; and the world overhears them. But it's horrible lonely not to hear someone else talk sometimes.

PROSERPINE. Wait until Mr Morell comes. He'll talk to you. (MARCHBANKS *shudders.*) Oh, you neednt make wry faces over him: he can talk better than you. (*With temper.*) He'd talk your little head off. (*She is going back angrily to her place, when he, suddenly enlightened, springs up and stops her.*)

MARCHBANKS. Ah! I understand now.

PROSERPINE (*reddening*). What do you understand?

MARCHBANKS. Your secret. Tell me: is it really and truly possible for a woman to love him?

PROSERPINE (*as if this were beyond all bounds*). Well!!

MARCHBANKS (*passionately*). No: answer me. I want to know: I must know. *I* cant understand it. I can see nothing in him but words, pious resolutions, what people call goodness. You cant love that.

PROSERPINE (*attempting to snub him by an air of cool propriety*). I simply dont know what youre talking about. I dont understand you.

MARCHBANKS (*vehemently*). You do. You lie.

PROSERPINE. Oh!

MARCHBANKS. You do understand; and you know. (*Determined to have an answer.*) Is it possible for a woman to love him?

PROSERPINE (*looking him straight in the face*). Yes. (*He covers his face with his hands.*) Whatever is the matter with you! (*He takes down his hands. Frightened at the tragic mask presented to her, she hurries past him at the utmost possible distance, keeping her eyes on his face until he turns from her and goes to the child's chair beside the hearth, where he sits in the deepest dejection. As she approaches the door, it opens and* BURGESS *enters. Seeing him, she ejaculates.*) Praise heaven! here's somebody (*and feels safe enough to resume her place at her table. She puts a fresh sheet of paper into the typewriter as* BURGESS *crosses to* EUGENE.)

BURGESS (*bent on taking care of the distinguished visitor*). Well: so this is the way they leave you to yourself, MR MORCHBANKS. Ive come to keep you company. (MARCHBANKS *looks up at him in consternation, which is quite lost on him.*) James is receivin a deppitation in the dinin room; and Candy is hupstairs heducating of a young stitcher gurl she's hinterested in. (*Condolingly.*) You must find it lonesome here with no one but the typist to talk to. (*He pulls round the easy chair, and sits down.*)

PROSERPINE (*highly incensed*). He'll be all right now that he has the advantage of your polished conversation: thats one comfort, anyhow. (*She begins to typewrite with clattering asperity.*)

BURGESS (*amazed at her audacity*). Hi was not addressin myself to you, young woman, that I'm awerr of.

PROSERPINE. Did you ever see worse manners, Mr Marchbanks?

BURGESS (*with pompous severity*). Mr. Morchbanks is a gentleman, and knows his place, which is more than some people do.

PROSERPINE (*fretfully*). It's well you and I are not ladies and gentlemen: I'd talk to you pretty straight if Mr. Marchbanks wasnt here. (*She pulls the letter out of the machine so crossly that it tears.*) There! now I've spoiled this letter! have to be done all over again! Oh, I cant contain myself: silly old fathead!

BURGESS (*rising, breathless with indignation*). Ho! I'm a silly ole fat'ead, am I? Ho, indeed (*gasping*)! Hall right, my gurl! Hall right. You just wait till I tell that to yore hemployer. You'll see. I'll teach you: see if I don't.

PROSERPINE (*conscious of having gone too far*). I—

BURGESS (*cutting her short*). Ho: youve done it now. No huse a-talkin to me. I'll let you know who I am. (PROSERPINE *shifts her paper carriage with a defiant bang, and disdainfully goes on with her work.*) Dont you take no notice of her, Mr Morchbanks. She's beneath it. (*He loftily sits down again.*)

MARCHBANKS (*miserably nervous and disconcerted*). Hadnt we better change the subject? I—I dont think Miss Garnett meant anything.

PROSERPINE (*with intense conviction*). Oh, didnt I though, just!

BURGESS. I wouldnt demean myself to take notice on her.

(*An electric bell rings twice.*)

PROSERPINE (*gathering up her note-book and papers*). Thats for me. (*She hurries out.*)

BURGESS (*calling after her*). Oh, we can spare you. (*Somewhat relieved by the triumph of having the last word, and yet half inclined to try to improve on it, he looks after her for a moment; then subsides into his seat by* EUGENE, *and addresses him very confidentially.*) Now we're alone, Mr Morchbanks, let me give you a friendly int that I wouldnt give to heverybody. Ow long ave you known my son-in-law James ere?

MARCHBANKS. I dont know. I never can remember dates. A few months, perhaps.

BURGESS. Ever notice hennythink queer about him?

MARCHBANKS. I dont think so.

BURGESS (*impressively*). No more you wouldnt. Thats the danger on it. Well, he's mad.

MARCHBANKS. Mad!

BURGESS. Mad as a Morch 'are. You take notice on him and youll see.

MARCHBANKS (*uneasily*). But surely that is only because his opinions—

BURGESS (*touching him on the knee with his forefinger, and pressing it to hold his attention*). Thats the same what I hused to think, Mr Morchbanks. Hi thought long enough that it was only his opinions; though, mind you, hopinions becomes vurry serious things when people takes to hactin on em as e does. But thats not what I go on. (*He looks round to make sure that they are alone, and bends over to* EUGENE'S *ear.*) What do you think he sez to me this mornin in this very room?

MARCHBANKS. What?

BURGESS. He sez to me—this is as sure as we're settin here now—he sez "I'm a fool," he sez; "and yore a scounderl." Me a scounderl, mind you! And then shook ands with me on it, as if it was to my credit! Do you mean to tell me as that man's sane?

MORELL (*outside, calling to* PROSERPINE *as he opens the door*). Get all their names and addresses, Miss Garnett.

PROSERPINE (*in the distance*). Yes, Mr Morell.

(MORELL *comes in, with the deputation's documents in his hands.*)

BURGESS (*aside to* MARCHBANKS). Yorr he is. Just you keep your heye on im and see. (*Rising momentously.*) I'm sorry, James, to ave to make a complaint to you. I dont want to do it; but I feel I oughter, as a matter o right and dooty.

MORELL. Whats the matter?

BURGESS. Mr. Morchbanks will bear me hout: he was a witness. (*Very solemnly.*) Yore young woman so far forgot herself as to call ma a silly ole fat'ead.

MORELL (*with tremendous heartiness*). Oh, now, isnt that exactly like Prossy? She's so frank: she cant contain herself! Poor Prossy! Ha! ha!

BURGESS (*trembling with rage*). And do you hexpec me to put up with it from the like of er?

MORELL. Pooh, nonsense! you cant take any notice of it. Never mind. (*He goes to the cellaret and puts the papers into one of the drawers.*)

BURGESS. Oh, Hi dont mind. Hi'm above it. But is it right? thats what I want to know. Is it right?

MORELL. That's a question for the Church, not for the laity. Has it done you any harm? thats the question for you, eh? Of course it hasnt. Think no more of it. (*He dismisses the subject by going to his place at the table and setting to work at his correspondence.*)

BURGESS (*aside to* MARCHBANKS). What did I tell you? Mad as a atter. (*He goes to the table and asks, with the sickly civility of a hungry man.*) When's dinner, James?

MORELL. Not for a couple of hours yet.

BURGESS (*with plaintive resignation*). Gimme a nice book to read over the fire, will you, James: thur's a good chap.

MORELL. What sort of book? A good one?

BURGESS (*with almost a yell of remonstrance*). Nah-oo! Summat pleasant, just to pass the time. (*Morell takes an illustrated paper from the table and offers it. He accepts it humbly.*) Thank yer, James. (*He goes back to the big chair at the fire, and sits there at his ease, reading.*)

MORELL (*as he writes*). Candida will come to entertain you presently. She has got rid of her pupil. She is filling the lamps.

MARCHBANKS (*starting up in the wildest consternation*). But that will soil her hands. I cant bear that, Morell: it's a shame. I'll go and fill them. (*He makes for the door.*)

MORELL. Youd better not. (MARCHBANKS *stops irresolutely.*) She'd only set you to clean my boots, to save me the trouble of doing it myself in the morning.

BURGESS (*with grave disapproval*). Dont you keep a servant now, James?

MORELL. Yes: but she isnt a slave; and the house looks as if I kept three. That means that everyone has to lend a hand. It's not a bad plan: Prossy and I can talk business after breakfast while we're washing up. Washing up's no trouble when there are two people to do it.

MARCHBANKS (*tormentedly*). Do you think every woman is as coarse-grained as Miss Garnett?

BURGESS (*emphatically*). Thats quite right, Mr. Morchbanks: thats quite right. She is coarse-grained.

MORELL (*quietly and significantly*). Marchbanks!

MARCHBANKS. Yes?

MORELL. How many servants does your father keep?

MARCHBANKS (*pettishly*). Oh, I dont know. (*He moves to the sofa, as if to get as far as possible from Morell's questioning, and sits down in great agony of spirit, thinking of the paraffin.*)

MORELL (*very gravely*). So many that you dont know! (*More aggressively.*) When theres anything coarse-grained to be done, you just ring the bell and throw it on to somebody else, eh?

MARCHBANKS. Oh, dont torture me. You dont even ring the bell. But your wife's beautiful fingers are dabbling in paraffin oil while you sit here comfortably preaching about it: everlasting preaching! preaching! words! words! words!

BURGESS (*intensely appreciating this retort*). Har, har! Devil a better! (*Radiantly.*) Ad you there, James, straight.

(CANDIDA *comes in, well aproned, with a reading lamp trimmed, filled, and ready for lighting. She places it on the table near* MORELL, *ready for use.*)

CANDIDA (*brushing her finger tips together with a slight twitch of her nose*). If you stay with us, Eugene, I think I will hand over the lamps to you.

MARCHBANKS. I will stay on condition that you hand over all the rough work to me.

CANDIDA. That's very gallant; but I think I should like to see how you do it first. (*Turning to* MORELL.) James: youve not been looking after the house properly.

MORELL. What have I done—or not done—my love?

CANDIDA (*with serious vexation*). My own particular pet scrubbing brush has been used for blackleading. (*A heart-breaking wail bursts from* MARCHBANKS. BURGESS *looks round, amazed.* CANDIDA *hurries to the sofa.*) Whats the matter? Are you ill, Eugene?

MARCHBANKS. No: not ill. Only horror! horror! horror! (*He bows his head on his hands.*)

BURGESS (*shocked*). What! Got the orrors, Mr. Morchbanks! Oh, thats bad, at your age. You must leave it off grajally.

CANDIDA (*reassured*). Nonsense, papa! Its only poetic horror, isn't it, Eugene (*petting him*)?

BURGESS (*abashed*). Oh, poetic orror, is it? I beg your pardon, I'm shore. (*He turns to the fire again, deprecating his hasty conclusion.*)

CANDIDA. What is it, Eugene? the scrubbing brush? (*He shudders.*) Well, there! never mind. (*She sits down beside him.*) Wouldnt you like to present me with a nice new one, with an ivory back inlaid with mother-of-pearl?

MARCHBANKS (*softly and musically, but sadly and longingly*). No, not a scrubbing brush, but a boat: a tiny shallop to sail away in, far from the world, where the marble floors are washed by the rain and dried by the sun; where the south wind dusts the beautiful green and purple carpets. Or a chariot! to carry us up into the sky, where the lamps are stars, and dont need to be filled with paraffin oil every day.

MORELL (*harshly*). And where there is nothing to do but to be idle, selfish, and useless.

CANDIDA (*jarred*). Oh James! how could you spoil it all?

MARCHBANKS (*firing up*). Yes, to be idle, selfish, and useless: that is, to be beautiful and free and happy: hasnt every man desired that with all his soul for the woman he loves? Thats my deal: whats yours, and that of all the dreadful people who live in these hideous rows of houses? Sermons and scrubbing brushes! With you to preach the sermon and your wife to scrub.

CANDIDA (*quaintly*). He cleans the boots, Eugene. You will have to clean them to-morrow for saying that about him.

MARCHBANKS. Oh, dont talk about boots! Your feet should be beautiful on the mountains.

CANDIDA. My feet would not be beautiful on the Hackney Road without boots.

BURGESS (*scandalized*). Come, Candy! dont be vulgar. Mr Morchbanks aint accustomed to it. Youre givin him the orrors again. I mean the poetic ones.

(MORELL *is silent. Apparently he is busy with his letters: really he is puzzling with misgiving over his new and alarming experience that the surer he is of his moral thrusts, the more swiftly and effectively Eugene parries them. To find himself beginning to fear a man whom he does not respect afflicts him bitterly.*)

(MISS GARNETT *comes in with a telegram.*)

PROSERPINE (*handing the telegram to* MORELL). Reply paid. The boy's waiting. (*To* CANDIDA, *coming back to her machine and sitting down*). Maria is ready for you now in the kitchen, Mrs Morell. (CANDIDA *rises.*) The onions have come.

MARCHBANKS (*convulsively*). Onions!

CANDIDA. Yes, onions. Not even Spanish ones: nasty little red onions. You shall help me to slice them. Come along.

(*She catches him by the wrist and runs out, pulling him after her,* BURGESS *rises in consternation, and stands aghast on the hearth-rug, staring after them.*)

BURGESS. Candy didn't oughter andle a hearl's nevvy like that. It's goin too fur with it. Lookee ere, James: do e often git taken queer like that?

MORELL (*shortly, writing a telegram*). I dont know.

BURGESS (*sentimentally*). He talks very pretty. I awlus had a turn for a bit of poetry. Candy takes arter me that-a-way. Huseter make me tell er fairy stories when she was only a little kiddy not that igh (*indicating a stature of two feet or thereabouts*).

MORELL (*preoccupied*). Ah, indeed. (*He blots the telegram and goes out.*)

PROSERPINE. Used you to make the fairy stories up out of your own head?

(BURGESS, *not deigning to reply, strikes an attitude of the haughtiest disdain on the hearth-rug.*)

PROSERPINE (*calmly*). I should never have supposed you had it in you. By the way, I'd better warn you, since youve taken such a fancy to Mr Marchbanks. He's mad.

BURGESS. Mad! What! Im too!!

PROSERPINE. Mad as a March hare. He did frighten me, I can tell you, just before you came in that time. Havent you noticed the queer things he says?

BURGESS. So thats what the poetic orrors means. Blame me if it didnt come into my ed once or twyst that he was a bit horff is chump! (*He crosses the room to the door, lifting up his voice as he goes.*) Well, this is a pretty sort of asylum for a man to be in, with no one but you to take care of him!

PROSERPINE (*as he passes her*). Yes, what a dreadful thing it would be if anything happened to you!

BURGESS (*loftily*). Dont you haddress no remarks to me. Tell your hemployer that Ive gone into the gorden for a smoke.

PROSERPINE (*mocking*). Oh!

(*Before* BURGESS *can retort,* MORELL *comes back.*)

BURGESS (*sentimentally*). Going for a turn in the gording to smoke, James.

MORELL (*brusquely*). Oh, all right, all right. (BURGESS *goes out pathetically in the character of a weary old man.* MORELL *stands at the table, turning over his papers, and adding, across to* PROSERPINE, *half humorously, half absently.*) Well, Miss Prossy, why have you been call-ing my father-in-law names?

PROSERPINE (*blushing fiery red, and looking quickly up at him, half scared, half reproachful*). I— (*She bursts into tears.*)

MORELL (*with tender gaiety, leaning across the table towards her, and consoling her*). Oh, come! come! come! Never mind, Pross: he is a silly old fathead, isn't he?

(*With an explosive sob, she makes a dash at the door, and vanishes, banging it.* MORELL, *shaking his head resignedly, sighs and goes wearily to his chair, where he sits down and sets to work, looking old and careworn.*)

(CANDIDA *comes in. She has finished her household work and taken off the apron. She at once notices his dejected appearance, and posts herself quietly at the visitors' chair, looking down at him attentively. She says nothing.*)

MORELL (*looking up, but with his pen raised ready to resume his work*). Well? Where is Eugene?

CANDIDA.   Washing his hands in the scullery under the tap. He will make an excellent cook if he can only get over his dread of Maria.

MORELL (*shortly*).   Ha! No doubt. (*He begins writing again.*)

CANDIDA (*going nearer, and putting her hand down softly on his to stop him as she says*).   Come here, dear. Let me look at you. (*He drops his pen and yields himself to her disposal. She makes him rise, and brings him a little away from the table, looking at him critically all the time.*) Turn your face to the light. (*She places him facing the window.*) My boy is not looking well. Has he been overworking?

MORELL.   Nothing more than usual.

CANDIDA.   He looks very pale, and grey, and wrinkled, and old. (*His melancholy deepens: and she attacks it with wilful gaiety.*) Here: (*pulling him towards the easy chair*) youve done enough writing for today. Leave Prossy to finish it. Come and talk to me.

MORELL.   But—

CANDIDA (*insisting*).   Yes, I must be talked to. (*She makes him sit down, and seats herself on the carpet beside his knee.*) Now (*patting his hand*) youre beginning to look better already. Why must you go out every night lecturing and talking? I hardly have one evening a week with you. Of course what you say is all very true; but it does no good: they dont mind what you say to them one little bit. They think they agree with you; but whats the use of their agreeing with you if they go and do just the opposite of what you tell them the moment your back is turned? Look at our congregation at St. Dominic's! Why do they come to hear you talking about Christianity every Sunday? Why, just because theyve been so full of business and money-making for six days that they want to forget all about it and have a rest on the seventh; so that they can go back fresh and make money harder than ever! You positively help them at it instead of hindering them.

MORELL (*with energetic seriousness*).   You know very well, Candida, that I often blow them up soundly for that. And if there is nothing in their churchgoing but rest and diversion, why dont they try something more amusing? more self-indulgent? There must be some good in the fact that they prefer St Dominic's to worse places on Sundays.

CANDIDA.   Oh, the worse places arnt open; and even if they were, they darent be seen going to them. Besides, James dear, you preach so splendidly that it's as good as a play for them. Why do you think the women are so enthusiastic?

MORELL (*shocked*).   Candida!

CANDIDA.   Oh, *I* know. You silly boy: you think it's your Socialism and your religion; but if it were that, theyd do what you tell them instead of only coming to look at you. They all have Prossy's complaint.

MORELL.   Prossy's complaint! What do you mean, Candida?

CANDIDA.   Yes, Prossy, and all the other secretaries you ever had. Why does Prossy condescend to wash up the things, and to peel potatoes and abase herself in all manner of ways for six shillings a week less than

Candida

she used to get in a city office? She's in love with you, James: thats the reason. Theyre all in love with you. And you are in love with preaching because you do it so beautifully. And you think it's all enthusiasm for the kingdom of Heaven on earth; and so do they. You dear silly!

MORELL. Candida: what deadful! what soul-destroying cynicism! Are you jesting? Or—can it be?—are you jealous?

CANDIDA (*with curious thoughtfulness*). Yes, I feel a little jealous sometimes.

MORELL (*incredulously*). Of Prossy?

CANDIDA (*laughing*). No, no, no, no. Not jealous of anybody. Jealous for somebody else, who is not loved as he ought to be.

MORELL. Me?

CANDIDA. You! Why, youre spoiled with love and worship: you get far more than is good for you. No: I mean Eugene.

MORELL (*startled*). Eugene!

CANDIDA. It seems unfair that all the love should go to you, and none to him; although he needs it so much more than you do. (*A convulsive movement shakes him in spite of himself.*) Whats the matter? Am I worrying you?

MORELL (*hastily*). Not at all. (*Looking at her with troubled intensity.*) You know that I have perfect confidence in you, Candida.

CANDIDA. You vain thing! Are you so sure of your irresistible attractions?

MORELL. Candida: you are shocking me. I never thought of my attractions. I thought of your goodness, of your purity. That is what I confide in.

CANDIDA. What a nasty uncomfortable thing to say to me! Oh, you are a clergyman, James: a thorough clergyman!

MORELL (*turning away from her, heart-stricken*). So Eugene says.

CANDIDA (*with lively interest, leaning over to him with her arms on his knee*). Eugene's always right. He's a wonderful boy: I have grown fonder and fonder of him all the time I was away. Do you know, James, that though he has not the least suspicion of it himself, he is ready to fall madly in love with me?

MORELL (*grimly*). Oh, he has no suspicion of it himself, hasnt he?

CANDIDA. Not a bit. (*She takes her arms from his knee, and turns thoughtfully, sinking into a more restful attitude with her hands in her lap.*) Some day he will know: when he is grown up and experienced, like you. And he will know that I must have known. I wonder what he will think of me then.

MORELL. No evil, Candida. I hope and trust, no evil.

CANDIDA (*dubiously*). That will depend.

MORELL (*bewildered*). Depend!

CANDIDA (*looking at him*). Yes: it will depend on what happens to him. (*He looks vacantly at her*). Dont you see? It will depend on how he comes to learn what love really is. I mean on the sort of woman who will teach it to him.

MORELL (*quite at a loss*). Yes. No. I don't know what you mean.

CANDIDA (*explaining*). If he learns it from a good woman, then it will be all right: he will forgive me.

MORELL. Forgive?

CANDIDA. But suppose he learns it from a bad woman, as so many men do, especially poetic men, who imagine all women are angels! Suppose he only discovers the value of love when he has thrown it away and degraded himself in his ignorance! Will he forgive me then, do you think?

MORELL. Forgive you for what?

CANDIDA (*realizing how stupid he is, and a little disappointed, though quite tenderly so*). Dont you understand? (*He shakes his head. She turns to him again, so as to explain with the fondest intimacy.*) I mean, will he forgive me for not teaching him myself? For abandoning him to the bad women for the sake of my goodness, of my purity, as you call it? Ah, James, how little you understand me, to talk of your confidence in my goodness and purity! I would give them both to poor Eugene as willingly as I would give my shawl to a beggar dying of cold, if there were nothing else to restrain me. Put your trust in my love for you, James; for if that went, I should care very little for your sermons: mere phrases that you cheat yourself and others with every day. (*She is about to rise.*)

MORELL. His words!

CANDIDA (*checking herself quickly in the act of getting up*). Whose words?

MORELL. Eugene's.

CANDIDA (*delighted*). He is always right. He understands you; he understands me; he understands Prossy; and you, darling, you understand nothing. (*She laughs, and kisses him to console him. He recoils as if stabbed, and springs up.*)

MORELL. How can you bear to do that when— Oh, Candida (*with anguish in his voice*) I had rather you had plunged a grappling iron into my heart than given me that kiss.

CANDIDA (*amazed*). My dear: whats the matter?

MORELL (*frantically waving her off*). Dont touch me.

CANDIDA. James !!!

(*They are interrupted by the entrance of* MARCHBANKS *with* BURGESS, *who stop near the door, staring.*)

MARCHBANKS. Is anything the matter?

MORELL (*deadly white, putting an iron constraint on himself*). Nothing but this: that either you were right this morning, or Candida is mad.

BURGESS (*in modest protest*). What! Candy mad too! Oh, come! come! come! (*He crosses the room to the fireplace, protesting as he goes, and knocks the ashes out of his pipe on the bars.*)

(MORELL *sits down at his table desperately, leaning forward to hide his face, and interlacing his fingers rigidly to keep them steady.*)

CANDIDA (*to* MORELL, *relieved and laughing*). Oh, youre only shocked! Is that all? How conventional all you unconventional people are! (*She sits gaily on the arm of the chair.*)

BURGESS. Come: be'ave yourself, Candy. Whatll Mr Morchbanks think of you?

CANDIDA. This comes of James teaching me to think for myself, and never to hold back out of fear of what other people may think of me. It works beautifully as long as I think the same things as he does. But now! because I have just thought something different! look at him! Just look! (*She points to* MORELL, *greatly amused.*)

(EUGENE *looks, and instantly presses his hand on his heart, as if some pain had shot through it. He sits down on the sofa like a man witnessing a tragedy.*)

BURGESS (*on the hearthrug*). Well, James, you certnly haint as himpressive lookin as usu'l.

MORELL (*with a laugh which is half a sob*). I suppose not. I beg all your pardons: I was not conscious of making a fuss. (*Pulling himself together.*) Well, well, well, well, well! (*He sets to work at his papers again with resolute cheerfulness.*)

CANDIDA (*going to the sofa and sitting beside* MARCHBANKS, *still in a bantering humor*). Well, Eugene: why are you so sad? Did the onions make you cry?

MARCHBANKS (*aside to her*). It is your cruelty. I hate cruelty. It is a horrible thing to see one person make another suffer.

CANDIDA (*petting him ironically*). Poor boy! have I been cruel? Did I make it slice nasty little red onions?

MARCHBANKS (*earnestly*). Oh, stop, stop: I dont mean myself. You have made him suffer frightfully. I feel his pain in my own heart. I know that it is not your fault: it is something that must happen; but don't make light of it. I shudder when you torture him and laugh.

CANDIDA (*incredulously*). *I* torture James! Nonsense, Eugene: how you exaggerate! Silly! (*She rises and goes to the table, a little troubled.*) Dont work any more, dear. Come and talk to us.

MORELL (*affectionately but bitterly*). Ah no: *I* can't talk. I can only preach.

CANDIDA (*caressing his hand*). Well, come and preach.

BURGESS (*strongly remonstrating*). Aw no, Candy. Ang it all!

(LEXY MILL *comes in, anxious and important.*)

LEXY (*hastening to shake hands with Candida*). How do you do, Mrs Morell? So glad to see you back again.

CANDIDA. Thank you, Lexy. You know Eugene, dont you?

LEXY. Oh yes. How do you do, Marchbanks?

MARCHBANKS. Quite well, thanks.

LEXY (*to* MORELL). Ive just come from the Guild of St Matthew. They are in the greatest consternation about your telegram.

CANDIDA. What did you telegraph about, James?

LEXY (*to* CANDIDA). He was to have spoken for them to-night.

Theyve taken the large hall in Mare Street and spent a lot of money on posters. Morell's telegram was to say he couldnt come. It came on them like a thunderbolt.

CANDIDA (*surprised, and beginning to suspect something wrong*). Given up an engagement to speak!

BURGESS. Fust time in his life, I'll bet. Aint it, Candy?

LEXY (*to* MORELL). They decided to send an urgent telegram to you asking whether you could not change your mind. Have you received it?

MORELL (*with restrained impatience*). Yes, yes: I got it.

LEXY. It was reply paid.

MORELL. Yes, I know. I answered it. I cant go.

CANDIDA. But why, James?

MORELL (*almost fiercely*). Because I dont choose. These people forget that I am a man: they think I am a talking machine to be turned on for their pleasure every evening of my life. May I not have one night at home, with my wife, and my friends?

(*They are all amazed at this outburst, except* EUGENE. *His expression remains unchanged.*)

CANDIDA. Oh, James, you mustnt mind what I said about that. And if you dont go youll have an attack of bad conscience tomorrow.

LEXY (*intimidated, but urgent*). I know, of course, that they make the most unreasonable demands on you. But they have been telegraphing all over the place for another speaker; and they can get nobody but the President of the Agnostic League.

MORELL (*promptly*). Well, an excellent man. What better do they want?

LEXY. But he always insists so powerfully on the divorce of Socialism from Christianity. He will undo all the good we have been doing. Of course you know best; but—(*he shrugs his shoulders and wanders to the hearth beside* BURGESS).

CANDIDA (*coaxingly*). Oh, do go, James. We'll all go.

BURGESS (*grumblingly*). Look ere, Candy! I say! Lets stay at home by the fire, comfortable. He wont need to be more'n a couple-o-hour away.

CANDIDA. Youll be just as comfortable at the meeting. We'll all sit on the platform and be great people.

EUGENE (*terrified*). Oh please dont let us go on the platform. No: everyone will stare at us: I couldn't. I'll sit at the back of the room.

CANDIDA. Dont be afraid. Theyll be too busy looking at James to notice you.

MORELL. Prossy's complaint, Candida! Eh?

CANDIDA (*gaily*). Yes: Prossy's complaint.

BURGESS (*mystified*). Prossy's complaint! What are you talking about, James?

MORELL (*not heeding him, rises; goes to the door; and holds it open, calling in a commanding tone*). Miss Garnett.

PROSERPINE (*in the distance*). Yes, Mr Morell. Coming.

(*They all wait, except* BURGESS, *who turns stealthily to* LEXY.)

BURGESS. Listen ere, Mr Mill. Whats Prossy's complaint? Whats wrong with er?

LEXY (*confidentially*). Well, I dont exactly know; but she spoke very strangely to me this morning. I'm afraid she's a little out of her mind sometimes.

BURGESS (*overwhelmed*). Why, it must be catchin! Four in the same ouse!

PROSERPINE (*appearing on the threshold*). What is it, Mr Morell?

MORELL. Telegraph to the Guild of St. Matthew that I am coming.

PROSERPINE (*surprised*). Dont they expect you?

MORELL (*peremptorily*). Do as I tell you.

(PROSERPINE, *frightened, sits down at her typewriter, and obeys.* MORELL, *now unaccountably resolute and forceful, goes across to* BURGESS. CANDIDA *watches his movements with growing wonder and misgiving.*)

MORELL. Burgess: you dont want to come.

BURGESS. Oh, dont put it like that, James. It's ony that it aint Sunday, you know.

MORELL. I'm sorry. I thought you might like to be introduced to the chairman. He's on the Works Committee of the County Council, and has some influence in the matter of contracts. (BURGESS *wakes up at once.*) Youll come?

BURGESS (*with enthusiasm*). Cawrse I'll come, James. Aint it awlus a pleasure to ear you!

MORELL (*turning to Prossy*). I shall want you to take some notes at the meeting, Miss Garnett, if you have no other engagement. (*She nods, afraid to speak.*) You are coming, Lexy, I suppose?

LEXY. Certainly.

CANDIDA. We're all coming, James.

MORELL. No: you are not coming; and Eugene is not coming. You will stay here and entertain him—to celebrate your return home. (EUGENE *rises, breathless.*)

CANDIDA. But, James—

MORELL (*authoritatively*). I insist. You do not want to come; and he does not want to come. (CANDIDA *is about to protest.*) Oh, dont concern yourselves: I shall have plenty of people without you: your chairs will be wanted by unconverted people who have never heard me before.

CANDIDA (*troubled*). Eugene: wouldnt you like to come?

MORELL. I should be afraid to let myself go before Eugene: he is so critical of sermons. (*Looking at him.*) He knows I am afraid of him: he told me as much this morning. Well, I shall shew him how much afraid I am by leaving him here in your custody, Candida.

MARCHBANKS (*to himself, with vivid feeling*). Thats brave. Thats beautiful.

CANDIDA (*with anxious misgiving*).   But—but—Is anything the matter, James? (*Greatly troubled.*) I cant understand—

MORELL (*taking her tenderly in his arms and kissing her on the forehead*).   Ah, I thought it was *I* who couldnt understand, dear.

ACT III

Past ten in the evening. The curtains are drawn, and the lamps lighted. The typewriter is in its case: the large table has been cleared and tidied: everything indicates that the day's work is over.

CANDIDA *and* MARCHBANKS *are sitting by the fire. The reading lamp is on the mantelshelf above* MARCHBANKS, *who is in the small chair, reading aloud. A little pile of manuscripts and a couple of volumes of poetry are on the carpet beside him.* CANDIDA *is in the easy chair. The poker, a light brass one, is upright in her hand. Leaning back and looking intently at the point of it, with her feet stretched towards the blaze, she is in a waking dream, miles away from her surroundings and completely oblivious of* EUGENE.

MARCHBANKS (*breaking off in his recitation*).   Every poet that ever lived has put that thought into a sonnet. He must: he cant help it. (*He looks to her for assent, and notices her absorption in the poker.*) Havent you been listening? (*No response.*) Mrs Morell!

CANDIDA (*starting*).   Eh?

MARCHBANKS.   Havent you been listening?

CANDIDA (*with a guilty excess of politeness*).   Oh yes. It's very nice. Go on, Eugene. I'm longing to hear what happens to the angel.

MARCHBANKS (*letting the manuscript drop from his hand to the floor*). I beg your pardon for boring you.

CANDIDA.   But you are not boring me, I assure you. Please go on. Do, Eugene.

MARCHBANKS.   I finished the poem about the angel quarter of an hour ago. Ive read you several things since.

CANDIDA (*remorsefully*).   I'm so sorry, Eugene. I think the poker must have hypnotized me. (*She puts it down.*)

MARCHBANKS.   It made me horribly uneasy.

CANDIDA.   Why didnt you tell me? I'd have put it down at once.

MARCHBANKS.   I was afraid of making you uneasy too. It looked as if it were a weapon. If I were a hero of old I should have laid my drawn sword between us. If Morell had come in he would have thought you had taken up the poker because there was no sword between us.

CANDIDA (*wondering*).   What? (*With a puzzled glance at him.*) I cant quite follow that. Those sonnets of yours have perfectly addled me. Why should there be a sword between us?

MARCHBANKS (*evasively*).   Oh, never mind. (*He stoops to pick up the manuscript.*)

CANDIDA. Put that down again, Eugene. There are limits to my appetite for poetry: even your poetry. Youve been reading to me for more than two hours, ever since James went out. I want to talk.

MARCHBANKS (*rising, scared*). No: I mustnt talk. (*He looks round him in his lost way, and adds, suddenly.*) I think I'll go out and take a walk in the park. (*He makes for the door.*)

CANDIDA. Nonsense: it's closed long ago. Come and sit down on the hearth-rug, and talk moonshine as you usually do. I want to be amused. Dont you want to?

MARCHBANKS (*half in terror, half enraptured*). Yes.

CANDIDA. Then come along. (*She moves her chair back a little to make room.*)

(*He hesitates; then timidly stretches himself on the hearth-rug, face upwards, and throws back his head across her knees, looking up at her.*)

MARCHBANKS. Oh, Ive been so miserable all the evening, because I was doing right. Now I'm doing wrong; and I'm happy.

CANDIDA (*tenderly amused at him*). Yes: I'm sure you feel a great grown-up wicked deceiver. Quite proud of yourself, arnt you?

MARCHBANKS (*raising his hand quickly and turning a little to look round at her*). Take care. I'm ever so much older than you, if you only knew. (*He turns quite over on his knees, with his hands clasped and his arms on her lap, and speaks with growing impulse, his blood beginning to stir.*) May I say some wicked things to you?

CANDIDA (*without the least fear or coldness, and with perfect respect for his passion, but with a touch of her wisehearted maternal humor*). No. But you may say anything you really and truly feel. Anything at all, no matter what it is. I am not afraid, so long as it is your real self that speaks, and not a mere attitude: a gallant attitude, or a wicked attitude, or even a poetic attitude. I put you on your honor and truth. Now say whatever you want to.

MARCHBANKS (*the eager expression vanishing utterly from his lips and nostrils as his eyes light up with pathetic spirituality*). Oh, now I cant say anything: all the words I know belong to some attitude or other—all except one.

CANDIDA. What one is that?

MARCHBANKS (*softly, losing himself in the music of the name*). Candida, Candida, Candida, Candida, Candida. I must say that now, because you have put me on my honor and truth; and I never think or feel Mrs Morell: it is always Candida.

CANDIDA. Of course. And what have you to say to Candida?

MARCHBANKS. Nothing but to repeat your name a thousand times. Dont you feel that every time is a prayer to you?

CANDIDA. Doesnt it make you happy to be able to pray?

MARCHBANKS. Yes, very happy.

CANDIDA. Well, that happiness is the answer to your prayer. Do you want anything more?

MARCHBANKS. No: I have come into Heaven, where want is unknown. (MORELL *comes in. He halts on the threshold, and takes in the scene at a glance.*)

MORELL (*grave and self-contained*). I hope I dont disturb you.

(CANDIDA *starts up violently, but without the smallest embarrassment, laughing at herself.* EUGENE, *capsized by her sudden movement, recovers himself without rising, and sits on the rug hugging his ankles, also quite unembarrassed.*)

CANDIDA. Oh, James, how you startled me! I was so taken up with Eugene that I didn't hear your latchkey. How did the meeting go off? Did you speak well?

MORELL. I have never spoken better in my life.

CANDIDA. That was first rate! How much was the collection?

MORELL. I forgot to ask.

CANDIDA (*to* EUGENE). He must have spoken splendidly, or he would never have forgotten that. (*To* MORELL.) Where are all the others?

MORELL. They left long before I could get away: I thought I should never escape. I believe they are having supper somewhere.

CANDIDA (*in her domestic business tone*). Oh, in that case, Maria may go to bed. I'll tell her. (*She goes out to the kitchen.*)

MORELL (*looking sternly down at* MARCHBANKS). Well?

MARCHBANKS (*squatting grotesquely on the hearth-rug, and actually at ease with* MORELL: *even impishly humorous*). Well?

MORELL. Have you anything to tell me?

MARCHBANKS. Only that I have been making a fool of myself here in private whist you have been making a fool of yourself in public.

MORELL. Hardly in the same way, I think.

MARCHBANKS (*eagerly, scrambling up*). The very, very, very same way. I have been playing the Good Man. Just like you. When you began your heroics about leaving me here with Candida—

MORELL (*involuntarily*). Candida!

MARCHBANKS. Oh yes: Ive got that far. But dont be afraid. Heroics are infectious: I caught the disease from you. I swore not to say a word in your absence that I would not have said a month ago in your presence.

MORELL. Did you keep your oath?

MARCHBANKS (*suddenly perching himself on the back of the easy chair*). It kept itself somehow until about ten minutes ago. Up to that moment I went on desperately reading to her—reading my own poems—anybody's poems—to stave off a conversation. I was standing outside the gate of Heaven, and refusing to go in. Oh, you cant think how heroic it was, and how uncomfortable! Then—

MORELL (*steadily controlling his suspense*). Then?

MARCHBANKS (*prosaically slipping down into a quite ordinary attitude on the seat of the chair*). Then she couldnt bear being read to any longer.

MORELL. And you approached the gate of Heaven at last?

MARCHBANKS. Yes.

MORELL. Well. (*Fiercely.*) Speak, man: have you no feeling for me?

MARCHBANKS (*softly and musically*). Then she became an angel; and there was a flaming sword that turned every way, so that I couldnt go in; for I saw that that gate was really the gate of Hell.

MORELL (*triumphantly*). She repulsed you!

MARCHBANKS (*rising in wild scorn*). No, you fool: if she had done that I should never have seen that I was in Heaven already. Repulsed me! You think that would have saved us! virtuous indignation! Oh, you are not worthy to live in the same world with her. (*He turns away contemptuously to the other side of the room.*)

MORELL (*who has watched him quietly without changing his place*). Do you think you make yourself more worthy by reviling me, Eugene?

MARCHBANKS. Here endeth the thousand and first lesson. Morell: I dont think much of your preaching after all: I believe I could do it better myself. The man I want to meet is the man that Candida married.

MORELL. The man that—? Do you mean me?

MARCHBANKS. I dont mean the Reverend James Mavor Morell, moralist and windbag. I mean the real man that the Reverend James must have hidden somewhere inside his black coat: the man that Candida loved. You cant make a woman like Candida love you by merely buttoning your collar at the back instead of in front.

MORELL (*boldly and steadily*). When Candida promised to marry me, I was the same moralist and windbag you now see. I wore my black coat; and my collar was buttoned behind instead of in front. Do you think she would have loved me any the better for being insincere in my profession?

MARCHBANKS (*on the sofa, hugging his ankles*). Oh, she forgave you, just as she forgives me for being a coward, and a weakling, and what you call a snivelling little whelp and all the rest of it. (*Dreamily.*) A woman like that has divine insight: she loves our souls, and not our follies and vanities and illusions, nor our collars and coats, nor any other of the rags and tatters we are rolled up in. (*He reflects on this for an instant: then turns intently to question* MORELL.) What I want to know is how you got past the flaming sword that stopped me.

MORELL. Perhaps because I was not interrupted at the end of ten minutes.

MARCHBANKS (*taken aback*). What!

MORELL. Man can climb to the highest summits; but he cannot dwell there long.

MARCHBANKS (*springing up*). It's false: there can he dwell for ever, and there only. It's in the other moments that he can find no rest, no sense of the silent glory of life. Where would you have me spend my moments, if not on the summits?

MORELL. In the scullery, slicing onions and filling lamps.

MARCHBANKS. Or in the pulpit, scrubbing cheap earthenware souls?

MORELL. Yes, that too. It was there that I earned my golden moment, and the right, in that moment, to ask her to love me. *I* did not take the moment on credit; or did I use it to steal another man's happiness.

MARCHBANKS (*rather disgustedly, trotting back towards the fireplace*). I have no doubt you conducted the transaction as honestly as if you were buying a pound of cheese. (*He stops on the brink of the hearth-rug, and adds, thoughtfully, to himself, with his back turned to* MORELL.) *I* could only go to her as a beggar.

MORELL (*staring*). A beggar dying of cold! asking for her shawl!

MARCHBANKS (*turning, surprised*). Thank you for touching up my poetry. Yes, if you like: a beggar dying of cold, asking for her shawl.

MORELL (*excitedly*). And she refused. Shall I tell you why she refused? I can tell you, on her own authority. It was because of—

MARCHBANKS. She didnt refuse.

MORELL. Not!

MARCHBANKS. She offered me all I chose to ask for: her shawl, her wings, the wreath of stars on her head, the lilies in her hand, the crescent moon beneath her feet—

MORELL (*seizing him*). Out with the truth, man: my wife is my wife: I want no more of your poetic fripperies. I know well that if I have lost her love and you have gained it, no law will bind her.

MARCHBANKS (*quaintly, without fear or resistance*). Catch me by the shirt collar, Morell: she will arrange it for me afterwards as she did this morning. (*With quiet rapture.*) I shall feel her hands touch me.

MORELL. You young imp, do you know how dangerous it is to say that to me? Or (*with a sudden misgiving*) has something made you brave?

MARCHBANKS. I'm not afraid now. I disliked you before: that was why I shrank from your touch. But I saw today—when she tortured you—that you love her. Since then I have been your friend: you may strangle me if you like.

MORELL (*releasing him*). Eugene: if that is not a heartless lie—if you have a spark of human feeling left in you—will you tell me what has happened during my absence?

MARCHBANKS. What happened! Why, the flaming sword (MORELL *stamps with impatience*)—Well, in plain prose, I loved her so exquisitely that I wanted nothing more than the happiness of being in such love. And before I had time to come down from the highest summits, you came in.

MORELL (*suffering deeply*). So it is still unsettled. Still the misery of doubt.

MARCHBANKS. Misery! I am the happiest of men. I desire nothing now but her happiness. (*In a passion of sentiment.*) Oh, Morell, let us both give her up. Why should she have to choose between a wretched little nervous disease like me, and a pig-headed parson like you? Let us go on a pilgrimage, you to the east and I to the west, in search of a worthy lover for her: some beautiful archangel with purple wings—

MORELL. Some fiddlestick! Oh, if she is mad enough to leave me for you, who will protect her? who will help her? who will work for her? who will be a father to her children? (*He sits down distractedly on the sofa, with his elbows on his knees and his head propped on his clenched fists.*)

MARCHBANKS (*snapping his fingers wildly*). She does not ask those silly questions. It is she who wants somebody to protect, to help, to work for: somebody to give her children to protect, to help and to work for. Some grown up man who has become as a little child again. Oh, you fool, you fool, you triple fool! I am the man, Morell: I am the man. (*He dances about excitedly, crying.*) You dont understand what a woman is. Send for her, Morell: send for her and let her choose between— (*The door opens and* CANDIDA *enters. He stops as if petrified.*)

CANDIDA (*amazed, on the threshold*). What on earth are you at, Eugene?

MARCHBANKS (*oddly*). James and I are having a preaching match; and he is getting the worst of it.

(CANDIDA *looks quickly round at* MORELL. *Seeing that he is distressed, she hurries down to him, greatly vexed.*)

CANDIDA. You have been annoying him. Now I wont have it, Eugene: do you hear? (*She puts her hand on* MORELL'S *shoulder, and quite forgets her wifely tact in her anger.*) My boy shall not be worried: I will protect him.

MORELL (*rising proudly*). Protect!

CANDIDA (*not heeding him: to* EUGENE). What have you been saying?

MARCHBANKS (*appalled*). Nothing. I—

CANDIDA. Eugene! Nothing?

MARCHBANKS (*piteously*). I mean—I—I'm very sorry. I wont do it again: indeed I wont. I'll let him alone.

MORELL (*indignantly, with an aggressive movement towards* EUGENE). Let me alone! You young—

CANDIDA (*stopping him*). Sh!—no: let me deal with him, James.

MARCHBANKS. Oh, youre not angry with me, are you?

CANDIDA (*severely*). Yes I am: very angry. I have a good mind to pack you out of the house.

MORELL (*taken aback by* CANDIDA'S *vigor, and by no means relishing the position of being rescued by her from another man*). Gently, Candida, gently. I am able to take care of myself.

CANDIDA (*petting him*). Yes, dear: of course you are. But you musnt be annoyed and made miserable.

MARCHBANKS (*almost in tears, turning to the door*). I'll go.

CANDIDA. Oh, you neednt go: I cant turn you out at this time of night. (*Vehemently.*) Shame on you! For shame!

MARCHBANKS (*desperately*). But what have I done?

CANDIDA. I know what you have done: as well as if I had been here all the time. Oh, it was unworthy! You are like a child: you cannot hold your tongue.

MARCHBANKS. I would die ten times over sooner than give you a moment's pain.

CANDIDA (*with infinite contempt for this puerility*). Much good your dying would do me!

MORELL. Candida, my dear: this altercation is hardly quite seemly. It is a matter between two men; and I am the right person to settle it.

CANDIDA. Two men! Do you call that a man! (*To* EUGENE.) You bad boy!

MARCHBANKS (*gathering a whimsically affectionate courage from the scolding*). If I am to be scolded like a boy, I must make a boy's excuse. He began it. And he's bigger than I am.

CANDIDA (*losing confidence a little as her concern for* MORELL'S *dignity takes the alarm*). That cant be true. (*To* MORELL.) You didn't begin it, James, did you?

MORELL (*contemptuously*). No.

MARCHBANKS (*indignant*). Oh!

MORELL (*to* EUGENE). You began it: this morning. (CANDIDA, *intantly connecting this with his mysterious allusion in the afternoon to* something told him by EUGENE *in the morning, looks at him with quick suspicion.* MORELL *proceeds, with the emphasis of offended superiority.*) But your other point is true. I am certainly the bigger of the two, and, I hope, the stronger, Candida. So you had better leave the matter in my hands.

CANDIDA (*again soothing him*). Yes, dear; but—(*troubled*) I dont understand about this morning.

MORELL (*gently snubbing her*). You need not understand, my dear.

CANDIDA. But James, I (*the street bell rings*)—Oh bother! Here they all come. (*She goes out to let them in.*)

MARCHBANKS (*running to* MORELL). Oh, Morell, isnt it dreadful? She's angry with us: she hates me. What shall I do?

MORELL (*with quaint desperation, walking up and down the middle of the room*). Eugene: my head is spinning round. I shall begin to laugh presently.

MARCHBANKS (*following him anxiously*). No, no: she'll think Ive thrown you into hysterics. Dont laugh.

(*Boisterous voices and laughter are heard approaching.* LEXY MILL, *his eyes sparkling, and his bearing denoting unwonted elevation of spirit, enters with* BURGESS, *who is greasy and self-complacent, but has all his wits about him.* MISS GARNETT, *with her smartest hat and jacket on, follows them; but though her eyes are brighter than before, she is evidently a prey to misgiving. She places herself with her back to her typewriting table, with one hand on it to steady herself, passing the other across her forehead as if she were a little tired and giddy.* MARCHBANKS *relapses into shyness and edges away into the corner near the window, where* MORELL'S *books are.*)

LEXY (*exhilarated*). Morell: I must congratulate you. (*Grasping his hand.*) What a noble, splendid, inspired address you gave us! You surpassed yourself.

BURGESS. So you did, James. It fair kep me awake to the lars' word. Didnt it, Miss Gornett?

PROSERPINE (*worriedly*). Oh, I wasnt minding you: I was trying to make notes. (*She takes out her notebook, and looks at her stenography, which nearly makes her cry.*)

MORELL. Did I go too fast, Pross?

PROSERPINE. Much too fast. You know I cant do more than ninety words a minute. (*She relieves her feelings by throwing her notebook angrily beside her machine, ready for use next morning.*)

MORELL (*soothingly*). Oh well, well, never mind, never mind, never mind. Have you all had supper?

LEXY. Mr. Burgess has been kind enough to give us a really splendid supper at the Belgrave.

BURGESS (*with effusive magnanimity*). Dont mention it, Mr Mill. (*Modestly.*) Youre arty welcome to my little treat.

PROSERPINE. We had champagne. I never tasted it before. I feel quite giddy.

MORELL (*surprised*). A champagne supper! That was very handsome. Was it my eloquence that produced all this extravagance?

LEXY (*rhetorically*). Your eloquence, and Mr Burgess's goodness of heart. (*With a fresh burst of exhilaration.*) And what a very fine fellow the chairman is, Morell! He came to supper with us.

MORELL (*with long drawn significance, looking at* BURGESS). O-o-o-h! the chairman. Now I understand.

(BURGESS *covers with a deprecatory cough a lively satisfaction with his own diplomatic cunning.* LEXY *folds his arms and leans against the head of the sofa in a high-spirited attitude after nearly losing his balance. Candida comes in with glasses, lemons, and a jug of hot water on a tray.*)

CANDIDA. Who will have some lemonade? You know our rules: total abstinence. (*She puts the tray on the table, and takes up the lemon squeezer, looking enquiringly round at them.*)

MORELL. No use, dear. Theyve all had champagne. Pross has broken her pledge.

CANDIDA (*to* PROSERPINE). You dont mean to say youve been drinking champagne!

PROSERPINE (*stubbornly*). Yes I do. I'm only a beer teetotaller, not a champagne teetotaller. I dont like beer. Are there any letters for me to answer, Mr Morell?

MORELL. No more tonight.

PROSERPINE. Very well. Goodnight, everybody.

LEXY (*gallantly*). Had I not better see you home, Miss Garnett?

PROSERPINE. No thank you. I shant trust myself with anybody tonight. I wish I hadnt taken any of that stuff. (*She takes uncertain aim at the door; dashes at it; and barely escapes without disaster.*)

BURGESS (*indignantly*). Stuff indeed! That gurl dunno what champagne is! Pommery and Greeno at twelve and six a bottle. She took two glasses amost straight horff.

MORELL (*anxious about her*). Go and look after her, Lexy.

LEXY (*alarmed*). But if she should really be— Suppose she began to sing in the street, or anything of that sort.

MORELL. Just so: she may. Thats why youd better see her safely home.

CANDIDA. Do, Lexy: theres a good fellow. (*She shakes his hand and pushes him gently to the door.*)

LEXY. It's evidently my duty to go. I hope it may not be necessary. Goodnight, Mrs. Morell. (*To the rest.*) Goodnight. (*He goes.* CANDIDA *shuts the door.*)

BURGESS. He was gushin with hextra piety hisself arter two sips. People carnt drink like they useter. (*Bustling across to the hearth.*) Well, James: it's time to lock up. Mr. Morchbanks: shall I ave the pleasure of your company for a bit o the way ome?

MARCHBANKS (*affrightedly*). Yes: I'd better go. (*He hurries towards the door; but* CANDIDA *places herself before it, barring his way.*)

CANDIDA (*with quiet authority*). You sit down. Youre not going yet.

MARCHBANKS (*quailing*). No: I—I didn't mean to. (*He sits down abjectly on the sofa.*)

CANDIDA. Mr Marchbanks will stay the night with us, papa.

BURGESS. Oh well, I'll say goodnight. So long, James. (*He shakes hands with* MORELL, *and goes over to* EUGENE.) Make em give you a nightlight by your bed, Mr. Morchbanks: itll comfort you if you wake up in the night with a touch of that complaint of yores. Goodnight.

MARCHBANKS. Thank you: I will. Goodnight, Mr. Burgess. (*They shake hands.* BURGESS *goes to the door.*)

CANDIDA (*intercepting* MORELL, *who is following* BURGESS). Stay here, dear: I'll put on papa's coat for him. (*She goes out with* BURGESS.)

MARCHBANKS (*rising and stealing over to* MORELL). Morell: theres going to be a terrible scene. Arnt you afraid?

MORELL. Not in the least.

MARCHBANKS. I never envied you your courage before. (*He puts his hand appealingly on* MORELL's *forearm.*) Stand by me, wont you?

MORELL (*casting him off resolutely*). Each for himself, Eugene. She must choose between us now.

(CANDIDA *returns.* EUGENE *creeps back to the sofa like a guilty school-boy.*)

CANDIDA (*between them, addressing* EUGENE). Are you sorry?

MARCHBANKS (*earnestly*). Yes. Heartbroken.

CANDIDA. Well then, you are forgiven. Now go off to bed like a good little boy: I want to talk to James about you.

MARCHBANKS (*rising in great consternation*). Oh, I cant do that, Morell. I must be here. I'll not go away. Tell her.

CANDIDA (*her suspicions confirmed*). Tell me what? (*His eyes avoid hers furtively. She turns and mutely transfers the question to* MORELL.)

MORELL (*bracing himself for the catastrophe*). I have nothing to tell her, except (*here his voice deepens to a measured and mournful tenderness*) that she is my greatest treasure on earth—if she is really mine.

CANDIDA (*coldly, offended by his yielding to his orator's instinct and treating her as if she were the audience at the Guild of St Matthew*). I am sure Eugene can say no less, if that is all.

MARCHBANKS (*discouraged*). Morell: she's laughing at us.

MORELL (*with a quick touch of temper*). There is nothing to laugh at. Are you laughing at us, Candida?

CANDIDA (*with quiet anger*). Eugene is very quick-witted, James. I hope I am going to laugh; but I am not sure that I am not going to be very angry. (*She goes to the fireplace, and stands there leaning with her arm on the mantelpiece, and her foot on the fender, whilst* EUGENE *steals to* MORELL *and plucks him by the sleeve.*)

MARCHBANKS (*whispering*). Stop, Morell. Dont let us say anything.

MORELL (*pushing* EUGENE *away without deigning to look at him*). I hope you dont mean that as a threat, Candida.

CANDIDA (*with emphatic warning*). Take care, James. Eugene: I asked you to go. Are you going?

MORELL (*putting his foot down*). He shall not go. I wish him to remain.

MARCHBANKS. I'll go. I'll do whatever you want. (*He turns to the door.*)

CANDIDA. Stop! (*He obeys.*) Didnt you hear James say he wished you to stay? James is master here. Dont you know that?

MARCHBANKS (*flushing with a young poet's rage against tyranny*). By what right is he master?

CANDIDA (*quietly*). Tell him, James.

MORELL (*taken aback*). My dear: I dont know of any right that makes me master. I assert no such right.

CANDIDA (*with infinite reproach*). You dont know! Oh, James! James! (*To* EUGENE, *musingly*.) I wonder do you understand, Eugene! (*He shakes his head helplessly, not daring to look at her.*) No: youre too young. Well, I give you leave to stay: to stay and learn. (*She comes away from the hearth and places herself between them.*) Now, James! whats the matter? Come: tell me.

MARCHBANKS (*whispering tremulously across to him*). Dont.

CANDIDA. Come. Out with it!

MORELL (*slowly*). I meant to prepare your mind carefully, Candida, so as to prevent misunderstanding.

CANDIDA. Yes, dear: I am sure you did. But never mind: I shant misunderstand.

MORELL. Well—er—(*he hesitates, unable to find the long explanation which he supposed to be available*).

CANDIDA. Well?

MORELL (*blurting it out badly*). Eugene declares that you are in love with him.

MARCHBANKS (*frantically*). No, no, no, no, never. I did not, Mrs Morell: it's not true. I said I loved you. I said I understood you, and that he couldn't. And it was not after what passed there before the fire that I spoke: it was not, on my word. It was this morning.

CANDIDA (*enlightened*). This morning!

MARCHBANKS. Yes. (*He looks at her, pleading for credence, and then adds simply.*) That was what was the matter with my collar.

CANDIDA. Your collar? (*Suddenly taking in his meaning she turns to* MORELL, *shocked.*) Oh, James: did you—(*she stops*)?

MORELL (*ashamed*). You know, Candida, that I have a temper to struggle with. And he said (*shuddering*) that you despised me in your heart.

CANDIDA (*turning quickly on* EUGENE). Did you say that?

MARCHBANKS (*terrified*). No.

CANDIDA (*almost fiercely*). Then James has just told me a falsehood. Is that what you mean?

MARCHBANKS. No, no: I—I—(*desperately*) it was David's wife. And it wasn't at home: it was when she saw him dancing before all the people.

MORELL (*taking the cue with a debater's adroitness*). Dancing before all the people, Candida; and thinking he was moving their hearts by his mission when they were only suffering from—Prossy's complaint. (*She is about to protest: he raises his hand to silence her.*) Don't try to look indignant, Candida—

CANDIDA. Try!

MORELL (*continuing*). Eugene was right. As you told me a few hours after, he is always right. He said nothing that you did not say far better yourself. He is the poet, who sees everything; and I am the poor parson, who understands nothing.

CANDIDA (*remorsefully*). Do you mind what is said by a foolish boy, because I said something like it in jest?

MORELL. That foolish boy can speak with the inspiration of a child and the cunning of a serpent. He has claimed that you belong to him and not to me; and, rightly or wrongly, I have come to fear that it may be true. I will not go about tortured with doubts and suspicions. I will not live with you and keep a secret from you. I will not suffer the intolerable degradation of jealousy. We have agreed—he and I—that you shall choose between us now. I await your decision.

CANDIDA (*slowly recoiling a step, her heart hardened by his rhetoric in spite of the sincere feeling behind it*). Oh! I am to choose am I? I suppose it is quite settled that I must belong to one or the other.

MORELL (*firmly*). Quite. You must choose definitely.

MARCHBANKS (*anxiously*). Morell: you dont understand. She means that she belongs to herself.

CANDIDA (*turning to him*). I mean that, and a good deal more, Master Eugene, as you will both find out presently. And pray, my lords and masters, what have you to offer for my choice? I am up for auction, it seems. What do you bid, James?

MORELL (*reproachfully*). Cand—(*He breaks down: his eyes and throat fill with tears: the orator becomes a wounded animal.*) I cant speak—

CANDIDA (*impulsively going to him*). Ah, dearest—

MARCHBANKS (*in wild alarm*). Stop: it's not fair. You mustnt shew her that you suffer, Morell. I am on the rack too; but I am not crying.

MORELL (*rallying all his forces*). Yes: you are right. It is not for pity that I am bidding. (*He disengages himself from* CANDIDA.)

CANDIDA (*retreating, chilled*). I beg your pardon, James: I did not mean to touch you. I am waiting to hear your bid.

MORELL (*with proud humility*). I have nothing to offer you but my strength for your defence, my honesty for your surety, my ability and industry for your livelihood, and my authority and position for your dignity. That is all it becomes a man to offer to a woman.

CANDIDA (*quite quietly*). And you, Eugene? What do you offer?

MARCHBANKS. My weakness. My desolation. My heart's need.

CANDIDA (*impressed*). Thats a good bid, Eugene. Now I know how to make my choice.

(*She pauses and looks curiously from one to the other, as if weighing them.* MORELL, *whose lofty confidence has changed into heartbreaking dread at* EUGENE's *bid, loses all power of concealing his anxiety.* EUGENE, *strung to the highest tension, does not move a muscle.*)

MORELL (*in a suffocated voice: the appeal bursting from the depths of his anguish*). Candida!

MARCHBANKS (*aside, in a flash of contempt*). Coward!

CANDIDA (*significantly*). I give myself to the weaker of the two.

(EUGENE *divines her meaning at once: his face whitens like steel in a furnace.*)

MORELL (*bowing his head with the calm of collapse*). I accept your sentence, Candida.

CANDIDA. Do you understand, Eugene?

MARCHBANKS. Oh, I feel I'm lost. He cannot bear the burden.

MORELL (*incredulously, raising his head and voice with comic abruptness*). Do you mean me, Candida?

CANDIDA (*smiling a little*). Let us sit and talk comfortably over it like three friends. (*To* MORELL.) Sit down, dear. (MORELL, *quite lost, takes the chair from the fireside: the children's chair.*) Bring me that chair, Eugene. (*She indicates the easy chair. He fetches it silently, even with something like cold strength, and places it next* MORELL, *a little behind him. She sits down. He takes the visitor's chair himself, and sits, inscrutable. When they are all settled she begins, throwing a spell of quietness on them by her calm, sane, tender tone.*) You remember what you told me about yourself, Eugene: how nobody has cared for you since your old nurse died: how those clever fashionable sisters and successful brothers of yours were your mother's and father's pets: how miserable you were at Eton: how your father is trying to starve you into returning to Oxford: how you have had to live without comfort or welcome or refuge: always lonely, and nearly always disliked and misunderstood, poor boy!

MARCHBANKS (*faithful to the nobility of his lot*). I had my books. I had Nature. And at last I met you.

CANDIDA. Never mind that just at present. Now I want you to look at this other boy here! my boy! spoiled from his cradle. We go once a fortnight to see his parents. You should come with us, Eugene, to see the pictures of the hero of that household. James as a baby! the most wonderful of all babies. James holding his first school prize, won at the ripe age of eight! James as the captain of his eleven! James in his first frock coat! James under all sorts of glorious circumstances! You know how strong he is (I hope he didnt hurt you): how clever he is: how happy. (*With deepening gravity.*) Ask James's mother and his three sisters what it cost to save James the trouble of doing anything but be strong and clever and happy. Ask me what it costs to be James's mother and three sisters and wife and mother to his children all in one. Ask Prossy and Maria how troublesome the house is even when we have no visitors to help us to slice the onions. Ask the tradesmen who want to worry James and spoil his beautiful sermons who it is that puts them off. When there is money to give, he gives it: when there is money to refuse, I refuse it. I build a castle of comfort and indulgence and love for him, and stand sentinel always to keep little vulgar cares out. I make him master here, though he does not know it, and could not tell you a moment ago how it came to be so. (*With sweet irony.*) And when he thought I might go away with you, his only anxiety was—what should become of me! And to tempt me to stay he offered me (*leaning forward to stroke his hair caressingly at each phrase*) his strength for my defence! his industry for my livelihood! his dignity for my position! his—(*relenting*) ah, I am mixing up your beautiful cadences and spoiling them, am I not, darling? (*She lays her cheek fondly against his.*)

MORELL (*quite overcome, kneeling beside her chair and embracing her with boyish ingenuousness*). It's all true, every word. What I am you have made me with the labor of your hands and the love of your heart. You are my wife, my mother, my sisters: you are the sum of all loving care to me.

CANDIDA (*in his arms, smiling, to* EUGENE). Am I your mother and sisters to you, Eugene?

MARCHBANKS (*rising with a fierce gesture of disgust*). Ah, never. Out, then, into the night with me!

CANDIDA (*rising quickly*). You are not going like that, Eugene?

MARCHBANKS (*with the ring of a man's voice—no longer a boy's—in the words*). I know the hour when it strikes. I am impatient to do what must be done.

MORELL (*who has also risen*). Candida: dont let him do anything rash.

CANDIDA (*confident, smiling at* EUGENE). Oh, there is no fear. He has learnt to live without happiness.

MARCHBANKS. I no longer desire happiness: life is nobler than that. Parson James: I give you my happiness with both hands: I love you because you have filled the heart of the woman I loved. Goodbye. (*He goes towards the door.*)

CANDIDA. One last word. (*He stops, but without turning to her. She goes to him.*) How old are you, Eugene?

MARCHBANKS. As old as the world now. This morning I was eighteen.

CANDIDA. Eighteen! Will you, for my sake, make a little poem out of the two sentences I am going to say to you? And will you promise to repeat it to yourself whenever you think of me?

MARCHBANKS (*without moving*). Say the sentences.

CANDIDA. When I am thirty, she will be forty-five. When I am sixty, she will be seventy-five.

MARCHBANKS (*turning to her*). In a hundred years, we shall be the same age. But I have a better secret than that in my heart. Let me go now. The night outside grows impatient.

CANDIDA. Goodbye. (*She takes his face in her hands; and as he divines her intention and falls on his knees, she kisses his forehead. Then he flies out into the night. She turns to* MORELL, *holding out her arms to him.*) Ah, James!

(*They embrace. But they do not know the secret in the poet's heart.*)

QUESTIONS

1. Ordinarily the break up of a happy marriage and a normal family would not be considered materials for comedy. By what means and devices does Shaw make the threatened break in Candida's and Morell's marriage comic?

2. In what ways is the characterization of Prossy and Prossy's situation related to the ideas about marriage?

3. Eugene, though in a number of ways a comic figure, is nevertheless to a degree a sympathetic character. How does Shaw make him sympathetic? What aspects of his character are comic?

4. Does Burgess have any function in the plot of the play? Why is he included among the characters? Can you state any reasons why in terms of the ideas of the play Shaw should give Candida such a ludicrous father?

5. Does Lexy have any function in the plot? Why is he included among the characters?

6. Among the comic devices which Shaw employs in the play is that of comic surprise. List the chief examples.

7. Self discovery is often an important part of a serious action. Shaw employs it in *Candida* for comic effects with several of his characters and notably with Morell. By what means does Shaw maintain the comic effect in Morell's self discovery?

8. Eugene's self discovery is likewise comic but with a difference. State the difference.

9. Is there any element of self discovery for Candida? Can you state it?

10. Candida is often interpreted as an entirely normative, even an ideal character. Is there any element of the comic in her characterization?

11. Shaw is to some extent ridiculing the crusading socialist in this play. How does he accomplish this? Does he satirize socialism as an idea?

12. At the end of the first and the second acts, Shaw builds two highly effective curtain climaxes. Trace the development of each. How does each forward audience interest?

THE CHERRY ORCHARD

Anton Chekhov

Anton Pavlovich Chekhov (1860–1904), whose grandfather had been a serf, was born in Taganrog in 1860 and received the M.D. degree from the University of Moscow in 1884. As a student he won considerable prominence for his short stories and thereby was able to meet Tolstoy, Gorky, and other literary figures of the day. Despite his continued and considerable work as a journalist and short-story writer, he considered himself a doctor and devoted himself to his medical practice until tuberculosis forced him to give up. As a young man, he was attracted to the writing of plays, but was doomed to bitter disappointment in the production of *Ivanov*, written for the Korsh Theatre in 1887; of *The Wood Demon*, presented by a private theatre in 1889; and finally by the complete failure of *The Sea-Gull* as produced in 1896 by the old-fashioned Alexandrinsky Imperial Theatre. Upon the latter occasion, he fled from the theatre before the final curtain, vowing never to write plays again. With considerable scepticism he finally in 1898 gave Constantine Stanislavsky *The Sea-Gull* to produce at his newly organized Moscow Art Theatre. The great success of this production in 1899 caused him to release *Uncle Vanya* and to write *The Three Sisters* and *The Cherry Orchard* for the Art Theatre. Chekhov died in the Crimea, where he had gone for his health, before the first production of *The Cherry Orchard* on 17 January 1904. The play proved an immense success.

A number of Chekhov's plays are one acts, some of them based on incidents or characters drawn from his short stories. His one-act plays include *On The High Road* (1884), *The Tragedian in Spite of Himself* (1888), *The Bear* (1888), *Tatyana Riepin* (1889), *The Swan Song* (1889), *The Proposal* (1889), *The Jubilee* (1903), and *The Wedding* (1903). *That Worthless Fellow Platonov* (1889) was left unfinished. His first long play was *Ivanov* (1887). Then followed *The Wood Demon* (1889), *The Sea-Gull* (1896), *Uncle Vanya* (1897, a revision of *The Wood Demon*), *The Three Sisters* (1900), and *The Cherry Orchard* (1904). Some of these are translated under slightly different English titles.

Chekhov called *The Cherry Orchard* a comedy. To a friend he wrote: "The play has turned out not a drama, but a comedy, in parts even farce. . . ." Yet in its first production, as David Margarshark in his biography of Chekhov has shown, Stanislavsky began that emphasis upon the play as a serious representation which has dominated stage interpretations to the present day. The misconception arises out of the nature of the play. Chekhov saw his central characters, and especially Madame Ranévsky, as a product, and as a kind of epitome, of a culture and a social order that was outmoded and largely useless, though still exquisite and lovely. The characters of the play exist between two worlds, the one dead though not buried, the other as yet powerless to be born. The cherry orchard is a right symbol for them, and like the cherry orchard, they must eventually be chopped down and replaced by less beautiful but more useful people. Necessary as their disappearance is in the face of change—change which by their very natures they cannot accept and to which they cannot accommodate—their departure and the disappearance of their order is not unmixed with sadness. Change may eventually bring from the crude new order another exquisite culture, which in turn will have to be replaced. People caught by the moment of change may be seen as pathetic victims or as ludicrous incompetents. While Chekhov can see the ludicrousness of a Gáyef, of the perpetual student Trophímof, of Ephikhódof and his thousand and one misfortunes, and of his other people, yet the playwright identifies with some of them enough to view them with sympathetic understanding even as they are comic. Though Chekhov was well aware of the grave injustices and evils of the old order, he was also aware of its accomplishments and of the beauties of its culture. Hence, though he could view its vestigial remains as somewhat ludicrous, he could also look back upon its heyday with a certain nostalgia.

It is right, then, that the element of seriousness is largely reflected in the atmosphere and mood of the play. The incidents, as well as the characters, are dominantly comic—some even, as Chekhov said, farcical. Gáyef's oration commending a piece of furniture is only one of many bits of comedy bordering on farce. Though the mood is sometimes serious, even sad, the thought is mainly comic. Even the speeches of the perpetual student Trophímof, with their doctrine of work (one of which has been often called Chekhov's prophetic vision of the new Russia), are, coming from his mouth, relatively ludicrous. To the characters who listen to them, they are just good talk. There is an element of the ludicrous, though also of slight pathos, in the way Old Firs looks after Gáyef, as though he were still a youngster. There is much ironic comedy in the situation of the lovely Madame Ranévsky, an idler in Paris, but the keeper of the beautiful cherry orchard in her Russian home. Even the inabilities of the various characters to work out their love affairs and marriages is ironically comic, especially in the peasant landowner, Simeónof-Píshtchik.

Perhaps it is the ending, with Old Firs left alone locked in the abandoned house, that causes some critics to see the play as dominantly serious. Yet that action is ironically revealing of the ludicrous self-centeredness of the major characters. It serves to highlight Chekhov's vision of them all.

CHARACTERS

MADAME RANÉVSKY, a landowner
ÁNYA, her daughter, aged seventeen
BARBARA, her adopted daughter,
     aged twenty-seven
LEONÍD GÁYEF, brother of Madame
     Ranévsky
LOPÁKHIN, a merchant
PETER TROPHÍMOF, a student
SIMEÓNOF-PÍSHTCHIK, a landowner

CHARLOTTE, a governess
EPHIKHÓDOF, a clerk
DUNYÁSHA, a housemaid
FIRS, man-servant, aged eighty-seven
YÁSHA, a young man-servant
TRAMP
Stationmaster, Post-Office Official,
     Guests, Servants, etc.

The action takes place on Madame Ranévsky's property.

ACT I

(*A room which is still called the nursery. One door leads to* ÁNYA'S *room. Dawn; the sun will soon rise. It is already May; the cherry trees are in blossom, but it is cold in the garden and there is a morning frost. The windows are closed.*)

(*Enter* DUNYÁSHA *with a candle, and* LOPÁKHIN *with a book in his hand.*)

LOPÁKHIN.   So the train has come in, thank Heaven. What is the time?

DUNYÁSHA.   Nearly two. (*Putting the candle out.*) It is light already.

LOPÁKHIN.   How late is the train? A couple of hours at least. (*Yawning and stretching.*) What do you think of me? A fine fool I have made of myself. I came on purpose to meet them at the station and then I went and fell asleep, fell asleep as I sat in my chair. What a nuisance it is! You might have woke me up anyway.

DUNYÁSHA.   I thought that you had gone. (*She listens.*) That sounds like them driving up.

LOPÁKHIN (*listening*).   No; they have got to get the luggage out and all that. (*A pause.*) Madame Ranévsky has been five years abroad. I wonder what she has become like. What a splendid creature she is! So easy and simple in her ways. I remember when I was a youngster of fifteen my old father (he used to keep the shop here in the village then) struck me in the face with his fist and set my nose bleeding. We had come, for some reason or other, I forget what, into the courtyard, and he had been drinking. Madame Ranévsky—I remember it like yesterday, still a young girl, and oh, so slender—brought me to the wash-hand stand, here, in this very room, in the nursery. "Don't cry, little peasant," she said, "it'll mend by your wedding." (*A pause.*) "Little peasant"! . . . My father, it is true, was a peasant, and here am I in a white waistcoat and brown boots; a silk purse out of a sow's ear, as you might say; just turned rich, with heaps of money, but when you come to look at it, still a peasant of the peasants. (*Turning over the pages of the book.*) Here's this book that I was reading and didn't understand a word of it; I just sat reading and fell asleep.

DUNYÁSHA. The dogs never slept all night; they knew that their master and mistress were coming.

LOPÁKHIN. What's the matter with you, Dunyásha? You're all . . .

DUNYÁSHA. My hands are trembling; I feel quite faint.

LOPÁKHIN. You are too refined, Dunyásha; that's what it is. You dress yourself like a young lady; and look at your hair! You ought not to do it; you ought to remember your place.

(*Enter* EPHIKHÓDOF *with a nosegay. He is dressed in a short jacket and brightly polished boots which squeak noisily. As he comes in he drops the nosegay.*)

EPHIKHÓDOF (*picking it up*). The gardener has sent this; he says it is to go in the dining-room. (*Handing it to* DUNYÁSHA.)

LOPÁKHIN. And bring me some quass.

DUNYÁSHA. Yes, sir. (*Exit* DUNYÁSHA.)

EPHIKHÓDOF. There's a frost this morning, three degrees, and the cherry trees all in blossom. I can't say I think much of our climate; (*Sighing.*) that is impossible. Our climate is not adapted to contribute; and I should like to add, with your permission, that only two days ago I bought myself a new pair of boots, and I venture to assure you they do squeak beyond all bearing. What am I to grease them with?

LOPÁKHIN. Get out; I'm tired of you.

EPHIKHÓDOF. Every day some misfortune happens to me; but do I grumble? No; I am used to it; I can afford to smile.

(*Enter* DUNYÁSHA, *and hands a glass of quass to* LOPÁKHIN.)

EPHIKHÓDOF. I must be going. (*He knocks against a chair, which falls to the ground.*) There you are! (*In a voice of triumph.*) You see, if I may venture on the expression, the sort of incidents *inter alia*. It really is astonishing! (*Exit* EPHIKHÓDOF.)

DUNYÁSHA. To tell you the truth, Yermolái Alexéyitch, Ephikhódof has made me a proposal.

LOPÁKHIN. Hmph!

DUNYÁSHA. I hardly know what to do. He is such a well-behaved young man, only so often when he talks one doesn't know what he means. It is all so nice and full of good feeling, but you can't make out what it means. I fancy I am rather fond of him. He adores me passionately. He is a most unfortunate man; every day something seems to happen to him. They call him "Twenty-two misfortunes," that's his nickname.

LOPÁKHIN (*listening*). There, surely that is them coming!

DUNYÁSHA. They're coming! Oh, what is the matter with me? I am all turning cold.

LOPÁKHIN. Yes, there they are, and no mistake. Let's go and meet them. Will she know me again, I wonder? It is five years since we met.

DUNYÁSHA. I am going to faint! . . . I am going to faint!

(*Two carriages are heard driving up to the house.* LOPÁKHIN *and* DUNYÁSHA *exeunt quickly. The stage remains empty. A hubbub begins in the neighboring rooms.* FIRS *walks hastily across the stage, leaning on a walking-stick. He had been to meet them at the station. He is wearing an old-fashioned livery and a tall hat; he mumbles something to himself, but not a word is audible. The noise behind the scenes grows louder and louder. A voice says: "Let's go this way."* Enter MADAME RANÉVSKY, ÁNYA, CHARLOTTE, *leading a little dog on a chain, all dressed in traveling-dresses;* BARBARA *in greatcoat, with a kerchief over her head,* GÁYEF, SIMEÓNOF-PÍSHTCHIK, LOPÁKHIN, DUNYÁSHA, *carrying parcel and umbrella, servants with luggage, all cross the stage.*)

ÁNYA. Come through this way. Do you remember what room this is, mamma?

MADAME RANÉVSKY (*joyfully through her tears*). The nursery.

BARBARA. How cold it is. My hands are simply frozen. (*To* MADAME RANÉVSKY.) Your two rooms, the white room and the violet room, are just the same as they were, mamma.

MADAME RANÉVSKY. My nursery, my dear, beautiful nursery! This is where I used to sleep when I was a little girl. (*Crying.*) I am like a little girl still. (*Kissing* GÁYEF *and* BARBARA *and then* GÁYEF *again.*) Barbara has not altered a bit; she is just like a nun; and I knew Dunyásha at once. (*Kissing* DUNYÁSHA.)

GÁYEF. Your train was two hours late. What do you think of that? There's punctuality for you!

CHARLOTTE (*to* SIMEÓNOF-PÍSHTCHIK). My little dog eats nuts.

PÍSHTCHIK (*astonished*). You don't say so! Well, I never!

(*Exeunt all but* ÁNYA *and* DUNYÁSHA.)

DUNYÁSHA. At last you've come! (*She takes off* ÁNYA's *overcoat and hat.*)

ÁNYA. I have not slept for four nights on the journey. I am frozen to death.

DUNYÁSHA. It was Lent when you went away. There was snow on the ground; it was freezing; but now! Oh, my dear! (*Laughing and kissing her.*) How I have waited for you, my joy, my light! Oh, I must tell you something at once, I cannot wait another minute.

ÁNYA (*without interest*). What, again?

DUNYÁSHA. Ephikhódof, the clerk, proposed to me in Easter Week.

ÁNYA. Same old story. . . . (*Putting her hair straight.*) All my hair-pins have dropped out. (*She is very tired, staggering with fatigue.*)

DUNYÁSHA. I hardly know what to think of it. He loves me! Oh, how he loves me!

ÁNYA (*looking into her bedroom, affectionately*). My room, my windows, just as if I had never gone away! I am at home again! When I wake up in the morning I shall run out into the garden. . . . Oh, if only I could get to sleep! I have not slept the whole journey from Paris, I was so nervous and anxious.

DUNYÁSHA. Monsieur Trophímof arrived the day before yesterday.

ÁNYA (*joyfully*). Peter?

DUNYÁSHA. He was sleeping outside in the bath-house; he is living there. He was afraid he might be in the way. (*Looking at her watch.*) I'd like to go and wake him, only Mamzelle Barbara told me not to. "Mind you don't wake him," she said.

(*Enter* BARBARA *with bunch of keys hanging from her girdle.*)

BARBARA. Dunyásha, go and get some coffee, quick. Mamma wants some coffee.

DUNYÁSHA. In a minute! (*Exit* DUNYÁSHA.)

BARBARA. Well, thank Heaven, you have come. Here you are at home again. (*Caressing her.*) My little darling is back! My pretty one is back!

ÁNYA. What I've had to go through!

BARBARA. I can believe you.

ÁNYA. I left here in Holy Week. How cold it was! Charlotte would talk the whole way and keep doing conjuring tricks. What on earth made you tie Charlotte round my neck?

BARBARA. Well, you couldn't travel alone, my pet! At seventeen!

ÁNYA. When we got to Paris, it was so cold! There was snow on the ground. I can't talk French a bit. Mamma was on the fifth floor of a big house. When I arrived there were a lot of Frenchmen with her, and ladies, and an old Catholic priest with a book, and it was very uncomfortable and full of tobacco smoke. I suddenly felt so sorry for mamma, oh so sorry! I took her head in my arms and squeezed it and could not let it go, and then mamma kept kissing me and crying.

BARBARA (*crying*). Don't go on; don't go on!

ÁNYA. She's sold her villa near Mentone already. She's nothing left, absolutely nothing; and I hadn't a farthing either. We only just managed to get home. And mamma won't understand! We get out at a station to have some dinner, and she asks for all the most expensive things and gives the waiters a florin each for a tip; and Charlotte does the same. And Yásha wanted his portion, too. It was too awful! Yásha is mamma's new man-servant. We have brought him back with us.

BARBARA. I've seen the rascal.

ÁNYA. Come, tell me all about everything! Has the interest on the mortgage been paid?

BARBARA.   How could it be?

ÁNYA.   Oh, dear! Oh, dear!

BARBARA.   The property will be sold in August.

ÁNYA.   Oh, dear! Oh, dear!

LOPÁKHIN (*looking in at the door and mooing like a cow*).   Moo-oo! (*He goes away again.*)

BARBARA (*laughing through her tears, and shaking her fist at the door*). Oh, I should like to give him one!

ÁNYA (*embracing BARBARA softly*).   Barbara, has he proposed to you? (*BARBARA shakes her head.*)

ÁNYA.   And yet I am sure he loves you. Why don't you come to an understanding? What are you waiting for?

BARBARA.   I don't think anything will come of it. He has so much to do; he can't be bothered with me; he hardly takes any notice. Confound the man, I can't bear to see him! Every one talks about our marriage; every one congratulates me; but, as a matter of fact, there is nothing in it; it's all a dream. (*Changing her tone.*) You've got on a brooch like a bee.

ÁNYA (*sadly*).   Mamma bought it me. (*Going into her room, talking gayly, like a child.*) When I was in Paris, I went up in a balloon!

BARBARA.   How glad I am you are back, my little pet! my pretty one!

(DUNYÁSHA *has already returned with a coffee-pot and begins to prepare the coffee.*)

BARBARA (*standing by the door*).   I trudge about all day looking after things and I think and think. What are we to do? If only we could marry you to some rich man it would be a load off my mind. I would go into a retreat, and then to Kief, to Moscow; I would tramp about from one holy place to another, always tramping and tramping. What bliss!

ÁNYA.   The birds are singing in the garden. What time is it now?

BARBARA.   It must be past two. It is time to go to bed, my darling. (*Following ÁNYA into her room.*) What bliss!

(*Enter YÁSHA with a shawl and a traveling-bag.*)

YÁSHA (*crossing the stage, delicately*).   May I pass this way, mademoiselle?

DUNYÁSHA.   One would hardly know you, Yásha. How you've changed abroad!

YÁSHA.   Ahem! And who may you be?

DUNYÁSHA.   When you left here I was a little thing like that. (*Indicating with her hand.*) My name is Dunyásha, Theodore Kozoyédof's daughter. Don't you remember me?

YÁSHA.   Ahem! You little cucumber! (*He looks round cautiously, then embraces her. She screams and drops a saucer. Exit YÁSHA hastily.*)

BARBARA (*in the doorway, crossly*).   What's all this?

DUNYÁSHA (*crying*).   I've broken a saucer.

BARBARA.   Well, it brings luck.

(*Enter ÁNYA from her room.*)

ÁNYA.   We must tell mamma that Peter's here.

BARBARA. I've told them not to wake him.

ÁNYA (*thoughtfully*). It's just six years since papa died. And only a month afterwards poor little Grisha was drowned in the river; my pretty little brother, only seven years old! It was too much for mamma; she ran away, ran away without looking back. (*Shuddering.*) How well I can understand her, if only she knew! (*A pause.*) Peter Trophímof was Grisha's tutor; he might remind her.

(*Enter* FIRS *in long coat and white waistcoat.*)

FIRS (*going over to the coffee-pot, anxiously*). My mistress is going to take coffee here. (*Putting on white gloves.*) Is the coffee ready? (*Sternly, to* DUNYÁSHA.) Here, girl, where's the cream?

DUNYÁSHA. Oh, dear! Oh, dear! (*Exit* DUNYÁSHA *hastily.*)

FIRS (*bustling about the coffee-pot*). Ah, you . . . job-lot! (*Mumbling to himself.*) She's come back from Paris. The master went to Paris once in a post-chaise. (*Laughing.*)

BARBARA. What is it, Firs?

FIRS. I beg your pardon? (*Joyfully.*) My mistress has come home; at last I've seen her. Now I'm ready to die.

(*He cries with joy. Enter* MADAME RANÉVSKY, LOPÁKHIN, GÁYEF, *and* PÍSHTCHIK; PÍSHTCHIK *in Russian breeches and coat of fine cloth.* GÁYEF *as he enters makes gestures as if playing billiards.*)

MADAME RANÉVSKY. What was the expression? Let me see. "I'll put the red in the corner pocket; double into the middle—"

GÁYEF. I'll chip the red in the right-hand top. Once upon a time, Lyuba, when we were children, we used to sleep here side by side in two little cots, and now I'm fifty-one, and can't bring myself to believe it.

LOPÁKHIN. Yes, time flies.

GÁYEF. Who's that?

LOPÁKHIN. Time flies, I say.

GÁYEF. There's a smell of patchouli!

ÁNYA. I am going to bed. Good-night, mamma. (*Kissing her mother.*)

MADAME RANÉVSKY. My beloved little girl! (*Kissing her hands.*) Are you glad you're home again? I can't come to my right senses.

ÁNYA. Good-night, uncle.

GÁYEF (*kissing her face and hands*). God bless you, little Ánya. How like your mother you are! (*To* MADAME RANÉVSKY.) You were just such another girl at her age, Lyuba.

(ÁNYA *shakes hands with* LOPÁKHIN *and* SIMEÓNOF-PÍSHTCHIK, *and exit, shutting her bedroom door behind her.*)

MADAME RANÉVSKY. She's very, very tired.

PÍSHTCHIK. It must have been a long journey.

BARBARA (*to* LOPÁKHIN *and* PÍSHTCHIK). Well, gentlemen, it's past two; time you were off.

MADAME RANÉVSKY (*laughing*). You haven't changed a bit, Barbara!

Job-lot. In the original, *nedotepa*, a word invented by Tchekhov, and now established as classical. Derived from *ne*, not, and *dotyapat*, to finish chopping. [Translator.]

(*Drawing her to herself and kissing her.*) I'll just finish my coffee, then
we'll all go. (Firs *puts a footstool under her feet.*) Thank you, friend. I'm
used to my coffee. I drink it day and night. Thank you, you dear old man.
(*Kissing* Firs.)

BARBARA.   I'll go and see if they've got all the luggage. (*Exit* BARBARA.)

MADAME RANÉVSKY.   Can it be me that's sitting here? (*Laughing.*) I
want to jump and wave my arms about. (*Pausing and covering her face.*)
Surely I must be dreaming! God knows I love my country. I love it tenderly. I couldn't see out of the window from the train, I was crying so.
(*Crying.*) However, I must drink my coffee. Thank you, Firs; thank you,
you dear old man. I'm so glad to find you still alive.

FIRS.   The day before yesterday.

GÁYEF.   He's hard of hearing.

LOPÁKHIN.   I've got to be off for Kharkof by the five-o'clock train.
Such a nuisance! I wanted to stay and look at you and talk to you. You're
as splendid as you always were.

PÍSHTCHIK (*sighing heavily*).   Handsomer than ever and dressed like
a Parisian . . . Perish my wagon and all its wheels!

LOPÁKHIN.   Your brother, Leoníd Andréyitch, says I'm a snob, a money-
grubber. He can say what he likes. I don't care a hang. Only I want you
to believe in me as you used to; I want your wonderful, touching eyes to
look at me as they used to. Merciful God in heaven! My father was your
father's serf, and your grandfather's serf before him; but you, you did so
much for me in the old days that I've forgotten everything, and I love you
like a sister—more than a sister.

MADAME RANÉVSKY.   I can't sit still! I can't do it! (*Jumping up and
walking about in great agitation.*) This happiness is more than I can bear.
Laugh at me! I am a fool! (*Kissing a cupboard.*) My darling old cupboard!
(*Caressing a table.*) My dear little table!

GÁYEF.   Nurse is dead since you went away.

MADAME RANÉVSKY (*sitting down and drinking coffee*).   Yes, Heaven
rest her soul. They wrote and told me.

GÁYEF.   And Anastási is dead. Squint-eyed Peter has left us and works
in the town at the Police Inspector's now. (GÁYEF *takes out a box of sugar
candy from his pocket, and begins to eat it.*)

PÍSHTCHIK.   My daughter Dáshenka sent her compliments.

LOPÁKHIN.   I long to say something charming and delightful to you.
(*Looking at his watch.*) I'm just off; there's no time to talk. Well, yes,
I'll put it in two or three words. You know that your cherry orchard is
going to be sold to pay the mortgage: the sale is fixed for the 22d of
August; but don't you be uneasy, my dear lady; sleep peacefully; there's
a way out of it. This is my plan. Listen to me carefully. Your property is
only fifteen miles from the town; the railway runs close beside it; and if
only you will cut up the cherry orchard and the land along the river into
building lots and let it off on lease for villas, you will get at least two thousand five hundred pounds a year out of it.

GÁYEF. Come, come! What rubbish you're talking!

MADAME RANÉVSKY. I don't quite understand what you mean, Yer-molái Alexéyitch.

LOPÁKHIN. You will get a pound a year at least for every acre from the tenants, and if you advertise the thing at once, I am ready to bet whatever you like, by the autumn you won't have a clod of that earth left on your hands. It'll all be snapped up. In two words, I congratulate you; you are saved. It's a first-class site, with a good deep river. Only, of course you will have to put it in order and clear the ground; you will have to pull down all the old buildings—this house, for instance, which is no longer fit for anything; you'll have to cut down the cherry orchard. . . .

MADAME RANÉVSKY. Cut down the cherry orchard! Excuse me, but you don't know what you are talking about. If there is one thing that's interesting, remarkable in fact, in the whole province, it's our cherry orchard.

LOPÁKHIN. There's nothing remarkable about the orchard except that it's a very big one. It only bears once every two years, and then you don't know what to do with the fruit. Nobody wants to buy it.

GÁYEF. Our cherry orchard is mentioned in Andréyevsky's Encyclo-paedia.

LOPÁKHIN (*looking at his watch*). If we don't make up our minds or think of any way, on the 22d of August the cherry orchard and the whole property will be sold by auction. Come, make up your mind! There's no other way out of it, I swear—absolutely none.

FIRS. In the old days, forty or fifty years ago, they used to dry the cherries and soak 'em and pickle 'em, and make jam of 'em; and the dried cherries . . .

GÁYEF. Shut up, Firs.

FIRS. The dried cherries used to be sent in wagons to Moscow and Kharkof. A heap of money! The dried cherries were soft and juicy and sweet and sweet-smelling then. They knew some way in those days.

MADAME RANÉVSKY. And why don't they do it now?

FIRS. They've forgotten. Nobody remembers how to do it.

PÍSHTCHIK (*to* MADAME RANÉVSKY). What about Paris? How did you get on? Did you eat frogs?

MADAME RANÉVSKY. Crocodiles.

PÍSHTCHIK. You don't say so! Well, I never!

LOPÁKHIN. Until a little while ago there was nothing but gentry and peasants in the villages; but now villa residents have made their appear-ance. All the towns, even the little ones, are surrounded by villas now. In another twenty years the villa resident will have multiplied like anything. At present he only sits and drinks tea on his veranda, but it is quite likely that he will soon take to cultivating his three acres of land, and then your old cherry orchard will become fruitful, rich and happy. . . .

GÁYEF (*angry*). What gibberish!

(*Enter* BARBARA *and* YÁSHA.)

BARBARA (*taking out a key and noisily unlocking an old-fashioned cupboard*). There are two telegrams for you, mamma. Here they are.

MADAME RANÉVSKY (*tearing them up without reading them*). They're from Paris. I've done with Paris.

GÁYEF. Do you know how old this cupboard is, Lyuba? A week ago I pulled out the bottom drawer and saw a date burnt in it. That cupboard was made exactly a hundred years ago. What do you think of that, eh? We might celebrate its jubilee. It's only an inanimate thing, but for all that it's a historic cupboard.

PÍSHTCHIK (*astonished*). A hundred years? Well, I never!

GÁYEF (*touching the cupboard*). Yes, it's a wonderful thing. . . . Beloved and venerable cupboard; honor and glory to your existence, which for more than a hundred years has been directed to the noble ideals of justice and virtue. Your silent summons to profitable labor has never weakened in all these hundred years. (*Crying.*) You have upheld the courage of succeeding generations of our humankind; you have upheld faith in a better future and cherished in us ideals of goodness and social consciousness. (*A pause.*)

LOPÁKHIN. Yes. . . .

MADAME RANÉVSKY. You haven't changed, Leoníd.

GÁYEF (*embarrassed*). Off the white in the corner, chip the red in the middle pocket!

LOPÁKHIN (*looking at his watch*). Well, I must be off.

YÁSHA (*handing a box to* MADAME RANÉVSKY). Perhaps you'll take your pills now.

PÍSHTCHIK. You oughtn't to take medicine, dear lady. It does you neither good nor harm. Give them here, my friend. (*He empties all the pills into the palm of his hand, blows on them, puts them in his mouth, and swallows them down with a draught of quass.*) There!

MADAME RANÉVSKY (*alarmed*). Have you gone off your head?

PÍSHTCHIK. I've taken all the pills.

LOPÁKHIN. Greedy feller!

(*Every one laughs.*)

FIRS (*mumbling*). They were here in Easter Week and finished off a gallon of pickled gherkins.

MADAME RANÉVSKY. What's he talking about?

BARBARA. He's been mumbling like that these three years. We've got used to it.

YÁSHA. Advancing age.

(CHARLOTTE *crosses in a white frock, very thin, tightly laced, with a lorgnette at her waist.*)

LOPÁKHIN. Excuse me, Charlotte Ivánovna, I've not paid my respects to you yet. (*He prepares to kiss her hand.*)

CHARLOTTE (*drawing her hand away*). If one allows you to kiss one's hand, you will want to kiss one's elbow next, and then one's shoulder.

LOPÁKHIN. I'm having no luck to-day. (*All laugh.*) Charlotte Ivánovna, do us a conjuring trick.

MADAME RANÉVSKY. Charlotte, do do us a conjuring trick.

CHARLOTTE. No, thank you. I'm going to bed. (*Exit* CHARLOTTE.)

LOPÁKHIN. We shall meet again in three weeks. (*Kissing* MADAME RANÉVSKY's *hand.*) Meanwhile, good-bye. I must be off. (*To* GÁYEF.) So-long. (*Kissing* PÍSHTCHIK.) Ta-ta. (*Shaking hands with* BARBARA, *then with* FIRS *and* YÁSHA.) I hate having to go. (*To* MADAME RANÉVSKY.) If you make up your mind about the villas, let me know, and I'll raise you five thousand pounds at once. Think it over seriously.

BARBARA (*angrily*). For Heaven's sake, do go!

LOPÁKHIN. I'm *going,* I'm *going.* (*Exit* LOPÁKHIN.)

GÁYEF. Snob! . . . However, *pardon!* Barbara's going to marry him; he's Barbara's young man.

BARBARA. You talk too much, uncle.

MADAME RANÉVSKY. Why, Barbara, I shall be very glad. He's a nice man.

PÍSHTCHIK. Not a doubt of it. . . . A most worthy individual. My Dáshenka, she says . . . oh, she says . . . lots of things. (*Snoring and waking up again at once.*) By the by, dear lady, can you lend me twenty-five pounds? I've got to pay the interest on my mortgage to-morrow.

BARBARA (*alarmed*). We can't! We can't!

MADAME RANÉVSKY. It really is a fact that I haven't any money.

PÍSHTCHIK. I'll find it somewhere. (*Laughing.*) I never lose hope. Last time I thought, "Now I really am done for, I'm a ruined man," when behold, they ran a railway over my land and paid me compensation. And so it'll be again; something will happen, if not to-day, then to-morrow. Dáshenka may win the twenty-thousand-pound prize; she's got a ticket in the lottery.

MADAME RANÉVSKY. The coffee's finished. Let's go to bed.

FIRS (*brushing* GÁYEF's *clothes, admonishingly*). You've put on the wrong trousers again. Whatever am I to do with you?

BARBARA (*softly*). Ánya is asleep. (*She opens the window quietly.*) The sun's up already; it isn't cold now. Look, mamma, how lovely the trees are. Heavens! what a sweet air! The starlings are singing!

GÁYEF (*opening the other window*). The orchard is all white. You've not forgotten it, Lyuba? This long avenue going straight on, straight on, like a ribbon between the trees? It shines like silver on moonlight nights. Do you remember? You've not forgotten?

MADAME RANÉVSKY (*looking out into the garden*). Oh, my childhood, my pure and happy childhood! I used to sleep in this nursery. I used to look out from here into the garden. Happiness awoke with me every morning; and the orchard was just the same then as it is now; nothing is altered. (*Laughing with joy.*) It is all white, all white! Oh, my cherry orchard! After the dark and stormy autumn and the frosts of winter you are young again and full of happiness; the angels of heaven have not abandoned you.

Oh! if only I could free my neck and shoulders from the stone that weighs them down! If only I could forget my past!

GÁYEF. Yes; and this orchard will be sold to pay our debts, however impossible it may seem. . . .

MADAME RANÉVSKY. Look! There's mamma walking in the orchard . . . in a white frock! (*Laughing with joy.*) There she is!

GÁYEF. Where?

BARBARA. Heaven help you!

MADAME RANÉVSKY. There's no one there really. It only looked like it; there on the right where the path turns down to the summer-house; there's a white tree that leans over and looks like a woman.

(*Enter* TROPHÍMOF *in a shabby student uniform and spectacles.*)

MADAME RANÉVSKY. What a wonderful orchard, with its white masses of blossom and the blue sky above!

TROPHÍMOF. Lyubóf Andráyevna! (*She looks round at him.*) I only want to say, "How do you do," and go away at once. (*Kissing her hand eagerly.*) I was told to wait till the morning, but I hadn't the patience.

(MADAME RANÉVSKY *looks at him in astonishment.*)

BARBARA (*crying*). This is Peter Trophímof.

TROPHÍMOF. Peter Trophímof; I was Grisha's tutor, you know. Have I really altered so much?

(MADAME RANÉVSKY *embraces him and cries softly.*)

GÁYEF. Come, come, that's enough, Lyuba!

BARBARA (*crying*). I told you to wait till to-morrow, you know, Peter.

MADAME RANÉVSKY. My little Grisha! My little boy! Grisha . . . my son. . . .

BARBARA. It can't be helped, mamma. It was the will of God.

TROPHÍMOF (*gently, crying*). There, there!

MADAME RANÉVSKY (*crying*). He was drowned. My little boy was drowned. Why? What was the use of that, my dear? (*In a softer voice.*) Ánya's asleep in there, and I am speaking so loud, and making a noise. . . . But tell me, Peter, why have you grown so ugly? Why have you grown so old?

TROPHÍMOF. An old woman in the train called me a "mouldy gentleman."

MADAME RANÉVSKY. You were quite a boy then, a dear little student, and now your hair's going and you wear spectacles. Are you really still a student? (*Going toward the door.*)

TROPHÍMOF. Yes, I expect I shall be a perpetual student.

MADAME RANÉVSKY (*kissing her brother and then* BARBARA). Well, go to bed. You've grown old too, Leoníd. Yes, yes; time for bed. Oh, oh, my gout! I'll stay the night here. Don't forget, Lyubóf Andréyevna, my angel, to-morrow morning . . . twenty-five.

GÁYEF. He's still on the same string.

PÍSHTCHIK. Twenty-five . . . to pay the interest on my mortgage.

MADAME RANÉVSKY. I haven't any money, my friend.

PÍSHTCHIK. I'll pay you back, dear lady. It's a trifling sum.

MADAME RANÉVSKY. Well, well, Leoníd will give it you. Let him have it, Leoníd.

GÁYEF (*ironical*). I'll give it him right enough! Hold your pocket wide!

MADAME RANÉVSKY. It can't be helped. . . . He needs it. He'll pay it back.

(*Exeunt* MADAME RANÉVSKY, TROPHÍMOF, PÍSHTCHIK, *and* FIRS, GÁYEF, BARBARA, *and* YÁSHA *remain.*)

GÁYEF. My sister hasn't lost her old habit of scattering the money. (*To* YÁSHA.) Go away, my lad! You smell of chicken.

YÁSHA (*laughing*). You're just the same as you always were, Leoníd Andréyevitch!

GÁYEF. Who's that? (*to* BARBARA.) What does he say?

BARBARA (*to* YÁSHA). Your mother's come up from the village. She's been waiting for you since yesterday in the servants' hall. She wants to see you.

YÁSHA. What a nuisance she is!

BARBARA. You wicked, unnatural son!

YÁSHA. Well, what do I want with her? She might just as well have waited till to-morrow. (*Exit* YÁSHA.)

BARBARA. Mamma is just like she used to be; she hasn't changed a bit. If she had her way, she'd give away everything she has.

GÁYEF. Yes. (*A pause.*) If people recommend very many cures for an illness, that means that the illness is incurable. I think and think, I batter my brains; I know of many remedies, very many, and that means really that there is none. How nice it would be to get a fortune left one by somebody! How nice it would be if Ánya could marry a very rich man! How nice it would be to go to Yaroslav and try my luck with my aunt the Countess. My aunt is very, very rich, you know.

BARBARA (*crying softly*). If only God would help us!

GÁYEF. Don't howl! My aunt is very rich, but she does not like us. In the first place, my sister married a solicitor, not a nobleman. (ÁNYA *appears in the doorway.*) She married a man who was not a nobleman, and it's no good pretending that she has led a virtuous life. She's a dear, kind, charming creature, and I love her very much, but whatever mitigating circumstances one may find for her, there's no getting round it that she's a sinful woman. You can see it in her every gesture.

BARBARA (*whispering*). Ánya is standing in the door!

GÁYEF. Who's that? (*A pause.*) It's very odd, something's got into my right eye. I can't see properly out of it. Last Thursday when I was down at the District Court . . .

(ÁNYA *comes down.*)

BARBARA. Why aren't you asleep, Ánya?

ÁNYA. I can't sleep. It's no good trying.

GÁYEF. My little pet! (*Kissing* ÁNYA's *hands and face.*) My little girl!

(*Crying.*) You're not my niece; you're my angel; you're my everything. Trust me, trust me. . . .

ÁNYA. I do trust you, uncle. Every one loves you, every one respects you; but dear, dear uncle, you ought to hold your tongue, only to hold your tongue. What were you saying just now about mamma?—about your own sister? What was the good of saying that?

GÁYEF. Yes, yes. (*Covering his face with her hand.*) You're quite right; it was awful of me! Lord, Lord! Save me from myself! And a little while ago I made a speech over a cupboard. What a stupid thing to do! As soon as I had done it, I knew it was stupid.

BARBARA. Yes, really, uncle. You ought to hold your tongue. Say nothing; that's all that's wanted.

ÁNYA. If only you would hold your tongue, you'd be so much happier!

GÁYEF. I will! I will! (*Kissing* ÁNYA'S *and* BARBARA'S *hands.*) I'll hold my tongue. But there's one thing I must say; it's business. Last Thursday, when I was down at the District Court, a lot of us were there together, we began to talk about this and that, one thing and another, and it seems I could arrange a loan on note of hand to pay the interest into the bank.

BARBARA. If only Heaven would help us!

GÁYEF. I'll go in on Tuesday and talk it over again. (*To* BARBARA.) Don't howl! (*To* ÁNYA.) Your mamma shall have a talk with Lopákhin. Of course he won't refuse her. And as soon as you are rested you must go to see your grandmother, the Countess, at Yaroslav. We'll operate from three points, and the trick is done. We'll pay the interest, I'm certain of it. (*Taking sugar candy.*) I swear on my honor, or whatever you will, the property shall not be sold. (*Excitedly.*) I swear by my hope of eternal happiness! There's my hand on it. Call me a base, dishonorable man if I let it go to auction. I swear by my whole being!

ÁNYA (*calm again and happy*). What a dear you are, uncle, and how clever! (*Embraces him.*) Now I'm easy again. I'm easy again! I'm happy!

(*Enter* FIRS.)

FIRS (*reproachfully*). Leoníd Andréyevitch, have you no fear of God? When are you going to bed?

GÁYEF. I'm just off—just off. You get along, Firs. I'll undress myself all right. Come, children, by-bye! Details to-morrow, but now let's go to bed. (*Kissing* ÁNYA *and* BARBARA.) I'm a good Liberal, a man of the eighties. People abuse the eighties, but I think that I may say I've suffered something for my convictions in my time. It's not for nothing that the peasants love me. We ought to know the peasants; we ought to know with what . . .

ÁNYA. You're at it again, uncle!

BARBARA. Why don't you hold your tongue, uncle?

FIRS (*angrily*). Leoníd Andréyevitch!

GÁYEF. I'm coming; I'm coming. Now go to bed. Off two cushions in the middle pocket! I start another life! . . . (*Exit, with* FIRS *hobbling after him.*)

ÁNYA. Now my mind is at rest. I don't want to go to Yaroslav; I don't like grandmamma; but my mind is at rest, thanks to Uncle Leoníd. (*She sits down.*)

BARBARA. Time for bed. I'm off. Whilst you were away there's been a scandal. You know that nobody lives in the old servants' quarters except the old people. Ephim, Pauline, Evstignéy, and old Karp. Well, they took to having in all sorts of queer fish to sleep there with them. I didn't say a word. But at last I heard they had spread a report that I had given orders that they were to have nothing but peas to eat; out of stinginess, you understand? It was all Evstignéy's doing. "Very well," I said to myself, "you wait a bit." So I sent for Evstignéy. (*Yawning.*) He comes. "Now then, Evstignéy," I said, "you old imbecile, how do you dare . . ." (*Looking at* ÁNYA.) Ánya, Ánya! (*A pause.*) She's asleep. (*Taking* ÁNYA's *arm.*) Let's go to bed. Come along. (*Leading her away.*) Sleep on, my little one! Come along; come along! (*They go towards* ÁNYA's *room. In the distance beyond the orchard a shepherd plays his pipe.* TROPHÍMOF *crosses the stage and, seeing* BARBARA *and* ÁNYA, *stops.*) 'Sh! She's asleep, she's asleep! Come along, my love.

ÁNYA (*drowsily*). I'm so tired! Listen to the bells! Uncle, dear uncle! Mamma! Uncle!

BARBARA. Come along, my love! Come along. (*Exeunt* BARBARA *and* ÁNYA *to the bedroom.*)

TROPHÍMOF (*with emotion*). My sunshine! My spring!

ACT II

(*In the open fields; an old crooked half-ruined shrine. Near it a well; big stones, apparently old tombstones; an old bench. Road to the estate beyond. On one side rise dark poplar trees. Beyond them begins the cherry orchard. In the distance a row of telegraph poles, and, far away on the horizon, the dim outlines of a big town, visible only in fine, clear weather. It is near sunset.*)

(CHARLOTTE, YÁSHA, *and* DUNYÁSHA *sit on the bench.* EPHIKHÓDOF *stands by them and plays on a guitar; they mediate.* CHARLOTTE *wears an old peaked cap. She has taken a gun from off her shoulders and is mending the buckle of the strap.*)

CHARLOTTE (*thoughtfully*). I have no proper passport. I don't know how old I am; I always feel I am still young. When I was a little girl my father and mother used to go about from one country fair to another, giving performances, and very good ones, too. I used to do the *salto mortale* and all sorts of tricks. When papa and mamma died, an old German lady adopted me and educated me. Good! When I grew up I became a governess. But where I come from and who I am, I haven't a notion. Who my

Furázhka, the commonest men's headgear in Russia, shaped like a yachting cap. [Translator.]

parents were—very likely they weren't married—I don't know. (*Taking a cucumber from her pocket and beginning to eat.*) I don't know anything about it. (*A pause.*) I long to talk so, and I have no one to talk to, I have no friends or relations.

EPHIKHÓDOF (*playing on the guitar and singing*).
    "What is the noisy world to me?
    Oh, what are friends and foes?"
How sweet it is to play upon a mandolin!

DUNYÁSHA.   That's a guitar, not a mandolin. (*She looks at herself in a hand-glass and powders her face.*)

EPHIKHÓDOF.   For the madman who loves, it is a mandolin. (*Singing.*)
    "Oh, that my heart were cheered
    By the warmth of requited love."

(YÁSHA *joins in.*)

CHARLOTTE.   How badly these people do sing! Foo! Like jackals howling!

DUNYÁSHA (*to* YÁSHA.)   What happiness it must be to live abroad!

YÁSHA.   Of course it is; I quite agree with you. (*He yawns and lights a cigar.*)

EPHIKHÓDOF.   It stands to reason. Everything abroad has attained a certain culnimation.

YÁSHA.   That's right.

EPHIKHÓDOF.   I am a man of cultivation; I have studied various remarkable books, but I cannot fathom the direction of my preferences; do I want to live or do I want to shoot myself, so to speak? But in order to be ready for all contingencies I always carry a revolver in my pocket. Here it is. (*Showing revolver.*)

CHARLOTTE.   That's done. I'm off. (*Slinging the rifle over her shoulder.*) You're a clever fellow, Ephikhódof, and very alarming. Women must fall madly in love with you. Brrr! (*Going.*) These clever people are all so stupid; I have no one to talk to. I am always alone, always alone; I have no friends or relations, and who I am, or why I exist, is a mystery. (*Exit slowly.*)

EPHIKHÓDOF.   Strictly speaking, without touching upon other matters, I must protest *inter alia* that destiny treats me with the utmost rigor, as a tempest might treat a small ship. If I labor under a misapprehension, how is it that when I woke up this morning, behold, so to speak, I perceived sitting on my chest a spider of preternatural dimensions, like that? (*Indicating with both hands.*) And if I go to take a draught of quass, I am sure to find something of the most indelicate character, in the nature of a cockroach. (*A pause.*) Have you read Buckle? (*A pause.—to* DUNYÁSHA.) I should like to trouble you, Avdotya Fëdorovna, for a momentary interview.

DUNYÁSHA.   Talk away.

Culnimation. This represents a similar blunder of Ephikhodof's in the original. [Translator.]

EPHIKHÓDOF.   I should prefer to conduct it *tête-à-tête*. (*Sighing.*)

DUNYÁSHA (*confused*).   Very well, only first please fetch me my cloak. It's by the cupboard. It's rather damp here.

EPHIKHÓDOF.   Very well, mademoiselle. I will go and fetch it, mademoiselle. Now I know what to do with my revolver. (*Takes his guitar and exit, playing.*)

YÁSHA.   Twenty-two misfortunes! Between you and me, he's a stupid fellow. (*Yawning.*)

DUNYÁSHA.   Heaven help him, he'll shoot himself! (*A pause.*) I have grown so nervous, I am always in a twitter. I was quite a little girl when they took me into the household, and now I have got quite disused to common life, and my hands are as white as white, like a lady's. I have grown so refined, so delicate and genteel, I am afraid of everything. I'm always frightened. And if you deceive me, Yásha, I don't know what will happen to my nerves.

YÁSHA (*kissing her*).   You little cucumber! Of course every girl ought to behave herself properly; there's nothing I dislike as much as when girls aren't proper in their behavior.

DUNYÁSHA.   I've fallen dreadfully in love with you. You're so educated; you can talk about anything! (*A pause.*)

YÁSHA (*yawning*).   Yes. . . . The way I look at it is this; if a girl falls in love with anybody, then I call her immoral. (*A pause.*) How pleasant it is to smoke one's cigar in the open air. (*Listening.*) There's some one coming. It's the missis and the rest of 'em. . . . (DUNYÁSHA *embraces him hastily.*) Go towards the house as if you'd just been for a bathe. Go by this path or else they'll meet you and think that I've been walking out with you. I can't stand that sort of thing.

DUNYÁSHA (*coughing softly*).   Your cigar has given me a headache.

(*Exit* DUNYÁSHA. YÁSHA *remains sitting by the shrine.*)

(*Enter* MADAME RANÉVSKY, GÁYEF, *and* LOPÁKHIN.)

LOPÁKHIN.   You must make up your minds once and for all. Time waits for no man. The question is perfectly simple. Are you going to let off the land for villas or not? Answer in one way; yes or no? Only one word!

MADAME RANÉVSKY.   Who's smoking horrible cigars here? (*She sits down.*)

GÁYEF.   How handy it is now they've built that railway. (*Sitting.*) We've been into town for lunch and back again. . . . Red in the middle! I must just go up to the house and have a game.

MADAME RANÉVSKY.   There's no hurry.

LOPÁKHIN.   Only one word—yes or no! (*Entreatingly.*) Come, answer the question!

GÁYEF (*yawninng.*)   Who's that?

MADAME RANÉVSKY (*looking into her purse*).   I had a lot of money yesterday, but there's hardly any left now. Poor Barbara tries to save money by feeding us all on milk soup; the old people in the kitchen get nothing but peas, and yet I go squandering aimlessly. . . . (*Dropping her purse and scattering gold coins; vexed.*) There, I've dropped it all!

YÁSHA.   Allow me, I'll pick it up. (*Collecting the coins.*)

MADAME RANÉVSKY.   Yes, please do, Yásha! Whatever made me go into town for lunch? I hate your horrid restaurant with the organ, and the tablecloths all smelling of soap. Why do you drink so much, Leoníd? Why do you eat so much? Why do you talk so much? You talked too much at the restaurant again, and and most unsuitably, about the seventies, and the decadents. And to whom? Fancy talking about decadents to the waiters!

LOPÁKHIN.   Quite true.

GÁYEF (*with a gesture*).   I'm incorrigible, that's plain. (*Irritably to* YÁSHA.) What do you keep dodging about in front of me for?

YÁSHA (*laughing*).   I can't hear your voice without laughing.

GÁYEF (*to* MADAME RANÉVSKY).   Either he or I . . .

MADAME RANÉVSKY.   Go away, Yásha; run along.

YÁSHA (*handing* MADAME RANÉVSKY *her purse*).   I'll go at once. (*Restraining his laughter with difficulty.*) This very minute. (*Exit* YÁSHA.)

LOPÁKHIN.   Derigánof, the millionaire, wants to buy your property. They say he'll come to the auction himself.

MADAME RANÉVSKY.   How did you hear?

LOPÁKHIN.   I was told so in town.

GÁYEF.   Our aunt at Yaroslav has promised to send something; but I don't know when, or how much.

LOPÁKHIN.   How much will she send? Ten thousand pounds? Twenty thousand pounds?

MADAME RANÉVSKY.   Oh, come. . . . A thousand or fifteen hundred at the most.

LOPÁKHIN.   Excuse me, but in all my life I never met anybody so frivolous as you two, so crazy and unbusinesslike! I tell you in plain Russian your property is going to be sold, and you don't seem to understand what I say.

MADAME RANÉVSKY.   Well, what are we to do? Tell us what you want us to do.

LOPÁKHIN.   Don't I tell you every day? Every day I say the same thing over and over again. You must lease off the cherry orchard and the rest of the estate for villas; you must do it at once, this very moment; the auction will be on you in two twos! Try and understand. Once you make up your mind there are to be villas, you can get all the money you want, and you're saved.

MADAME RANÉVSKY.   Villas and villa residents, oh, please, . . . it's so vulgar!

GÁYEF.   I quite agree with you.

LOPÁKHIN.   I shall either cry, or scream, or faint. I can't stand it! You'll be the death of me. (*To* GÁYEF.) You're an old woman!

GÁYEF.   Who's that?

LOPÁKHIN.   You're an old woman! (*Going.*)

MADAME RANÉVSKY (*frightened*). No; don't go. Stay here, there's a dear! Perhaps we shall think of some way.

LOPÁKHIN. What's the good of thinking!

MADAME RANÉVSKY. Please don't go; I want you. At any rate, it's gayer when you're here. (*A pause.*) I keep expecting something to happen, as if the house were going to tumble down about our ears.

GÁYEF (*in deep abstraction*). Off the cushion on the corner; double into the middle pocket . . .

MADAME RANÉVSKY. We have been very, very sinful!

LOPÁKHIN. You! What sins have you committed?

GÁYEF (*eating candy*). They say I've devoured all my substance in sugar candy. (*Laughing.*)

MADAME RANÉVSKY. Oh, the sins that I have committed . . . I've always squandered money at random like a mad-woman; I married a man who made nothing but debts. My husband drank himself to death on champagne; he was a fearful drinker. Then for my sins I fell in love and went off with another man; and immediately—that was my first punishment—a blow full on the head . . . here, in this very river . . . my little boy was drowned; and I went abroad, right, right away, never to come back any more, never to see this river again. . . . I shut my eyes and ran, like a mad thing, and *he* came after me, pitiless and cruel. I bought a villa at Mentone, because he fell ill there, and for three years I knew no rest day or night; the sick man tormented and wore down my soul. Then, last year, when my villa was sold to pay my debts, I went off to Paris, and he came and robbed me of everything, left me and took up with another woman, and I tried to poison myself. . . . It was all so stupid, so humiliating. . . . Then suddenly I longed to be back in Russia, in my own country, with my little girl. . . . (*Wiping away her tears.*) Lord, Lord, be merciful to me; forgive my sins! Do not punish me any more! (*Taking a telegram from her pocket.*) I got this to-day from Paris. . . . He asks to be forgiven, begs me to go back. . . . (*Tearing up the telegram.*) Isn't that music that I hear? (*Listening.*)

GÁYEF. That's our famous Jewish band. You remember? Four fiddles, a flute, and a double bass.

MADAME RANÉVSKY. Does it still exist? We must make them come up sometime; we'll have a dance.

LOPÁKHIN (*listening*). I don't hear anything. (*Singing softly.*)
        "The Germans for a fee will turn
        A Russ into a Frenchman."
(*Laughing.*) I saw a very funny piece at the theater last night; awfully funny!

MADAME RANÉVSKY. It probably wasn't a bit funny. You people oughtn't to go and see plays; you ought to try to see yourselves; to see what a dull life you lead, and how much too much you talk.

LOPÁKHIN. Quite right. To tell the honest truth, our life's an imbecile affair. (*A pause.*) My papa was a peasant, an idiot; he understood nothing; he taught me nothing; all he did was to beat me, when he was drunk, with a walking-stick. As a matter of fact I'm just as big a blockhead and idiot as he was. I never did any lessons; my handwriting's abominable; I write so badly I'm ashamed before people; like a pig.

MADAME RANÉVSKY. You ought to get married.

LOPÁKHIN. Yes, that's true.

MADAME RANÉVSKY. Why not marry Barbara? She's a nice girl.

LOPÁKHIN. Yes.

MADAME RANÉVSKY. She's a nice straight-forward creature; works all day; and what's most important, she loves you. You've been fond of her for a long time.

LOPÁKHIN. Well, why not? I'm quite willing. She's a very nice girl. (*A pause.*)

GÁYEF. I've been offered a place in a bank. Six hundred pounds a year. Do you hear?

MADAME RANÉVSKY. You in a bank! Stay where you are.

(*Enter* FIRS, *carrying an overcoat.*)

FIRS (*to* GÁYEF). Put this on, please, master; it's getting damp.

GÁYEF (*putting on the coat*). What a plague you are, Firs!

FIRS. What's the use. . . . You went off and never told me. (*Examining his clothes.*)

MADAME RANÉVSKY. How old you've got, Firs!

FIRS. I beg your pardon?

LOPÁKHIN. She says how old you've got!

FIRS. I've been alive a long time. When they found me a wife, your father wasn't even born yet. (*Laughing.*) And when the Liberation came I was already chief valet. But I wouldn't have any Liberation then; I stayed with the master. (*A pause.*) I remember how happy everybody was, but why they were happy they didn't know themselves.

LOPÁKHIN. It was fine before then. Anyway they used to flog 'em.

FIRS (*mishearing him*). I should think so! The peasants minded the masters, and the masters minded the peasants, but now it's all higgledy-piggledy; you can't make head or tail of it.

GÁYEF. Shut up, Firs. I must go into town again to-morrow. I've been promised an introduction to a general who'll lend money on a bill.

LOPÁKHIN. You'll do no good. You won't even pay the interest; set your mind at ease about that.

MADAME RANÉVSKY (*to* LOPÁKHIN). He's only talking nonsense. There's no such general at all.

(*Enter* TROPHÍMOF, ÁNYA, *and* BARBARA.)

GÁYEF. Here come the others.

ÁNYA. Here's mamma.

MADAME RANÉVSKY (*tenderly*). Come along, come along . . . my little ones. . . . (*Embracing* ÁNYA *and* BARBARA.) If only you knew how much I love you both! Sit beside me . . . there, like that.

(*Every one sits.*)

LOPÁKHIN. The Perpetual Student's always among the girls.

TROPHÍMOF. It's no affair of yours.

LOPÁKHIN. He's nearly fifty and still a student.

TROPHÍMOF. Stop your idiotic jokes!

LOPÁKHIN. What are you losing your temper for, silly?

TROPHÍMOF. Why can't you leave me alone?

LOPÁKHIN (*laughing*). I should like to know what your opinion is of me.

TROPHÍMOF. My opinion of you, Yermolái Alexéyitch, is this. You're a rich man; you'll soon be a millionaire. Just as a beast of prey which devours everything that comes in its way is necessary for the conversion of matter, so you are necessary, too.

(*All laugh.*)

BARBARA. Tell us something about the planets, Peter, instead.

MADAME RANÉVSKY. No. Let's go on with the conversation we were having yesterday.

TROPHÍMOF. What about?

GÁYEF. About the proud man.

TROPHÍMOF. We had a long talk yesterday, but we didn't come to any conclusion. There is something mystical in the proud man in the sense in which you use the words. You may be right from your point of view, but, if we look at it simple-mindedly, what room is there for pride? Is there any sense in it, when man is so poorly constructed from the physiological point of view, when the vast majority of us are so gross and stupid and profoundly unhappy? We must give up admiring ourselves. The only thing to do is to work.

GÁYEF. We shall die all the same.

TROPHÍMOF. Who knows? And what does it mean, to die? Perhaps man has a hundred senses, and when he dies only the five senses that we know perish with him, and the other ninety-five remain alive.

MADAME RANÉVSKY. How clever you are, Peter!

LOPÁKHIN (*ironically*). Oh, extraordinary!

TROPHÍMOF. Mankind marches forward, perfecting its strength. Everything that is unattainable for us now will one day be near and clear; but we must work; we must help with all our force those who seek for truth. At present only a few men work in Russia. The vast majority of the educated people that I know seek after nothing, do nothing, and are as yet incapable of work. They call themselves the "Intelligentsia," they say "thou" and "thee" to the servants, they treat the peasants like animals, learn nothing, read nothing serious, do absolutely nothing, only talk about science, and understand little or nothing about art. They are all serious; they all have solemn faces; they only discuss important subjects; they philosophize; but meanwhile the vast majority of us, ninety-nine per cent, live like savages; at the least thing they curse and punch people's heads; they eat like beasts and sleep in dirt and bad air; there are bugs everywhere, evil smells, damp and moral degradation. . . . It's plain that all our clever conversations are only meant to distract our own attention and other people's. Show me where those crèches are, that they're always talking so much about; or those reading-rooms. They are only things people write about in novels; they don't really exist at all. Nothing exists but dirt, vulgarity, and Asiatic ways. I am afraid of solemn faces; I dislike them; I am afraid of solemn conversations. Let us rather hold our tongues.

LOPÁKHIN. Do you know, I get up at five every morning; I work from morning till night; I am always handling my own money or other people's, and I see the sort of men there are about me. One only has to begin to do anything to see how few honest and decent people there are. Sometimes, as I lie awake in bed, I think: "O Lord, you have given us mighty forests, boundless fields and immeasurable horizons, and, we living in their midst, ought really to be giants."

MADAME RANÉVSKY. Oh, dear, you want giants! They are all very well in fairy stories; but in real life they are rather alarming.

(EPHIKHÓDOF *passes at the back of the scene, playing on his guitar.*)

MADAME RANÉVSKY (*pensively*). There goes Ephikhódof.

ÁNYA (*pensively*). There goes Ephikhódof.

GÁYEF. The sun has set.

TROPHÍMOF. Yes.

GÁYEF (*as if declaiming, but not loud*). O Nature, wonderful Nature, you glow with eternal light; beautiful and indifferent, you whom we call our mother, uniting in yourself both life and death, you animate and you destroy . . .

BARBARA (*entreatingly*). Uncle!

ÁNYA. You're at it again, uncle.

TROPHÍMOF. You'd far better double the red into the middle pocket.

GÁYEF. I'll hold my tongue! I'll hold my tongue!

(*They all sit pensively. Silence reigns, broken only by the mumbling of old* FIRS. *Suddenly a distant sound is heard as if from the sky, the sound of a string breaking, dying away, melancholy.*)

MADAME RANÉVSKY. What's that?

LOPÁKHIN. I don't know. It's a lifting-tub given way somewhere away in the mines. It must be a long way off.

GÁYEF. Perhaps it's some sort of bird . . . a heron, or something.

TROPHÍMOF. Or an owl. . . .

MADAME RANÉVSKY (*shuddering*). There is something uncanny about it!

FIRS. The same thing happened before the great misfortune: the owl screeched and the samovar kept humming.

GÁYEF. What great misfortune?

FIRS. The Liberation. (*A pause.*)

MADAME RANÉVSKY. Come, every one, let's go in; it's getting late. (*To* ÁNYA.) You've tears in your eyes. What is it, little one? (*Embracing her.*)

ÁNYA. Nothing, mamma. I'm all right.

TROPHÍMOF. There's some one coming.

(A TRAMP *appears in a torn white peaked cap and overcoat. He is slightly drunk.*)

TRAMP. Excuse me, but can I go through this way straight to the station?

GÁYEF. Certainly. Follow this path.

TRAMP. I am uncommonly obliged to you, sir. (*Coughing.*) We're having lovely weather. (*Declaiming.*) "Brother, my suffering brother" . . . "Come forth to the Volga. Who moans?" . . . (*To* BARBARA.) Mademoiselle, please spare a sixpence for a hungry fellow-countryman.

(BARBARA, *frightened, screams.*)

LOPÁKHIN (*angrily*). There's a decency for every indecency to observe!

MADAME RANÉVSKY. Take this; here you are. (*Fumbling in her purse.*) I haven't any silver. . . . Never mind, take this sovereign.

TRAMP. I am uncommonly obliged to you, madame. (*Exit* TRAMP. *Laughter.*)

BARBARA (*frightened*). I'm going! I'm going! Oh, mamma, there's nothing for the servants to eat at home, and you've gone and given this man a sovereign.

MADAME RANÉVSKY. What's to be done with your stupid old mother? I'll give you up everything I have when I get back. Yermolái Alexéyitch, lend me some more money.

LOPÁKHIN. Very good.

MADAME RANÉVSKY. Come along, every one; it's time to go in. We've settled all about your marriage between us, Barbara. I wish you joy.

BARBARA (*through her tears*). You mustn't joke about such things, mamma.

LOPÁKHIN. Amelia, get thee to a nunnery, go!

GÁYEF. My hands are all trembling; it's ages since I had a game of billiards.

LOPÁKHIN. Amelia, nymphlet, in thine orisons remember me.

MADAME RANÉVSKY. Come along. It's nearly supper-time.

BARBARA. How he frightened me! My heart is simply throbbing.

LOPÁKHIN. Allow me to remind you, the cherry orchard is to be sold on the 22d of August. Bear that in mind; bear that in mind!

(*Exeunt* OMNES *except* TROPHÍMOF *and* ÁNYA.)

ÁNYA (*laughing*). Many thanks to the Tramp for frightening Barbara; at last we are alone.

TROPHÍMOF. Barbara's afraid we shall go and fall in love with each other. Day after day she never leaves us alone. With her narrow mind she cannot understand that we are above love. To avoid everything petty, everything illusory, everything that prevents one from being free and happy, that is the whole meaning and purpose of our life. Forward! We march on irresistibly towards that bright star which burns far, far before us! Forward! Don't tarry, comrades!

ÁNYA (*clasping her hands*). What beautiful things you say! (*A pause.*) Isn't it enchanting here to-day!

TROPHÍMOF. Yes, it's wonderful weather.

ÁNYA. What have you done to me, Peter? Why is it that I no longer love the cherry orchard as I did? I used to love it so tenderly; I thought there was no better place on earth than our garden.

TROPHÍMOF. All Russia is our garden. The earth is great and beautiful; it is full of wonderful places. (*A pause.*) Think, Ánya, your grandfather, your great-grandfather and all your ancestors were serf owners, owners of living souls. Do not human spirits look out at you from every tree in the orchard, from every leaf and every stem? Do you not hear human voices? . . . Oh! it is terrible. Your orchard frightens me. When I walk through it in the evening or at night, the rugged bark on the trees glows with a dim light, and the cherry trees seem to see all that happened a hundred and two hundred years ago in painful and oppressive dreams. Well, well, we have fallen at least two hundred years behind the times. We have achieved nothing at all as yet; we have not made up our minds how we stand with the past; we only philosophize, complain of boredom, or drink vodka. It is so plain that, before we can live in the present, we must first redeem the past, and have done with it; and it is only by suffering that we can redeem it, only by strenuous, unremitting toil. Understand that, Ánya.

ÁNYA. The house we live in has long since ceased to be our house; and I shall go away, I give you my word.

TROPHÍMOF. If you have the household keys, throw them in the well and go away. Be free, be free as the wind.

ÁNYA (*enthusiastically*). How beautifully you put it!

TROPHÍMOF. Believe what I say, Ánya; believe what I say. I'm not thirty yet; I am still young, still a student; but what I have been through! I am hungry as the winter; I am sick, anxious, poor as a beggar. Fate has tossed me hither and thither; I have been everywhere, everywhere. But wherever I have been, every minute, day and night, my soul has been full of mysterious anticipations. I feel the approach of happiness, Ánya; I see it coming. . . .

ÁNYA (*pensively*). The moon is rising.

(EPHIKHÓDOF *is heard still playing the same sad tune on his guitar. The moon rises. Somewhere beyond the poplar trees,* BARBARA *is heard calling for* ÁNYA: "*Ánya, where are you?*")

TROPHÍMOF. Yes, the moon is rising. (*A pause.*) There it is, there is happiness; it is coming towards us, nearer and nearer; I can hear the sound of its footsteps. . . . And if we do not see it, if we do not know it, what does it matter? Others will see it.

BARBARA (*without*). Ánya? Where are you?

TROPHÍMOF. There's Barbara again! (*Angrily.*) It really is too bad!

ÁNYA. Never mind. Let us go down to the river. It's lovely there.

TROPHÍMOF. Come on!

(*Exeunt* ÁNYA *and* TROPHÍMOF.)

BARBARA (*without*). Ánya! Ánya!

ACT III

(*A sitting-room separated by an arch from a big drawing-room behind. Chandelier lighted. The Jewish band mentioned in Act II is heard playing on the landing. Evening. In the drawing-room they are dancing the grand rond.* SIMEÓNOF-PÍSHTCHIK *is heard crying,* "Promenade à une paire!")
   (*The dancers come down into the sitting-room. The first pair consists of* PÍSHTCHIK *and* CHARLOTTE; *the second of* TROPHÍMOF *and* MADAME RANÉVSKY; *the third of* ÁNYA *and the* POST-OFFICE OFFICIAL; *the fourth of* BARBARA *and the* STATIONMASTER, *etc., etc.* BARBARA *is crying softly and wipes away the tears as she dances. In the last pair comes* DUNYÁSHA. *They cross the sitting-room.*)

PÍSHTCHIK.   "Grand rond, balancez . . . Les cavaliers à genou et remerciez vos dames."
   (FIRS *in evening dress carries seltzer water across on a tray.* PÍSHTCHIK *and* TROPHÍMOF *come down into the sitting-room.*)

PÍSHTCHIK.   I am a full-blooded man; I've had two strokes already; it's hard work dancing, but, as the saying goes. "If you run with the pack, bark or no, but anyway wag your tail." I'm as strong as a horse. My old father, who was fond of his joke, rest his soul, used to say, talking of our pedigree, that the ancient stock of the Simeónof-Píshtchiks was descended from that very horse that Caligula made a senator. . . . (*Sitting.*) But the worst of it is, I've got no money. A hungry dog believes in nothing but meat. (*Snoring and waking up again at once.*) I'm just the same . . . It's nothing but money, money, with me.

TROPHÍMOF.   Yes, it's quite true, there is something horse-like about your build.

PÍSHTCHIK.   Well, well . . . a horse is a jolly creature . . . you can sell a horse.
   (*A sound of billiards being played in the next room.* BARBARA *appears in the drawing-room beyond the arch.*)

TROPHÍMOF (*teasing her*).   Madame Lopákhin! Madame Lopákhin.

BARBARA (*angrily*).   Mouldy gentleman!

TROPHÍMOF.   Yes, I'm a mouldy gentleman, and I'm proud of it.

BARBARA (*bitterly*).   We've hired the band, but where's the money to pay for it? (*Exit* BARBARA.)

TROPHÍMOF (*to* PÍSHTCHIK).   If the energy which you have spent in the course of your whole life in looking for money to pay the interest on your loans had been diverted to some other purpose, you would have had enough of it, I dare say, to turn the world upside down.

PÍSHTCHIK.   Nietzsche the philosopher, a very remarkable man, very famous, a man of gigantic intellect, says in his works that its quite right to forge bank notes.

TROPHÍMOF.   What, have you read Nietzsche?

PÍSHTCHIK.   Well . . . Dáshenka told me. . . . But I'm in such a hole, I'd forge 'em for twopence. I've got to pay thirty-one pounds the day after to-morrow. . . . I've got thirteen pounds already. (*Feeling his pockets; alarmed.*) My money's gone! I've lost my money! (*Crying.*) Where's my money got to? (*Joyfully.*) Here it is, inside the lining. . . . It's thrown me all in a perspiration.

(*Enter* MADAME RANÉVSKY *and* CHARLOTTE.)

MADAME RANÉVSKY (*humming a lezginka*). Why is Leoníd so long? What can he be doing in the town? (*To* DUNYÁSHA.) Dunyásha, ask the musicians if they'll have some tea.

TROPHÍMOF. The sale did not come off, in all probability.

MADAME RANÉVSKY. It was a stupid day for the musicians to come; it was a stupid day to have this dance. . . . Well, well, it doesn't matter. . . . (*She sits down and sings softly to herself.*)

CHARLOTTE (*giving* PÍSHTCHIK *a pack of cards*). Here is a pack of cards. Think of any card you like.

PÍSHTCHIK. I've thought of one.

CHARLOTTE. Now shuffle the pack. That's all right. Give them here, oh, most worthy Mr. Píshtchik. Ein, zwei, drei! Now look and you'll find it in your side pocket.

PÍSHTCHIK (*taking a card from his side pocket*). The Eight of Spades! You're perfectly right. (*Astonished.*) Well, I never!

CHARLOTTE (*holding the pack on the palm of her hand, to* TROPHÍMOF). Say quickly, what's the top card?

TROPHÍMOF. Well, say the Queen of Spades.

CHARLOTTE. Right! (*To* PÍSHTCHIK.) Now, then, what's the top card?

PÍSHTCHIK. Ace of Hearts.

CHARLOTTE. Right! (*She claps her hands; the pack of cards disappears.*) What a beautiful day we've been having.

(*A mysterious female* VOICE *answers her as if from under the floor:* "Yes, indeed, a charming day, mademoiselle.")

CHARLOTTE. You are my beautiful ideal.

THE VOICE. "*I think you also ferry peautiful, mademoiselle.*"

STATIONMASTER (*applauding*). Bravo, Miss Ventriloquist!

PÍSHTCHIK (*astonished*). Well, I never! Bewitching Charlotte Ivánovna, I'm head over ears in love with you.

CHARLOTTE. In love! (*Shrugging her shoulders.*) Are you capable of love? Guter Mensch, aber schlechter Musikant!

TROPHÍMOF (*slapping* PÍSHTCHIK *on the shoulder*). You old horse!

CHARLOTTE. Now, attention, please; one more trick. (*Taking a shawl from a chair.*) Now here's a shawl, and a very pretty shawl; I'm going to sell this very pretty shawl. (*Shaking it.*) Who'll buy? who'll buy?

PÍSHTCHIK (*astonished*). Well, I never!

CHARLOTTE. Ein, zwei, drei! (*She lifts the shawl quickly; behind it stands* ÁNYA, *who drops a curtsy, runs to her mother, kisses her, then runs up into the drawing-room amid general applause.*)

Lezginka. A lively Caucasian dance in two-four-time, popularized by Glinka, and by Rubinstein in his opera, *Demon.*

MADAME RANÉVSKY (*applauding*). Bravo! bravo!

CHARLOTTE. Once more. Ein, zwei, drei! (*She lifts up the shawl; behind it stands* BARBARA, *bowing.*)

PÍSHTCHIK (*astonished*). Well, I never!

CHARLOTTE. That's all. (*She throws the shawl over* PÍSHTCHIK, *makes a curtsy and runs up into the drawing-room.*)

PÍSHTCHIK (*hurrying after her*). You little rascal . . . there's a girl for you, there's a girl. . . . (*Exit.*)

MADAME RANÉVSKY. And still no sign of Leoníd. What he's doing in the town so long, I can't understand. It must be all over by now; the property's sold; or the auction never came off; why does he keep me in suspense so long?

BARBARA (*trying to soothe her*). Uncle has bought it, I am sure of that.

TROPHÍMOF (*mockingly*). Of course he has.

BARBARA. Grannie sent him a power of attorney to buy it in her name and transfer the mortgage. She's done it for Ánya's sake. I'm perfectly sure that Heaven will help us and uncle will buy it.

MADAME RANÉVSKY. Your Yaroslav grannie sent fifteen hundred pounds to buy the property in her name—she doesn't trust us—but it wouldn't be enough even to pay the interest. (*Covering her face with her hands.*) My fate is being decided to-day, my fate. . . .

TROPHÍMOF (*teasing* BARBARA). Madame Lopákhin!

BARBARA (*angrily*). Perpetual Student! He's been sent down twice from the University.

MADAME RANÉVSKY. Why do you get angry, Barbara? He calls you Madame Lopákhin for fun. Why not? You can marry Lopákhin if you like; he's a nice, interesting man; you needn't if you don't; nobody wants to force you, my pet.

BARBARA. I take it very seriously, mamma, I must confess. He's a nice man and I like him.

MADAME RANÉVSKY. Then marry him. There's no good putting it off that I can see.

BARBARA. But, mamma, I can't propose to him myself. For two whole years everybody's been talking about him to me, every one; but he either says nothing or makes a joke of it. I quite understand. He's making money; he's always busy; he can't be bothered with me. If I only had some money, even a little, even ten pounds, I would give everything up and go right away. I would go into a nunnery.

TROPHÍMOF (*mocking*). What bliss!

BARBARA (*to* TROPHÍMOF). A student ought to be intelligent. (*In a gentler voice, crying.*) How ugly you've grown, Peter; how old you've grown! (*She stops crying; to* MADAME RANÉVSKY.) But I can't live without work, mamma. I must have something to do every minute of the day.

(*Enter* YÁSHA.)

YÁSHA (*trying not to laugh*). Ephikhódof has broken a billiard cue. (*Exit* YÁSHA.)

BARBARA. What's Ephikhódof doing here? Who gave him leave to play billiards? I don't understand these people. (*Exit* BARBARA.)

MADAME RANÉVSKY. Don't tease her, Peter. Don't you see that she's unhappy enough already.

TROPHÍMOF. I wish she wouldn't be so fussy, always meddling in other people's affairs. The whole summer she's given me and Ánya no peace; she is afraid we'll work up a romance between us. What business is it of hers? I'm sure I never gave her any grounds; I'm not likely to be so commonplace. We are above love!

MADAME RANÉVSKY. Then I suppose I must be beneath love. (*Deeply agitated.*) Why doesn't Leoníd come? Oh, if only I knew whether the property's sold or not! It seems such an impossible disaster, that I don't know what to think. . . . I'm bewildered . . . I shall burst out screaming, I shall do something idiotic. Save me, Peter; say something to me, say something. . . .

TROPHÍMOF. Whether the property is sold to-day or whether it's not sold, surely it's all one? It's all over with it long ago; there's no turning back; the path is overgrown. Be calm, dear Lyubóf Andréyevna. You mustn't deceive yourself any longer; for once you must look the truth straight in the face.

MADAME RANÉVSKY. What truth? You can see what's truth, and what's untruth, but I seem to have lost the power of vision; I see nothing. You settle every important question so boldly; but tell me, Peter, isn't that because you're young, because you have never solved any question of your own as yet by suffering? You look boldly ahead; isn't it only that you don't see or divine anything terrible in the future; because life is still hidden from your young eyes? You are bolder, honester, deeper than we are, but reflect, show me just a finger's breadth of consideration, take pity on me. Don't you see? I was born here, my father and mother lived here, and my grandfather; I love this house; without the cherry orchard my life has no meaning for me, and if it *must* be sold, then for Heaven's sake, sell me too! (*Embracing* TROPHÍMOF *and kissing him on the forehead.*) My little boy was drowned here. (*Crying.*) Be gentle with me, dear, kind Peter.

TROPHÍMOF. You know I sympathize with all my heart.

MADAME RANÉVSKY. Yes, yes, but you ought to say it somehow differently. (*Taking out her handkerchief and dropping a telegram.*) I am so wretched to-day, you can't imagine! All this noise jars on me, my heart jumps at every sound. I tremble all over; but I can't shut myself up; I am afraid of the silence when I'm alone. Don't be hard on me, Peter; I love you like a son. I would gladly let Ánya marry you, I swear it; but you must work, Peter; you must get your degree. You do nothing; Fate tosses you about from place to place; and that's not right. It's true what I say, isn't it? And you must do something to your beard to make it grow better. (*Laughing.*) I can't help laughing at you.

TROPHÍMOF (*picking up the telegram*). I don't wish to be an Adonis.

MADAME RANÉVSKY. It's a telegram from Paris. I get them every day.

One came yesterday, another to-day. That savage is ill again; he's in a bad way. . . . He asks me to forgive him, he begs me to come; and I really ought to go to Paris and be with him. You look at me sternly; but what am I to do, Peter? What as I to do? He's ill, he's lonely, he's unhappy. Who is to look after him? Who is to keep him from doing stupid things? Who is to give him his medicine when it's time? After all, why should I be ashamed to say it? I love him, that's plain. I love him, I love him. . . . My love is like a stone tied round my neck; it's dragging me down to the bottom; but I love my stone. I can't live without it. (*Squeezing* TROPHÍMOF's *hand.*) Don't think ill of me, Peter; don't say anything! Don't say anything!

TROPHÍMOF (*crying*).   Forgive my bluntness, for Heaven's sake; but the man has simply robbed you.

MADAME RANÉVSKY.   No, no, no! (*Stopping her ears.*) You mustn't say that!

TROPHÍMOF.   He's a rascal; everybody sees it but yourself; he's a petty rascal, a ne'er-do-well . . .

MADAME RANÉVSKY (*angry but restrained*).   You're twenty-six or twenty-seven, and you're still a Lower School boy!

TROPHÍMOF.   Who cares?

MADAME RANÉVSKY.   You ought to be a man by now; at your age you ought to understand people who love. You ought to love some one yourself, you ought to be in love! (*Angrily.*) Yes, yes! It's not purity with you; it's simply you're a smug, a figure of fun, a freak. . . .

TROPHÍMOF (*horrified*).   What does she say?

MADAME RANÉVSKY.   "I am above love!" You're not above love; you're simply what Firs calls a "job-lot." At your age you ought to be ashamed not to have a mistress!

TROPHÍMOF (*aghast*).   This is awful! What does she say? (*Going quickly up into the drawing-room, clasping his head with his hands.*) This is something awful! I can't stand it; I'm off . . . (*Exit, but returns at once.*) All is over between us! (*Exit to landing.*)

MADAME RANÉVSKY (*calling after him*).   Stop, Peter! Don't be ridiculous; I was only joking! Peter!

(TROPHÍMOF *is heard on the landing going quickly down the stairs, and suddenly falling down them with a crash.* ÁNYA *and* BARBARA *scream. A moment later the sound of laughter.*)

MADAME RANÉVSKY.   What has happened?

(ÁNYA *runs in.*)

ÁNYA (*laughing*).   Peter's tumbled downstairs. (*She runs out again.*)

MADAME RANÉVSKY.   What a ridiculous fellow he is!

(*The* STATIONMASTER *stands in the middle of the drawing-room beyond the arch and recites Alexey Tolstoy's poem, "The Sinner." Everybody stops to listen, but after a few lines the sound of a waltz is heard from the landing and he breaks off. All dance.* TROPHÍMOF, ÁNYA, BARBARA, *and* MADAME RANÉVSKY *enter from the landing.*)

558 The Nature of Drama

MADAME RANÉVSKY. Come, Peter, come, you pure spirit. . . . I beg your pardon. Let's have a dance. (*She dances with* TROPHÍMOF. ÁNYA *and* BARBARA *dance.*)

(*Enter* FIRS, *and stands his walking-stick by the side door. Enter* YÁSHA *by the drawing-room; he stands looking at the dancers.*)

YÁSHA. Well, grandfather?

FIRS. I'm not feeling well. In the old days it was generals and barons and admirals that danced at our dances, but now we send for the Postmaster and the Stationmaster, and even they make a favor of coming. I'm sort of weak all over. The old master, their grandfather, used to give us all sealing wax, when we had anything the matter. I've taken sealing wax every day for twenty years and more. Perhaps that's why I'm still alive.

YÁSHA. I'm sick of you, grandfather. (*Yawning.*) I wish you'd die and have done with it.

FIRS. Ah! you . . . job-lot. (*He mumbles to himself.*)

(TROPHÍMOF *and* MADAME RANÉVSKY *dance beyond the arch and down into the sitting-room.*)

MADAME RANÉVSKY. Merci. I'll sit down. (*Sitting.*) I'm tired.

(*Enter* ÁNYA.)

ÁNYA (*agitated*). There was somebody in the kitchen just now saying that the cherry orchard was sold to-day.

MADAME RANÉVSKY. Sold? Who to?

ÁNYA. He didn't say who to. He's gone. (*She dances with* TROPHÍMOF. *Both dance up into the drawing-room.*)

YÁSHA. It was some old fellow chattering; a stranger.

FIRS. And still Leoníd Andréyitch doesn't come. He's wearing his light overcoat, *demi-saison;* he'll catch cold as like as not. Ah, young wood, green wood!

MADAME RANÉVSKY. This is killing me. Yásha, go and find out who it was sold to.

YÁSHA. Why, he's gone long ago, the old man. (*Laughs.*)

MADAME RANÉVSKY (*vexed*). What are you laughing at? What are you glad about?

YÁSHA. He's a ridiculous fellow is Ephikhódof. Nothing in him. Twenty-two misfortunes!

MADAME RANÉVSKY. Firs, if the property is sold, where will you go to?

FIRS. Wherever you tell me, there I'll go.

MADAME RANÉVSKY. Why do you look like that? Are you ill? You ought to be in bed.

FIRS (*ironically*). Oh, yes, I'll go to bed, and who'll hand the things around, who'll give orders? I've the whole house on my hands.

YÁSHA. Lyubóf Andréyevna! Let me ask a favor of you; be so kind; if you go to Paris again, take me with you, I beseech you. It's absolutely impossible for me to stay here. (*Looking about; sotto voce.*) What's the use of talking? You can see for yourself this is a barbarous country; the people have no morals; and the boredom! The food in the kitchen is something shocking, and on the top of it old Firs going about mumbling irrelevant nonsense. Take me back with you; be so kind!

(*Enter* Píshtchik.)

Píshtchik. May I have the pleasure . . . a bit of a waltz, charming lady? (Madame Ranévsky *takes his arm.*) All the same, enchanting lady, you must let me have eighteen pounds. (*Dancing.*) Let me have . . . eighteen pounds. (*Exeunt dancing through the arch.*)

Yásha (*singing to himself*).

"Oh, wilt thou understand
The turmoil of my soul?"

(*Beyond the arch appears a figure in gray tall hat and check trousers, jumping and waving its arms. Cries of "Bravo, Charlotte Ivánovna."*)

Dunyásha (*stopping to powder her face*). Mamselle Ánya tells me I'm to dance; there are so many gentlemen and so few ladies. But dancing makes me giddy and makes my heart beat, Firs Nikoláyevitch; and just now the gentleman from the postoffice said something so nice to me, oh so nice! It quite took my breath away.

(*The music stops.*)

Firs. What did he say to you?

Dunyásha. He said, "You are like a flower."

Yásha (*yawning*). Cad! (*Exit* Yásha.)

Dunyásha. Like a flower! I am so ladylike and refined, I dote on compliments.

Firs. You'll come to a bad end.

(*Enter* Ephikhódof.)

Ephikhódof. You are not pleased to see me, Avdótya Fyódorovna, no more than if I were some sort of insect. (*Sighing.*) Ah! Life! Life!

Dunyásha. What do you want?

Ephikhódof. Undoubtedly perhaps you are right. (*Sighing.*) But of course, if one regards it, so to speak, from the point of view, if I may allow myself the expression, and with apologies for my frankness, you have finally reduced me to a state of mind. I quite appreciate my destiny; every day some misfortune happens to me, and I have long since grown accustomed to it, and face my fortune with a smile. You have passed your word to me, and although I . . .

Dunyásha. Let us talk of this another time, if you please; but now leave me in peace. I am busy meditating. (*Playing with her fan.*)

Ephikhódof. Every day some misfortune befalls me, and yet if I may venture to say so, I meet them with smiles and even laughter.

(*Enter* Barbara *from the drawing-room.*)

Barbara (*to* Ephikhódof). Haven't you gone yet, Simeon? You seem to pay no attention to what you're told. (*To* Dunyásha.) You get out of here, Dunyásha. (*To* Ephikhódof.) First you play billiards and break a cue, and then you march about the drawing-room as if you were a guest!

Ephikhódof. Allow me to inform you that it's not your place to call me to account.

BARBARA. I'm not calling you to account; I'm merely talking to you. All you can do is to walk about from one place to another, without ever doing a stroke of work; and why on earth we keep a clerk at all Heaven only knows.

EPHIKHÓDOF (*offended*). Whether I work, or whether I walk, or whether I eat, or whether I play billiards is a question to be decided only by my elders and people who understand.

BARBARA (*furious*). How dare you talk to me like that! How dare you! I don't understand things, don't I? You clear out of here this minute! Do you hear me? This minute!

EPHIKHÓDOF (*flinching*). I must beg you to express yourself in genteeler language.

BARBARA (*beside herself*). You clear out this instant second! Out you go! (*Following him as he retreats towards the door.*) Twenty-two misfortunes! Make yourself scarce! Get out of my sight!

(*Exit* EPHIKHÓDOF.)

EPHIKHÓDOF (*without*). I shall lodge a complaint against you.

BARBARA. What! You're coming back, are you? (*Seizing the walking-stick left at the door by* FIRS.) Come on! Come on! Come on! I'll teach you! Are you coming? Are you coming? Then take that. (*She slashes with the stick.*)

(*Enter* LOPÁKHIN.)

LOPÁKHIN. Many thanks; much obliged.

BARBARA (*still angry, but ironical*). Sorry!

LOPÁKHIN. Don't mention it. I'm very grateful for your warm reception.

BARBARA. It's not worth thanking me for. (*She walks away, then looks round and asks in a gentle voice:*) I didn't hurt you?

LOPÁKHIN. Oh, no, nothing to matter. I shall have a bump like a goose's egg, that's all.

(*Voices from the drawing-room: "Lopákhin has arrived! Yermolái Alexéyitch!"*)

PÍSHTCHIK. Let my eyes see him, let my ears hear him! (*He and* LOPÁKHIN *kiss.*) You smell of brandy, old man. We're having a high time, too.

(*Enter* MADAME RANÉVSKY.)

MADAME RANÉVSKY. Is it you, Yermolái Alexéyitch? Why have you been so long? Where is Leoníd?

LOPÁKHIN. Leoníd Andréyitch came back with me. He's just coming.

MADAME RANÉVSKY (*agitated*). What happened? Did the sale come off? Tell me, tell me!

LOPÁKHIN (*embarrassed, afraid of showing his pleasure*). The sale was all over by four o'clock. We missed the train and had to wait till half-past eight. (*Sighing heavily.*) Ouf! I'm rather giddy. . . .

(*Enter* GÁYEF. *In one hand he carries parcels; with the other he wipes away his tears.*)

MADAME RANÉVSKY. What happened, Lénya? Come, Lénya? (*Impatiently, crying.*) Be quick, be quick, for Heaven's sake!

GÁYEF (*answering her only with an up-and-down gesture of the hand; to* FIRS, *crying*). Here, take these. . . . Here are some anchovies and Black Sea herrings. I've had nothing to eat all day. Lord, what I've been through! (*Through the open door of the billiard-room comes the click of the billiard balls and* YÁSHA's *voice: "Seven, eighteen!"* GÁYEF's *expression changes; he stops crying.*) I'm frightfully tired. Come and help me change, Firs. (*He goes up through the drawing-room,* FIRS *following.*)

PÍSHTCHIK. What about the sale? Come on, tell us all about it.

MADAME RANÉVSKY. Was the cherry orchard sold?

LOPÁKHIN. Yes.

MADAME RANÉVSKY. Who bought it?

LOPÁKHIN. I did. (*A pause.* MADAME RANÉVSKY *is overwhelmed at the news. She would fall to the ground but for the chair and table by her.* BARBARA *takes the keys from her belt, throws them on the floor in the middle of the sitting-room, and exit.*) I bought it. Wait a bit; don't hurry me; my head's in a whirl; I can't speak. . . . (*Laughing.*) When we got to the sale, Derigánof was there already. Leoníd Andréyitch had only fifteen hundred pounds, and Derigánof bid three thousand more than the mortgage right away. When I saw how things stood, I went for him and bid four thousand. He said four thousand five hundred. I said five thousand five hundred. He went up by five hundreds, you see, and I went up by thousands. . . . Well, it was soon over. I bid nine thousand more than the mortgage, and got it; and now the cherry orchard is mine! Mine! (*Laughing.*) Heavens alive! Just think of it! The cherry orchard is mine! Tell me that I'm drunk; tell me that I'm off my head; tell me that it's all a dream! . . . (*Stamping his feet.*) Don't laugh at me! If only my father and my grandfather could rise from their graves and see the whole affair, how their Yermolái, their flogged and ignorant Yermolái, who used to run about barefooted in the winter, how this same Yermolái had bought a property that hasn't its equal for beauty anywhere in the whole world! I have bought the property where my father and grandfather were slaves, where they weren't even allowed into the kitchen. I'm asleep, it's only a vision, it isn't real. . . . 'Tis the fruit of imagination, wrapped in the mists of ignorance. (*Picking up the keys and smiling affectionately.*) She's thrown down her keys; she wants to show that she's no longer mistress here. . . . (*Jingling them together.*) Well, well, what's the odds? (*The musicians are heard tuning up.*) Hey, musicians, play! I want to hear you. Come, every one, and see Yermolái Lopákhin lay his axe to the cherry orchard, come and see the trees fall down! We'll fill the place with villas; our grandsons and great-grandsons shall see a new life here. . . . Strike up, music!

(*The band plays.* MADAME RANÉVSKY *sinks into a chair and weeps bitterly.*)

LOPÁKHIN (*reproachfully*). Oh, why, why, didn't you listen to me? You can't put the clock back now, poor dear. (*Crying.*) Oh, that all this were past and over! Oh, that our unhappy topsy-turvy life were changed!

PÍSHTCHIK (*taking him by the arm, sotto voce*). She's crying. Let's go into the drawing-room and leave her alone to . . . Come on. (*Taking him by the arm, and going up toward the drawing-room.*)

LOPÁKHIN. What's up? Play your best, musicians! Let everything be as I want. (*Ironically.*) Here comes the new squire, the owner of the cherry orchard! (*Knocking up by accident against a table and nearly throwing down the candelabra.*) Never mind, I can pay for everything!

(*Exit with* PÍSHTCHIK. *Nobody remains in the drawing-room or sitting-room except* MADAME RANÉVSKY, *who sits huddled together, weeping bitterly. The band plays softly.*)

(*Enter* ÁNYA *and* TROPHÍMOF *quickly.* ÁNYA *goes to her mother and kneels before her.* TROPHÍMOF *stands in the entry to the drawing-room.*)

ÁNYA. Mamma! Are you crying, mamma? My dear, good, sweet mamma! Darling, I love you! I bless you! The cherry orchard is sold; it's gone; it's quite true, it's quite true. But don't cry, mamma, you've still got life before you, you've still got your pure and lovely soul. Come with me, darling; come away from here. We'll plant a new garden, still lovelier than this. You will see it and understand, and happiness, deep tranquil happiness will sink down on your soul, like the sun at even-tide, and you'll smile, mamma. Come, darling, come with me!

ACT IV

(*Same scene as Act I. There are no window curtains, no pictures. The little furniture left is stacked in a corner, as if for sale. A feeling of emptiness. By the door to the hall and at the back of the scene are piled portmanteaux, bundles, etc. The door is open and the voices of* BARBARA *and* ÁNYA *are audible.*)

(LOPÁKHIN *stands waiting.* YÁSHA *holds a tray with small tumblers full of champagne.* EPHIKHÓDOF *is tying up a box in the hall. A distant murmur of voices behind the scene; the* PEASANTS *have come to say good-bye.*)

GÁYEF (*without*). Thank you, my lads, thank you.

YÁSHA. The common people have come to say good-bye. I'll tell you what I think, Yermolái Alexéyitch; they're good fellows but rather stupid. (*The murmur of voices dies away.*)

(*Enter* MADAME RANÉVSKY *and* GÁYEF *from the hall. She is not crying, but she is pale, her face twitches, she cannot speak.*)

GÁYEF. You gave them your purse, Lyuba. That was wrong, very wrong!

MADAME RANÉVSKY. I couldn't help it. I couldn't help it! (*Exeunt both.*)

LOPÁKHIN (*calling after them through the doorway*). Please come here! Won't you come here? Just a glass to say good-bye. I forgot to bring any from the town, and could only raise one bottle at the station.

Come along. (*A pause.*) What, won't you have any? (*Returning from the door.*) If I'd known, I wouldn't have bought it. I shan't have any either. (YÁSHA *sets the tray down carefully on a chair.*) Drink it yourself, Yásha.

YÁSHA.   Here's to our departure! Good luck to them that stay! (*Drinking.*) This isn't real champagne, you take my word for it.

LOPÁKHIN.   Sixteen shillings a bottle. (*A pause.*) It's devilish cold in here.

YÁSHA.   The fires weren't lighted to-day; we're all going away. (*He laughs.*)

LOPÁKHIN.   What are you laughing for?

YÁSHA.   Just pleasure.

LOPÁKHIN.   Here we are in October, but it's as calm and sunny as summer. Good building weather. (*Looking at his watch and speaking off.*) Don't forget that there's only forty-seven minutes before the train goes. You must start for the station in twenty minutes. Make haste.

(*Enter* TROPHÍMOF *in an overcoat, from out of doors.*)

TROPHÍMOF.   I think it's time we were off. The carriages are round. What the deuce has become of my goloshes? I've lost 'em. (*Calling off.*) Ánya, my goloshes have disappeared. I can't find them anywhere!

LOPÁKHIN.   I've got to go to Kharkof. I'll start in the same train with you. I'm going to spend the winter at Kharkof. I've been loafing about all this time with you people, eating my head off for want of work. I can't live without work, I don't know what to do with my hands; they dangle about as if they didn't belong to me.

TROPHÍMOF.   Well, we're going now, and you'll be able to get back to your beneficent labors.

LOPÁKHIN.   Have a glass.

TROPHÍMOF.   Not for me.

LOPÁKHIN.   Well, so you're off to Moscow?

TROPHÍMOF.   Yes, I'll see them into the town, and go on to Moscow to-morrow.

LOPÁKHIN.   Well, well, . . . I suppose the professors haven't started their lectures yet; they're waiting till you arrive.

TROPHÍMOF.   It's no affair of yours.

LOPÁKHIN.   How many years have you been up at the University?

TROPHÍMOF.   Try and think of some new joke; this one's getting a bit flat. (*Looking for his goloshes.*) Look here, I dare say we shan't meet again, so let me give you a bit of advice as a keepsake: Don't flap your hands about! Get out of the habit of flapping. Building villas, prophesying that villa residents will turn into small freeholders, all that sort of thing is flapping, too. Well, when all's said and done, I like you. You have thin, delicate, artist fingers; you have a delicate artist soul.

LOPÁKHIN (*embracing him*).   Good-bye, old chap. Thank you for everything. Take some money off me for the journey if you want it.

TROPHÍMOF.   What for? I don't want it.

LOPÁKHIN.   But you haven't got any.

TROPHÍMOF.   Yes, I have. Many thanks. I got some for a translation.
Here it is, in my pocket. (*Anxiously.*) I can't find my goloshes anywhere!
  BARBARA (*from the next room*).   Here, take your garbage away! (*She
throws a pair of goloshes on the stage.*)
  TROPHÍMOF.   What are you so cross about, Barbara? Humph! . . .
But those aren't *my* goloshes!
  LOPÁKHIN.   In the spring I sowed three thousand acres of poppy and
I have cleared four thousand pounds net profit. When my poppies were
in flower, what a picture they made! So you see, I cleared four thousand
pounds; and I wanted to lend you a bit because I've got it to spare.
What's the good of being stuck up? I'm a peasant. . . . As man to man . . .
  TROPHÍMOF.   Your father was a peasant; mine was a chemist; it
doesn't prove anything. (LOPÁKHIN *takes out his pocket-book with paper
money.*) Shut up, shut up. . . . If you offered me twenty thousand
pounds I would not take it. I am a free man; nothing that you value so
highly, all of you, rich and poor, has the smallest power over me; it's like
thistledown floating on the wind. I can do without you; I can go past you;
I'm strong and proud. Mankind marches forward to the highest truth, to
the highest happiness possible on earth, and I march in the foremost
ranks.
  LOPÁKHIN.   Will you get there?
  TROPHÍMOF.   Yes. (*A pause.*) I will get there myself, or I will show
others the way.
  (*The sound of axes hewing is heard in the distance.*)
  LOPÁKHIN.   Well, good-bye, old chap; it is time to start. Here we
stand swaggering to each other, and life goes by all the time without
heeding us. When I work for hours without getting tired, I get easy in
my mind and I seem to know why I exist. But God alone knows what
most of the people in Russia were born for. . . . Well, who cares? It
doesn't affect the circulation of work? They say Leoníd Andréyitch has
got a place; he's going to be in a bank and get six hundred pounds a year.
. . . He won't sit it out, he's too lazy.
  ÁNYA (*in the doorway*).   Mamma says, will you stop them cutting
down the orchard till she has gone?
  TROPHÍMOF.   Really, haven't you got tact enough for that? (*Exit
TROPHÍMOF by the hall.*)
  LOPÁKHIN.   Of course, I'll stop them at once.—What fools they are!
(*Exit after TROPHÍMOF.*)
  ÁNYA.   Has Firs been sent to the hospital?
  YÁSHA.   I told 'em this morning. They're sure to have sent him.
  ÁNYA (*to EPHIKHÓDOF, who crosses*).   Simeon Pantaléyitch, please find
out if Firs has been sent to the hospital.
  YÁSHA (*offended*).   I told George this morning. What's the good of
asking a dozen times?
  EPHIKHÓDOF.   Our centenarian friend, in my conclusive opinion, is
hardly worth tinkering; it's time he was despatched to his forefathers. I

can only say I envy him. (*Putting down a portmanteau on a bandbox and crushing it flat.*) There you are! I knew how it would be! (*Exit.*)

YÁSHA (*jeering*). Twenty-two misfortunes!

BARBARA (*without*). Has Firs been sent to the hospital?

ÁNYA. Yes.

BARBARA. Why didn't they take the note to the doctor?

ÁNYA. We must send it after them. (*Exit ÁNYA.*)

BARBARA (*from the next room*). Where's Yásha? Tell him his mother is here. She wants to say good-bye to him.

YÁSHA (*with a gesture of impatience*). It's enough to try the patience of a saint!

(DUNYÁSHA *has been busying herself with the luggage. Seeing* YÁSHA *alone, she approaches him.*)

DUNYÁSHA. You might just look once at me, Yásha. You are going away, you are leaving me. (*Crying and throwing her arms round his neck.*)

YÁSHA. What's the good of crying? (*Drinking champagne.*) In six days I shall be back in Paris. To-morrow we take the express, off we go, and that's the last of us! I can hardly believe it's true. *Vive la France!* This place don't suit me. I can't bear it . . . it can't be helped. I have had enough barbarism; I'm fed up. (*Drinking champagne.*) What's the good of crying? You be a good girl, and you'll have no call to cry.

DUNYÁSHA (*powdering her face and looking into a glass*). Write me a letter from Paris. I've been so fond of you, Yásha, ever so fond! I am a delicate creature, Yásha.

YÁSHA. Here's somebody coming. (*He busies himself with luggage, singing under his breath.*)

(*Enter* MADAME RANÉVSKY, GÁYEF, ÁNYA, *and* CHARLOTTE.)

GÁYEF. We'll have to be off; it's nearly time. (*Looking at* YÁSHA.) Who is it smells of red herring?

MADAME RANÉVSKY. We must take our seats in ten minutes. (*Looking round the room.*) Good-bye dear old house; good-bye, grandpapa! When winter is past and spring comes again, you will be here no more; they will have pulled you down. Oh, think of all these walls have seen! (*Kissing* ÁNYA *passionately.*) My treasure, you look radiant, your eyes flash like two diamonds. Are you happy?—very happy?

ÁNYA. Very, very happy. We're beginning a new life, mamma.

GÁYEF (*gaily*). She's quite right; everything's all right now. Till the cherry orchard was sold we were all agitated and miserable; but once the thing was settled finally and irrevocably, we all calmed down and got jolly again. I'm a bank clerk now; I'm a financier . . . red in the middle! And you, Lyuba, whatever you may say, you're looking ever so much better, not a doubt about it.

MADAME RANÉVSKY. Yes, my nerves are better; it's quite true. (*She is helped on with her hat and coat.*) I sleep well now. Take my things out, Yásha. We must be off. (*To* ÁNYA.) We shall soon meet again, darling. . . . I'm off to Paris; I shall live on the money your grandmother sent from Yaroslav to buy the property. God bless your grandmother! I'm afraid it won't last long.

ÁNYA. You'll come back very, very soon, won't you, mamma? I'm going to work and pass the examination at the Gymnase and get a place and help you. We'll read all sorts of books together, won't we, mamma? (*Kissing her mother's hands.*) We'll read in the long autumn evenings, we'll read heaps of books, and a new, wonderful world will open up before us. (*Meditating.*) . . . Come back, mamma!

MADAME RANÉVSKY. I'll come back, my angel. (*Embracing her.*)

(*Enter* LOPÁKHIN. CHARLOTTE *sings softly.*)

GÁYEF. Happy Charlotte, she's singing.

CHARLOTTE (*taking a bundle of rags, like a swaddled baby.*) Hush-a-bye, baby, on the tree-top . . . (*The baby answers,* "*Wah, wah.*") Hush, my little one, hush, my pretty one! ("*Wah, wah.*") You'll break your mother's heart. (*She throws the bundle down on the floor again.*) Don't forget to find me a new place, please. I can't do without it.

LOPÁKHIN. We'll find you a place, Charlotte Ivánovna, don't be afraid.

GÁYEF. Everybody's deserting us. Barbara's going. Nobody seems to want us.

CHARLOTTE. There's nowhere for me to live in the town. I'm obliged to go. (*Hums a tune.*) What's the odds?

(*Enter* PÍSHTCHIK.)

LOPÁKHIN. Nature's masterpiece!

PÍSHTCHIK (*panting*). Oy, oy, let me get my breath again! . . . I'm done up! . . . My noble friends! . . . Give me some water.

GÁYEF. Wants some money, I suppose. No, thank you; I'll keep out of harm's way. (*Exit.*)

PÍSHTCHIK. It's ages since I have been here, fairest lady. (*To* LOPÁKHIN.) You here? Glad to see you, you man of gigantic intellect. Take this; it's for you. (*Givivng* LOPÁKHIN *money.*) Forty pounds! I still owe you eighty-four.

LOPÁKHIN (*amazed, shrugging his shoulders*). It's like a thing in a dream! Where did you get it from?

PÍSHTCHIK. Wait a bit. . . . I'm hot. . . . A most remarkable thing! Some Englishmen came and found some sort of white clay on my land. (*To* MADAME RANÉVSKY.) And here's forty pounds for you, lovely, wonderful lady. (*Giving her money.*) The rest another time. (*Drinking water.*) Only just now a young man in the train was saying that some . . . some great philosopher advises us all to jump off roofs. . . . Jump, he says, and there's an end of it. (*With an astonished air.*) Just think of that! More water!

LOPÁKHIN. Who were the Englishmen?

PÍSHTCHIK. I leased them the plot with the clay on it for twenty-four years. But I haven't any time now . . . I must be getting on. I must go to Znoikof's, to Kardamónof's. . . . I owe everybody money. (*Drinking.*) Good-bye to every one; I'll look in on Thursday.

MADAME RANÉVSKY. We're just moving into town, and to-morrow I go abroad.

PÍSHTCHIK. What! (*Alarmed.*) What are you going into town for? Why, what's happened to the furniture? . . . Trunks? . . . Oh, it's all right. (*Crying.*) It's all right. People of powerful intellect . . . those Englishmen. It's all right. Be happy . . . God be with you . . . it's all right. Everything in this world has to come to an end. (*Kissing* MADAME RANÉVSKY's *hand.*) If ever the news reaches you that *I* have come to an end, give a thought to the old . . . horse, and say, "Once there lived a certain Simeónof-Píshtchik, Heaven rest his soul." . . . Remarkable weather we're having. . . . Yes. . . . (*Goes out deeply moved. Returns at once and says from the doorway:*) Dáshenka sent her compliments. (*Exit.*)

MADAME RANÉVSKY. Now we can go. I have only two things on my mind. One is poor old Firs. (*Looking at her watch.*) We can still stay five minutes.

ÁNYA. Firs has ben sent to the hospital already, mamma. Yásha sent him off this morning.

MADAME RANÉVSKY. My second anxiety is Barbara. She's used to getting up early and working, and now that she has no work to do she's like a fish out of water. She has grown thin and pale and taken to crying, poor dear. . . . (*A pause.*) You know very well, Yermolái Alexéyitch, I always hoped . . . to see her married to you, and as far as I can see, you're looking out for a wife. (*She whispers to* ÁNYA, *who nods to* CHARLOTTE, *and both exeunt.*) She loves you; you like her; and I can't make out why you seem to fight shy of each other. I don't understand it.

LOPÁKHIN. I don't understand it either, to tell you the truth. It all seems so odd. If there's still time I'll do it this moment. Let's get it over and have done with it; without you there, I feel as if I should never propose to her.

MADAME RANÉVSKY. A capital idea! After all, it doesn't take more than a minute. I'll call her at once.

LOPÁKHIN. And here's the champagne all ready. (*Looking at the glasses.*) Empty; some one's drunk it. (YÁSHA *coughs.*) That's what they call lapping it up and no mistake!

MADAME RANÉVSKY (*animated*). Capital! We'll all go away. . . . *Allez*, Yásha. I'll call her. (*At the door.*) Barbara, leave all that and come here. Come along! (*Exeunt* MADAME RANÉVSKY *and* YÁSHA.)

LOPÁKHIN (*looking at his watch*). Yes.

(*A pause. A stifled laugh behind the door; whispering; at last enter* BARBARA.)

BARBARA (*examining the luggage*). Very odd; I can't find it anywhere . . .

LOPÁKHIN. What are you looking for?

BARBARA. I packed it myself, and can't remember. (*A pause.*)

LOPÁKHIN. Where are you going to-day, Varvára Mikháilovna?

BARBARA. Me? I'm going to the Ragulins. I'm engaged to go and keep house for them, to be housekeeper or whatever it is.

LOPÁKHIN. Oh, at Yáshnevo? That's about fifty miles from here. (*A pause.*) Well, so life in this house is over now.

BARBARA (*looking at the luggage*). Wherever can it be? Perhaps I put it in the trunk. . . . Yes, life here is over now; there won't be any more . . .

LOPÁKHIN. And I'm off to Kharkof at once . . . by the same train. A lot of business to do. I'm leaving Ephikhódof to look after this place. I've taken him on.

BARBARA. Have you?

LOPÁKHIN. At this time last year snow was falling already, if you remember; but now it's fine and sunny. Still, it's cold for all that. Three degrees of frost.

BARBARA. Were there? I didn't look. (*A pause.*) Besides, the thermometer's broken. (*A pause.*)

A VOICE (*at the outer door*). Yermolái Alexéyitch!

LOPÁKHIN (*as if he had only been waiting to be called*). I'm just coming! (*Exit* LOPÁKHIN *quickly.*)

(BARBARA *sits on the floor, puts her head on a bundle and sobs softly. The door opens and* MADAME RANÉVSKY *comes in cautiously.*)

MADAME RANÉVSKY. Well? (*A pause.*) We must be off.

BARBARA (*no longer crying, wiping her eyes*). Yes, it's time, mamma. I shall get to the Ragulins all right to-day, so long as I don't miss the train.

MADAME RANÉVSKY (*calling off*). Put on your things, Ánya.

(*Enter* ÁNYA, *then* GÁYEF *and* CHARLOTTE. GÁYEF *wears a warm overcoat with a hood. The servants and drivers come in.* EPHIKHÓDOF *busies himself about the luggage.*)

MADAME RANÉVSKY. Now we can start on our journey.

ÁNYA (*delighted*). We can start on our journey!

GÁYEF. My friends, my dear, beloved friends! Now that I am leaving this house forever, can I keep silence? Can I refrain from expressing those emotions which fill my whole being at such a moment?

ÁNYA (*pleadingly*). Uncle!

BARBARA. Uncle, what's the good?

GÁYEF (*sadly*). Double the red in the middle pocket. I'll hold my tongue.

(*Enter* TROPHÍMOF, *then* LOPÁKHIN.)

TROPHÍMOF. Come along, it's time to start.

LOPÁKHIN. Ephikhódof, my coat.

MADAME RANÉVSKY. I must sit here another minute. It's just as if I had never noticed before what the walls and ceilings of the house were like. I look at them hungrily, with such tender love . . .

GÁYEF. I remember, when I was six years old, how I sat in this window on Trinity Sunday, and watched father starting out for church.

MADAME RANÉVSKY. Has everything been cleared out?

LOPÁKHIN. . . . Apparently everything. (*To* EPHIKHÓDOF, *putting on his overcoat.*) See that everything's in order, Ephikhódof.

EPHIKHÓDOF (*in a hoarse voice*). You trust me, Yermolái Alexéyitch.

LOPÁKHIN. What's up with your voice?

EPHIKHÓDOF. I was just having a drink of water. I swallowed something.

YÁSHA (*contemptuously*). Cad!

MADAME RANÉVSKY. We're going, and not a soul will be left here.

LOPÁKHIN. Until the spring.

(BARBARA *pulls an umbrella out of a bundle of rugs, as if she were brandishing it to strike.* LOPÁKHIN *pretends to be frightened.*)

BARBARA. Don't be so silly! I never thought of such a thing.

TROPHÍMOF. Come, we'd better go and get in. It's time to start. The train will be in immediately.

BARBARA. There are your goloshes, Peter, by that portmanteau. (*Crying.*) What dirty old things they are!

TROPHÍMOF (*putting on his goloshes*). Come along.

GÁYEF (*much moved, afraid of crying*). The train . . . the station . . . double the red in the middle; doublette to pot the white in the corner. . . .

MADAME RANÉVSKY. Come on!

LOPÁKHIN. Is every one here? No one left in there? (*Locking the door.*) There are things stacked in there; I must lock them up. Come on!

ÁNYA. Good-bye, house! Good-bye, old life!

TROPHÍMOF. Welcome, new life!

(*Exit with* ÁNYA. BARBARA *looks round the room, and exit slowly. Exeunt* YÁSHA, *and* CHARLOTTE *with her dog.*)

LOPÁKHIN. Till the spring, then. Go on, everybody. So-long! (*Exit.*)

(MADAME RANÉVSKY *and* GÁYEF *remain alone. They seem to have been waiting for this, throw their arms around each other's necks and sob restrainedly and gently, afraid of being overheard.*)

GÁYEF (*in despair*). My sister! my sister!

MADAME RANÉVSKY. Oh, my dear, sweet, lovely orchard! My life, my youth, my happiness, farewell! Farewell!

ÁNYA (*calling gayly, without*). Mamma!

TROPHÍMOF (*gay and excited*). Aoo!

MADAME RANÉVSKY. One last look at the walls and the windows. . . . Our dear mother used to love to walk up and down this room.

GÁYEF. My sister! my sister!

ÁNYA (*without*). Mamma!

TROPHÍMOF (*without*). Aoo!

MADAME RANÉVSKY. We're coming.

(*Exeunt. The stage is empty. One hears all the doors being locked, and the carriages driving away. All is quiet. Amid the silence the thud of the axes on the trees echoes sad and lonely. The sound of footsteps.* FIRS *appears in the doorway, right. He is dressed, as always, in his long coat and white waistcoat; he wears slippers. He is ill.*)

---

doublette: If you make your ball hit the cushion and run across into a pocket, it is a double; if I hit the cushion myself and pot you on the rebound, it is a doublette.

Firs (*going to the door, left, and trying the handle*). Locked. They've gone. (*Sitting on the sofa.*) They've forgotten me. Never mind! I'll sit here. Leoníd Andréyitch is sure to put on his cloth coat instead of his fur. (*He sighs anxiously.*) He hadn't me to see. Young wood, green wood! (*He mumbles something incomprehensible.*) Life has gone by as if I'd never lived. (*Lying down.*) I'll lie down. There's no strength left in you; there's nothing, nothing. Ah, you . . . job-lot!

(*He lies motionless. A distant sound is heard, as if from the sky, the sound of a string breaking, dying away, melancholy. Silence ensues, broken only by the stroke of the axe on the trees far away in the cherry orchard.*)

QUESTIONS

1. Could the opening scene of the play be staged for comic effects? What interpretations and emphases would be required so to stage it? Which other scenes or episodes in the action are obviously and dominantly comic?

2. Each of the characters in the play has some degree of abnormality. With some of these, this amounts to definite ludicrousness. Point out the ludicrous traits of each of the main characters. Certain of the characters are at the same time made sympathetic. How?

3. Despite the comic incidents and character traits, there is a mood or atmosphere of nostalgia and even melancholy enveloping certain scenes and much of the action. Cite as many ways as you can discover by which Chekov creates this mood.

4. The plot is largely constructed out of what goes on inside the characters. Since the main characters are largely incapable of definitive decision, the plot does not obviously move forward through a series of antecedents and consequences as does the plot of *The Wild Duck*. Yet there are incidents arranged in the relation of antecedents to consequences. Point out the main examples. Does this arrangement determine the outcome of the action?

5. Does the play have a major complication, a crisis, and a resolution? If it does, trace these.

6. Since the characters are incapable of making basic discoveries and determinant decisions, they cannot bring about a reversal in their fortunes. Yet there are episodic discoveries throughout the play. Point out the chief examples.

7. One of the conditions necessary to Chekhov's conception in this play is the inability of the characters to adjust to change. How many instances of this inability can you find?

8. Certain critics have called this "a plotless play," which is an impossibility. Why? Do the analyses made in connection with the preceding questions throw light on what these critics mean by "a plotless play"?

9. What aspects of the nature of man were of chief interest to Chekhov in this play?

10. What conceptions do you find in the play of an order within the human universe?

SIX CHARACTERS
IN SEARCH OF
AN AUTHOR

Luigi Pirandello

Luigi Pirandello (1867–1936), Italy's greatest modern playwright, was born at Girgenti, Sicily, in 1867, and was educated at the Universities of Palermo, Rome, and Bonn. The loss of his family's fortune forced him to take a position as a professor in the Higher Normal School for Women in Rome, a position that irked him though he was forced by necessity to hold it from 1907 to 1923. Misfortunes dogged his heels through early manhood and middle age. His wife went insane after the birth of their third child. Unable to afford a private sanitorium and unwilling to send her to a state institution, he kept her in his house and looked after her for many years. In his youth he was a liberal socialist but later gave up his liberal beliefs. The discovery of the corruption of the government in Rome made him cynical about all government.

Pirandello began his career as a writer of cheerful poems and tales in the realistic style ("verismo"). In addition to many volumes of short stories, he wrote seven novels. Later in life, after he had turned from the realistic to the so-called school of the grotesque, which is somewhat similar to German expressionism, he gave up prose fiction for drama. A number of his early plays are dramatizations of short stories. In 1925 in Rome he founded his own theatre (*Teatro Odescalchi*) and toured with his company in Europe and America. His influence upon a disillusioned post-war generation was profound. In 1934 he was awarded the Nobel Prize for literature. His training in philosophy, and his acceptance of naturalistic principles of literature somewhat modified by his later use of the grotesque, are strongly reflected in all his plays. By the time of his death in 1936 he was one of the most celebrated of modern European playwrights.

Pirandello wrote over thirty plays, some in one act, and many revised or made into new pieces. His plays are as follows: *Scamandra* (1910), *Sicilian Limes* (1910), *The Vise* (1910), *If Not Thus* (1911; revised as *The Rights of Others*, 1915), *The Doctor's Duty* (1911), *Just Think, Giacomino* (1914), *The Pleasures of Honesty* (1914), *At The Gate*

(1914), *Cap and Bells* (1915), *Chee-Chee* (1915), *The Imbecile* (1915), *Liola* (1916), *Right You Are, If You Think So* (1916), *Grafting* (1917), *The Patient* (1918), *Each of Us His Own Part* (1918), *But It Is Not A Serious Affair* (1918), *Man, Beast, and Virtue* (1919), *All for the Best* (1920), *Signora Moreli, One and Two* (1920; revised as *Two in One*, 1922), *As Before and Better* (1920), *By Judgment of the Court* (1920), *Six Characters in Search of An Author* (1921), *Henry IV* (1922), *Naked* (1922), *The Life I Gave Thee* (1923), *The Man with a Flower in His Mouth* (1923), *Each in His Own Way* (1924), *The Consecration of Our Lord of the Ship* (1925), *The Jar* (1925), *The House with a Column* (1925), *Diana and la Tuda* (1926), *Friendship of Women* (1927), *The New Colony* (1927), *Lassarus* (1929), *One's or Nobody's* (1929), *As You Desire Me* (1930), *Tonight We Improvise* (1930), *Finding Oneself* (1932).

Many of Pirandello's plays, including *Six Characters in Search of an Author* (often called his best), deal with the problems of personality and the relativity of reality. He sees personality not as static and fixed, centering on a dominant, unchanging ego, but rather as a constantly changing series of roles which a man is called upon to play by his conception of himself and (equally) by other peoples' conceptions of him. A human being is not a fixed, ego-centered, and finished pattern but, chameleon like, changes with changing associates and environments. Characters created by artists are more stable and enduring than personalities in life, which constantly vary with growth, change, and conditions. Through change, the very appearance of reality is constantly seen in new aspects.

If man lacks a dominant, central ego, he cannot control his choices and his actions through the exercise of will; hence he cannot be held morally responsible for what he does. His life is ever changing; hence it cannot be completely and finally tragic. Pirandello therefore usually writes tragi-comedies or comedies. What happens in his plays may seem serious, even deeply distressing, to some of the characters while to others it appears ludicrous. Life to those emotionally involved may be movingly tragic, while to the detached it remains a charade or an intriguing paradox. Distressing as is the sordid story unfolded by the six characters (actually seven), it remains merely a play for the actors. Hence it raises profound but unanswerable questions about the nature of reality and of art.

Critics have said that this play represents the ultimate dissolution of the ego in modern drama, and there is truth in the assertion. And yet, if assertion of the ego is an act of will, where in literature can be found a stronger though paradoxical assertion of ego than in these seven characters willing themselves to come to life, argue an obstinate stage manager into letting them enact their story, and disputing with "real" human beings questions of reality and existence? Pirandello is a master of such paradoxes. Like Wilde and Shaw, he employs them for comic effects, but he employs them chiefly to raise questions about the nature of man and of reality.

CHARACTERS OF THE COMEDY IN THE MAKING

THE FATHER	THE SON
THE MOTHER	THE BOY } (*These two do*
THE STEPDAUGHTER	THE CHILD } *not speak*)
	MADAME PACE

ACTORS OF THE COMPANY

THE MANAGER	OTHER ACTORS AND ACTRESSES
LEADING LADY	PROPERTY MAN
LEADING MAN	PROMPTER
SECOND LADY	MACHINIST
LEAD	MANAGER'S SECRETARY
L'INGÉNUE	DOOR-KEEPER
JUVENILE LEAD	SCENE-SHIFTERS

DAYTIME: *The Stage of a Theater.*

ACT I

N. B. *The Comedy is without acts or scenes. The performance is interrupted once, without the curtain being lowered, when* THE MANAGER *and the chief characters withdraw to arrange the scenario. A second interruption of the action takes place when, by mistake, the stage hands let the curtain down.*

The spectators will find the curtain raised and the stage as it usually is during the daytime. It will be half dark, and empty, so that from the beginning the public may have the impression of an impromptu performance.

PROMPTER's *box and a small table and chair for* THE MANAGER.

Two other small tables and several chairs scattered about as during rehearsals.

The ACTORS and ACTRESSES of the company enter from the back of the stage:

First one, then another, then two together: nine or ten in all. They are about to rehearse a Pirandello play: Mixing It Up. Some of the company move off towards their dressing rooms. The PROMPTER who has the "book" under his arm, is waiting for THE MANAGER in order to begin the rehearsal.

The ACTORS and ACTRESSES, some standing, some sitting, chat and smoke. One perhaps reads a paper; another cons his part.

Finally, THE MANAGER enters and goes to the table prepared for him. His SECRETARY brings him his mail, through which he glances. The PROMPTER takes his seat, turns on a light, and opens the "book."

THE MANAGER (*throwing a letter down on the table*).   I can't see. (*To* PROPERTY MAN.) Let's have a little light, please!

PROPERTY MAN.   Yes sir, yes, at once. (*A light comes down on to the stage.*)

THE MANAGER (*clapping his hands*). Come along! Come along! Second act of *Mixing It Up*. (*Sits down.*)

(*The* ACTORS *and* ACTRESSES *go from the front of the stage to the wings, all except the three who are to begin the rehearsal.*)

THE PROMPTER (*reading the "book"*). "Leo Gala's house. A curious room serving as dining-room and study."

THE MANAGER (*to* PROPERTY MAN). Fix up the old red room.

PROPERTY MAN (*noting it down*) Red set. All right!

THE PROMPTER (*continuing to read from the "book"*). "Table already laid and writing desk with books and papers. Bookshelves. Exit rear to Leo's bedroom. Exit left to kitchen. Principal exit to right."

THE MANAGER (*energetically*). Well, you understand: The principal exit over there; here, the kitchen. (*Turning to* ACTOR *who is to play the part of Socrates.*) You make *your entrances and exits here*. (*To* PROPERTY MAN.) The baize doors at the rear, and curtains.

PROPERTY MAN (*noting it down*). Right-o!

PROMPTER (*reading as before*). "When the curtain rises, Leo Gala, dressed in cook's cap and apron, is busy beating an egg in a cup. Philip, also dressed as a cook, is beating another egg. Guido Venanzi is seated and listening."

LEADING MAN (*to* MANAGER). Excuse me, but must I absolutely wear a cook's cap?

THE MANAGER (*annoyed*). I imagine so. It says so there anyway. (*Pointing to the "book."*)

LEADING MAN. But it's ridiculous!

THE MANAGER (*annoyed*). I imagine so. It ridiculous? Ridiculous? Is it my fault if France won't send us any more good comedies, and we are reduced to putting on Pirandello's works, where nobody understands anything, and where the author plays the fool with us all? (*The* ACTORS *grin.* THE MANAGER *goes to* LEADING MAN *and shouts.*) Yes sir, you put on the cook's cap and beat eggs. Do you suppose that with all this egg-beating business you are on an ordinary stage? Get that out of your head. You represent the shell of the eggs you are beating! (*Laughter and comments among the* ACTORS.) Silence! and listen to my explanations, please! (*To* LEADING MAN.) "The empty form of reason without the fullness of instinct, which is blind"—You stand for reason, your wife is instinct. It's a mixing up of the parts, according to which you who act your own part become the puppet of yourself. Do you understand?

LEADING MAN. I'm hanged if I do.

THE MANAGER. Neither do I. But let's get on with it. It's sure to be a glorious failure anyway. (*Confidentially.*) But I say, please face three-quarters. Otherwise, what with the abstruseness of the dialogue, and the public that won't be able to hear you, the whole thing will go to hell. Come on! come on!

PROMPTER. Pardon sir, may I get into my box? There's a bit of a draught.

THE MANAGER. Yes, yes, of course!

(*At this point, the* DOOR-KEEPER *has entered from the stage door and advances towards* THE MANAGER'S *table, taking off his braided cap. During this maneuver, the* SIX CHARACTERS *enter, and stop by the door at back of stage, so that when the* DOOR-KEEPER *is about to announce their coming to* THE MANAGER, *they are already on the stage. A tenuous light surrounds them, almost as if irradiated by them—the faint breath of their fantastic reality.*

This light will disappear when they come forward towards the ACTORS. *They preserve, however, something of the dream lightness in which they seem almost suspended; but this does not detract from the essential reality of their forms and expressions.*

He who is known as THE FATHER *is a man of about 50: hair, reddish in color, thin at the temples; he is not bald, however; thick moustaches, falling over his still fresh mouth, which often opens in an empty and uncertain smile. He is fattish, pale; with an especially wide forehead. He has blue, oval-shaped eyes, very clear and piercing. Wears light trousers and a dark jacket. He is alternatively mellifluous and violent in his manner.*

THE MOTHER *seems crushed and terrified as if by an intolerable weight of shame and abasement. She is dressed in modest black and wears a thick widow's veil of crêpe. When she lifts this, she reveals a wax-like face. She always keeps her eyes downcast.*

THE STEPDAUGHTER *is dashing, almost impudent, beautiful. She wears mourning too, but with great elegance. She shows contempt for the timid half-frightened manner of the wretched* BOY (*14 years old, and also dressed in black*); *on the other hand, she displays a lively tenderness for her little sister,* THE CHILD (*about four*), *who is dressed in white, with a black silk sash at the waist.*

THE SON (*22*) *tall, severe in his attitude of contempt for* THE FATHER, *supercilious and indifferent to the* MOTHER. *He looks as if he had come on the stage against his will.*)

DOORKEEPER (*cap in hand*).   Excuse me, sir . . .

THE MANAGER (*rudely*).   Eh? What is it?

DOORKEEPER (*timidly*).   These people are asking for you, sir.

THE MANAGER (*furious*).   I am rehearsing, and you know perfectly well no one's allowed to come in during rehearsals! (*Turning to the* CHARACTERS.) Who are you, please? What do you want?

THE FATHER (*coming forward a little, followed by the others who seem embarrassed*).   As a matter of fact . . . we have come here in search of an author. . . .

THE MANAGER (*half angry, half amazed*).   An author? What author?

THE FATHER.   Any author, sir.

THE MANAGER.   But there's no author here. We are not rehearsing a new piece.

THE STEPDAUGHTER (*vivaciously*).   So much the better, so much the better! We can be your new piece.

AN ACTOR (*coming forward from the others*). Oh, do you hear that?

THE FATHER (*to* STEPDAUGHTER). Yes, but if the author isn't here . . . (*To* MANAGER.) . . . unless you would be willing . . .

THE MANAGER. You are trying to be funny.

THE FATHER. No, for Heaven's sake, what are you saying? We bring you a drama, sir.

THE STEPDAUGHTER. We may be your fortune.

THE MANAGER. Will you oblige me by going away? We haven't time to waste with mad people.

THE FATHER (*mellifluously*). Oh sir, you know well that life is full of infinite absurdities, which, strangely enough, do not even need to appear plausible, since they are true.

THE MANAGER. What the devil is he talking about?

THE FATHER. I say that to reverse the ordinary process may well be considered a madness: that is, to create credible situations, in order that they may appear true. But permit me to observe that if this be madness, it is the sole *raison d'être* of your profession, gentlemen. (THE ACTORS *look hurt and perplexed.*)

THE MANAGER (*getting up and looking at him*). So our profession seems to you one worthy of madmen then?

THE FATHER. Well, to make seem true that which isn't true . . . without any need . . . for a joke as it were . . . Isn't that your mission, gentlemen: to give life to fantastic characters on the stage?

THE MANAGER (*interpreting the rising anger of the* COMPANY.) But I would beg you to believe, my dear sir, that the profession of the comedian is a noble one. If today, as things go, the playwrights give us stupid comedies to play and puppets to represent instead of men, remember we are proud to have given life to immortal works here on these very boards! (*The* ACTORS, *satisfied, applaud their* MANAGER.)

THE FATHER (*interrupting furiously*). Exactly, perfectly, to living beings more alive than those who breathe and wear clothes: being less real perhaps, but truer! I agree with you entirely. (*The* ACTORS *look at one another in amazement.*)

THE MANAGER. But what do you mean? Before, you said . . .

THE FATHER. No, excuse me, I meant it for you, sir, who were crying out that you had no time to lose with madmen, while no one better than yourself knows that nature uses the instrument of human fantasy in order to pursue her high creative purpose.

THE MANAGER. Very well—but where does all this take us?

THE FATHER. Nowhere! It is merely to show you that one is born to life in many forms, in many shapes, as tree, or as stone, as water, as butterfly, or as woman. So one may also be born a character in a play.

THE MANAGER (*with feigned comic dismay*). So you and these other friends of yours have been born characters?

THE FATHER. Exactly, and alive as you see! (MANAGER *and* ACTORS *burst out laughing.*)

THE FATHER (*hurt*). I am sorry you laugh, because we carry in us a drama, as you can guess from this woman here veiled in black.

THE MANAGER (*losing patience at last and almost indignant*). Oh, chuck it! Get away please! Clear out of here! (*To* PROPERTY MAN.) For Heaven's sake, turn them out!

THE FATHER (*resisting*). No, no, look here, we . . .

THE MANAGER (*roaring*). We come here to work, you know.

LEADING ACTOR. One cannot let oneself be made such a fool of.

THE FATHER (*determined, coming forward*). I marvel at your incredulity, gentlemen. Are you not accustomed to see the characters created by an author spring to life in yourselves and face each other? Just because there is no "book" (*pointing to the* PROMPTER's *box*) which contains us, you refuse to believe . . .

THE STEPDAUGHTER (*advances towards* MANAGER, *smiling and coquettish*). Believe me, we are really six most interesting characters, sir; sidetracked however.

THE FATHER. Yes, that is the word! (*To* MANAGER *all at once.*) In the sense, that is, that the author who created us alive no longer wished, or was no longer able, materially to put us into a work of art. And this was a real crime, sir; because he who has had the luck to be born a character can laugh even at death. He cannot die. The man, the writer, the instrument of the creation will die, but his creation does not die. And to live for ever, it does not need to have extraordinary gifts or to be able to work wonders. Who was Sancho Panza? Who was Don Abbondio? Yet they live eternally because—live germs as they were—they had the fortune to find a fecundating matrix, a fantasy which could raise and nourish them: make them live for ever!

THE MANAGER. That is quite all right. But what do you want here, all of you?

THE FATHER. We want to live.

THE MANAGER (*ironically*). For Eternity?

THE FATHER. No, sir, only for a moment . . . in you.

AN ACTOR. Just listen to him!

LEADING LADY. They want to live, in us! . . .

JUVENILE LEAD (*pointing to the* STEPDAUGHTER). I've no objection, as far as that one is concerned!

THE FATHER. Look here! Look here! The comedy has to be made. (*To the* MANAGER.) But if you and your actors are willing, we can soon concert it among ourselves.

THE MANAGER (*annoyed*). But what do you want to concert? We don't go in for concerts here. Here we play dramas and comedies!

THE FATHER. Exactly! That is just why we have come to you.

THE MANAGER. And where is the "book"?

THE FATHER. It is in us! (*The* ACTORS *laugh.*) The drama is in us, and we are the drama. We are impatient to play it. Our inner passion drives us on to this.

THE STEPDAUGHTER (*disdainful, alluring, treacherous, full of impudence*). My passion, sir! Ah, if you only knew! My passion for him! (*Points to the* FATHER *and makes a pretence of embracing him. Then she breaks out into a loud laugh.*)

THE FATHER (*angrily*). Behave yourself! And please don't laugh in that fashion.

THE STEPDAUGHTER. With your permission, gentlemen, I, who am a two months' orphan, will show you how I can dance and sing. (*Sings and then dances* Prenez garde à Tchou-Thin-Tchou.)

> Les chinois sont un peuple malin,
> De Shangaî à Pékin,
> Ils ont mis des écriteaux partout:
> Prenez garde à Tchou-Thin-Tchou.

ACTORS and ACTRESSES.   Bravo! Well done! Tip-top!

THE MANAGER.   Silence! This isn't a café concert, you know! (*Turning to the* FATHER *in consternation.*) Is she mad?

THE FATHER.   Mad? No, she's worse than mad.

THE STEPDAUGHTER (*to* MANAGER). Worse? Worse? Listen! Stage this drama for us at once! Then you will see that at a certain moment I . . . when this little darling here . . . (*Takes the* CHILD *by the hand and leads her to the* MANAGER.) Isn't she a dear? (*Takes her up and kisses her.*) Darling! Darling! (*Puts her down again and adds feelingly.*) Well, when God suddenly takes this dear little child away from that poor mother there; and this imbecile here (*seizing hold of the* BOY *roughly and pushing him forward*) does the stupidest things, like the fool he is, you will see me run away. Yes, gentlemen, I shall be off. But the moment hasn't arrived yet. After what has taken place between him and me (*indicates the* FATHER *with a horrible wink*) I can't remain any longer in this society, to have to witness the anguish of this mother here for that fool . . . (*Indicates the* SON.) Look at him! Look at him! See how indifferent, how frigid he is, because he is the legitimate son. He despises me, despises him (*pointing to the* BOY), despises this baby here; because . . . we are bastards. (*Goes to the* MOTHER *and embraces her.*) And he doesn't want to recognize her as his mother—she who is the common mother of us all. He looks down upon her as if she were only the mother of us three bastards. Wretch! (*She says all this very rapidly, excitedly. At the word "bastards" she raises her voice, and almost spits out the final "Wretch!"*)

THE MOTHER (*to the* MANAGER, *in anguish*). In the name of these two little children, I beg you . . . (*She grows faint and is about to fall.*) Oh God!

THE FATHER (*coming forward to support her as do some of the* ACTORS). Quick, a chair, a chair for this poor widow!

THE ACTORS.   Is it true? Has she really fainted?

THE MANAGER.   Quick, a chair! Here!

(*One of the* ACTORS *brings a chair, the others proffer assistance. The*

MOTHER *tries to prevent the* FATHER *from lifting the veil which covers her face.*)

THE FATHER. Look at her! Look at her!

THE MOTHER. No, no; stop it please!

THE FATHER (*raising her veil*). Let them see you!

THE MOTHER (*rising and covering her face with her hands, in desperation*). I beg you, sir, to prevent this man from carrying out his plan which is loathsome to me.

THE MANAGER (*dumbfounded*). I don't understand at all. What is the situation? Is this lady your wife? (*To the* FATHER.)

THE FATHER. Yes, gentlemen: my wife!

THE MANAGER. But how can she be a widow if you are alive? (*The* ACTORS *find relief for their astonishment in a loud laugh.*)

THE FATHER. Don't laugh! Don't laugh like that, for Heaven's sake. Her drama lies just here in this: she has had a lover, a man who ought to be here.

THE MOTHER (*with a cry*). No! No!

THE STEPDAUGHTER. Fortunately for her, he is dead. Two months ago as I said. We are in mourning, as you see.

THE FATHER. He isn't here you see, not because he is dead. He isn't here—look at her a moment and you will understand—because her drama isn't a drama of the love of two men for whom she was incapable of feeling anything except possibly a little gratitude—gratitude not for me but for the other. She isn't a woman, she is a mother, and her drama—powerful sir, I assure you—lies, as a matter of fact, all in these four children she has had by two men.

THE MOTHER. I had them? Have you got the courage to say that I wanted them? (*To the* COMPANY.) It was his doing. It was he who gave me that other man, who forced me to go away with him.

THE STEPDAUGHTER. It isn't true.

THE MOTHER (*startled*). Not true, isn't it?

THE STEPDAUGHTER. No, it isn't true, it just isn't true.

THE MOTHER. And what can you know about it?

THE STEPDAUGHTER. It isn't true. Don't believe it. (*To* MANAGER.) Do you know why she says so? For that fellow there. (*Indicates the* SON.) She tortures herself, destroys herself on account of the neglect of that son there; and she wants him to believe that if she abandoned him when he was only two years old, it was because he (*indicates the* FATHER) made her do so.

THE MOTHER (*vigorously*). He forced me to it, and I call God to witness it. (*To the* MANAGER.) Ask him (*indicates the* FATHER) if it isn't true. Let him speak. You (*to* DAUGHTER) are not in a position to know anything about it.

THE STEPDAUGHTER. I know you lived in peace and happiness with my father while he lived. Can you deny it?

THE MOTHER. No, I don't deny it . . .

THE STEPDAUGHTER.   He was always full of affection and kindness for you. (*To the* BOY, *angrily.*) It's true, isn't it? Tell them! Why don't you speak, you little fool?

THE MOTHER.   Leave the poor boy alone. Why do you want to make me appear ungrateful, daughter? I don't want to offend your father. I have answered him that I didn't abandon my house and my son through any fault of mine, nor from any wilful passion.

THE FATHER.   It is true. It was my doing.

LEADING MAN (*to the* COMPANY).   What a spectacle!

LEADING LADY.   We are the audience this time.

JUVENILE LEAD.   For once, in a way.

THE MANAGER (*beginning to get really interested*).   Let's hear them out. Listen!

THE SON.   Oh yes, you're going to hear a fine bit now. He will talk to you of the Demon of Experiment.

THE FATHER.   You are a cynical imbecile. I've told you so already a hundred times. (*To the* MANAGER.) He tries to make fun of me on account of this expression which I have found to excuse myself with.

THE SON (*with disgust*).   Yes, phrases! phrases!

THE FATHER.   Phrases! Isn't everyone consoled when faced with a trouble or fact he doesn't understand, by a word, some simple word, which tells us nothing and yet calms us?

THE STEPDAUGHTER.   Even in the case of remorse. In fact, especially then.

THE FATHER.   Remorse? No, that isn't true. I've done more than use words to quieten the remorse in me.

THE STEPDAUGHTER.   Yes, there was a bit of money too. Yes, yes, a bit of money. There were the hundred lire he was about to offer me in payment, gentlemen. . . . (*Sensation of horror among the* ACTORS.)

THE SON (*to the* STEPDAUGHTER).   This is vile.

THE STEPDAUGHTER.   Vile? There they were in a pale blue envelope on a little mahogany table in the back of Madame Pace's shop. You know Madame Pace—one of those ladies who attract poor girls of good family into their ateliers, under the pretext of their selling *robes et manteaux.*

THE SON.   And he thinks he has bought the right to tyrannize over us all with those hundred lire he was going to pay; but which, fortunately— note this, gentlemen—he had no chance of paying.

THE STEPDAUGHTER.   It was a near thing, though, you know! (*Laughs ironically.*)

THE MOTHER (*protesting*).   Shame, my daughter, shame!

THE STEPDAUGHTER.   Shame indeed! This is my revenge! I am dying to live that scene. . . . The room . . . I see it . . . Here is the window with the mantles exposed, there the divan, the looking-glass, a screen, there in front of the window the little mahogany table with the blue envelope containing one hundred lire. I see it. I see it. I could take hold of it . . . But you, gentlemen, you ought to turn your backs now: I am almost nude, you know. But I don't blush: I leave that to him. (*Indicating* FATHER.)

THE MANAGER.   I don't understand this at all.

THE FATHER.   Naturally enough. I would ask you, sir, to exercise your authority a little here, and let me speak before you believe all she is trying to blame me with. Let me explain.

THE STEPDAUGHTER.   Ah yes, explain it in your own way.

THE FATHER.   But don't you see that the whole trouble lies here. In words, words. Each one of us has within him a whole world of things, each man of us his own special world. And how can we ever come to an understanding if I put in the words I utter the sense and value of things as I see them; while you who listen to me must inevitably translate them according to the conception of things each one of you has within himself. We think we understand each other, but we never really do. Look here! This woman (*indicating the* MOTHER) takes all my pity for her as a specially ferocious form of cruelty.

THE MOTHER.   But you drove me away.

THE FATHER.   Do you hear her? I drove her away! She believes I really sent her away.

THE MOTHER.   You know how to talk, and I don't; but, believe me sir (*to* MANAGER), after he had married me . . . who knows why? . . . I was a poor insignificant woman . . .

THE FATHER.   But, good Heaven! it was just for your humility that I married you. I loved this simplicity in you. (*He stops when he sees she makes signs to contradict him, opens his arms wide in sign of desperation, seeing how hopeless it is to make himself understood.*) You see she denies it. Her mental deafness, believe me, is phenomenal, the limit (*touches his forehead*): deaf, deaf, mentally deaf! She has plenty of feeling. Oh yes, a good heart for the children; but the brain—deaf, to the point of desperation——!

THE STEPDAUGHTER.   Yes, but ask him how his intelligence has helped us.

THE FATHER.   If we could see all the evil that may spring from good, what should we do? (*At this point the* LEADING LADY *who is biting her lips with rage at seeing the* LEADING MAN *flirting with the* STEPDAUGHTER, *comes forward and says to the* MANAGER.)

LEADING LADY.   Excuse me, but are we going to rehearse today?

MANAGER.   Of course, of course; but let's hear them out.

JUVENILE LEAD.   This is something quite new.

L'INGENUE.   Most interesting!

LEADING LADY.   Yes, for the people who like that kind of thing. (*Casts a glance at* LEADING MAN.)

THE MANAGER (*to* FATHER).   You must please explain yourself quite clearly. (*Sits down.*)

THE FATHER.   Very well then: listen! I had in my service a poor man, a clerk, a secretary of mine, full of devotion, who became friends with her.

(*Indicating the* MOTHER.) They understood one another, were kindred souls in fact, without, however, the least suspicion of any evil existing. They were incapable even of thinking of it.

THE STEPDAUGHTER.   So he thought of it—for them!

THE FATHER.   That's not true. I meant to do good to them—and to myself, I confess, at the same time. Things had come to the point that I could not say a word to either of them without their making a mute appeal, one to the other, with their eyes. I could see them silently asking each other how I was to be kept in countenance, how I was to be kept quiet. And this, believe me, was just about enough of itself to keep me in a constant rage, to exasperate me beyond measure.

THE MANAGER.   And why didn't you send him away then—this secretary of yours?

THE FATHER.   Precisely what I did, sir. And then I had to watch this poor woman drifting forlornly about the house like an animal without a master, like an animal one has taken in out of pity.

THE MOTHER.   Ah yes! . . .

THE FATHER (*suddenly turning to the* MOTHER). It's true about the son anyway, isn't it?

THE MOTHER.   He took my son away from me first of all.

THE FATHER.   But not from cruelty. I did it so that he should grow up healthy and strong by living in the country.

THE STEPDAUGHTER (*pointing to him ironically*).   As one can see.

THE FATHER (*quickly*).   Is it my fault if he has grown up like this? I sent him to a wet nurse in the country, a peasant, as *she* did not seem to me strong enough, though she is of humble origin. That was, anyway, the reason I married her. Unpleasant all this may be, but how can it be helped? My mistake possibly, but there we are! All my life I have had these confounded aspirations towards a certain moral sanity. (*At this point the* STEPDAUGHTER *bursts out into a noisy laugh.*) Oh, stop it! Stop it! I can't stand it.

THE MANAGER.   Yes, please stop it, for Heaven's sake.

THE STEPDAUGHTER.   But imagine moral sanity from him, if you please —the client of certain ateliers like that of Madame Pace!

THE FATHER.   Fool! That is the proof that I am a man! This seeming contradiction, gentlemen, is the strongest proof that I stand here a live man before you. Why, it is just for this very incongruity in my nature that I have had to suffer what I have. I could not live by the side of that woman (*indicating the* MOTHER) any longer; but not so much for the boredom she inspired me with as for the pity I felt for her.

THE MOTHER.   And so he turned me out—.

THE FATHER.   —well provided for! Yes, I sent her to that man, gentlemen . . . to let her go free of me.

THE MOTHER.   And to free himself.

THE FATHER.   Yes, I admit it. It was also a liberation for me. But great evil has come of it. I meant well when I did it; and I did it more for her sake than mine. I swear it. (*Crosses his arms on his chest; then turns suddenly to the* MOTHER.) Did I ever lose sight of you until that other man carried you off to another town, like the angry fool he was? And on account of my pure interest in you . . . my pure interest, I repeat, that had no base motive in it . . . I watched with the tenderest concern the new family that grew up around her. She can bear witness to this. (*Points to the* STEPDAUGHTER.)

THE STEPDAUGHTER. Oh yes, that's true enough. When I was a kiddie, so so high, you know, with plaits over my shoulders and knickers longer than my skirts, I used to see him waiting outside the school for me to come out. He came to see how I was growing up.

THE FATHER. This is infamous, shameful!

THE STEPDAUGHTER. No. Why?

THE FATHER. Infamous! Infamous! (*Then excitedly to* MANAGER *explaining.*) After she (*indicating* MOTHER) went away, my house seemed suddenly empty. She was my incubus, but she filled my house. I was like a dazed fly alone in the empty rooms. This boy here (*indicating the* SON) was educated away from home, and when he came back, he seemed to me to be no more mine. With no mother to stand between him and me, he grew up entirely for himself, on his own, apart, with no tie of intellect or affection binding him to me. And then—strange but true—I was driven, by curiosity at first and then by some tender sentiment, towards her family, which had come into being through my will. The thought of her began gradually to fill up the emptiness I felt all around me. I wanted to know if she were happy in living out the simple daily duties of life. I wanted to think of her as fortunate and happy because far away from the complicated torments of my spirit. And so, to have proof of this, I used to watch that child coming out of school.

THE STEPDAUGHTER. Yes, yes. True. He used to follow me in the street and smiled at me, waved his hand, like this. I would look at him with interest, wondering who he might be. I told my mother, who guessed at once. (*The* MOTHER *agrees with a nod.*) Then she didn't want to send me to school for some days; and when I finally went back, there he was again —looking so ridiculous—with a paper parcel in his hands. He came close to me, caressed me, and drew out a fine straw hat from the parcel, with a bouquet of flowers—all for me!

THE MANAGER. A bit discursive this, you know!

THE SON (*contemptuously*). Literature! Literature!

THE FATHER. Literature indeed! This is life, this is passion!

THE MANAGER. It may be, but it won't act.

THE FATHER. I agree. This is only the part leading up. I don't suggest this should be staged. She (*pointing to the* STEPDAUGHTER), as you see, is no longer the flapper with plaits down her back—.

THE STEPDAUGHTER. —and the knickers showing below the skirt!

THE FATHER. The drama is coming now, sir; something new, complex, most interesting.

THE STEPDAUGHTER. As soon as my father died . . .

THE FATHER. —there was absolute misery for them. They came back here, unknown to me. Through her stupidity! (*Pointing to the* MOTHER.) It is true she can barely write her own name; but she could anyhow have got her daughter to write to me that they were in need. . . .

THE MOTHER. And how was I to divine all this sentiment in him?

THE FATHER. That is exactly your mistake, never to have guessed any of my sentiments.

THE MOTHER. After so many years apart, and all that had happened . . .

THE FATHER. Was it my fault if that fellow carried you away? It happened quite suddenly; for after he had obtained some job or other, I could find no trace of them; and so, not unnaturally, my interest in them dwindled. But the drama culminated unforeseen and violent on their return, when I was impelled by my miserable flesh that still lives . . . Ah! what misery, what wretchedness is that of the man who is alone and disdains debasing *liaisons!* Not old enough to do without women, and not young enough to go and look for one without shame. Misery? It's worse than misery; it's a horror; for no woman can any longer give him love; and when a man feels this . . . One ought to do without, you say? Yes, yes, I know. Each of us when he appears before his fellows is clothed in a certain dignity. But every man knows what unconfessable things pass within the secrecy of his own heart. One gives way to the temptation, only to rise from it again, afterwards, with a great eagerness to reestablish one's dignity, as if it were a tombstone to place on the grave of one's shame, and a monument to hide and sign the memory of our weaknesses. Everybody's in the same case. Some folks haven't the courage to say certain things, that's all!

THE STEPDAUGHTER. All appear to have the courage to do them though.

THE FATHER. Yes, but in secret. Therefore, you want more courage to say these things. Let a man but speak these things out, and folks at once label him a cynic. But it isn't true. He is like all the others, better indeed, because he isn't afraid to reveal with the light of the intelligence the red shame of human bestiality on which most men close their eyes so as not to see it. Woman—for example, look at her case! She turns tantalizing inviting glances on you. You seize her. No sooner does she feel herself in your grasp than she closes her eyes. It is the sign of her mission, the sign by which she says to man: "Blind yourself, for I am blind."

THE STEPDAUGHTER. Sometimes she can close them no more: when she no longer feels the need of hiding her shame to herself, but dry-eyed and dispassionately, sees only that of the man who has blinded himself without love. Oh, all these intellectual complications make me sick, disgust me—all this philosophy that uncovers the beast in man, and then seeks to save him, excuse him . . . I can't stand it, sir. When a man seeks to "simplify" life bestially, throwing aside every relic of humanity, every chaste aspiration, every pure feeling, all sense of ideality, duty, modesty, shame

. . . then nothing is more revolting and nauseous than a certain kind of remorse—crocodiles' tears, that's what it is.

THE MANAGER. Let's come to the point. This is only discussion.

THE FATHER. Very good, sir! But a fact is like a sack which won't stand up when it is empty. In order that it may stand up, one has to put into it the reason and sentiment which have caused it to exist. I couldn't possibly know that after the death of that man, they had decided to return here, that they were in misery, and that she (*pointing to the* MOTHER) had gone to work as a modiste, and at a shop of the type of that of Madame Pace.

THE STEPDAUGHTER. A real high-class modiste, you must know, gentlemen. In appearance, she works for the leaders of the best society; but she arranges matters so that these elegant ladies serve her purpose . . . without prejudice to other ladies who are . . . well . . . only so so.

THE MOTHER. You will believe me, gentlemen, that it never entered my mind that the old hag offered me work because she had her eye on my daughter.

THE STEPDAUGHTER. Poor mamma! Do you know, sir, what that woman did when I brought her back the work my mother had finished? She would point out to me that I had torn one of my frocks, and she would give it back to my mother to mend. It was I who paid for it, always I; while this poor creature here believed she was sacrificing herself for me and these two children here, sitting up at night sewing Madame Pace's robes.

THE MANAGER. And one day you met there . . .

THE STEPDAUGHTER. Him, him. Yes sir, an old client. There's a scene for you to play! Superb!

THE FATHER. She, the Mother arrived just then . . .

THE STEPDAUGHTER (*treacherously*). Almost in time!

THE FATHER (*crying out*). No, in time! in time! Fortunately I recognized her . . . in time. And I took them back home with me to my house. You can imagine now her position and mine: she, as you see her; and I who cannot look her in the face.

THE STEPDAUGHTER. Absurd! How can I possibly be expected—after that—to be a modest young miss, a fit person to go with his confounded aspirations for "a solid moral sanity"?

THE FATHER. For the drama lies all in this—in the conscience that I have, that each one of us has. We believe this conscience to be a single thing, but it is many-sided. There is one for this person, and another for that. Diverse consciences. So we have this illusion of being one person for all, of having a personality that is unique in all our acts. But it isn't true. We perceive this when, tragically perhaps, in something we do, we are as it were, suspended, caught up in the air on a kind of hook. Then we perceive that all of us was not in that act, and that it would be an atrocious injustice to judge us by that action alone, as if all our existence were summed up in that one deed. Now do you understand the perfidy of this girl? She surprised me in a place, where she ought not to have known me, just as I could not exist for her; and she now seeks to attach to me a reality such as I could never suppose I should have to assume for her in a shameful and fleeting moment of my life. I feel this above all else. And the drama, you will see, acquires a tremendous value from this point. Then there is the position of the others . . . his . . . (*Indicating the* SON.)

THE SON (*shrugging his shoulders scornfully*). Leave me alone! I don't come into this.

THE FATHER. What? You don't come into this?

THE SON. I've got nothing to do with it, and don't want to have; because you know well enough I wasn't made to be mixed up in all this with the rest of you.

THE STEPDAUGHTER. We are only vulgar folk! He is the fine gentleman. You may have noticed, Mr. Manager, that I fix him now and again with a look of scorn while he lowers his eyes—for he knows the evil he has done me.

THE SON (*scarcely looking at her*). I?

THE STEPDAUGHTER. You! you! I owe my life on the streets to you. Did you or did you not deny us, with your behavior, I won't say the intimacy of home, but even that mere hospitality which makes guests feel at their ease? We were intruders who had come to disturb the kingdom of your legitimacy. I should like to have you witness, Mr. Manager, certain scenes between him and me. He says I have tyrannized over everyone. But it was just his behavior which made me insist on the reason for which I had come into the house—this reason he calls "vile"—into his house, with my mother who is his mother too. And I came as mistress of the house.

THE SON. It's easy for them to put me always in the wrong. But imagine, gentlemen, the position of a son, whose fate it is to see arrive one day at his home a young woman of impudent bearing, a young woman who inquires for his father, with whom who knows what business she has. This young man has then to witness her return bolder than ever, accompanied by that child there. He is obliged to watch her treat his father in an equivocal and confidential manner. She asks money of him in a way that lets one suppose he must give it her, *must*, do you understand, because he has every obligation to do so.

THE FATHER. But I have, as a matter of fact, this obligation. I owe it to your mother.

THE SON. How should I know? When had I ever seen or heard of her? One day there arrive with her (*indicating* STEPDAUGHTER) that lad and this baby here. I am told: "This is *your* mother too, you know." I divine from her manner (*indicating* STEPDAUGHTER *again*) why it is they have come home. I had rather not say what I feel and think about it. I shouldn't even care to confess to myself. No action can therefore be hoped for from me in this affair. Believe me, MR. MANAGER, I am an "unrealized" character, dramatically speaking; and I find myself not at all at ease in their company. Leave me out of it, I beg you.

THE FATHER. What? It is just because you are so that . . .

THE SON. How do you know what I am like? When did you ever bother your head about me?

THE FATHER. I admit it. I admit it. But isn't that a situation in itself? This aloofness of yours which is so cruel to me and to your mother, who returns home and sees you almost for the first time grown up, who doesn't recognize you but knows you are her son . . . (*Pointing out the* MOTHER *to the* MANAGER.) See, she's crying!

THE STEPDAUGHTER (*angrily, stamping her foot*). Like a fool!

THE FATHER (*indicating* STEPDAUGHTER). She can't stand him you know. (*Then referring again to the* SON.) He says he doesn't come into the affair, whereas he is really the hinge of the whole action. Look at that lad who is always clinging to his mother, frightened and humiliated. It is on account of this fellow here. Possibly his situation is the most painful of all. He feels himself a stranger more than the others. The poor little chap feels mortified, humiliated at being brought into a home out of charity as it were. (*In confidence*)—: He is the image of his father. Hardly talks at all. Humble and quiet.

THE MANAGER. Oh, we'll cut him out. You've no notion what a nuisance boys are on the stage . . .

THE FATHER. He disappears soon, you know. And the baby too. She is the first to vanish from the scene. The drama consists finally in this: when that mother re-enters my house, her family born outside of it, and shall we say superimposed on the original, ends with the death of the little girl, the tragedy of the boy and the flight of the elder daughter. It cannot go on, because it is foreign to its surroundings. So after much torment, we three remain: I, the mother, that son. Then, owing to the disappearance of that extraneous family, we too find ourselves strange to one another. We find we are living in an atmosphere of mortal desolation which is the revenge, as he (*indicating* SON) scornfully said of the Demon of Experiment, that unfortunately hides in me. Thus, sir, you see when faith is lacking, it becomes impossible to create certain states of happiness, for we lack the necessary humility. Vaingloriously, we try to substitute ourselves for this faith, creating thus for the rest of the world a reality which we believe after their fashion, while, actually, it doesn't exist. For each one of us has his own reality to be respected before God, even when it is harmful to one's very self.

THE MANAGER. There is something in what you say. I assure you all this interests me very much. I begin to think there's the stuff for a drama in all this, and not a bad drama either.

THE STEPDAUGHTER (*coming forward*). When you've got a character like me.

THE FATHER (*shutting her up, all excited to learn the decision of the* MANAGER). You be quiet!

THE MANAGER (*reflecting, heedless of interruption*). It's new . . . hem . . . yes . . .

THE FATHER. Absolutely new!

THE MANAGER. You've got a nerve though, I must say, to come here and fling it at me like this . . .

THE FATHER. You will understand, sir, born as we are for the stage . . .

THE MANAGER. Are you amateur actors then?

THE FATHER. No, I say born for the stage, because . . .

THE MANAGER. Oh, nonsense. You're an old hand, you know.

THE FATHER. No sir, no. We act that rôle for which we have been cast, that rôle which we are given in life. And in my own case, passion itself, as usually happens, becomes a trifle theatrical when it is exalted.

THE MANAGER. Well, well, that will do. But you see, without an author . . . I could give you the address of an author if you like . . .

THE FATHER. No, no. Look here! You must be the author.

THE MANAGER. I? What are you talking about?

THE FATHER. Yes, you, you! Why not?

THE MANAGER. Because I have never been an author: that's why.

THE FATHER. Then why not turn author now? Everybody does it. You don't want any special qualities. Your task is made much easier by the fact that we are all here alive before you . . .

THE MANAGER. It won't do.

THE FATHER. What? When you see us live our drama . . .

THE MANAGER. Yes, that's all right. But you want someone to write it.

THE FATHER. No, no. Someone to take it down, possibly, while we play it, scene by scene! It will be enough to sketch it out at first, and then try it over.

THE MANAGER. Well . . . I am almost tempted. It's a bit of an idea. One might have a shot at it.

THE FATHER. Of course. You'll see what scenes will come out of it. I can give you one, at once . . .

THE MANAGER. By Jove, it tempts me. I'd like to have a go at it. Let's try it out. Come with me to my office. (*Turning to the* ACTORS.) You are at liberty for a bit, but don't stop out of the theater for long. In a quarter of an hour, twenty minutes, all back here again! (*To the* FATHER.) We'll see what can be done. Who knows if we don't get something really extraordinary out of it?

THE FATHER. There's no doubt about it. They (*indicating the* CHARACTERS) had better come with us too, hadn't they?

THE MANAGER. Yes, yes. Come on! come on! (*Moves away and then turning to the* ACTORS.) Be punctual, please! (MANAGER *and the* SIX CHARACTERS *cross the stage and go off. The other* ACTORS *remain, looking at one another in astonishment.*)

LEADING MAN. Is he serious? What the devil does he want to do?

JUVENILE LEAD. This is rank madness.

THIRD ACTOR. Does he expect to knock up a drama in five minutes?

JUVENILE LEAD. Like the improvisers!

LEADING LADY. If he thinks I'm going to take part in a joke like this . . .

JUVENILE LEAD. I'm out of it anyway.

FOURTH ACTOR. I should like to know who they are. (*Alludes to* CHARACTERS.)

THIRD ACTOR. What do you suppose? Madmen or rascals!

JUVENILE LEAD. And he takes them seriously!

L'INGÉNAL. Vanity! He fancies himself as an author now.

LEADING MAN. It's absolutely unheard of. If the stage has come to this . . . well I'm . . .

FIFTH ACTOR. It's rather a joke.

THIRD ACTOR. Well, we'll see what's going to happen next.

(*Thus talking, the* ACTORS *leave the stage; some going out by the little door at the back; others retiring to their dressing-rooms.*
The curtain remains up.
The action of the play is suspended for twenty minutes.)

ACT II

(*The stage call-bells ring to warn the company that the play is about to begin again.*)

THE STEPDAUGHTER (*comes out of the* MANAGER'S *office along with* THE CHILD *and* THE BOY. *As she comes out of the office, she cries.*)   Nonsense! Nonsense! Do it yourselves! I'm not going to mix myself up in this mess. (*Turning to the* CHILD *and coming quickly with her on to the stage.*) Come on, Rosetta, let's run!

(THE BOY *follows them slowly, remaining a little behind and seeming perplexed.*)

THE STEPDAUGHTER (*stops, bends over the* CHILD *and takes the latter's face between her hands*). My little darling! You're frightened, aren't you? You don't know where we are, do you? (*Pretending to reply to a question of the* CHILD.) What is the stage? It's a place, baby, you know, where people play at being serious, a place where they act comedies. We've got to act a comedy now, dead serious, you know; and you're in it also, little one. (*Embraces her, pressing the little head to her breast, and rocking the* CHILD *for a moment.*)   Oh darling, darling, what a horrid comedy you've got to play! What a wretched part they've found for you! A garden . . . a fountain . . . look . . . just suppose, kiddie, it's here. Where, you say? Why, right here in the middle. It's all pretence you know. That's the trouble, my pet: it's all make-believe here. It's better to imagine it though, because if they fix it up for you, it'll only be painted cardboard, painted cardboard for the rockery, the water, the plants . . . Ah, but I think a baby like this one would sooner have a make-believe fountain than a real one, so she could play with it. What a joke it'll be for the others! But for you, alas! not quite such a joke: you who are real, baby dear, and really play by a real fountain that is big and green and beautiful, with ever so many bamboos around it that are reflected in the water, and a whole lot of little ducks swimming about . . . No, Rosetta, no, your mother doesn't bother about you on account of that wretch of a son there. I'm in the devil of a temper, and as for that lad . . . (*Seizes* BOY *by the arm to force him to take one of his hands out of his pockets.*) What have you got there? What are you hiding? (*Pulls his hand out of his pocket, looks into it and catches the glint of a revolver.*) Ah! where did you get this? (THE BOY, *very pale in the face, looks at her, but does not answer.*) Idiot! If I'd been in your place, instead of killing myself, I'd have shot one of those two, or both of them: father and son.

> (THE FATHER *enters from the office, all excited from his work.* THE MANAGER *follows him.*)

THE FATHER.   Come on, come on, dear! Come here for a minute! We've arranged everything. It's all fixed up.

THE MANAGER (*also excited*).   If you please, young lady, there are one or two points to settle still. Will you come along?

THE STEPDAUGHTER (*following him towards the office*).   Ouff! what's the good, if you've arranged everything.

> (THE FATHER, MANAGER *and* STEPDAUGHTER *go back into the office again* [*off*] *for a moment. At the same time,* THE SON *followed by* THE MOTHER, *comes out.*)

THE SON (*looking at the three entering office*).   Oh this is fine, fine! And to think I can't even get away!

> (THE MOTHER *attempts to look at him, but lowers her eyes immediately when he turns away from her. She then sits down.* THE BOY *and* THE CHILD *approach her. She casts a glance again at the* SON, *and speaks with humble tones, trying to draw him into conversation.*)

THE MOTHER.   And isn't my punishment the worst of all? (*Then seeing from the* SON'S *manner that he will not bother himself about her.*) My God! Why are you so cruel? Isn't it enough for one person to support all this torment? Must you then insist on others seeing it also?

THE SON (*half to himself, meaning the* MOTHER *to hear, however*). And they want to put it on the stage! If there was at least a reason for it! He thinks he has got at the meaning of it all. Just as if each one of us in every circumstance of life couldn't find his own explanation of it! (*Pauses.*) He complains he was discovered in a place where he ought not to have been seen, in a moment of his life which ought to have remained hidden and kept out of the reach of that convention which he has to maintain for other people. And what about my case? Haven't I had to reveal what no son ought ever to reveal: how father and mother live and are man and wife for themselves quite apart from that idea of father and mother which we give them? When this idea is revealed, our life is then linked at one point only to that man and that woman; and as such it should shame them, shouldn't it?

(THE MOTHER *hides her face in her hands. From the dressing-rooms and the little door at the back of the stage the* ACTORS *and* STAGE MANAGER *return, followed by the* PROPERTY MAN, *and the* PROMPTER. *At the same moment,* THE MANAGER *comes out of his office, accompanied by the* FATHER *and the* STEPDAUGHTER.)

THE MANAGER.   Come on, come on, ladies and gentlemen! Heh! you there, machinist!

MACHINIST.   Yes sir?

THE MANAGER.   Fix up the white parlor with the floral decorations. Two wings and a drop with a door will do. Hurry up!

(THE MACHINIST *runs off at once to prepare the scene, and arranges it while* THE MANAGER *talks with the* STAGE MANAGER, *the* PROPERTY MAN, *and the* PROMPTER *on matters of detail.*)

THE MANAGER (*to* PROPERTY MAN).   Just have a look, and see if there isn't a sofa or divan in the wardrobe . . .

PROPERTY MAN.   There's the green one.

THE STEPDAUGHTER.   No no! Green won't do. It was yellow, ornamented with flowers—very large! and most comfortable!

PROPERTY MAN.   There isn't one like that.

THE MANAGER.   It doesn't matter. Use the one we've got.

THE STEPDAUGHTER.   Doesn't matter? It's most important!

THE MANAGER.   We're only trying it now. Please don't interfere. (*To* PROPERTY MAN.) See if we've got a shop window—long and narrowish.

THE STEPDAUGHTER.   And the little table! The little mahogany table for the pale blue envelope!

PROPERTY MAN (*to* MANAGER).   There's that little gilt one.

THE MANAGER.   That'll do fine.

THE FATHER.   A mirror.

THE STEPDAUGHTER.   And the screen! We must have a screen. Otherwise how can I manage?

PROPERTY MAN.   That's all right, Miss. We've got any amount of them.

THE MANAGER (*to the* STEPDAUGHTER).   We want some clothes pegs too, don't we?

THE STEPDAUGHTER.   Yes, several, several!

THE MANAGER.   See how many we've got and bring them all.

PROPERTY MAN.   All right!

(*The* PROPERTY MAN *hurries off to obey his orders. While he is putting the things in their places, the* MANAGER *talks to the* PROMPTER *and then with the* CHARACTERS *and the* ACTORS.)

THE MANAGER (*to* PROMPTER).   Take your seat. Look here: this is the outline of the scenes, act by act. (*Hands him some sheets of paper.*) And now I'm going to ask you to do something out of the ordinary.

PROMPTER.   Take it down in shorthand?

THE MANAGER (*pleasantly surprised*).   Exactly! Can you do shorthand?

PROMPTER.   Yes, a little.

MANAGER. Good! (*Turning to a stage hand.*) Go and get some paper from my office, plenty, as much as you can find.

(*The* STAGE HAND *goes off, and soon returns with a handful of paper which he gives to the* PROMPTER.)

THE MANAGER (*to* PROMPTER). You follow the scenes as we play them, and try and get the points down, at any rate the most important ones. (*Then addressing the* ACTORS.) Clear the stage, ladies and gentlemen! Come over here (*Pointing to the Left*) and listen attentively.

LEADING LADY. But, excuse me, we . . .

THE MANAGER (*guessing her thought*). Don't worry! You won't have to improvise.

LEADING MAN. What have we to do then?

THE MANAGER. Nothing. For the moment you just watch and listen. Everybody will get his part written out afterwards. At present we're going to try the thing as best we can. They're going to act now.

THE FATHER (*as if fallen from the clouds into the confusion of the stage*). We? What do you mean, if you please, by a rehearsal?

THE MANAGER. A rehearsal for them. (*Points to the* ACTORS.)

THE FATHER. But since we are the characters . . .

THE MANAGER. All right: "characters" then, if you insist on calling yourselves such. But here, my dear sir, the characters don't act. Here the actors do the acting. The characters are there, in the "book"—(*Pointing towards* PROMPTER's *box*) when there is a "book"!

THE FATHER. I won't contradict you; but excuse me, the actors aren't the characters. They want to be, they pretend to be, don't they? Now if these gentlemen here are fortunate enough to have us alive before them . . .

THE MANAGER. Oh this is grand! You want to come before the public yourselves then?

THE FATHER. As we are . . .

THE MANAGER. I can assure you it would be a magnificent spectacle!

LEADING MAN. What's the use of us here anyway then?

THE MANAGER. You're not going to pretend that you can act? It makes me laugh! (*The* ACTORS *laugh.*) There, you see, they are laughing at the notion. But, by the way, I must cast the parts. That won't be difficult. They cast themselves. (*To the* SECOND LADY LEAD.) You play the Mother. (*To the* FATHER.) We must find her a name.

THE FATHER. Amalia, sir.

THE MANAGER. But that is the real name of your wife. We don't want to call her by her real name.

THE FATHER. Why ever not, if it is her name? . . . Still, perhaps, if that lady must . . . (*Makes a slight motion of the hand to indicate the* SECOND LADY LEAD.) I see this woman here (*means the* MOTHER) as Amalia. But do as you like. (*Gets more and more confused.*) I don't know what to say to you. Already, I begin to hear my own words ring false, as if they had another sound . . .

THE MANAGER. Don't you worry about it. It'll be our job to find the right tones. And as for her name, if you want her Amalia, Amalia it shall be; and if you don't like it, we'll find another! For the moment though, we'll call the characters in this way: (*to* JUVENILE LEAD.) You are the Son; (*to the* LEADING LADY.) You naturally are the Stepdaughter . . .

THE STEPDAUGHTER (*excitedly*). What? what? I, that woman there? (*Bursts out laughing.*)

THE MANAGER (*angrily*). What is there to laugh at?

LEADING LADY (*indignant*). Nobody has ever dared to laugh at me. I insist on being treated with respect; otherwise I go away.

THE STEPDAUGHTER. No, no, excuse me . . . I am not laughing at you . . .

THE MANAGER (*to* STEPDAUGHTER). You ought to feel honored to be played by . . .

LEADING LADY (*at once, contemptuously*). "That woman there" . . .

THE STEPDAUGHTER. But I wasn't speaking of you, you know. I was speaking of myself—whom I can't see at all in you! That is all. I don't know . . . but . . . you . . . aren't in the least like me . . .

THE FATHER. True. Here's the point. Look here, sir, our temperaments, our souls . . .

THE MANAGER. Temperament, soul, be hanged! Do you suppose the spirit of the piece is in you? Nothing of the kind!

THE FATHER. What, haven't we our own temperaments, our own souls?

THE MANAGER. Not at all. Your soul or whatever you like to call it takes shape here. The actors give body and form to it, voice and gesture. And my actors—I may tell you—have given expression to much more lofty material than this little drama of yours, which may or may not hold up on the stage. But if it does, the merit of it, believe me, will be due to my actors.

THE FATHER. I don't dare contradict you, sir; but, believe me, it is a terrible suffering for us who are as we are, with these bodies of ours, these features to see . . .

THE MANAGER (*cutting him short and out of patience*). Good heavens! The make-up will remedy all that, man, the make-up . . .

THE FATHER. Maybe. But the voice, the gestures . . .

THE MANAGER. Now, look here! On the stage, you as yourself, cannot exist. The actor here acts you, and that's an end to it!

THE FATHER. I understand. And now I think I see why our author who conceived us as we are, all alive, didn't want to put us on the stage after all. I haven't the least desire to offend your actors. Far from it! But when I think that I am to be acted by . . . I don't know by whom . . .

LEADING MAN (*on his dignity*). By me, if you've no objection!

THE FATHER (*humbly, mellifluously*). Honored, I assure you, sir. (*Bows.*) Still, I must say that try as this gentleman may, with all his good will and wonderful art, to absorb me into himself . . .

LEADING MAN.   Oh chuck it! "Wonderful art!" Withdraw that, please!

THE FATHER.   The performance he will give, even doing his best with make-up to look like me . . .

LEADING MAN.   It will certainly be a bit difficult! (*The* ACTORS *laugh.*)

THE FATHER.   Exactly! It will be difficult to act me as I really am. The effect will be rather—apart from the make-up—according as to how he supposes I am, as he senses me—if he does sense me—and not as I inside of myself feel myself to be. It seems to me then that account should be taken of this by everyone whose duty it may become to criticize us . . .

THE MANAGER.   Heavens! The man's starting to think about the critics now! Let them say what they like. It's up to us to put on the play if we can. (*Looking around.*) Come on! come on! Is the stage set? (*To the* ACTORS *and* CHARACTERS.) Stand back—stand back! Let me see, and don't let's lose any more time! (*To the* STEPDAUGHTER.) Is it all right as it is now?

THE STEPDAUGHTER.   Well, to tell the truth, I don't recognize the scene.

THE MANAGER.   My dear lady, you can't possibly suppose that we can construct that shop of Madame Pace piece by piece here? (*To the* FATHER.) You said a white room with flowered wall paper, didn't you?

THE FATHER.   Yes.

THE MANAGER.   Well then. We've got the furniture right more or less. Bring that little table a bit further forward. (*The stage hands obey the order. To* PROPERTY MAN.) You go and find an envelope, if possible, a pale blue one; and give it to that gentleman. (*Indicates* FATHER.)

PROPERTY MAN.   An ordinary envelope?

MANAGER AND FATHER.   Yes, yes, an ordinary envelope.

PROPERTY MAN.   At once, sir. (*Exit.*)

THE MANAGER.   Ready, everyone! First scene—the Young Lady. (*The* LEADING LADY *comes forward.*) No, no, you must wait. I meant her. (*Indicating the* STEPDAUGHTER.) You just watch—

THE STEPDAUGHTER (*adding at once*).   How I shall play it, how I shall live it! . . .

LEADING LADY (*offended*).   I shall live it also, you may be sure, as soon as I begin!

THE MANAGER (*with his hands to his head*).   Ladies and gentlemen, if you please! No more useless discussions! Scene I: the young lady with Madame Pace: Oh! (*Looks around as if lost.*) And this Madame Pace, where is she?

THE FATHER.   She isn't with us, sir.

THE MANAGER.   Then what the devil's to be done?

THE FATHER.   But she is alive too.

THE MANAGER.   Yes, but where is she?

THE FATHER.   One minute. Let me speak! (*Turning to the* ACTRESSES.) If these ladies would be so good as to give me their hats for a moment . . .

THE ACTRESSES (*half surprised, half laughing, in chorus*).   What?

Why?

Our hats?

What does he say?

THE MANAGER.   What are you going to do with the ladies' hats? (*The* ACTORS *laugh.*)

THE FATHER.   Oh nothing. I just want to put them on these pegs for a moment. And one of the ladies will be so kind as to take off her mantle . . .

THE ACTORS.   Oh, what d'you think of that?

Only the mantle?

He must be mad.

SOME ACTRESSES.   But why?

Mantles as well?

THE FATHER.   To hang them up here for a moment. Please be so kind, will you?

THE ACTRESSES (*taking off their hats, one or two also their cloaks, and going to hang them on the racks*).   After all, why not?

There you are!

This is really funny.

We've got to put them on show.

THE FATHER.   Exactly; just like that, on show.

THE MANAGER.   May we know why?

THE FATHER.   I'll tell you. Who knows if, by arranging the stage for her, she does not come here herself, attracted by the very articles of her trade? (*Inviting the* ACTORS *to look towards the exit at back of stage.*) Look! Look!

(*The door at the back of stage opens and* MADAME PACE *enters and takes a few steps forward. She is a fat, oldish woman with puffy oxygen-ated hair. She is rouged and powdered, dressed with a comical elegance in black silk. Round her waist is a long silver chain from which hangs a pair of scissors. The* STEPDAUGHTER *runs over to her at once amid the stupor of the* ACTORS.)

THE STEPDAUGHTER (*turning towards her*).   There she is! There she is!

THE FATHER. (*Radiant*).   It's she! I said so, didn't I? There she is!

THE MANAGER (*conquering his surprise, and then becoming indignant*). What sort of a trick is this?

LEADING MAN (*almost at the same time*).   What's going to happen next?

JUVENILE LEAD.   Where does *she* come from?

L'INGÉNUE.   They've been holding her in reserve, I guess.

LEADING LADY.   A vulgar trick!

THE FATHER (*Dominating the protests*).   Excuse me, all of you! Why are you so anxious to destroy in the name of a vulgar, commonplace sense of truth, this reality which comes to birth attracted and formed by the magic of the stage itself, which has indeed more right to live here than you, since it is much truer than you—if you don't mind my saying so? Which is the actress among you who is to play Madame Pace? Well, here is Madame Pace herself. And you will allow, I fancy, that the actress who acts her will be less true than this woman here, who is herself in person. You see my daughter recognized her and went over to her at once. Now you're going to witness the scene!

(*But the scene between the* STEPDAUGHTER *and* MADAME PACE *has already begun despite the protest of the* ACTORS *and the reply of* THE FATHER. *It has begun quietly, naturally, in a manner impossible for the stage. So when the* ACTORS, *called to attention by* THE FATHER, *turn round and see* MADAME PACE, *who has placed one hand under the* STEPDAUGHTER's *chin to raise her head, they observe her at first with great attention, but hearing her speak in an unintelligible manner their interest begins to wane.*)

THE MANAGER.   Well? well?

LEADING MAN.   What does she say?

LEADING LADY.   One can't hear a word.

JUVENILE LEAD.   Louder! Louder please!

THE STEPDAUGHTER (*leaving* MADAME PACE, *who smiles a Sphinx-like smile, and advancing towards the* ACTORS). Louder? Louder? What are you talking about? These aren't matters which can be shouted at the top of one's voice. If I have spoken them out loud, it was to shame him and have my revenge. (*Indicates* FATHER.) But for Madame it's quite a different matter.

THE MANAGER.   Indeed? indeed? But here, you know, people have got to make themselves heard, my dear. Even we who are on the stage can't hear you. What will it be when the public's in the theater? And anyway, you can very well speak up now among yourselves, since we shan't be present to listen to you as we are now. You've got to pretend to be alone in a room at the back of a shop where no one can hear you.

(*The* STEPDAUGHTER *coquettishly and with a touch of malice makes a sign of disagreement two or three times with her finger.*)

THE MANAGER.   What do you mean by no?

THE STEPDAUGHTER (*Sotto voce, mysteriously*). There's someone who will hear us if she (*indicating* MADAME PACE) speaks out loud.

THE MANAGER (*in consternation*). What? Have you got someone else to spring on us now? (*The* ACTORS *burst out laughing.*)

THE FATHER.   No, no sir. She is alluding to me. I've got to be here— there behind that door, in waiting; and Madame Pace knows it. In fact, if you will allow me, I'll go there at once, so I can be quite ready. (*Moves away.*)

THE MANAGER (*stopping him*). No! Wait! wait! We must observe the conventions of the theater. Before you are ready . . .

THE STEPDAUGHTER (*interrupting him*). No, get on with it at once! I'm just dying, I tell you, to act this scene. If he's ready, I'm more than ready.

THE MANAGER (*shouting*). But, my dear young lady, first of all, we must have the scene between you and this lady . . . (*Indicates* MADAME PACE.) Do you understand? . . .

THE STEPDAUGHTER.   Good Heavens! She's been telling me what you know already: that mamma's work is badly done again, that the material's ruined; and that if I want her to continue to help us in our misery I must be patient . . .

MADAME PACE (*coming forward with an air of great importance*). Yes indeed, sir, I no wanta take advantage of her, I no wanta be hard . . .

(*Note:* MADAME PACE *is supposed to talk in a jargon half Italian, half Spanish.*)

THE MANAGER (*alarmed*).   What? What? she talks like that? (*The* ACTORS *burst out laughing again.*)

THE STEPDAUGHTER (*also laughing*).   Yes yes, that's the way she talks, half English, half Italian! Most comical it is!

MADAME PACE.   Itta seem not verra polite gentlemen laugha atta me eef I trya best speaka English.

THE MANAGER.   *Diamine!* Of course! Of course! Let her talk like that! Just what we want. Talk just like that, Madame, if you please! The effect will be certain. Exactly what was wanted to put a little comic relief into the crudity of the situation. Of course she talks like that! Magnificent!

THE STEPDAUGHTER.   Magnificent? Certainly! When certain suggestions are made to one in language of that kind, the effect is certain, since it seems almost a joke. One feels inclined to laugh when one hears her talk about an "old signore" "who wanta talka nicely with you." Nice old signore, eh, Madame?

MADAME PACE.   Not so old, my dear, not so old! And even if you no lika him, he won't make any scandal!

THE MOTHER (*jumping up amid the amazement and consternation of the* ACTORS *who had not been noticing her. They move to restrain her.*). You old devil! You murderess!

THE STEPDAUGHTER (*running over to calm her* MOTHER).   Calm yourself, mother, calm yourself! Please don't . . .

THE FATHER (*going to her also at the same time*).   Calm yourself! Don't get excited! Sit down now!

THE MOTHER.   Well then, take that woman away out of my sight!

THE STEPDAUGHTER (*to* MANAGER).   It is impossible for my mother to remain here.

THE FATHER (*to* MANAGER).   They can't be here together. And for this reason, you see: that woman there was not with us when we came . . . If they are on together, the whole thing is given away inevitably, as you see.

THE MANAGER.   It doesn't matter. This is only a first rough sketch—just to get an idea of the various points of the scene, even confusedly . . . (*Turning to the* MOTHER *and leading her to her chair.*) Come along, my dear lady, sit down now, and let's get on with the scene . . .

(*Meanwhile, the* STEPDAUGHTER, *coming forward again, turns to* MADAME PACE.)

THE STEPDAUGHTER.   Come on, Madame, come on!

MADAME PACE (*offended*).   No, no, *grazie*. I not do anything witha your mother present.

THE STEPDAUGHTER.   Nonsense! Introduce this "old signore" who wants to talk nicely to me. (*Addressing the company imperiously.*) We've got to do this scene one way or another, haven't we? Come on! (*To* MADAME PACE.) You can go!

MADAME PACE.   Ah yes! I go'way! I go'way! Certainly! (*Exits furious.*)

THE STEPDAUGHTER (*to the* FATHER).   Now you make your entry. No, you needn't go over here. Come here. Let's suppose you've already come in. Like that, yes! I'm here with bowed head, modest like. Come on! Out with your voice! Say "Good morning, Miss" in that peculiar tone, that special tone . . .

THE MANAGER.   Excuse me, but are you the Manager, or am I? (*To the* FATHER, *who looks undecided and perplexed.*) Get on with it, man! Go down there to the back of the stage. You needn't go off. Then come right forward here.

(THE FATHER *does as he is told, looking troubled and perplexed at first. But as soon as he begins to move, the reality of the action affects him, and he begins to smile and to be more natural. The* ACTORS *watch intently.*)

THE MANAGER (*Sotto voce, quickly to the* PROMPTER *in his box*). Ready! ready? Get ready to write now.

THE FATHER (*coming forward and speaking in a different tone*).   Good afternoon, Miss!

THE STEPDAUGHTER (*head bowed down slightly, with restrained disgust*).   Good afternoon!

THE FATHER (*looks under her hat which partly covers her face. Perceiving she is very young, he makes an exclamation, partly of surprise, partly of fear lest he compromise himself in a risky adventure*).   Ah . . . but . . . ah . . . I say . . . this is not the first time that you have come here, is it?

THE STEPDAUGHTER (*modestly*).   No sir.

THE FATHER.   You've been here before, eh? (*Then seeing her nod agreement.*) More than once? (*Waits for her to answer, looks under her hat, smiles, and then says.*) Well then, there's no need to be so shy, is there? May I take off your hat?

THE STEPDAUGHTER (*anticipating him and with veiled disgust*).   No sir . . . I'll do it myself. (*Takes it off quickly.*)

(THE MOTHER, *who watches the progress of the scene with* THE SON *and the other two* CHILDREN *who cling to her, is on thorns; and follows with varying expressions of sorrow, indignation, anxiety, and horror the words and actions of the other two. From time to time she hides her face in her hands and sobs.*)

THE MOTHER.   Oh, my God, my God!

THE FATHER (*playing his part with a touch of gallantry*).   Give it to me! I'll put it down. (*Takes hat from her hands.*) But a dear little head like yours ought to have a smarter hat. Come and help me choose one from the stock, won't you?

L'INGÉNUE (*interrupting*).   I say . . . those are our hats you know.

THE MANAGER (*furious*).   Silence! silence! Don't try and be funny, if you please . . . We're playing the scene now I'd have you notice. (*To the* STEPDAUGHTER.) Begin again, please!

THE STEPDAUGHTER (*continuing*).   No thank you, sir.

THE FATHER.   Oh, come now. Don't talk like that. You must take it. I shall be upset if you don't. There are some lovely little hats here; and then—Madame will be pleased. She expects it, anyway, you know.

THE STEPDAUGHTER.   No, no! I couldn't wear it!

THE FATHER.   Oh, you're thinking about what they'd say at home if they saw you come in with a new hat? My dear girl, there's always a way round these little matters, you know.

THE STEPDAUGHTER (*all keyed up*).   No, it's not that. I couldn't wear it because I am . . . as you see . . . you might have noticed . . . (*showing her black dress.*)

THE FATHER.   . . . in mourning! Of course: I beg your pardon: I'm frightfully sorry . . .

THE STEPDAUGHTER (*forcing herself to conquer her indignation and nausea*).   Stop! Stop! It's I who must thank you. There's no need for you to feel mortified or specially sorry. Don't think any more of what I've said. (*Tries to smile.*) I must forget that I am dressed so . . .

THE MANAGER (*interrupting and turning to the* PROMPTER).   Stop a minute! Stop! Don't write that down. Cut out that last bit. (*Then to the* FATHER *and* STEPDAUGHTER.) Fine! it's going fine! (*To the* FATHER *only.*) And now you can go on as we arranged. (*To the* ACTORS.) Pretty good that scene, where he offers her the hat, eh?

THE STEPDAUGHTER.   The best's coming now. Why can't we go on?

THE MANAGER.   Have a little patience! (*To the* ACTORS.) Of course, it must be treated rather lightly.

LEADING MAN.   Still, with a bit of go in it!

LEADING LADY.   Of course! It's easy enough! (*To* LEADING MAN.) Shall you and I try it now?

LEADING MAN.   Why, yes! I'll prepare my entrance. (*Exit in order to make his entrance.*)

THE MANAGER (*to* LEADING LADY).   See here! The scene between you and Madame Pace is finished. I'll have it written out properly after. You remain here . . . oh, where are you going?

LEADING LADY.   One minute. I want to put my hat on again. (*Goes over to hat-rack and puts her hat on her head.*)

THE MANAGER.   Good! You stay here with your head bowed down a bit.

THE STEPDAUGHTER.   But she isn't dressed in black.

LEADING LADY.   But I shall be, and much more effectively than you.

THE MANAGER (*to* STEPDAUGHTER).   Be quiet please and watch!

You'll be able to learn something. (*Clapping his hands.*) Come on! come on! Entrance, please!

> (*The door at rear of stage opens, and the* LEADING MAN *enters with the lively manner of an old gallant. The rendering of the scene by the* ACTORS *from the very first words is seen to be quite a different thing, though it has not in any way the air of a parody. Naturally, the* STEPDAUGHTER *and the* FATHER, *not being able to recognize themselves in the* LEADING LADY *and the* LEADING MAN, *who deliver their words in different tones and with a different psychology, express, sometimes with smiles, sometimes with gestures, the impression they receive.*)

LEADING MAN. Good afternoon, Miss . . .

THE FATHER (*at once unable to contain himself*). No! no!

(THE STEPDAUGHTER *noticing the way the* LEADING MAN *enters, bursts out laughing.*)

THE MANAGER (*furious*). Silence! And you please just stop that laughing. If we go on like this, we shall never finish.

THE STEPDAUGHTER. Forgive me, sir, but it's natural enough. This lady (*indicating* LEADING LADY) stands there still; but if she is supposed to be me, I can assure you that if I heard anyone say "Good afternoon" in that manner and in that tone, I should burst out laughing as I did.

THE FATHER. Yes, yes, the manner, the tone . . .

THE MANAGER. Nonsense! Rubbish! Stand aside and let me see the action.

LEADING MAN. If I've got to represent an old fellow who's coming into a house of an equivocal character . . .

THE MANAGER. Don't listen to them, for Heaven's sake! Do it again! It goes fine. (*Waiting for the* ACTORS *to begin again.*) Well?

LEADING MAN. Good afternoon, Miss.

LEADING LADY. Good afternoon.

LEADING MAN (*imitating the gesture of the* FATHER *when he looked under the hat, and then expressing quite clearly first satisfaction and then fear*). Ah, but . . . I say . . . this is not the first time that you have come here, is it?

THE MANAGER. Good, but not quite so heavily. Like this. (*Acts himself.*) "This isn't the first time that you have come here" . . . (*To* LEADING LADY.) And you say: "No, sir."

LEADING LADY. No, sir.

LEADING MAN. You've been here before, more than once.

THE MANAGER. No, no, stop! Let her nod "yes" first. "You've been here before, eh?" (*The* LEADING LADY *lifts up her head slightly and closes her eyes as though in disgust. Then she inclines her head twice.*)

THE STEPDAUGHTER (*unable to contain herself*). Oh my God! (*Puts a hand to her mouth to prevent herself from laughing.*)

THE MANAGER (*turning round*). What's the matter?

THE STEPDAUGHTER. Nothing, nothing!

THE MANAGER (*to* LEADING MAN). Go on!

LEADING MAN. You've been here before, eh? Well then, there's no need to be so shy, is there? May I take off your hat?

(*The* LEADING MAN *says this last speech in such a tone and with such gestures that the* STEPDAUGHTER, *though she has her hand to her mouth, cannot keep from laughing.*)

LEADING LADY (*indignant*). I'm not going to stop here to be made a fool of by that woman there.

LEADING MAN. Neither am I! I'm through with it!

THE MANAGER (*shouting to* STEPDAUGHTER). Silence! for once and all, I tell you!

THE STEPDAUGHTER. Forgive me! forgive me!

THE MANAGER. You haven't any manners: that's what it is! You go too far.

THE FATHER (*endeavoring to intervene*). Yes, it's true, but excuse her . . .

THE MANAGER. Excuse what? It's absolutely disgusting.

THE FATHER. Yes, sir, but believe me, it has such a strange effect when . . .

THE MANAGER. Strange? Why strange? Where is it strange?

THE FATHER. No, sir; I admire your actors—this gentleman here, this lady; but they are certainly not us!

THE MANAGER. I should hope not. Evidently they cannot be you, if they are actors.

THE FATHER. Just so: actors! Both of them act our parts exceedingly well. But, believe me, it produces quite a different effect on us. They want to be us, but they aren't, all the same.

THE MANAGER. What is it then anyway?

THE FATHER. Something that is . . . that is theirs—and no longer ours . . .

THE MANAGER. But naturally, inevitably. I've told you so already.

THE FATHER. Yes, I understand . . . I understand . . .

THE MANAGER. Well then, let's have no more of it! (*Turning to the* ACTORS.) We'll have the rehearsals by ourselves, afterwards, in the ordinary way. I never could stand rehearsing with the author present. He's never satisfied! (*Turning to* FATHER *and* STEPDAUGHTER.) Come on! Let's get on with it again; and try and see if you can't keep from laughing.

THE STEPDAUGHTER. Oh, I shan't laugh any more. There's a nice little bit coming for me now: you'll see.

THE MANAGER. Well then: when she says "Don't think any more of what I've said. I must forget, etc.," you (*addressing the* FATHER) come in sharp with "I understand, I understand"; and then you ask her . . .

THE STEPDAUGHTER (*interrupting*). What?

THE MANAGER. Why she is in mourning.

THE STEPDAUGHTER. Not at all! See here: when I told him that it was useless for me to be thinking about my wearing mourning, do you know how he answered me? "Ah well," he said, "then let's take off this little frock."

THE MANAGER. Great! Just what we want, to make a riot in the theater!

THE STEPDAUGHTER. But it's the truth!

THE MANAGER. What does that matter? Acting is our business here. Truth up to a certain point, but no further.

THE STEPDAUGHTER. What do you want to do then?

THE MANAGER. You'll see, you'll see! Leave it to me.

THE STEPDAUGHTER. No sir! What you want to do is to piece together a little romantic sentimental scene out of my disgust, out of all the reasons, each more cruel and viler than the other, why I am what I am. He is to ask me why I'm in mourning; and I'm to answer with tears in my eyes, that it is just two months since papa died. No sir, no! He's got to say to me; as he did say: "Well, let's take off this little dress at once." And I; with my two months' mourning in my heart, went there behind that screen, and with these fingers tingling with shame . . .

THE MANAGER (*running his hands through his hair*). For Heaven's sake! What are you saying?

THE STEPDAUGHTER (*crying out excitedly*). The truth! The truth!

THE MANAGER. It may be. I don't deny it, and I can understand all your horror; but you must surely see that you can't have this kind of thing on the stage. It won't go.

THE STEPDAUGHTER. Not possible, eh? Very well! I'm much obliged to you—but I'm off!

THE MANAGER. Now be reasonable! Don't lose your temper!

THE STEPDAUGHTER. I won't stop here! I won't! I can see you've fixed it all up with him in your office. All this talk about what is possible for the stage . . . I understand! He wants to get at his complicated "cerebral drama," to have his famous remorses and torments acted; but I want to act my part, *my part!*

THE MANAGER (*annoyed, shaking his shoulders*). Ah! Just *your* part! But, if you will pardon me, there are other parts than yours: his (*indicating the* FATHER) and hers! (*Indicating the* MOTHER.) On the stage you can't have a character becoming too prominent and overshadowing all the others. The thing is to pack them all into a neat little framework and then act what is actable. I am aware of the fact that everyone has his own interior life which he wants very much to put forward. But the difficulty lies in this fact: to set out just so much as is necessary for the stage, taking the other characters into consideration, and at the same time hint at the unrevealed interior life of each. I am willing to admit, my dear young lady, that from your point of view it would be a fine idea if each character could tell the public all his troubles in a nice monologue or a regular one-hour lecture. (*Good humoredly.*) You must restrain yourself, my dear, and in your own interest, too; because this fury of yours, this exaggerated disgust you show, may make a bad impression, you know. After you have confessed to me that there were others before him at Madame Pace's and more than once . . .

THE STEPDAUGHTER (*bowing her head, impressed*). It's true. But remember those others mean him for me all the same.

THE MANAGER (*not understanding*). What? The others? What do you mean?

THE STEPDAUGHTER. For one who has gone wrong, sir, he who was responsible for the first fault is responsible for all that follow. He is responsible for my faults, was, even before I was born. Look at him, and see if it isn't true!

THE MANAGER. Well, well! And does the weight of so much responsibility seem nothing to you? Give him a chance to act it, to get it over!

THE STEPDAUGHTER. How? How can he act all his "noble remorses" all his "moral torments," if you want to spare him the horror of being discovered one day—after he had asked her what he did ask her—in the arms of her, that already fallen woman, that child, sir, that child he used to watch come out of school? (*She is moved.*)

(THE MOTHER *at this point is overcome with emotion, and breaks out into a fit of crying. All are touched. A long pause.*)

THE STEPDAUGHTER (*as soon as the* MOTHER *becomes a little quieter, adds resolutely and gravely*). At present, we are unknown to the public. Tomorrow, you will act us as you wish, treating us in your own manner. But do you really want to see drama, do you want to see it flash out as it really did?

THE MANAGER. Of course! That's just what I do want, so I can use as much of it as is possible.

THE STEPDAUGHTER. Well then, ask that Mother there to leave us.

THE MOTHER (*changing her low plaint into a sharp cry*). No! No! Don't permit it, sir, don't permit it!

THE MANAGER. But it's only to try it.

THE MOTHER. I can't bear it. I can't.

THE MANAGER. But since it has happened already . . . I don't understand!

THE MOTHER. It's taking place now. It happens all the time. My torment isn't a pretended one. I live and feel every minute of my torture. Those two children there—have you heard them speak? They can't speak any more. They cling to me to keep my torment actual and vivid for me. But for themselves, they do not exist, they aren't any more. And she (*indicating* STEPDAUGHTER) has run away, she has left me, and is lost. If I now see her here before me, it is only to renew for me the tortures I have suffered for her too.

THE FATHER. The eternal moment! She (*indicating the* STEPDAUGHTER) is here to catch me, fix me, and hold me eternally in the stocks for that one fleeting and shameful moment of my life. She can't give it up! And you sir, cannot either fairly spare me it.

THE MANAGER. I never said I didn't want to act it. It will form, as a matter of fact, the nucleus of the whole first act right up to her surprise. (*Indicating the* MOTHER.)

THE FATHER. Just so! This is my punishment: the passion in all of us that must culminate in her final cry.

THE STEPDAUGHTER. I can hear it still in my ears. It's driven me mad, that cry!—You can put me on as you like; it doesn't matter. Fully dressed, if you like—provided I have at least the arm bare; because, standing like this (*she goes close to the* FATHER *and leans her head on his breast*) with my head so, and my arms round his neck, I saw a vein pulsing in my arm here; and then, as if that live vein had awakened disgust in me, I closed my eyes like this, and let my head sink on his breast. (*Turning to the* MOTHER.) Cry out, mother! Cry out! (*Buries head in* FATHER's *breast, and with her shoulders raised as if to prevent her hearing the cry, adds in tones of intense emotion.*) Cry out as you did then!

THE MOTHER (*coming forward to separate them*). No! My daughter, my daughter! (*And after having pulled her away from him.*) You brute! you brute! She is my daughter! Don't you see she's my daughter?

THE MANAGER (*walking backwards towards footlights*). Fine! fine! Damned good! And then, of course—curtain!

THE FATHER (*going towards him excitedly*). Yes, of course, because that's the way it really happened.

THE MANAGER (*convinced and pleased*). Oh, yes, no doubt about it. Curtain here, curtain!

(*At the reiterated cry of* THE MANAGER, THE MACHINIST *lets the curtain down, leaving* THE MANAGER *and* THE FATHER *in front of it before the footlights.*)

THE MANAGER. The darned idiot! I said "curtain" to show the act should end there, and he goes and lets it down in earnest. (*To the* FATHER, *while he pulls the curtain back to go on to the stage again.*) Yes, yes, it's all right. Effect certain! That's the right ending. I'll guarantee the first act at any rate.

ACT III

When the curtain goes up again, it is seen that the stage hands have shifted the bit of scenery used in the last part, and have rigged up instead at the back of the stage a drop, with some trees, and one or two wings. A portion of a fountain basin is visible. THE MOTHER is sitting on the Right with the two children by her side. THE SON is on the same side, but away from the others. He seems bored, angry, and full of shame. THE FATHER and THE STEPDAUGHTER are also seated towards the Right front. On the other side [Left] are the ACTORS, much in the positions they occupied before the curtain was lowered. Only THE MANAGER is standing up in the middle of the stage, with his hand closed over his mouth in the act of meditating.

THE MANAGER (*shaking his shoulders after a brief pause*).   Ah yes: the second act! Leave it to me, leave it all to me as we arranged, and you'll see! It'll go fine!

THE STEPDAUGHTER.   Our entry into his house (*indicates* FATHER) in spite of him . . . (*indicates the* SON).

THE MANAGER (*out of patience*).   Leave it to me, I tell you!

THE STEPDAUGHTER.   Do let it be clear, at any rate, that it is in spite of my wishes.

THE MOTHER (*from her corner, shaking her head*).   For all the good that's come of it . . .

THE STEPDAUGHTER (*turning towards her quickly*).   It doesn't matter. The more harm done us, the more remorse for him.

THE MANAGER (*impatiently*).   I understand! Good Heavens! I understand! I'm taking it into account.

THE MOTHER (*supplicatingly*).   I beg you, sir, to let it appear quite plain that for conscience sake I did try in every way . . .

THE STEPDAUGHTER (*interrupting indignantly and continuing for the* MOTHER).   . . . to pacify me, to dissuade me from spiting him. (*To* MANAGER.) Do as she wants: satisfy her, because it is true! I enjoy it immensely. Anyhow, as you can see, the meeker she is, the more she tries to get at his heart, the more distant and aloof does he become.

THE MANAGER.   Are we going to begin this second act or not?

THE STEPDAUGHTER.   I'm not going to talk any more now. But I must tell you this: you can't have the whole action take place in the garden, as you suggest. It isn't possible!

THE MANAGER.   Why not?

THE STEPDAUGHTER.   Because he (*indicates the* SON *again*) is always shut up alone in his room. And then there's all the part of that poor dazed-looking boy there which takes place indoors.

THE MANAGER.   Maybe! On the other hand, you will understand—we can't change scenes three or four times in one act.

THE LEADING MAN.   They used to once.

THE MANAGER.   Yes, when the public was up to the level of that child there.

THE LEADING LADY.   It makes the illusion easier.

THE FATHER (*irritated*).   The illusion! For Heaven's sake, don't say illusion. Please don't use that word, which is particularly painful for us.

THE MANAGER (*astounded*).   And why, if you please?

THE FATHER.   It's painful, cruel, really cruel; and you ought to understand that.

THE MANAGER.   But why? What ought we to say then? The illusion, I tell you, sir, which we've got to create for the audience . . .

THE LEADING MAN.   With our acting.

THE MANAGER.   The illusion of a reality.

THE FATHER.   I understand; but you, perhaps, do not understand us. Forgive me! You see . . . here for you and your actors, the thing is only— and rightly so . . . a kind of game . . .

THE LEADING LADY (*interrupting indignantly*). A game! We're not children here, if you please! We are serious actors.

THE FATHER. I don't deny it. What I mean is the game, or play, of your art, which has to give, as the gentleman says, a perfect illusion of reality.

THE MANAGER. Precisely——!

THE FATHER. Now, if you consider the fact that we (*indicates himself and the other five* CHARACTERS), as we are, have no other reality outside of this illusion . . .

THE MANAGER (*astonished, looking at his* ACTORS, *who are also amazed*). And what does that mean?

THE FATHER (*after watching them for a moment with a wan smile*). As I say, sir, that which is a game of art for you is our sole reality. (*Brief pause. He goes a step or two nearer the* MANAGER *and adds.*) But not only for us, you know, by the way. Just you think it over well. (*Looks him in the eyes.*) Can you tell me who you are?

THE MANAGER (*perplexed, half smiling*). What? Who am I? I am myself.

THE FATHER. And if I were to tell you that that isn't true, because you are I? . . .

THE MANAGER. I should say you were mad——! (*The* ACTORS *laugh.*)

THE FATHER. You're quite right to laugh: because we are all making believe here. (*To* MANAGER.) And you can therefore object that it's only for a joke that that gentleman there (*indicates the* LEADING MAN), who naturally is himself, has to be me, who am on the contrary myself—this thing you see here. You see I've caught you in a trap! (*The* ACTORS *laugh.*)

THE MANAGER (*annoyed*). But we've had all this over once before. Do you want to begin again?

THE FATHER. No, no! That wasn't my meaning! In fact, I should like to request you to abandon this game of art (*looking at the* LEADING LADY *as if anticipating her*) which you are accustomed to play here with your actors, and to ask you seriously once again: who are you?

THE MANAGER (*astonished and irritated, turning to his* ACTORS). If this fellow here hasn't got a nerve! A man who calls himself a character comes and asks me who I am!

THE FATHER (*with dignity, but not offended*). A character, sir, may always ask a man who he is. Because a character has really a life of his own, marked with his especial characteristics; for which reason he is always "somebody." But a man—I'm not speaking of you now—may very well be "nobody."

THE MANAGER. Yes, but you are asking these questions of me, the boss, the manager! Do you understand?

THE FATHER. But only in order to know if you, as you really are now, see yourself as you once were with all the illusions that were yours then, with all the things both inside and outside of you as they seemed to you

—as they were then indeed for you. Well, sir, if you think of all those illusions that mean nothing to you now, of all those things which don't even *seem* to you to exist any more, while once they *were* for you, don't you feel that—I won't say these boards—but the very earth under your feet is sinking away from you when you reflect that in the same way this *you* as you feel it today—all this present reality of yours—is fated to seem a mere illusion to you tomorrow?

THE MANAGER (*without having understood much, but astonished by the specious argument*).   Well, well! And where does all this take us anyway?

THE FATHER.   Oh, nowhere! It's only to show you that if we (*indicating the* CHARACTERS) have no other reality beyond illusion, you too must not count overmuch on your reality as you feel it today, since, like that of yesterday, it may prove an illusion for you tomorrow.

THE MANAGER (*determining to make fun of him*).   Ah, excellent! Then you'll be saying next that you, with this comedy of yours that you brought here to act, are truer and more real than I am.

THE FATHER (*with the greatest seriousness*).   But of course; without doubt!

THE MANAGER.   Ah, really?

THE FATHER.   Why, I thought you'd understand that from the beginning.

THE MANAGER.   More real than I?

THE FATHER.   If your reality can change from one day to another . . .

THE MANAGER.   But everyone knows it can change. It is always changing, the same as anyone else's.

THE FATHER (*with a cry*).   No, sir, not ours! Look here! That is the very difference! Our reality doesn't change: it can't change! It can't be other than what it is, because it is already fixed for ever. It's terrible. Ours is an immutable reality which should make you shudder when you approach us if you are really conscious of the fact that your reality is a mere transitory and fleeting illusion, taking this form today and that tomorrow, according to the conditions, according to your will, your sentiments, which in turn are controlled by an intellect that shows them to you today in one manner and tomorrow . . . who knows how? . . . Illusions of reality represented in this fatuous comedy of life that never ends, nor can ever end! Because if tomorrow it were to end . . . then why, all would be finished.

THE MANAGER.   Oh for God's sake, will you *at least* finish with this philosophizing and let us try and shape this comedy which you yourself have brought me here? You argue and philosophize a bit too much, my dear sir. You know you seem to me almost, almost . . . (*Stops and looks him over from head to foot.*) Ah, by the way, I think you introduced yourself to me as a—what shall . . . we say—a "character," created by an author who did not afterwards care to make a drama of his own creations.

THE FATHER.   It is the simple truth, sir.

THE MANAGER.   Nonsense! Cut that out, please! None of us believes it, because it isn't a thing, as you must recognize yourself, which one can believe seriously. If you want to know, it seems to me you are trying to imitate the manner of a certain author whom I heartily detest—I warn you—although I have unfortunately bound myself to put on one of his works. As a matter of fact, I was just starting to rehearse it, when you arrived. (*Turning to the* ACTORS.) And this is what we've gained—out of the frying-pan into the fire!

THE FATHER.   I don't know to what author you may be alluding, but believe me I feel what I think; and I seem to be philosophizing only for those who do not think what they feel, because they blind themselves with their own sentiment. I know that for many people this self-blinding seems much more "human"; but the contrary is really true. For man never reasons so much and becomes so introspective as when he suffers; since he is anxious to get at the cause of his sufferings, to learn who has produced them, and whether it is just or unjust that he should have to bear them. On the other hand, when he is happy, he takes his happiness as it comes and doesn't analyze it, just as if happiness were his right. The animals suffer without reasoning about their sufferings. But take the case of a man who suffers and begins to reason about it. Oh no! it can't be allowed! Let him suffer like an animal, and then—ah yes, he is "human!"

THE MANAGER.   Look here! Look here! You're off again, philosophizing worse than ever.

THE FATHER.   Because I suffer, sir! I'm not philosophizing: I'm crying aloud the reason of my sufferings.

THE MANAGER (*makes brusque movement as he is taken with a new idea*).   I should like to know if anyone has ever heard of a character who gets right out of his part and perorates and speechifies as you do. Have you ever heard of a case? I haven't.

THE FATHER.   You have never met such a case, sir, because authors, as a rule, hide the labor of their creations. When the characters are really alive before their author, the latter does nothing but follow them in their action, in their words, in the situations which they suggest to him; and he has to will them the way they will themselves—for there's trouble if he doesn't. When a character is born, he acquires at once such an independence, even of his own author, that he can be imagined by everybody even in many other situations where the author never dreamed of placing him; and so he acquires for himself a meaning which the author never thought of giving him.

THE MANAGER.   Yes, yes, I know this.

THE FATHER.   What is there then to marvel at in us? Imagine such a misfortune for characters as I have described to you: to be born of an author's fantasy, and be denied life by him; and then answer me if these characters left alive, and yet without life, weren't right in doing what they did do and are doing now, after they have attempted everything in their power to persuade him to give them their stage life. We've all tried him in turn, I, she (*indicating the* STEPDAUGHTER) and she. (*Indicating the* MOTHER.)

THE STEPDAUGHTER. It's true. I too have sought to tempt him, many, many times, when he has been sitting at his writing table, feeling a bit melancholy, at the twilight hour. He would sit in his armchair too lazy to switch on the light, and all the shadows that crept into his room were full of our presence coming to tempt him. (*As if she saw herself still there by the writing table, and was annoyed by the presence of the* ACTORS.) Oh, if you would only go away, go away and leave us alone—mother here with that son of hers—I with that Child—that Boy there always alone—and then I with him (*just hints at the* FATHER)—and then I alone, alone . . . in those shadows! (*Makes a sudden movement as if in the vision she has of herself illuminating those shadows she wanted to seize hold of herself.*) Ah! my life! my life! Oh, what scenes we proposed to him—and I tempted him more than any of the others!

THE FATHER. Maybe. But perhaps it was your fault that he refused to give us life: because you were too insistent, too troublesome.

THE STEPDAUGHTER. Nonsense! Didn't he make me so himself? (*Goes close to the* MANAGER *to tell him as if in confidence.*) In my opinion he abandoned us in a fit of depression, of disgust for the ordinary theater as the public knows it and likes it.

THE SON. Exactly what it was, sir; exactly that!

THE FATHER. Not at all! Don't believe it for a minute. Listen to me! You'll be doing quite right to modify, as you suggest, the excesses both of this girl here, who wants to do too much, and of this young man, who won't do anything at all.

THE SON. No, nothing!

THE MANAGER. You too get over the mark occasionally, my dear sir, if I may say so.

THE FATHER. I? When? Where?

THE MANAGER. Always! Continuously! Then there's this insistence of yours in trying to make us believe you are a character. And then too, you must really argue and philosophize less, you know, much less.

THE FATHER. Well, if you want to take away from me the possibility of representing the torment of my spirit which never gives me peace, you will be suppressing me: that's all. Every true man, sir, who is a little above the level of the beasts and plants does not live for the sake of living, without knowing how to live; but he lives so as to give a meaning and a value of his own to life. For me this is *everything*. I cannot give up this, just to represent a mere fact as she (*indicating the* STEPDAUGHTER) wants. It's all very well for her, since her "vendetta" lies in the "fact." I'm not going to do it. It destroys my *raison d'être*.

THE MANAGER. Your *raison d'être*! Oh, we're going ahead fine! First she starts off, and then you jump in. At this rate, we'll never finish.

THE FATHER. Now, don't be offended! Have it your own way—provided, however, that within the limits of the parts you assign us each one's sacrifice isn't too great.

THE MANAGER. You've got to understand that you can't go on arguing at your own pleasure. Drama is action, sir, action and not confounded philosophy.

THE FATHER.   All right. I'll do just as much arguing and philosophizing as everybody does when he is considering his own torments.

THE MANAGER.   If the drama permits! But for Heaven's sake, man, let's get along and come to the scene.

THE STEPDAUGHTER.   It seems to me we've got too much action with our coming into his house. (*Indicating* FATHER.) You said, before, you couldn't change the scene every five minutes.

THE MANAGER.   Of course not. What we've got to do is to combine and group up all the facts in one simultaneous, close-knit, action. We can't have it as you want, with your little brother wandering like a ghost from room to room, hiding behind doors and meditating a project which—what did you say it did to him?

THE STEPDAUGHTER.   Consumes him, sir, wastes him away!

THE MANAGER.   Well, it may be. And then at the same time, you want the little girl there to be playing in the garden . . . one in the house, and the other in the garden: isn't that it?

THE STEPDAUGHTER.   Yes, in the sun, in the sun! That is my only pleasure: to see her happy and careless in the garden after the misery and squalor of the horrible room where we all four slept together. And I had to sleep with her—I, do you understand?—with my vile contaminated body next to hers; with her folding me fast in her loving little arms. In the garden, whenever she spied me, she would run to take me by the hand. She didn't care for the big flowers, only the little ones; and she loved to show me them and pet me.

THE MANAGER.   Well then, we'll have it in the garden. Everything shall happen in the garden; and we'll group the other scenes there. (*Calls a stage hand.*) Here, a back-cloth with trees and something to do as a fountain basin. (*Turning round to look at the back of the stage.*) Ah, you've fixed it up. Good! (*To* STEPDAUGHTER.) This is just to give an idea, of course. The Boy, instead of hiding behind the doors, will wander about here in the garden, hiding behind the trees. But it's going to be rather difficult to find a child to do that scene with you where she shows you the flowers. (*Turning to the* YOUTH.) Come forward a little, will you please? Let's try it now! Come along! come along! (*Then seeing him come shyly forward, full of fear and looking lost.*) It's a nice business, this lad here. What's the matter with him? We'll have to give him a word or two to say. (*Goes close to him, puts a hand on his shoulders, and leads him behind one of the trees.*) Come on! come on! Let me see you a little! Hide here . . . yes, like that. Try and show your head just a little as if you were looking for someone . . . (*Goes back to observe the effect, when the* BOY *at once goes through the action.*) Excellent! fine! (*Turning to* STEPDAUGHTER.) Suppose the little girl there were to surprise him as he looks round, and run over to him, so we could give him a word or two to say?

THE STEPDAUGHTER. It's useless to hope he will speak, as long as that fellow there is here . . . (*Indicates the* SON.) You must send him away first.

THE SON (*jumping up*). Delighted! delighted! I don't ask for anything better. (*Begins to move away.*)

THE MANAGER (*at once stopping him*). No! No! Where are you going? Wait a bit!

(*The* MOTHER *gets up alarmed and terrified at the thought that he is really about to go away. Instinctively she lifts her arms to prevent him, without, however, leaving her seat.*)

THE SON (*to* MANAGER *who stops him*). I've got nothing to do with this affair. Let me go please! Let me go!

THE MANAGER. What do you mean by saying you've got nothing to do with this?

THE STEPDAUGHTER (*calmly, with irony*). Don't bother to stop him: he won't go away.

THE FATHER. He has to act the terrible scene in the garden with his mother.

THE SON (*suddenly resolute and with dignity*). I shall act nothing at all. I've said so from the very beginning. (*To the* MANAGER.) Let me go!

THE STEPDAUGHTER (*going over to the* MANAGER). Allow me? (*Puts down the* MANAGER's *arm which is restraining the* SON.) Well, go away then, if you want to! (*The* SON *looks at her with contempt and hatred. She luaghs and says.*) You see, he can't, he can't go away! He is obliged to stay here, indissolubly bound to the chain. If I, who fly off when that happens which has to happen, because I can't bear him—if I am still here and support that face and expression of his, you can well imagine that he is unable to move. He has to remain here, has to stop with that nice father of his, and that mother whose only son he is. (*Turning to the* MOTHER.) Come on, mother, come along! (*Turning to* MANAGER *to indicate her.*) You see, she was getting up to keep him back. (*To the* MOTHER, *beckoning her with her hand.*) Come on! come on! (*Then to* MANAGER.) You can imagine how little she wants to show these actors of yours what she really feels; but so eager is she to get near him that . . . There, you see? She is willing to act her part. (*And in fact, the* MOTHER *approaches him; and as soon as the* STEPDAUGHTER *has finished speaking, opens her arms to signify that she consents.*)

THE SON (*suddenly*). No! no! If I can't go away, then I'll stop here; but I repeat: I act nothing!

THE FATHER (*to* MANAGER *excitedly*). You can force him, sir.

THE SON. Nobody can force me.

THE FATHER. I can.

THE STEPDAUGHTER. Wait a minute, wait . . . First of all, the baby has to go to the fountain . . . (*Runs to take the* CHILD *and leads her to the fountain.*)

THE MANAGER. Yes, yes of course; that's it. Both at the same time.

(*The second* LADY LEAD *and the* JUVENILE LEAD *at this point separate themselves from the group of* ACTORS. *One watches the* MOTHER *attentively; the other moves about studying the movements and manner of the* SON *whom he will have to act.*)

THE SON (*to* MANAGER). What do you mean by both at the same time? It isn't right. There was no scene between me and her. (*Indicates the* MOTHER.) Ask her how it was!

THE MOTHER. Yes, it's true. I had come into his room . . .

THE SON. Into my room, do you understand? Nothing to do with the garden.

THE MANAGER. It doesn't matter. Haven't I told you we've got to group the action?

THE SON (*observing the* JUVENILE LEAD *studying him*). What do you want?

THE JUVENILE LEAD. Nothing! I was just looking at you.

THE SON (*turning towards the* SECOND LADY LEAD). Ah! she's at it too: to re-act her part. (*Indicating the* MOTHER.)!

THE MANAGER. Exactly! And it seems to me that you ought to be grateful to them for their interest.

THE SON. Yes, but haven't you yet perceived that it isn't possible to live in front of a mirror which not only freezes us with the image of ourselves, but throws our likeness back at us with a horrible grimace?

THE FATHER. That is true, absolutely true. You must see that.

THE MANAGER (*to* SECOND LADY LEAD *and* JUVENILE LEAD). He's right! Move away from them!

THE SON. Do as you like. I'm out of this!

THE MANAGER. Be quiet, you, will you? And let me hear your mother! (*To* MOTHER.) You were saying you had entered . . .

THE MOTHER. Yes, into his room, because I couldn't stand it any longer. I went to empty my heart to him of all the anguish that tortures me . . . But as soon as he saw me come in . . .

THE SON. Nothing happened! There was no scene. I went away, that's all! I don't care for scenes!

THE MOTHER. It's true, true. That's how it was.

THE MANAGER. Well now, we've got to do this bit between you and him. It's indispensable.

THE MOTHER. I'm ready . . . when you are ready. If you could only find a chance for me to tell him what I feel here in my heart.

THE FATHER (*going to* SON *in a great rage*). You'll do this for your mother, for your mother, do you understand?

THE SON (*quite determined*). I do nothing!

THE FATHER (*taking hold of him and shaking him*). For God's sake, do as I tell you! Don't you hear your mother asking you for a favor? Haven't you even got the guts to be a son?

THE SON (*taking hold of the* FATHER). No! No! And for God's sake stop it, or else . . . (*General agitation. The* MOTHER, *frightened, tries to separate them.*)

THE MOTHER (*pleading*). Please! please!

THE FATHER (*not leaving hold of the* SON). You've got to obey, do you hear?

THE SON (*almost crying from rage*). What does it mean, this madness you've got? (*They separate*). Have you no decency, that you insist on showing everyone our shame? I won't do it! I won't! And I stand for the will of our author in this. He didn't want to put us on the stage, after all!

THE MANAGER. Man alive! You came here . . .

THE SON (*indicating* FATHER). *He* did! I didn't!

THE MANAGER. Aren't you here now?

THE SON. It was his wish, and he dragged us along with him. He's told you not only the things that did happen, but also things that have never happened at all.

THE MANAGER. Well, tell me then what did happen. You went out of your room without saying a word?

THE SON. Without a word, so as to avoid a scene!

THE MANAGER. And then what did you do?

THE SON. Nothing . . . walking in the garden . . . (*Hesitates for a moment with expression of gloom.*)

THE MANAGER (*coming closer to him, interested by his extraordinary reserve*). Well, well . . . walking in the garden . . .

THE SON (*exasperated*). Why on earth do you insist? It's horrible! (*The* MOTHER *trembles, sobs, and looks towards the fountain.*)

THE MANAGER (*slowly observing the glance and turning towards the* SON *with increasing apprehension*). The baby?

THE SON. There in the fountain . . .

THE FATHER (*pointing with tender pity to the* MOTHER). She was following him at the moment . . .

THE MANAGER (*to the* SON *anxiously*). And then you . . .

THE SON. I ran over to her; I was jumping in to drag her out when I saw something that froze my blood . . . the boy there standing stock still, with eyes like a madman's, watching his little drowned sister, in the fountain! (*The* STEPDAUGHTER *bends over the fountain to hide the* CHILD. *She sobs.*) Then . . . (*A revolver shot rings out behind the trees where the* BOY *is hidden.*)

THE MOTHER (*with a cry of terror runs over in that direction together with several of the* ACTORS *amid general confusion*). My son! My son! (*Then amid the cries and exclamations one hears her voice.*) Help! Help!

THE MANAGER (*pushing the* ACTORS *aside while they lift up the* BOY *and carry him off*). Is he really wounded?

SOME ACTORS. He's dead! dead!

OTHER ACTORS. No, no, it's only make believe, it's only pretence!

THE FATHER (*with a terrible cry*). Pretence? Reality, sir, reality!

THE MANAGER. Pretence? Reality? To hell with it all! Never in my life has such a thing happened to me. I've lost a whole day over these people, a whole day! CURTAIN

QUESTIONS

1. In the first scene, Pirandello is concerned to establish the complete realness of the Stage Manager and the actors, even in the sense of the ordinary and commonplace. How does he accomplish this? Why is it necessary?

2. Later the Father argues that "Characters" are more real than living persons. What arguments does he advance for this claim? Within the play can you find the word real or reality used in more than one sense?

3. The story which the Six Characters (actually seven) seek to tell is distressing, even sordid; hence it has definite elements of the serious. By what means is it made serious?

4. Yet also in this story are elements of the ludicrous and elements of impermanence which prevent the story from being entirely, immutably serious. Point out all such elements.

5. The story of the Six Characters is fragmentary and incomplete. Why? What effects are created by its incompleteness?

6. A chief concern in this play is the nature of reality (question 2 above). Another is the difference between art and reality. State as explicitly as you can the differences Pirandello brings out.

7. In a sense Pirandello is saying that the theatre and theatricality can never actually capture and render reality. Reality will destroy theatricality as theatricality will inhibit, if not destroy, reality. How is this argument presented? Is there a fallacy in it concerning the nature of art? If so, what is it?

8. Can you point out any relations of this fallacy to the realistic-naturalistic conception of art?

9. Pirandello's characterizations are in harmony with certain developments in the modern psychology of personality. He sees human character as a composite of various roles required of individual men, and also of certain irrational elements. Do you find elements of irrationality in any of the Six Characters? If so, state them as explicitly as possible.

10. The play ends in a paradox or question. Is the ending effective to the author's purpose? Why?

11. If you were producing the play, what kinds of effects upon audiences would you attempt to create?

JUNO AND THE PAYCOCK

Sean O'Casey

Born in Dublin in 1884, Sean O'Casey, the youngest child of seven, had little formal schooling and was reared in the Dublin slums. He began work early in life as a common laborer. Like Shaw, he came of a Protestant family living in a dominantly Catholic society. The church, socialism and the Gaelic League were early influences in his life, but eventually his interest in the League was supplanted by membership and interest in the Irish Transport and General Workers Union. As a prisoner of the British during the Easter Week Uprising of 1900, he was once stood up against a wall for execution, but escaped in a scuffle that diverted the soldiers for a moment. He did not learn to read and write until he was about thirteen; yet at seventeen he wrote his first play, *Frost in The Flower*, which was rejected by a little theatre and by the Abbey Theatre. Other plays were likewise rejected by the Abbey. After the Rebellion of 1916, O'Casey began to give more time to writing and less to union and political activities. But it was not until the season of 1923–24, more than twenty years after his first attempt, that his first plays were accepted and produced by the Abbey Theatre. The first performance of his third play to be produced by the Abbey, *The Plough and the Stars* (1926), resulted in a terrible riot. Shortly thereafter O'Casey moved with his bride, Eileen Reynolds, to England, where he continues to reside. Two years later his new play, *The Silver Tassie*, was uncompromisingly rejected by William Butler Yeats, Director of the Abbey, and thus came about the breach between that theatre and its greatest playwright.

The first three O'Casey plays to be produced by the Abbey, *The Shadow of a Gunman* (1923), *Juno and the Paycock* (1924), *The Plough and The Stars* (1926), were realistic depictions of Dublin tenement folk and slum life under the frightful tensions and sufferings of rebellion and civil strife. *The Silver Tassie* (1928), partly realistic and partly expressionistic, is about World War I and is completely anti-war. As O'Casey came more and more to accept communist doctrines, he turned from realism toward symbolism, fantasy, and expressionism. His remaining plays are: *Within the Gates* (1933), *Purple Dust* (1940), *The Stars Turn Red* (1940), *Oak Leaves and Lavender* (1946), *Red Roses for Me* (1947), *Cock-a-doodle Dandy* (1949), *The Bishop's Bonfire* (1954). Two one-act plays, *The End of The Beginning* and *A Pound on Demand*, were written just before World War II. O'Casey has also written and published a series of critical and autobiographical works.

Juno and The Paycock bears the subtitle, "A Tragedy in Three Acts." It is nevertheless a realistic tragicomedy, and once more shows the in-

FROM *Collected Plays of Sean O'Casey*. Reprinted by permission of Macmillan & Company, Ltd., and St. Martin's Press.

ability of many modern dramatists to see man and his conduct as significant and noble enough for sustained tragedy. The central complication of the play, arising from the supposed inheritance of wealth by characters such as these, is essentially comic, even farcical. Certain of the characters, notably "Captain" Boyle and Joxer, are completely ludicrous, and all of them produce laughter in certain of their traits or actions. Yet several, notably Johnny, Mary, and especially Juno, are dominantly sympathetic, and their predicament elicits pathos and even an element of tragic pity. Juno, like certain other O'Casey women, is admirable in her unyielding devotion to her ideals, especially maternal ideals. She nevertheless takes a large part in the comic incidents. The situation of her son, Johnny, is wholly serious. It adds tension ending in his murder, and results in Juno's grief and bereavement. Until the major discovery and reversal, Mary's situation is largely comic, though in the end it proves quite serious for her. It is through juxtaposing these with the completely ludicrous characters—Boyle, Joxer, and Masie Madigan—that O'Casey highlights man's inhumanity to man and satirizes the verbose rhetoric of Irish nationalism. Through the contrast of these two groups he brings out forcefully the ludicrousness of human pretenses and something of the goodness of natural human conduct free of pretense.

The play gains in artistic effectiveness through the juxtaposition of serious and comic incidents. The comedy contrasts with and illuminates the serious. The comic incidents are not only effective as comedy but also reveal and emphasize O'Casey's ideas and his views of man. His view is almost completely antithetical to the romantically heroic conceptions of Yeats, Synge, Lady Gregory, and other leading figures of the Celtic Revival. To him the Cathleen ni Hoolihan, Deirdre, Playboy of the Western World conception of Irish character and human nature was a delusion built largely upon pretense similar to the delusion of "Captain" Boyle. Hence the central complication of the play, the delusion of inherited wealth, is organic to the idea. Nor did O'Casey make the opposite mistake of many socialist writers by glorifying his slum dwellers. He saw them with an eye too uncompromisingly realistic for that.

His diction is admirably suited to the purpose and effect of the drama. The Irish idiom enhances both his characterizations and the comic powers of the play. The dialogue has a strangeness and a rhythm that heightens interest. In O'Casey's hands, it becomes powerfully effective in the serious as well as the comic situations. In this early drama he moulded all the six parts of a play, and ordered them into an artistic unity expressive of his particular vision of man.

CHARACTERS

"Captain" Jack Boyle	"Joxer" Daly	
Juno Boyle, *his wife*	Mrs. Maisie Madigan	*Residents in*
Johnny Boyle ⎱ *their children*	"Needle" Nugent, *a tailor*	*the Tenement*
Mary Boyle ⎰	Mrs. Tancred	

Juno and the Paycock 617

JERRY DEVINE
CHARLIE BENTHAM, *a school teacher*
AN IRREGULAR MOBILIZER
TWO IRREGULARS

A COAL-BLOCK VENDOR
A SEWING MACHINE MAN
TWO FURNITURE REMOVAL MEN
TWO NEIGHBOURS

SCENE

ACT I.—The living apartment of a two-roomed tenancy of the Boyle family, in a tenement house in Dublin.

ACT II.—The same.

ACT III.—The same.

A few days elapse between Acts I and II, and two months between Acts II and III.

During Act III the curtain is lowered for a few minutes to denote the lapse of one hour.

Period of the play, 1922.

ACT I

The living room of a two-room tenancy occupied by the BOYLE *family in a tenement house in Dublin. Left, a door leading to another part of the house; left of door a window looking into the street; at back a dresser; farther to right at back, a window looking into the back of the house. Between the window and the dresser is a picture of the Virgin; below the picture, on a bracket, is a crimson bowl in which a floating votive light is burning. Farther to the right is a small bed partly concealed by cretonne hangings strung on a twine. To the right is the fireplace; near the fireplace is a door leading to the other room. Beside the fireplace is a box containing coal. On the mantelshelf is an alarm clock lying on its face. In a corner near the window looking into the back is a galvanized bath. A table and some chairs. On the table are breakfast things for one. A teapot is on the hob and a frying-pan stands inside the fender. There are a few books on the dresser and one on the table. Leaning against the dresser is a long-handled shovel—the kind invariably used by labourers when turning concrete or mixing mortar.* JOHNNY BOYLE *is sitting crouched beside the fire.* MARY *with her jumper off—it is lying on the back of a chair—is arranging her hair before a tiny mirror perched on the table. Beside the mirror is stretched out the morning paper, which she looks at when she isn't gazing into the mirror. She is a well-made and good-looking girl of twenty-two. Two forces are working in her mind—one, through the circumstances of her life, pulling her back; the other, through the influence of books she has read, pushing her forward. The opposing forces are apparent in her speech and her manners, both of which are degraded by her environment, and improved by her acquaintance—slight though it be—with literature. The time is early forenoon.*

MARY (*looking at the paper*). On a little bye-road, out beyant Finglas, he was found.

(MRS. BOYLE *enters by door on right; she has been shopping and carries a small parcel in her hand. She is forty-five years of age, and twenty years ago she must have been a pretty woman; but her face has now assumed that look which ultimately settles down upon the faces of the women of the working-class; a look of listless monotony and harassed anxiety, blending with an expression of mechanical resistance. Were circumstances favourable, she would probably be a handsome, active and clever woman.*)

MRS. BOYLE. Isn't he come in yet?

MARY. No, mother.

MRS. BOYLE. Oh, he'll come in when he likes; struttin' about the town like a paycock with Joxer, I suppose. I hear all about Mrs. Tancred's son is in this mornin's paper.

MARY. The full details are in it this mornin'; seven wounds he had—one entherin' the neck, with an exit wound beneath the left shoulder-blade; another in the left breast penethratin' the heart, an' . . .

JOHNNY (*springing up from the fire*). Oh, quit that readin', for God's sake! Are yous losin' all your feelin's? It'll soon be that none of yous'll read anythin' that's not about butcherin'! (*He goes quickly into the room on left.*)

MARY. He's gettin' very sensitive, all of a sudden!

MRS. BOYLE. I'll read it myself, Mary, by an' by, when I come home. Everybody's sayin' that he was a die-hard—thanks be to God that Johnny had nothin' to do with him this long time. . . . (*Opening the parcel and taking out some sausages, which she places on a plate.*) Ah, then, if that father o' yours doesn't come in soon for his breakfast, he may go without any; I'll not wait much longer for him.

MARY. Can't you let him get it himself when he comes in?

MRS. BOYLE. Yes, an' let him bring in Joxer Daly along with him? Ay, that's what he'd like, an' that's what he's waitin' for—till he thinks I'm gone to work, an' then sail in with the boul' Joxer, to burn all the coal an' dhrink all the tea in the place, to show them what a good Samaritan he is! But I'll stop here till he comes in, if I have to wait till to-morrow mornin'.

VOICE OF JOHNNY (*inside*). Mother!

MRS. BOYLE. Yis?

VOICE OF JOHNNY. Bring us in a dhrink o' wather.

MRS. BOYLE. Bring in that fella a dhrink o' wather, for God's sake, Mary.

MARY. Isn't he big an' able enough to come out an' get it himself?

MRS. BOYLE. If you weren't well yourself you'd like somebody to bring you in a dhrink o' wather. (*She brings in drink and returns.*)

MRS. BOYLE. Isn't it terrible to have to be waitin' this way! You'd think he was bringin' twenty poun's a week into the house the way he's goin' on. He wore out the Health Insurance long ago, he's afther wearin' out the unemployment dole, an', now, he's thryin' to wear out me! An' constantly singin', no less, when he ought always to be on his knees offerin' up a Novena for a job!

MARY (*tying a ribbon, fillet-wise around her head*). I don't like this ribbon, ma; I think I'll wear the green—it looks betther than the blue.

MRS. BOYLE. Ah, wear whatever ribbon you like, girl, only don't be botherin' me. I don't know what a girl on strike wants to be wearin' a ribbon round her head for or silk stockin's on her legs either; it's wearin' them things that make the employers think they're givin' yous too much money.

MARY. The hour is past now when we'll ask the employers' permission to wear what we like.

MRS. BOYLE. I don't know why you wanted to walk out for Jennie Claffey; up to this you never had a good word for her.

MARY. What's the use of belongin' to a Trades Union if you won't stand up for your principles? Why did they sack her? It was a clear case of victimization. We couldn't let her walk the streets, could we?

MRS. BOYLE. No, of course yous couldn't—yous wanted to keep her company. Wan victim wasn't enough. When the employers sacrifice wan victim, the Trades Unions go wan betther be sacrificin' a hundred.

MARY. It doesn't matther what you say, ma—a principle's a principle.

MRS. BOYLE. Yis; an' when I go into oul' Murphy's to-morrow, an' he gets to know that, instead o' payin' all, I'm goin' to borry more, what'll he say when I tell him a principle's a principle? What'll we do if he refuses to give us any more on tick?

MARY. He daren't refuse—if he does, can't you tell him he's paid?

MRS. BOYLE. It's lookin' as if he was paid, whether he refuses or no.

(JOHNNY *appears at the door on left. He can be plainly seen now; he is a thin delicate fellow, something younger than* MARY. *He has evidently gone through a rough time. His face is pale and drawn; there is a tremulous look of indefinite fear in his eyes. The left sleeve of his coat is empty, and he walks with a slight halt.*)

JOHNNY. I was lyin' down; I thought yous were gone. Oul' Simon Mackay is thrampin' about like a horse over me head, an' I can't sleep with him—they're like thunder-claps in me brain! The curse o'—God forgive me for goin' to curse!

MRS. BOYLE. There, now; go back an' lie down again, an' I'll bring you in a nice cup o' tay.

JOHNNY. Tay, tay, tay! You're always thinkin' o' tay. If a man was dyin', you'd thry to make him swally a cup o' tay! (*He goes back.*)

MRS. BOYLE. I don't know what's goin' to be done with him. The bullet he got in the hip in Easter Week was bad enough, but the bomb that shatthered his arm in the fight in O'Connell Street put the finishin' touch on him. I knew he was makin' a fool of himself. God knows I went down on me bended knees to him not to go agen the Free State.

MARY. He stuck to his principles, an', no matther how you may argue, ma, a principle's a principle.

VOICE OF JOHNNY.   Is Mary goin' to stay here?

MARY.   No, I'm not goin' to stay here; you can't expect me to be always at your beck an' call, can you?

VOICE OF JOHNNY.   I won't stop here be meself!

MRS. BOYLE.   Amn't I nicely handicapped with the whole o' yous! I don't know what any o' yous ud do without your ma. (*To* JOHNNY.) Your father'll be here in a minute, an' if you want anythin', he'll get it for you.

JOHNNY.   I hate assin' him for anythin'. . . . He hates to be assed to stir. . . . Is the light lightin' before the picture o' the Virgin?

MRS. BOYLE.   Yis, yis! The wan inside to St. Anthony isn't enough, but he must have another wan to the Virgin here!

(JERRY DEVINE *enters hastily. He is about twenty-five, well set, active and earnest. He is a type, becoming very common now in the Labour Movement, of a mind knowing enough to make the mass of his associates, who know less, a power, and too little to broaden that power for the benefit of all.* MARY *seizes her jumper and runs hastily into room left.*)

JERRY (*breathless*).   Where's the Captain, Mrs. Boyle; where's the Captain?

MRS. BOYLE.   You may well ass a body that: he's wherever Joxer Daly is—dhrinkin' in some snug or another.

JERRY.   Father Farrell is just afther stoppin' to tell me to run up an' get him to go to the new job that's goin' on in Rathmines; his cousin is foreman o' the job, an' Father Farrell was speakin' to him about poor Johnny an' his father bein' idle so long, an' the foreman told Father Farrell to send the Captain up an' he'd give him a start—I wondher where I'd find him?

MRS. BOYLE.   You'll find he's ayther in Ryan's or Foley's.

JERRY.   I'll run round to Ryan's—I know it's a great house o' Joxer's. (*He rushes out.*)

MRS. BOYLE (*piteously*).   There now, he'll miss that job, or I know for what! If he gets win' o' the word, he'll not come back till evenin', so that it'll be too late. There'll never be any good got out o' him so long as he goes with that shouldher-shruggin' Joxer. I killin' meself workin', an' he sthruttin' about from mornin' till night like a paycock!

(*The steps of two persons are heard coming up a flight of stairs. They are the footsteps of* CAPTAIN BOYLE *and* JOXER. CAPTAIN BOYLE *is singing in a deep, sonorous, self-honouring voice.*)

THE CAPTAIN.   Sweet Spirit, hear me prayer! Hear . . . oh . . . hear . . . me prayer . . . hear, oh, hear . . . Oh, he . . . ar . . . oh, he . . . ar . . . me . . . pray . . . er!

JOXER (*outside*).   Ah, that's a darlin' song, a daaarlin' song!

MRS. BOYLE (*viciously*).   Sweet spirit hear his prayer! Oh, then, I'll take me solemn affeydavey, it's not for a job he's prayin'!

(*She sits down on the bed so that the cretonne hangings hide her from the view of those entering.*)

(THE CAPTAIN *comes slowly in. He is a man of about sixty; stout, grey-haired and stocky. His neck is short, and his head looks like a stone ball that one sometimes sees on top of a gatepost. His cheeks, reddish-purple, are puffed out, as if he were always repressing an almost irrepressible ejaculation. On his upper lip is a crisp, tightly cropped moustache; he carries himself with the upper part of his body slightly thrown back, and his stomach slightly thrust forward. His walk is a slow, consequential strut. His clothes are dingy, and he wears a faded seaman's cap with a glazed peak.*)

BOYLE (*to* JOXER, *who is still outside*). Come on, come on in, Joxer; she's gone out long ago, man. If there's nothing else to be got, we'll furrage out a cup o' tay, anyway. It's the only bit I get in comfort when she's away. 'Tisn't Juno should be her pet name at all, but Deirdre of the Sorras, for she's always grousin'.

(JOXER *steps cautiously into the room. He may be younger than* THE CAPTAIN *but he looks a lot older. His face is like a bundle of crinkled paper; his eyes have a cunning twinkle; he is spare and loosely built; he has a habit of constantly shrugging his shoulders with a peculiar twitching movement, meant to be ingratiating. His face is invariably ornamented with a grin.*)

JOXER. It's a terrible thing to be tied to a woman that's always grousin'. I don't know how you stick it—it ud put years on me. It's a good job she has to be so ofen away, for (*with a shrug*) when the cat's away, the mice can play!

BOYLE (*with a commanding and complacent gesture*). Pull over to the fire, Joxer, an' we'll have a cup o' tay in a minute.

JOXER. Ah, a cup o' tay's a darlin' thing, a daaarlin' thing—the cup that cheers but doesn't . . .

(JOXER'S *rhapsody is cut short by the sight of* JUNO *coming forward and confronting the two cronies. Both are stupefied.*)

MRS. BOYLE (*with sweet irony—poking the fire, and turning her head to glare at* JOXER). Pull over to the fire, Joxer Daly, an' we'll have a cup o' tay in a minute! Are you sure, now, you wouldn't like an egg?

JOXER. I can't stop, Mrs. Boyle; I'm in a desperate hurry, a desperate hurry.

MRS. BOYLE. Pull over to the fire, Joxer Daly; people is always far more comfortabler here than they are in their own place.

(JOXER *makes hastily for the door.* BOYLE *stirs to follow him; thinks of something to relieve the situation—stops, and says suddenly*):
Joxer!

JOXER (*at door ready to bolt*). Yis?

BOYLE. You know the foreman o' that job that's goin' on down in Killesther, don't you, Joxer?

JOXER (*puzzled*). Foreman—Killesther?

BOYLE (*with a meaning look*). He's a butty o' yours, isn't he?

JOXER (*the truth dawning on him*). The foreman at Killesther—oh, yis, yis. He's an oul' butty o' mine—oh, he's a darlin' man, a daarlin' man.

BOYLE.   Oh, then, it's a sure thing. It's a pity we didn't go down at breakfast first thing this mornin'—we might ha' been working now; but you didn't know it then.

JOXER (*with a shrug*).   It's betther late than never.

BOYLE.   It's nearly time we got a start, anyhow; I'm fed up knockin' round, doin' nothin'. He promised you—gave you the straight tip?

JOXER.   Yis. "Come down on the blow o' dinner," says he, "an' I'll start you, an' any friend you like to brin' with you." Ah, says I, you're a darlin' man, a daaarlin' man.

BOYLE.   Well, it couldn't come at a betther time—we're a long time waitin' for it.

JOXER.   Indeed we were; but it's a long lane that has no turnin'.

BOYLE.   The blow up for dinner is at one—wait till I see what time it 'tis. (*He goes over to the mantelpiece, and gingerly lifts the clock.*)

MRS. BOYLE.   Min' now, how you go on fiddlin' with that clock—you know the least little thing sets it asthray.

BOYLE.   The job couldn't come at a betther time; I'm feelin' in great fettle, Joxer. I'd hardly believe I ever had a pain in me legs, an' last week I was nearly crippled with them.

JOXER.   That's betther and betther; ah, God never shut wan door but he opened another!

BOYLE.   It's only eleven o'clock; we've lashins o' time. I'll slip on me oul' moleskins afther breakfast, an' we can saunther down at our ayse. (*Putting his hand on the shovel.*) I think, Joxer, we'd betther bring our shovels?

JOXER.   Yis, Captain, yis; it's betther to go fully prepared, an ready for all eventualities. You bring your long-tailed shovel, an' I'll bring me navvy. We mighten' want them, an', then agen, we might: for want of a nail the shoe was lost, for want of a shoe the horse was lost, an' for want of a horse the man was lost—aw, that's a darlin' proverb, a daarlin' . . .

(*As* JOXER *is finishing his sentence,* MRS. BOYLE *approaches the door and* JOXER *retreats hurriedly. She shuts the door with a bang.*)

BOYLE (*suggestively*).   We won't be long pullin' ourselves together agen when I'm working for a few weeks.

(MRS. BOYLE *takes no notice.*)

BOYLE.   The foreman on the job is an oul' butty o' Joxer's; I have an idea that I know him meself. (*Silence.*) . . . There's a button off the back o' me moleskin trousers. . . . If you leave out a needle an' thread I'll sew it on meself. . . . Thanks be to God, the pains in me legs is gone, anyhow!

MRS. BOYLE (*with a burst*).   Look here, Mr. Jacky Boyle, them yarns won't go down with Juno. I know you an' Joxer Daly of an oul' date, an', if you think you're able to come it over me with them fairy tales, you're in the wrong shop.

BOYLE (*coughing subduedly to relieve the tenseness of the situation*). U-u-u-ugh.

MRS. BOYLE.   Butty o' Joxer's! Oh, you'll do a lot o' good as long as you continue to be a butty o' Joxer's!

BOYLE.   U-u-u-ugh.

MRS. BOYLE.   Shovel! Ah, then, me boyo, you'd do far more work with a knife an' fork than ever you'll do with a shovel! If there was e'er a genuine job goin' you'd be dh'other way about—not able to lift your arms with the pains in your legs! Your poor wife slavin' to keep the bit in your mouth, an' you gallivantin' about all the day like a paycock!

BOYLE.   It ud be betther for a man to be dead, betther for a man to be dead.

MRS. BOYLE (*ignoring the interruption*).   Everybody callin' you "Captain," an' you only wanst on the wather, in an oul' collier from here to Liverpool, when anybody, to listen or look at you, ud take you for a second Christo For Columbus!

BOYLE.   Are you never goin' to give us a rest?

MRS. BOYLE.   Oh, you're never tired o' lookin' for a rest.

BOYLE.   D'ye want to dhrive me out o' the house?

MRS. BOYLE.   It ud be easier to dhrive you out o' the house than to dhrive you into a job. Here, sit down an' take your breakfast—it may be the last you'll get, for I don't know where the next is goin' to come from.

BOYLE.   If I get this job we'll be all right.

MRS. BOYLE.   Did ye see Jerry Devine?

BOYLE (*testily*).   No, I didn't see him.

MRS. BOYLE.   No, but you seen Joxer. Well, he was here lookin' for you.

BOYLE.   Well, let him look!

MRS. BOYLE.   Oh, indeed, he may well look, for it ud be hard for him to see you, an' you stuck in Ryan's snug.

BOYLE.   I wasn't in Ryan's snug—I don't go into Ryan's.

MRS. BOYLE.   Oh, is there a mad dog there? Well, if you weren't in Ryan's you were in Foley's.

BOYLE.   I'm telling you for the last three weeks I haven't tasted a dhrop of intoxicatin' liquor. I wasn't in ayther wan snug or dh'other—I could swear that on a prayer-book—I'm as innocent as the child unborn!

MRS. BOYLE.   Well, if you'd been in for your breakfast you'd ha' seen him.

BOYLE (*suspiciously*).   What does he want me for?

MRS. BOYLE.   He'll be back any minute an' then you'll soon know.

BOYLE.   I'll dhrop out an' see if I can meet him.

MRS. BOYLE.   You'll sit down an' take your breakfast, an' let me go to me work, for I'm an hour late already waitin' for you.

BOYLE.   You needn't ha' waited, for I'll take no breakfast—I've a little spirit left in me still!

MRS. BOYLE.   Are you goin' to have your breakfast—yes or no?

BOYLE (*too proud to yield*).   I'll have no breakfast—yous can keep your breakfast. (*Plaintively.*) I'll knock out a bit somewhere, never fear.

MRS. BOYLE.   Nobody's goin' to coax you—don't think that. (*She vigorously replaces the pan and the sausages in the press.*)

BOYLE.   I've a little spirit left in me still.

(JERRY DEVINE *enters hastily.*)

JERRY.   Oh, here you are at last! I've been searchin' for you everywhere. The foreman in Foley's told me you hadn't left the snug with Joxer ten minutes before I went in.

MRS. BOYLE.   An' he swearin' on the holy prayer-book that he wasn't in no snug!

BOYLE (*to* JERRY).   What business is it o' yours whether I was in a snug or no? What do you want to be gallopin' about afther me for? Is a man not to be allowed to leave his house for a minute without havin' a pack o' spies, pimps an' informers cantherin' at his heels?

JERRY.   Oh, you're takin' a wrong view of it, Mr. Boyle; I simply was anxious to do you a good turn. I have a message for you from Father Farrell: he says that if you go to the job that's on in Rathmines, an' ask for Foreman Mangan, you'll get a start.

BOYLE.   That's all right, but I don't want the motions of me body to be watched the way an asthronomer ud watch a star. If you're folleyin' Mary aself, you've no pereeogative to be folleyin' me. (*Suddenly catching his thigh.*) U-ugh, I'm afther gettin' a terrible twinge in me right leg!

MRS. BOYLE.   Oh, it won't be very long now till it travels into your left wan. It's miraculous that whenever he scents a job in front of him, his legs begin to fail him! Then, me bucko, if you lose this chance, you may go an' furrage for yourself!

JERRY.   This job'll last for some time, too, Captain, an' as soon as the foundations are in, it'll be cushy enough.

BOYLE.   Won't it be a climbin' job? How d'ye expect me to be able to go up a ladder with these legs? An', if I get up aself, how am I goin' to get down agen?

MRS. BOYLE (*viciously*).   Get wan o' the labourers to carry you down in a hod! You can't climb a laddher, but you can skip like a goat into a snug!

JERRY.   I wouldn't let meself be let down that easy, Mr. Boyle; a little exercise, now, might do you all the good in the world.

BOYLE.   It's a docthor you should have been, Devine—maybe you know more about the pains in me legs than meself that has them?

JERRY (*irritated*).   Oh, I know nothin' about the pains in your legs; I've brought the message that Father Farrell gave me, an' that's all I can do.

MRS. BOYLE.   Here, sit down an' take your breakfast, an' go an' get ready; an' don't be actin' as if you couldn't pull a wing out of a dead bee.

BOYLE.   I want no breakfast, I tell you; it ud choke me afther all that's been said. I've a little spirit left in me still.

MRS. BOYLE.   Well, let's see your spirit, then, an' go in at wanst an' put on your moleskin trousers!

BOYLE (*moving towards the door on left*). It ud be betther for a man to be dead! U-ugh! There's another twinge in me other leg! Nobody but meself knows the sufferin' I'm goin' through with the pains in these legs o' mine! (*He goes into the room on left as* MARY *comes out with her hat in her hand.*)

MRS. BOYLE. I'll have to push off now, for I'm terrible late already, but I was determined to stay an' hunt that Joxer this time. (*She goes off.*)

JERRY. Are you going out, Mary?

MARY. It looks like it when I'm putting on my hat, doesn't it?

JERRY. The bitther word agen, Mary.

MARY. You won't allow me to be friendly with you; if I thry, you deliberately misundherstand it.

JERRY. I didn't always misundherstand it; you were ofen delighted to have the arms of Jerry around you.

MARY. If you go on talkin' like this, Jerry Devine, you'll make me hate you!

JERRY. Well, let it be either a weddin' or a wake! Listen, Mary, I'm standin' for the Secretaryship of our Union. There's only one opposin' me; I'm popular with all the men, an' a good speaker—all are sayin' that I'll get elected.

MARY. Well?

JERRY. The job's worth three hundred an' fifty pounds a year, Mary. You an' I could live nice an' cosily on that; it would lift you out o' this place an' . . .

MARY. I haven't time to listen to you now—I have to go. (*She is going out when* JERRY *bars the way.*)

JERRY (*appealingly*). Mary, what's come over you with me for the last few weeks? You hardly speak to me, an' then only a word with a face o' bittherness on it. Have you forgotten, Mary, all the happy evenin's that were as sweet as the scented hawthorn that sheltered the sides o' the road as we saunthered through the country?

MARY. That's all over now. When you get your new job, Jerry, you won't be long findin' a girl far betther than I am for your sweetheart.

JERRY. Never, never, Mary! No matther what happens you'll always be the same to me.

MARY. I must be off; please let me go, Jerry.

JERRY. I'll go a bit o' the way with you.

MARY. You needn't, thanks; I want to be by meself.

JERRY (*catching her arm*). You're goin' to meet another fella; you've clicked with some one else, me lady!

MARY. That's no concern o' yours, Jerry Devine; let me go!

JERRY. I saw yous comin' out o' the Cornflower Dance Class, an' you hangin' on his arm—a thin, lanky strip of a Micky Dazzler, with a walkin'-stick an' gloves!

VOICE OF JOHNNY (*loudly*). What are you doin' there—pullin' about everything!

VOICE OF BOYLE (*loudly and viciously*). I'm puttin' on me moleskin trousers!

MARY. You're hurtin' me arm! Let me go, or I'll scream, an' then you'll have the oul' fella out on top of us!

JERRY. Don't be so hard on a fella, Mary, don't be so hard.

BOYLE (*appearing at the door*). What's the meanin' of all this hilla-baloo?

MARY. Let me go, let me go!

BOYLE. D'ye hear me—what's all this hillabaloo about?

JERRY (*plaintively*). Will you not give us one kind word, one kind word, Mary?

BOYLE. D'ye hear me talkin' to yous? What's all this hillabaloo for?

JERRY. Let me kiss your hand, your little, tiny, white hand!

BOYLE. Your little, tiny, white hand—are you takin' leave o' your senses, man?

(MARY *breaks away and rushes out.*)

BOYLE. This is nice goin's on in front of her father!

JERRY. Ah, dhry up, for God's sake! (*He follows* MARY.)

BOYLE. Chiselurs don't care a damn now about their parents, they're bringin' their fathers' grey hairs down with sorra to the grave, an' laughin' at it, laughin' at it. Ah, I suppose it's just the same everywhere—the whole worl's in a state o' chassis! (*He sits by the fire.*) Breakfast! Well, they can keep their breakfast for me. Not if they went down on their bended knees would I take it—I'll show them I've a little spirit left in me still! (*He goes over to the press, takes out a plate and looks at it.*) Sassige! Well, let her keep her sassige. (*He returns to the fire, takes up the teapot and gives it a gentle shake.*) The tay's wet right enough. (*A pause; he rises, goes to the press, takes out the sausage, puts it on the pan, and puts both on the fire. He attends the sausage with a fork.*)

BOYLE (*singing*):
When the robins nest agen,
And the flowers are in bloom,
When the Springtime's sunny smile seems to banish all sorrow an' gloom;
Then me bonny blue-ey'd lad, if me heart be true till then—
He's promised he'll come back to me,
When the robins nest agen!

(*He lifts his head at the high note, and then drops his eyes to the pan.*)

BOYLE (*singing*):
When the . . .

(*Steps are heard approaching; he whips the pan off the fire and puts it under the bed, then sits down at the fire. The door opens and a bearded man looking in says*):
You don't happen to want a sewin' machine?

BOYLE (*furiously*). No, I don't want e'er a sewin' machine! (*He returns the pan to the fire, and commences to sing again.*)

BOYLE (*singing*):
When the robins nest agen,
And the flowers they are in bloom,
He's . . .
(*A thundering knock is heard at the street door.*)

BOYLE. There's a terrible tatheraraa—that's a stranger—that's nobody belongin' to the house. (*Another loud knock.*)

JOXER (*sticking his head in at the door*). Did ye hear them tatherarahs?

BOYLE. Well, Joxer, I'm not deaf.

JOHNNY (*appearing in his shirt and trousers at the door on left; his face is anxious and his voice is tremulous*). Who's that at the door; who's that at the door? Who gave that knock—d'ye yous hear me—are yous deaf or dhrunk or what?

BOYLE (*to* JOHNNY). How the hell do I know who 'tis? Joxer, stick your head out o' the window an' see.

JOXER. An' mebbe get a bullet in the kisser? Ah, none o' them thricks for Joxer! It's betther to be a coward than a corpse!

BOYLE (*looking cautiously out of the window*). It's a fella in a thrench coat.

JOHNNY. Holy Mary, Mother o' God, I . . .

BOYLE. He's goin' away—he must ha' got tired knockin'.

(JOHNNY *returns to the room on left.*)

BOYLE. Sit down an' have a cup o' tay, Joxer.

JOXER. I'm afraid the missus ud pop in on us agen before we'd know where we are. Somethin's tellin' me to go at wanst.

BOYLE. Don't be superstitious, man; we're Dublin men, an' not boyos that's only afther comin' up from the bog o' Allen—though if she did come in, right enough, we'd be caught like rats in a thrap.

JOXER. An' you know the sort she is—she wouldn't listen to reason—an' wanse bitten twice shy.

BOYLE (*going over to the window at back*). If the worst came to the worst, you could dart out here, Joxer; it's only a dhrop of a few feet to the roof of the return room, an' the first minute she goes into dh'other room, I'll give you the bend, an' you can slip in an' away.

JOXER (*yielding to the temptation*). Ah, I won't stop very long any-how. (*Picking up a book from the table.*) Whose is the buk?

BOYLE. Aw, one o' Mary's; she's always readin' lately—nothin' but thrash, too. There's one I was lookin' at dh'other day: three stories, The Doll's House, Ghosts, an' The Wild Duck—buks only fit for chiselurs!

JOXER. Didja ever rade *Elizabeth, or Th' Exile o' Sibayria* . . . ah, it's a darlin' story, a daarlin' story!

BOYLE. You eat your sassige, an' never min' *Th' Exile o' Sibayria.*

(*Both sit down;* BOYLE *fills out tea, pours gravy on* JOXER's *plate, and keeps the sausage for himself.*)

JOXER. What are you wearin' your moleskin trousers for?

BOYLE. I have to go to a job, Joxer. Just afther you'd gone, Devine kem runnin' in to tell us that Father Farrell said if I went down to the job that's goin' on in Rathmines I'd get a start.

JOXER.   Be the holy, that's good news!

BOYLE.   How is it good news? I wondher if you were in my condition, would you call it good news?

JOXER.   I thought . . .

BOYLE.   You thought! You think too sudden sometimes, Joxer. D'ye know, I'm hardly able to crawl with the pains in me legs!

JOXER.   Yis, yis; I forgot the pains in your legs. I know you can do nothin' while they're at you.

BOYLE.   You forgot; I don't think any of yous realize the state I'm in with the pains in me legs. What ud happen if I had to carry a bag o' cement?

JOXER.   Ah, any man havin' the like of them pains id be down an' out, down an' out.

BOYLE.   I wouldn't mind if he had said it to meself; but, no, oh no, he rushes in an' shouts it out in front o' Juno, an' you know what Juno is, Joxer. We all know Devine knows a little more than the rest of us, but he doesn't act as if he did; he's a good boy, sober, able to talk an' all that, but still . . .

JOXER.   Oh ay; able to argufy, but still . . .

BOYLE.   If he's runnin' afther Mary, aself, he's not goin' to be runnin' afther me. Captain Boyle's able to take care of himself. Afther all, I'm not gettin' brought up on Virol. I never heard him usin' a curse; I don't believe he was ever dhrunk in his life—sure he's not like a Christian at all!

JOXER.   You're afther takin' the word out o' me mouth—afther all, a Christian's natural, but he's unnatural.

BOYLE.   His oul' fella was just the same—a Wicklow man.

JOXER.   A Wicklow man! That explains the whole thing. I've met many a Wicklow man in me time, but I never met wan that was any good.

BOYLE.   "Father Farrell," says he, "sent me down to tell you." Father Farrell! . . . D'ye know, Joxer, I never like to be beholden to any o' the clergy.

JOXER.   It's dangerous, right enough.

BOYLE.   If they do anything for you, they'd want you to be livin' in the Chapel. . . . I'm goin' to tell you somethin', Joxer, that I wouldn't tell to anybody else—the clergy always had too much power over the people in this unfortunate country.

JOXER.   You could sing that if you had an air to it!

BOYLE (*becoming enthusiastic*).   Didn't they prevent the people in '47 from seizin' the corn, an' they starvin'; didn't they down Parnell; didn't they say that hell wasn't hot enough nor eternity long enough to punish the Fenians? We don't forget, we don't forget them things, Joxer. If they've taken everything else from us, Joxer, they've left us our memory.

JOXER (*emotionally*).   For mem'ry's the only friend that grief can call its own, that grief . . . can . . . call . . . its own!

BOYLE. Father Farrell's beginnin' to take a great intherest in Captain Boyle; because of what Johnny did for his country, says he to me wan day. It's a curious way to reward Johnny be makin' his poor oul' father work. But, that's what the clergy want, Joxer—work, work, work for me an' you; havin' us mulin' from mornin' till night, so that they may be in betther fettle when they come hoppin' round for their dues! Job! Well, let him give his job to wan of his hymn-singin', prayer-spoutin', craw-thumpin' Confraternity men!

(*The voice of a coal-block vendor is heard chanting in the street.*)

VOICE OF COAL VENDOR. Blocks . . . coal-blocks! Blocks . . . coal-blocks!

JOXER. God be with the young days when you were steppin' the deck of a manly ship, with the win' blowin' a hurricane through the masts, an' the only sound you'd hear was, "Port your helm!" an' the only answer, "Port it is, sir!"

BOYLE. Them was days, Joxer, them was days. Nothin' was too hot or too heavy for me then. Sailin' from the Gulf o' Mexico to the Antarctic Ocean. I seen things, I seen things, Joxer, that no mortal man should speak about that knows his Catechism. Ofen, an' ofen, when I was fixed to the wheel with a marlin-spike, an' the win's blowin' fierce an' the waves lashin' an' lashin', till you'd think every minute was goin' to be your last, an' it blowed, an' blowed—blew is the right word, Joxer, but blowed is what the sailors use. . . .

JOXER. Aw, it's a darlin' word, a daarlin' word.

BOYLE. An', as it blowed an' blowed, I ofen looked up at the sky an' assed meself the question—what is the stars, what is the stars?

VOICE OF COAL VENDOR. Any blocks, coal-blocks; blocks, coal-blocks!

JOXER. Ah, that's the question, that's the question—what is the stars?

BOYLE. An' then, I'd have another look, an' I'd ass meself—what is the moon?

JOXER. Ah, that's the question—what is the moon, what is the moon?

(*Rapid steps are heard coming towards the door.* BOYLE *makes desperate efforts to hide everything;* JOXER *rushes to the window in a frantic effort to get out;* BOYLE *begins to innocently lilt—"Oh, me darlin' Jennie, I will be thrue to thee," when the door is opened, and the black face of the* COAL VENDOR *appears.*)

THE COAL VENDOR. D'yes want any blocks?

BOYLE (*with a roar*). No, we don't want any blocks!

JOXER (*coming back with a sigh of relief*). That's afther puttin' the heart across me—I could ha' sworn it was Juno. I'd betther be goin', Captain; you couldn't tell the minute Juno'd hop in on us.

BOYLE. Let her hop in; we may as well have it out first as at last. I've made up me mind—I'm not goin' to do only what she damn well likes.

JOXER. Them sentiments does you credit, Captain; I don't like to say anything as between man an' wife, but I say as a butty, as a butty, Captain, that you've stuck it too long, an' that it's about time you showed a little spunk

How can a man die betther than facin' fearful odds,
For th' ashes of his fathers an' the temples of his gods.

BOYLE.   She has her rights—there's no one denyin' it, but haven't I me rights too?

JOXER.   Of course you have—the sacred rights o' man!

BOYLE.   To-day, Joxer, there's goin' to be issued a proclamation be me, establishin' an independent Republic, an' Juno'll have to take an oath of allegiance.

JOXER.   Be firm, be firm, Captain; the first few minutes'll be the worst: —if you gently touch a nettle it'll sting you for your pains; grasp it like a lad of mettle, an's as soft as silk remains!

VOICE OF JUNO (*outside*).   Can't stop, Mrs. Madigan—I haven't a minute!

JOXER (*flying out of the window*).   Holy God, here she is!

BOYLE (*packing the things away with a rush in the press*).   I knew that fella ud stop till she was in on top of us! (*He sits down by the fire.*)

(JUNO *enters hastily; she is flurried and excited.*)

JUNO.   Oh, you're in—you must have been only afther comin' in?

BOYLE.   No, I never went out.

JUNO.   It's curious, then, you never heard the knockin'. (*She puts her coat and hat on bed.*)

BOYLE.   Knockin'? Of course I heard the knockin'.

JUNO.   An' why didn't you open the door, then? I suppose you were so busy with Joxer that you hadn't time.

BOYLE.   I haven't seen Joxer since I seen him before. Joxer! What ud bring Joxer here?

JUNO.   D'ye mean to tell me that the pair of yous wasn't collogin' together here when me back was turned?

BOYLE.   What ud we be collogin' together about? I have somethin' else to think of besides collogin' with Joxer. I can swear on all the holy prayer-books . . .

MRS. BOYLE.   That you weren't in no snug! Go on in at wanst now, an' take aff that moleskin trousers o' yours, an' put on a collar an' tie to smarten yourself up a bit. There's a visitor comin' with Mary in a minute, an' he has great news for you.

BOYLE.   A job, I suppose; let us get wan first before we start lookin' for another.

MRS. BOYLE.   That's the thing that's able to put the win' up you. Well, it's no job, but news that'll give you the chance o' your life.

BOYLE.   What's all the mystery about?

MRS. BOYLE.   G'win an' take off the moleskin trousers when you're told!

(BOYLE *goes into room on left,* MRS. BOYLE *tidies up the room, puts the shovel under the bed, and goes to the press.*)

MRS. BOYLE.   Oh, God bless us, looka the way everythin's thrun about! Oh, Joxer was here, Joxer was here!

(MARY *enters with* CHARLIE BENTHAM; *he is a young man of twenty-five, tall, good-looking, with a very high opinion of himself generally. He is dressed in a brown coat, brown knee-breeches, grey stockings, a brown sweater, with a deep blue tie; he carries gloves and a walking-stick.*)

MRS. BOYLE (*fussing round*). Come in, Mr. Bentham; sit down, Mr. Bentham, in this chair; it's more comfortabler than that, Mr. Bentham. Himself'll be here in a minute; he's just takin' off his trousers.

MARY. Mother!

BENTHAM. Please don't put yourself to any trouble, Mrs. Boyle—I'm quite all right here, thank you.

MRS. BOYLE. An' to think of you knowin' Mary, an' she knowin' the news you had for us, an' wouldn't let on; but it's all the more welcomer now, for we were on our last lap!

VOICE OF JOHNNY (*inside*). What are you kickin' up all the racket for?

BOYLE (*roughly*). I'm takin' off me moleskin trousers!

JOHNNY. Can't you do it, then, without lettin' th' whole house know you're takin' off your trousers? What d'ye want puttin' them on an' takin' them off again?

BOYLE. Will you let me alone, will you let me alone? Am I never goin' to be done thryin' to please th' whole o' yous?

MRS BOYLE (*to* BENTHAM). You must excuse th' state o' th' place, Mr. Bentham; th' minute I turn me back that man o' mine always makes a litther o' th' place, a litther o' th' place.

BENTHAM. Don't worry, Mrs. Boyle; it's all right, I assure . . .

BOYLE (*inside*). Where's me braces; where in th' name o' God did I leave me braces. . . . Ay, did you see where I put me braces?

JOHNNY (*inside, calling out*). Ma, will you come in here an' take da away ou' o' this or he'll dhrive me mad.

MRS. BOYLE (*going towards door*). Dear, dear, dear, that man'll be lookin' for somethin' on th' day o' Judgment. (*Looking into room and calling to* BOYLE.) Look at your braces, man, hangin' round your neck!

BOYLE (*inside*). Aw, Holy God!

MRS. BOYLE (*calling*). Johnny, Johnny, come out here for a minute.

JOHNNY. Oh, leave Johnny alone, an' don't be annoyin' him!

MRS. BOYLE. Come on, Johnny, till I inthroduce you to Mr. Bentham. (*To* BENTHAM.) Me son, Mr. Bentham; he's afther goin' through the mill. He was only a chiselur of a Boy Scout in Easter Week, when he got hit in the hip; and his arm was blew off in the fight in O'Connell Street. (JOHNNY *comes in.*) Here he is, Mr. Bentham; Mr. Bentham. Iohnny. None can deny he done his bit for Irelan', if that's going to do him any good.

JOHNNY (*boastfully*). I'd do it agen, ma, I'd do it agen; for a principle's a principle.

MRS. BOYLE. Ah, you lost your best principle, me boy, when you lost your arm; them's the only sort o' principles that's any good to a workin' man.

JOHNNY.   Ireland only half free'll never be at peace while she has a son left to pull a trigger.

MRS. BOYLE.   To be sure, to be sure—no bread's a lot betther than half a loaf. (*Calling loudly in to* BOYLE.) Will you hurry up there?

(BOYLE *enters in his best trousers, which aren't too good, and looks very uncomfortable in his collar and tie.*)

MRS. BOYLE.   This is me husband; Mr. Boyle, Mr. Bentham.

BENTHAM.   Ah, very glad to know you, Mr. Boyle. How are you?

BOYLE.   Ah, I'm not too well at all; I suffer terrible with pains in me legs. Juno can tell you there what . . .

MRS. BOYLE.   You won't have many pains in your legs when you hear what Mr. Bentham has to tell you.

BENTHAM.   Juno! What an interesting name! It reminds one of Homer's glorious story of ancient gods and heroes.

BOYLE.   Yis, doesn't it? You see, Juno was born an' christened in June I met her in June; we were married in June, an' Johnny was born in June, so wan day I says to her, "You should ha' been called Juno," an' the name stuck to her ever since.

MRS. BOYLE.   Here, we can talk o' them things agen; let Mr. Bentham say what he has to say now.

BENTHAM.   Well, Mr. Boyle, I suppose you'll remember a Mr. Ellison of Santry—he's a relative of yours, I think.

BOYLE (*viciously*).   Is it that prognosticator an' procrastinator! Of course I remember him.

BENTHAM.   Well, he's dead, Mr. Boyle . . .

BOYLE.   Sorra many'll go into mournin' for him.

MRS. BOYLE.   Wait till you hear what Mr. Bentham has to say, an' then, maybe, you'll change your opinion.

BENTHAM.   A week before he died he sent for me to write his will for him. He told me that there were two only that he wished to leave his property to: his second cousin Michael Finnegan of Santry, and John Boyle, his first cousin of Dublin.

BOYLE (*excitedly*).   Me, is it me, me?

BENTHAM.   You, Mr. Boyle; I'll read a copy of the will that I have here with me, which has been duly filed in the Court of Probate. (*He takes a paper from his pocket and reads*):

6th February 1922.

This is the last Will and Testament of William Ellison, of Santry, in the County of Dublin. I hereby order and wish my property to be sold and divided as follows:—

£ 20 to the St. Vincent De Paul Society.

£ 60 for Masses for the repose of my soul (5s. for Each Mass).

The rest of my property to be divided between my first and second cousins.

I hereby appoint Timothy Buckly, of Santry, and Hugh Brierly, of Coolock, to be my Executors.

(*Signed*)

WILLIAM ELLISON.
HUGH BRIERLY.
TIMOTHY BUCKLY.
CHARLES BENTHAM, N.T.

BOYLE (*eagerly*). An' how much'll be comin' out of it, Mr. Bentham?

BENTHAM. The Executors told me that half of the property would be anything between £ 1500 and £ 2000.

MARY. A fortune, father, a fortune!

JOHNNY. We'll be able to get out o' this place now, an' go somewhere we're not known.

MRS. BOYLE. You won't have to trouble about a job for a while, Jack.

BOYLE (*fervently*). I'll never doubt the goodness o' God agen.

BENTHAM. I congratulate you, Mr. Boyle. (*They shake hands.*)

BOYLE. An' now, Mr. Bentham, you'll have to have a wet.

BENTHAM. A wet?

BOYLE. A wet—a jar—a boul!

MRS. BOYLE. Jack, you're speakin' to Mr. Bentham, an' not to Joxer.

BOYLE (*solemnly*). Juno ... Mary ... Johnny ... we'll have to go into mournin' at wanst. . . . I never expected that poor Bill ud die so sudden. . . . Well, we all have to die some day ... you, Juno, to-day ... an' me, maybe, to-morrow. . . . It's sad, but it can't be helped. . . . Requiescat in pace ... or, usin' our oul' tongue like St. Patrick or St. Briget, Guh sayeree jeea ayera!

MARY. Oh, father, that's not Rest in Peace; that's God save Ireland.

BOYLE. U-u-ugh, it's all the same—isn't it a prayer? . . . Juno, I'm done with Joxer; he's nothin' but a prognosticator an' a . . .

JOXER (*climbing angrily through the window and bounding into the room*). You're done with Joxer, are you? Maybe you thought I'd stop on the roof all the night for you! Joxer out on the roof with the win' blowin' through him was nothin' to you an' your friend with the collar an' tie!

MRS. BOYLE. What in the name o' God brought you out on the roof; what were you doin' there?

JOXER (*ironically*). I was dhreamin' I was standin' on the bridge of a ship, an' she sailin' the Antarctic Ocean, an' it blowed, an' blowed, an' I lookin' up at the sky an' sayin', what is the stars, what is the stars?

MRS. BOYLE (*opening the door and standing at it*). Here, get ou' o' this, Joxer Daly; I was always thinkin' you had a slate off.

JOXER (*moving to the door*). I have to laugh every time I look at the deep sea sailor; an' a row on a river ud make him sea-sick!

BOYLE. Get ou' o' this before I take the law into me own hands!

JOXER (*going out*). Say aw rewaeawr, but not good-bye. Lookin' for work, an' prayin' to God he won't get it! (*He goes.*)

MRS. BOYLE.   I'm tired tellin' you what Joxer was; maybe now you see yourself the kind he is.

BOYLE.   He'll never blow the froth off a pint o' mine agen, that's a sure thing. Johnny . . . Mary . . . you're to keep yourselves to yourselves for the future. Juno, I'm done with Joxer. . . . I'm a new man from this out. . . . (*Clasping* JUNO's *hand, and singing emotionally*):

> Oh, me darlin' Juno, I will be thrue to thee;
> Me own, me darlin' Juno, you're all the world to me.

CURTAIN

ACT II

SCENE.   *The same, but the furniture is more plentiful, and of a vulgar nature. A glaringly upholstered arm-chair and lounge; cheap pictures and photos everywhere. Every available spot is ornamented with huge vases filled with artificial flowers. Crossed festoons of coloured paper chains stretch from end to end of ceiling. On the table is an old attaché case. It is about six in the evening, and two days after the First Act.* BOYLE, *in his shirt sleeves, is voluptuously stretched on the sofa; he is smoking a clay pipe. He is half asleep. A lamp is lighting on the table. After a few moments' pause the voice of* JOXER *is heard singing softly outside at the door*—"Me pipe I'll smoke, as I dhrive me moke—are you there, Mor . . . ee . . . ar . . . i . . . teel."

BOYLE (*leaping up, takes a pen in his hand and busies himself with papers*).   Come along, Joxer, me son, come along.

JOXER (*putting his head in*).   Are you be yourself?

BOYLE.   Come on, come on; that doesn't matther; I'm masther now, an' I'm goin' to remain masther.

(JOXER *comes in.*)

JOXER.   How d'ye feel now, as a man o' money?

BOYLE (*solemnly*).   It's a responsibility, Joxer, a great responsibility.

JOXER.   I suppose 'tis now, though you wouldn't think it.

BOYLE.   Joxer, han' me over that attackey case on the table there. (JOXER *hands the case.*) Ever since the Will was passed I've run hundhreds o' dockyments through me han's—I tell you, you have to keep your wits about you. (*He busies himself with papers.*)

JOXER.   Well, I won't disturb you; I'll dhrop in when . . .

BOYLE (*hastily*).   It's all right, Joxer, this is the last one to be signed today. (*He signs a paper, puts it into the case, which he shuts with a snap, and sits back pompously in the chair.*) Now, Joxer, you want to see me; I'm at your service—what can I do for you, me man?

JOXER.   I've just dhropped in with the £3 : 5s. that Mrs. Madigan riz on the blankets an' table for you, and she says you're to be in no hurry payin' it back.

BOYLE. She won't be long without it; I expect the first cheque for a couple o' hundhred any day. There's the five bob for yourself—go on, take it, man; it'll not be the last you'll get from the Captain. Now an' agen we have our differ, but we're there together all the time.

JOXER. Me for you, an' you for me, like the two Musketeers.

BOYLE. Father Farrell stopped me to-day an' tole me how glad he was I fell in for the money.

JOXER. He'll be stoppin' you often enough now; I suppose it was "Mr." Boyle with him?

BOYLE. He shuk me be the han'. . . .

JOXER (*ironically*). I met with Napper Tandy, an' he shuk me be the han'!

BOYLE. You're seldom asthray, Joxer, but you're wrong shipped this time. What you're sayin' of Father Farrell is very near to blasfeemey. I don't like any one to talk disrespectful of Father Farrell.

JOXER. You're takin' me up wrong, Captain; I wouldn't let a word be said agen Father Farrell—the heart o' the rowl, that's what he is; I always said he was a darlin' man, a daarlin' man.

BOYLE. Comin' up the stairs who did I meet but that bummer, Nugent. "I seen you talkin' to Father Farrell," says he, with a grin on him. "He'll be folleyin' you," says he, "like a Guardian Angel from this out"— all the time the oul' grin on him, Joxer.

JOXER. I never seen him yet but he had that oul' grin on him!

BOYLE. "Mr. Nugent," says I, "Father Farrell is a man o' the people, an', as far as I know the History o' me country, the priests was always in the van of the fight for Irelan's freedom."

JOXER (*fervently*):

> Who was it led the van, Soggart Aroon?
> Since the fight first began, Soggart Aroon?

BOYLE. "Who are you tellin'?" says he. "Didn't they let down the Fenians, an' didn't they do in Parnell? An' now . . ." "You ought to be ashamed o' yourself," says I, interruptin' him, "not to know the History o' your country." An' I left him gawkin' where he was.

JOXER. Where ignorance 's bliss 'tis folly to be wise; I wondher did he ever read the Story o' Irelan'.

BOYLE. Be J. L. Sullivan? Don't you know he didn't?

JOXER. Ah, it's a darlin' buk, a daarlin' buk!

BOYLE. You'd betther be goin', now, Joxer, his Majesty, Bentham, 'll be here any minute, now.

JOXER. Be the way things is lookin', it'll be a match between him an' Mary. She's thrun over Jerry altogether. Well, I hope it will, for he's a darlin' man.

BOYLE. I'm glad you think so—I don't. (*Irritably.*) What's darlin' about him?

JOXER (*nonplussed*). I only seen him twiced; if you want to know me, come an' live with me.

BOYLE. He's too ignified for me—to hear him talk you'd think he knew as much as a Boney's Oraculum. He's given up his job as teacher, an' is goin' to become a solicitor in Dublin—he's been studyin' law. I suppose he thinks I'll set him up, but he's wrong shipped. An' th' other fella—Jerry's as bad. The two o' them ud give you a pain in your face, listenin' to them; Jerry believin' in nothin', an' Bentham believin' in everythin'. One that says all is God an' no man; an' th' other that says all is man an' no God!

JOXER. Well, I'll be off now.

BOYLE. Don't forget to dhrop down afther a while; we'll have a quiet jar, an' a song or two.

JOXER. Never fear.

BOYLE. An' tell Mrs. Madigan that I hope we'll have the pleasure of her organization at our little entherthainment.

JOXER. Righto; we'll come down together. (*He goes out.*)

(JOHNNY *comes from room on left, and sits down moodily at the fire.* BOYLE *looks at him for a few moments, and shakes his head. He fills his pipe.*)

VOICE OF JUNO AT THE DOOR. Open the door, Jack; this thing has me nearly kilt with the weight.

(BOYLE *opens the door.* JUNO *enters carrying the box of a gramophone, followed by* MARY *carrying the horn, and some parcels.* JUNO *leaves the box on the table and flops into a chair.*)

JUNO. Carryin' that from Henry Street was no joke.

BOYLE. U-u-ugh, that's a grand lookin' insthrument—how much was it?

JUNO. Pound down, an' five to be paid at two shillin's a week.

BOYLE. That's reasonable enough.

JUNO. I'm afraid we're runnin' into too much debt; first the furniture, an' now this.

BOYLE. The whole lot won't be much out of £2000.

MARY. I don't know what you wanted a gramophone for—I know Charlie hates them; he says they're destructive of real music.

BOYLE. Desthructive of music—that fella ud give you a pain in your face. All a gramophone wants is to be properly played; its thrue wondher is only felt when everythin's quiet—what a gramophone wants is dead silence!

MARY. But, father, Jerry says the same; afther all, you can only appreciate music when your ear is properly trained.

BOYLE. That's another fella ud give you a pain in your face. Properly thrained! I suppose you couldn't appreciate football unless your fut was properly thrained.

MRS. BOYLE (*to* MARY). Go on in ower that an' dress, or Charlie 'll be in on you, an' tay nor nothin' 'll be ready.

(MARY *goes into room left.*)

MRS. BOYLE (*arranging table for tea*). You didn't look at our new gramophone, Johnny?

JOHNNY. 'Tisn't gramophones I'm thinking of.

MRS. BOYLE. An' what is it you're thinkin' of, allanna?

JOHNNY. Nothin', nothin', nothin'.

MRS. BOYLE. Sure, you must be thinkin' of somethin'; it's yourself that has yourself the way y'are; sleepin' wan night in me sisther's, an' the nex' in your father's brother's—you'll get no rest goin' on that way.

JOHNNY. I can rest nowhere, nowhere, nowhere.

MRS. BOYLE. Sure, you're not thryin' to rest anywhere.

JOHNNY. Let me alone, let me alone, let me alone, for God's sake.

(*A knock at street door.*)

MRS. BOYLE (*in a flutter*). Here he is; here's Mr. Bentham!

BOYLE. Well, there's room for him; it's a pity there's not a brass band to play him in.

MRS. BOYLE. We'll han' the tay round, an' not be clusthered round the table, as if we never seen nothin'.

(*Steps are heard approaching, and* JUNO, *opening the door, allows* BENTHAM *to enter.*)

JUNO. Give your hat an' stick to Jack, there . . . sit down, Mr. Bentham . . . no, not there . . . in th' easy chair be the fire . . . there, that's betther. Mary'll be out to you in a minute.

BOYLE (*solemnly*). I seen be the paper this mornin' that Consols was down half per cent. That's serious, min' you, an' shows the whole counthry's in a state o' chassis.

MRS. BOYLE. What's Consols, Jack?

BOYLE. Consols? Oh, Consols is—oh, there's no use tellin' women what Consols is—th' wouldn't undherstand.

BENTHAM. It's just as you were saying, Mr. Boyle . . .

(MARY *enters charmingly dressed.*)

BENTHAM. Oh, good evening, Mary; how pretty you're looking!

MARY (*archly*). Am I?

BOYLE. We were just talkin' when you kem in, Mary, I was tellin' Mr. Bentham that the whole counthry's in a state o' chassis.

MARY (*to* BENTHAM). Would you prefer the green or the blue ribbon round me hair, Charlie?

MRS. BOYLE. Mary, your father's speakin'.

BOYLE (*rapidly*). I was jus' tellin' Mr. Bentham that the whole counthry's in a state o' chassis.

MARY. I'm sure you're frettin', da, whether it is or no.

MRS. BOYLE. With all our churches an' religions, the worl's not a bit the betther.

BOYLE (*with a commanding gesture*). Tay!

(MARY *and* MRS. BOYLE *dispense the tea.*)

MRS. BOYLE. An' Irelan's takin' a leaf out o' the worl's buk; when we got the makin' of our own laws I thought we'd never stop to look behind us, but instead of that we never stopped to look before us! If the people ud folley up their religion betther there'd be a betther chance for us—what do you think, Mr. Bentham?

BENTHAM.   I'm afraid I can't venture to express an opinion on that point, Mrs. Boyle; dogma has no attraction for me.

MRS. BOYLE.   I forgot you didn't hold with us: what's this you said you were?

BENTHAM.   A Theosophist, Mrs. Boyle.

MRS. BOYLE.   An' what in the name o' God's a Theosophist?

BOYLE.   A Theosophist, Juno, 's a—tell her, Mr. Bentham, tell her.

BENTHAM.   It's hard to explain in a few words: Theosophy's founded on The Vedas, the religious books of the East. Its central theme is the existence of an all-pervading Spirit—the Life-Breath. Nothing really exists but this one Universal Life-Breath. And whatever even seems to exist separately from this Life-Breath, doesn't really exist at all. It is all vital force in man, in all animals, and in all vegetation. This Life-Breath is called the Prawna.

MRS. BOYLE.   The Prawna! What a comical name!

BOYLE.   Prawna; yis, the Prawna. (*Blowing gently through his lips.*) That's the Prawna!

MRS. BOYLE.   Whist, whist, Jack.

BENTHAM.   The happiness of man depends upon his sympathy with this Spirit. Men who have reached a high state of excellence are called Yogi. Some men become Yogi in a short time, it may take others millions of years.

BOYLE.   Yogi! I seen hundhreds of them in the streets o' San Francisco.

BENTHAM.   It is said by these Yogi that if we practise certain mental exercises that we would have powers denied to others—for instance, the faculty of seeing things that happen miles and miles away.

MRS. BOYLE.   I wouldn't care to meddle with that sort o' belief; it's a very curious religion, altogether.

BOYLE.   What's curious about it? Isn't all religions curious? If they weren't, you wouldn't get any one to believe them. But religions is passin' away—they've had their day like everything else. Take the real Dublin people, f'rinstance: they know more about Charlie Chaplin an' Tommy Mix than they do about SS. Peter an' Paul!

MRS. BOYLE.   You don't believe in ghosts, Mr. Bentham?

MARY.   Don't you know he doesn't, mother?

BENTHAM.   I don't know that, Mary. Scientists are beginning to think that what we call ghosts are sometimes seen by persons of a certain nature. They say that sensational actions, such as the killing of a person, demand great energy, and that that energy lingers in the place where the action occurred. People may live in the place and see nothing, when some one may come along whose personality has some peculiar connection with the energy of the place, and, in a flash, the person sees the whole affair.

JOHNNY (*rising swiftly, pale and affected*).   What sort o' talk is this to be goin' on with? Is there nothin' betther to be talkin' about but the killin' o' people? My God, isn't it bad enough for these things to happen without talkin' about them! (*He hurriedly goes into the room on left.*)

BENTHAM. Oh, I'm very sorry, Mrs. Boyle; I never thought . . .

MRS. BOYLE (*apologetically*). Never mind, Mr. Bentham, he's very touchy. (*A frightened scream is heard from* JOHNNY *inside.*)

MRS. BOYLE. Mother of God? What's that?

(*He rushes out again, his face pale, his lips twitching, his limbs trembling.*)

JOHNNY. Shut the door, shut the door, quick, for God's sake! Great God, have mercy on me! Blessed Mother o' God, shelter me, shelter your son!

MRS. BOYLE (*catching him in her arms*). What's wrong with you? What ails you? Sit down, sit down, here, on the bed . . . there now . . . there now.

MARY. Johnny, Johnny, what ails you?

JOHNNY. I seen him, I seen him . . . kneelin' in front o' the statue . . . merciful Jesus, have pity on me!

MRS. BOYLE (*to* BOYLE). Get him a glass o' whisky . . . quick, man, an' don't stand gawkin'.

(BOYLE *gets the whisky.*)

JOHNNY. Sit here, sit here, mother . . . between me an' the door.

MRS. BOYLE. I'll sit beside you as long as you like, only tell me what was it came across you at all?

JOHNNY (*after taking some drink*). I seen him. . . . I seen Robbie Tancred kneelin' down before the statue . . . an' the red light shinin' on him . . . an' when I went in . . . he turned an' looked at me . . . an' I seen the woun's bleedin' in his breast. . . . Oh, why did he look at me like that . . . it wasn't my fault that he was done in. . . . Mother o' God, keep him away from me!

MRS. BOYLE. There, there, child, you've imagined it all. There was nothin' there at all—it was the red light you seen, an' the talk we had put all the rest into your head. Here, dhrink more o' this—it'll do you good. . . . An', now, stretch yourself down on the bed for a little. (*To* BOYLE.) Go in, Jack, an' show him it was only in his own head it was.

BOYLE (*making no move*). E-e-e-eh; it's all nonsense; it was only a shadda he saw.

MARY. Mother o' God, he made me heart lep!

BENTHAM. It was simply due to an overwrought imagination—we all get that way at times.

MRS. BOYLE. There, dear, lie down in the bed, an' I'll put the quilt across you . . . e-e-e-eh, that's it . . . you'll be as right as the mail in a few minutes.

JOHNNY. Mother, go into the room an' see if the light's lightin' before the statue.

MRS. BOYLE (*to* BOYLE). Jack, run in, an' see if the light's lightin' before the statue.

BOYLE (*to* MARY). Mary, slip in an' see if the light's lightin' before the statue.

(MARY *hesitates to go in.*)

BENTHAM. It's all right; Mary, I'll go. (*He goes into the room; remains for a few moments, and returns.*)

BENTHAM. Everything's just as it was—the light burning bravely before the statue.

BOYLE. Of course; I knew it was all nonsense.

(*A knock at the door.*)

BOYLE (*going to open the door*). E-e-e-e-eh. (*He opens it, and* JOXER, *followed by* MRS. MADIGAN, *enters.* MRS. MADIGAN *is a strong, dapper little woman of about forty-five; her face is almost always a widespread smile of complacency. She is a woman who, in manner at least, can mourn with them that mourn, and rejoice with them that do rejoice. When she is feeling comfortable, she is inclined to be reminiscent; when others say anything, or following a statement made by herself, she has a habit of putting her head a little to one side, and nodding it rapidly several times in succession, like a bird pecking at a hard berry. Indeed, she has a good deal of the bird in her, but the bird instinct is by no means a melodious one. She is ignorant, vulgar and forward, but her heart is generous withal. For instance, she would help a neighbour's sick child; she would probably kill the child, but her intentions would be to cure it; she would be more at home helping a drayman to lift a fallen horse. She is dressed in a rather soiled grey dress and a vivid purple blouse; in her hair is a huge comb, ornamented with huge coloured beads. She enters with a gliding step, beaming smile and nodding head.* BOYLE *receives them effusively.*)

BOYLE. Come on in, Mrs. Madigan; come on in; I was afraid you weren't comin'. . . . (*Slyly.*) There's some people able to dhress, ay, Joxer?

JOXER. Fair as the blossoms that bloom in the May, an' sweet as the scent of the new mown hay. . . . Ah, well she may wear them.

MRS. MADIGAN (*looking at* MARY). I know some as are as sweet as the blossoms that bloom in the May—oh, no names, no pack dhrill!

BOYLE. An', now, I'll inthroduce the pair o' yous to Mary's intended: Mr. Bentham, this is Mrs. Madigan, an oul' back-parlour neighbour, that, if she could help it at all, ud never see a body shuk!

BENTHAM (*rising, and tentatively shaking the hand of* MRS. MADIGAN). I'm sure, it's a great pleasure to know you, Mrs. Madigan.

MRS. MADIGAN. An' I'm goin' to tell you, Mr. Bentham, you're goin' to get as nice a bit o' skirt in Mary, there, as ever you seen in your puff. Not like some of the dhressed up dolls that's knockin' about lookin' for men when it's a skelpin' they want. I remember as well as I remember yesterday, the day she was born—of a Tuesday, the 25th o' June, in the year 1901, at thirty-three minutes past wan in the day be Foley's clock, the pub at the corner o' the street. A cowld day it was too, for the season o' the year, an' I remember sayin' to Joxer, there, who I met comin' up th' stairs, that the new arrival in Boyle's ud grow up a hardy chiselur if it lived, an' that she'd be somethin' one o' these days that nobody suspected, an' so signs on it, here she is to-day, goin' to be married to a young man lookin' as if he'd be fit to commensurate in any position in life it ud please God to call him!

BOYLE (*effusively*). Sit down, Mrs. Madigan, sit down, me oul' sport. (*To* BENTHAM.) This is Joxer Daly, Past Chief Ranger of the Dear Little Shamrock Branch of the Irish National Foresters, an' oul' front-top neighbour, that never despaired, even in the darkest days of Ireland's sorra.

JOXER. Nil desperandum, Captain, nil desperandum.

BOYLE. Sit down, Joxer, sit down. The two of us was ofen in a tight corner.

MRS. BOYLE. Ay, in Foley's snug!

JOXER. An' we kem out of it flyin', we kem out of it flyin', Captain.

BOYLE. An', now, for a dhrink—I know yous won't refuse an oul' friend.

MRS. MADIGAN (*to* JUNO). Is Johnny not well, Mrs. . . .

MRS. BOYLE (*warningly*). S-s-s-sh.

MRS. MADIGAN. Oh, the poor darlin'

BOYLE. Well, Mrs. Madigan, is it tay or what?

MRS. MADIGAN. Well, speakin' for meself, I jus' had me tea a minute ago, an' I'm afraid to dhrink any more—I'm never the same when I dhrink too much tay. Thanks, all the same, Mr. Boyle.

BOYLE. Well, what about a bottle o' stout or a dhrop o' whisky?

MRS. MADIGAN. A bottle o' stout ud be a little too heavy for me stummock afther me tay. . . . A-a-ah, I'll thry the ball o' malt.

(BOYLE *prepares the whisky.*)

MRS. MADIGAN. There's nothin' like a ball o' malt occasional like—too much of it isn't good. (*To* BOYLE, *who is adding water.*) Ah, God, Johnny, don't put too much wather on it! (*She drinks.*) I suppose yous'll be lavin' this place.

BOYLE. I'm looking for a place near the sea; I'd like the place that you might say was me cradle, to be me grave as well. The sea is always callin' me.

JOXER. She is callin', callin', callin', in the win' an' on the sea.

BOYLE. Another dhrop o' whisky, Mrs. Madigan?

MRS. MADIGAN. Well, now, it ud be hard to refuse seein' the suspicious times that's in it.

BOYLE (*with a commanding gesture*). Song! . . . Juno . . . Mary . . . "Home to Our Mount'ins"!

MRS. MADIGAN (*enthusiastically*). Hear, hear!

JOXER. Oh, tha's a darlin' song, a daarlin' song!

MARY (*bashfully*). Ah, no, da; I'm not in a singin' humour.

MRS. MADIGAN. Gawn with you, child, an' you only goin' to be marrid; I remember as well as I remember yestherday,—it was on a lovely August evenin', exactly, accordin' to date, fifteen years ago, come the Tuesday folleyin' the nex' that's comin' on, when me own man (the Lord be good to him) an' me was sittin' shy together in a doty little nook on a counthry road, adjacent to The Stiles. "That'll scratch your lovely, little white neck," says he, ketchin' hould of a danglin' bramble branch, holdin' clusters of the loveliest flowers you ever seen, an' breakin' it off, so that his arm fell, accidental like, roun' me waist, an' as I felt it tightenin', an' tightenin', an' tightenin', I thought me buzzum was every minute goin' to burst out into a roystherin' song about

> The little green leaves that were shakin' on the threes,
> The gallivantin' buttherflies, an' buzzin' o' the bees!

BOYLE. Ordher for the song!

JUNO. Come on, Mary—we'll do our best. (JUNO *and* MARY *stand up, and choosing a suitable position, sing simply* "Home to Our Mountains.")

(*They bow to company, and return to their places.*)

BOYLE (*emotionally, at the end of the song*). Lull . . . me . . . to . . . rest!

JOXER (*clapping his hands*). Bravo, bravo! Darlin' girulls, darlin' girulls!

MRS. MADIGAN. Juno, I never seen you in betther form.

BENTHAM. Very nicely rendered indeed.

MRS. MADIGAN. A noble call, a noble call!

MRS. BOYLE. What about yourself, Mrs. Madigan? (*After some coaxing,* MRS. MADIGAN *rises, and in a quavering voice sings the following verse*):

> If I were a blackbird I'd whistle and sing;
> I'd follow the ship that my thrue love was in;
> An' on the top riggin', I'd there build me nest,
> An' at night I would sleep on me Willie's white breast!

(*Becoming husky, amid applause, she sits down.*)

MRS. MADIGAN. Ah, me voice is too husky now, Juno; though I remember the time when Maisie Madigan could sing like a nightingale at matin' time. I remember as well as I remember yestherday, at a party given to celebrate the comin' of the first chiselur to Annie an' Benny Jimeson—who was the barber, yous may remember, in Henrietta Street, that, after Easter Week, hung out a green, white an' orange pole, an', then, when the Tans started their Jazz dancin', whipped it in agen, an' stuck out a red, white an' blue wan instead, given as an excuse that a barber's pole was strictly non-political—singin' "An' You'll Remember Me," with the top notes quiverin' in a dead hush of pethrified attention, folleyed by a clappin' o' han's that shuk the tumblers on the table, an' capped be Jimeson, the barber, sayin' that it was the best rendherin' of "You'll Remember Me" he ever heard in his natural!

BOYLE (*peremptorily*). Ordher for Joxer's song!

JOXER. Ah, no, I couldn't; don't ass me, Captain.

BOYLE. Joxer's song, Joxer's song—give us wan of your shut-eyed wans. (JOXER *settles himself in his chair; takes a drink; clears his throat; solemnly closes his eyes, and begins to sing in a very querulous voice*):

She is far from the lan' where her young hero sleeps,
An' lovers around her are sighing (*He hesitates*)
An' lovers around her are sighin' . . . sighin' . . . sighin' . . . (*A pause.*)

BOYLE (*imitating* JOXER):

And lovers around her are sighing!

What's the use of you thryin' to sing the song if you don't know it?

MARY. Thry another one, Mr. Daly—maybe you'd be more fortunate.

MRS. MADIGAN. Gawn, Joxer, thry another wan.

JOXER (*starting again*):

I have heard the mavis singin' his love song to the morn;
I have seen the dew-dhrop clingin' to the rose jus' newly born;
but . . . but . . . (*frantically*) to the rose jus' newly born
. . . newly born . . . born.

JOHNNY. Mother, put on the gramophone, for God's sake, an' stop Joxer's bawlin'.

BOYLE (*commandingly*). Gramophone! . . . I hate to see fellas thryin' to do what they're not able to do. (BOYLE *arranges the gramophone, and is about to start it, when voices are heard of persons descending the stairs.*)

MRS. BOYLE (*warningly*). Whisht, Jack, don't put it on, don't put it on yet; this must be poor Mrs. Tancred comin' down to go to the hospital —I forgot all about them bringin' the body to the church to-night. Open the door, Mary, an' give them a bit o' light.

(MARY *opens the door, and* MRS. TANCRED—*a very old woman, obviously shaken by the death of her son—appears, accompanied by several neighbours. The first few phrases are spoken before they appear.*)

FIRST NEIGHBOUR. It's a sad journey we're goin' on, but God's good, an' the Republicans won't be always down.

MRS. TANCRED. Ah, what good is that to me now? Whether they're up or down—it won't bring me darlin' boy from the grave.

MRS. BOYLE. Come in an' have a hot cup o' tay, Mrs. Tancred, before you go.

MRS. TANCRED. Ah, I can take nothin' now, Mrs. Boyle—I won't be long afther him.

FIRST NEIGHBOUR. Still an' all, he died a noble death, an' we'll bury him like a king.

MRS. TANCRED. An' I'll go on livin' like a pauper. Ah, what's the pains I suffered bringin' him into the world to carry him to his cradle, to the pains I'm sufferin' now, carryin' him out o' the world to bring him to his grave!

MARY. It would be better for you not to go at all, Mrs. Tancred, but to stay at home beside the fire with some o' the neighbours.

MRS. TANCRED.   I seen the first of him, an' I'll see the last of him.

MRS. BOYLE.   You'd want a shawl, Mrs. Tancred; it's a cowld night, an' the win's blowin' sharp.

MRS. MADIGAN (*rushing out*).   I've a shawl above.

MRS. TANCRED.   Me home is gone, now; he was me only child, an' to think that he was lyin' for a whole night stretched out on the side of a lonely counthry lane, with his head, his darlin' head, that I ofen kissed an' fondled, half hidden in the wather of a runnin' brook. An' I'm told he was the leadher of the ambush where me nex' door neighbour, Mrs. Mannin', lost her Free State soldier son. An' now here's the two of us oul' women, standin' one on each side of a scales o' sorra, balanced be the bodies of our two dead darlin' sons. (MRS. MADIGAN *returns, and wraps a shawl around her*.) God bless you, Mrs. Madigan. . . . (*She moves slowly towards the door*.) Mother o' God, Mother o' God, have pity on the pair of us! . . . O Blessed Virgin, where were you when me darlin' son was riddled with bullets, when me darlin' son was riddled with bullets! . . . Sacred Heart of the Crucified Jesus, take away our hearts o' stone . . . an' give us hearts o' flesh! . . . Take away this murdherin' hate . . . an' give us Thine own eternal love! (*They pass out of the room*.)

MRS. BOYLE (*explanatorily to* BENTHAM).   That was Mrs. Tancred of the two-pair back; her son was found, e'er yesterday, lyin' out beyant Finglas riddled with bullets. A die-hard he was, be all accounts. He was a nice quiet boy, but lattherly he went to hell, with his Republic first, an' Republic last an' Republic over all. He ofen took tea with us here, in the oul' days, an' Johnny, there, an' him used to be always together.

JOHNNY.   Am I always to be havin' to tell you that he was no friend o' mine? I never cared for him, an' he could never stick me. It's not because he was Commandant of the Battalion that I was Quarther-Masther of, that we were friends.

MRS. BOYLE.   He's gone, now—the Lord be good to him! God help his poor oul' creature of a mother, for no matther whose friend or enemy he was, he was her poor son.

BENTHAM.   The whole thing is terrible, Mrs. Boyle; but the only way to deal with a mad dog is to destroy him.

MRS. BOYLE.   An' to think of me forgettin' about him bein' brought to the church to-night, an' we singin' an' all, but it was well we hadn't the gramophone goin', anyhow.

BOYLE.   Even if we had aself. We've nothin' to do with these things, one way or t'other. That's the Government's business, an' let them do what we're payin' them for doin'.

MRS. BOYLE.   I'd like to know how a body's not to mind these things; look at the way they're afther leavin' the people in this very house. Hasn't the whole house, nearly, been massacreed? There's young Mrs. Dougherty's husband with his leg off; Mrs. Travers that had her son blew up be a mine in Inchegeela, in Co. Cork; Mrs. Mannin' that lost wan of her sons in an ambush a few weeks ago, an' now, poor Mrs. Tancred's only child gone

West with his body made a collandher of. Sure, if it's not our business, I don't know whose business it is.

BOYLE. Here, there, that's enough about them things; they don't affect us, an' we needn't give a damn. If they want a wake, well, let them have a wake. When I was a sailor, I was always resigned to meet with a wathery grave; an', if they want to be soldiers, well, there's no use o' them squealin' when they meet a soldier's fate.

JOXER. Let me like a soldier fall—me breast expandin' to th' ball!

MRS. BOYLE. In wan way, she deserves all she got; for lately, she let th' die-hards make an open house of th' place; an' for th' last couple of months, either when th' sun was risin', or when th' sun was settin', you had C.I.D. men burstin' into your room, assin' you where were you born, where were you christened, where were you married, an' where would you be buried!

JOHNNY. For God's sake, let us have no more o' this talk.

MRS. MADIGAN. What about Mr. Boyle's song before we start th' gramophone?

MARY (*getting her hat, and putting it on*). Mother, Charlie and I are goin' out for a little sthroll.

MRS. BOYLE. All right, darlin'.

BENTHAM (*going out with* MARY). We won't be long away, Mrs. Boyle.

MRS. MADIGAN. Gwan, Captain, gwan.

BOYLE. E-e-e-e-eh, I'd want to have a few more jars in me, before I'd be in fettle for singin'.

JOXER. Give us that poem you writ t'other day. (*To the rest.*) Aw, it's a darlin' poem, a daarlin' poem.

MRS. BOYLE. God bless us, is he startin' to write poetry!

BOYLE (*rising to his feet*). E-e-e-e-eh. (*He recites in an emotional, consequential manner the following verses*):

Shawn an' I were friends, sir, to me he was all in all.
His work was very heavy and his wages were very small.
None betther on th' beach as Docker, I'll go bail,
'Tis now I'm feelin' lonely, for to-day he lies in jail.
He was not what some call pious—seldom at church or prayer;
For the greatest scoundrels I know, sir, goes every Sunday there.
Fond of his pint—well, rather, but hated the Boss by creed
But never refused a copper to comfort a pal in need.
E-e-e-e-eh. (*He sits down.*)

MRS. MADIGAN. Grand, grand; you should folley that up, you should folley that up.

JOXER. It's a daarlin' poem!

BOYLE (*delightedly*). E-e-e-e-eh.

JOHNNY. Are yous goin' to put on th' gramophone to-night, or are yous not?

MRS. BOYLE. Gwan, Jack, put on a record.

MRS. MADIGAN. Gwan, Captain, gwan.

BOYLE. Well, yous'll want to keep a dead silence. (*He sets a record, starts the machine, and it begins to play "If you're Irish, come into the Parlour." As the tune is in full blare, the door is suddenly opened by a brisk, little bald-headed man, dressed circumspectly in a black suit; he glares fiercely at all in the room; he is "*NEEDLE NUGENT,*" a tailor. He carries his hat in his hands.*)

NUGENT (*loudly, above the noise of the gramophone*). Are yous goin' to have that thing bawlin' an' the funeral of Mrs. Tancred's son passin' the house? Have none of yous any respect for the Irish people's National regard for the dead?

(BOYLE *stops the gramophone.*)

MRS. BOYLE. Maybe, Needle Nugent, it's nearly time we had a little less respect for the dead, an' a little more regard for the livin'.

MRS. MADIGAN. We don't want you, Mr. Nugent, to teach us what we learned at our mother's knee. You don't look yourself as if you were dyin' of grief; if y'ass Maisie Madigan anything, I'd call you a real thrue die-hard an' live-soft Republican, attendin' Republican funerals in the day, an' stoppin' up half the night makin' suits for the Civic Guards! (*Persons are heard running down to the street, some saying, "Here it is, here it is."* NUGENT *withdraws, and the rest, except* JOHNNY, *go to the window looking into the street, and look out. Sounds of a crowd coming nearer are heard; portion are singing*):

To Jesus' Heart all burning
With fervent love for men,
My heart with fondest yearning
Shall raise its joyful strain.
While ages course along,
Blest be with loudest song,
The Sacred Heart of Jesus
By every heart and tongue.

MRS. BOYLE. Here's the hearse, here's the hearse!

BOYLE. There's t'oul' mother walkin' behin' the coffin.

MRS. MADIGAN. You can hardly see the coffin with the wreaths.

JOXER. Oh, it's a darlin' funeral, a daarlin' funeral!

MRS. MADIGAN. We'd have a betther view from the street.

BOYLE. Yes—this place ud give you a crick in your neck. (*They leave the room, and go down.* JOHNNY *sits moodily by the fire.*)

(*A young man enters; he looks at* JOHNNY *for a moment.*)

THE YOUNG MAN. Quarther-Masther Boyle.

JOHNNY (*with a start*). The Mobilizer!

THE YOUNG MAN. You're not at the funeral?

JOHNNY. I'm not well.

THE YOUNG MAN. I'm glad I've found you; you were stoppin' at your aunt's; I called there but you'd gone. I've to give you an ordher to attend a Battalion Staff meetin' the night afther to-morrow.

JOHNNY. Where?

THE YOUNG MAN. I don't know; you're to meet me at the Pillar at eight o'clock; then we're to go to a place I'll be told of to-night; there we'll meet a mothor that'll bring us to the meeting. They think you might be able to know somethin' about them that gave the bend where Commandant Tancred was shelterin'.

JOHNNY. I'm not goin', then. I know nothing about Tancred.

THE YOUNG MAN (*at the door*). You'd betther come for your own sake —remember your oath.

JOHNNY (*passionately*). I won't go! Haven't I done enough for Ireland! I've lost me arm, an' me hip's desthroyed so that I'll never be able to walk right agen! Good God, haven't I done enough for Ireland?

THE YOUNG MAN. Boyle, no man can do enough for Ireland! (*He goes.*) (*Faintly in the distance the crowd is heard saying:*)

> Hail, Mary, full of grace, the Lord is with Thee;
> Blessed art Thou amongst women, and blessed, etc.

CURTAIN

ACT III

SCENE. *The same as Act Two. It is about half-past six on a November evening; a bright fire is burning in the grate; MARY, dressed to go out, is sitting on a chair by the fire, leaning forward, her hands under her chin, her elbows on her knees. A look of dejection, mingled with uncertain anxiety, is on her face. A lamp, turned low, is lighting on the table. The votive light under the picture of the Virgin, gleams more redly than ever. MRS. BOYLE is putting on her hat and coat. It is two months later.*

MRS. BOYLE. An' has Bentham never even written to you since—not one line for the past month?

MARY (*tonelessly*). Not even a line, mother.

MRS. BOYLE. That's very curious. . . . What came between the two of yous at all? To leave you so sudden, an' yous so great together. . . . To go away t' England, an' not to even leave you his address. . . . The way he was always bringin' you to dances, I thought he was mad afther you. Are you sure you said nothin' to him?

MARY. No, mother—at least nothing that could possibly explain his givin' me up.

MRS. BOYLE. You know you're a bit hasty at times, Mary, an' say things you shouldn't say.

MARY. I never said to him what I shouldn't say, I'm sure of that.

MRS. BOYLE. How are you sure of it?

MARY. Because I love him with all my heart and soul, mother. Why, I don't know; I often thought to myself that he wasn't the man poor Jerry was, but I couldn't help loving him, all the same.

MRS. BOYLE.   But you shouldn't be frettin' the way you are; when a woman loses a man, she never knows what she's afther losin', to be sure, but, then, she never knows what she's afther gainin', either. You're not the one girl of a month ago—you look like one pinin' away. It's long ago I had a right to bring you to the doctor, instead of waitin' till to-night.

MARY.   There's no necessity, really, mother, to go to the doctor; nothing serious is wrong with me—I'm run down and disappointed, that's all.

MRS. BOYLE.   I'll not wait another minute; I don't like the look of you at all. . . . I'm afraid we made a mistake in throwin' over poor Jerry. . . . He'd have been betther for you than that Bentham.

MARY.   Mother, the best man for a woman is the one for whom she has the most love, and Charlie had it all.

MRS. BOYLE.   Well, there's one thing to be said for him—he couldn't have been thinkin' of the money, or he wouldn't ha' left you . . . it must ha' been somethin' else.

MARY (*wearily*).   I don't know . . . I don't know, mother . . . only I think . . .

MRS. BOYLE.   What d'ye think?

MARY.   I imagine . . . he thought . . . we weren't . . . good enough for him.

MRS. BOYLE.   An' what was he himself, only a school teacher? Though I don't blame him for fightin' shy of people like that Joxer fella an' that oul' Madigan wan—nice sort o' people for your father to inthroduce to a man like Mr. Bentham. You might have told me all about this before now, Mary; I don't know why you like to hide everything from your mother; you knew Bentham, an' I'd ha' known nothin' about it if it hadn't bin for the Will; an' it was only to-day, afther long coaxin', that you let out that he'd left you.

MARY.   It would have been useless to tell you—you wouldn't understand.

MRS. BOYLE (*hurt*).   Maybe not. . . . Maybe I wouldn't understand. . . . Well, we'll be off now. (*She goes over to the door left, and speaks to* BOYLE *inside.*)

MRS. BOYLE.   We're goin' now to the doctor's. Are you goin' to get up this evenin'?

BOYLE (*from inside*).   The pains in me legs is terrible! It's me should be poppin' off to the doctor instead o' Mary, the way I feel.

MRS. BOYLE.   Sorra mend you! A nice way you were in last night—carried in a frog's march, dead to the world. If that's the way you'll go on when you get the money it'll be the grave for you, an asylum for me and the Poorhouse for Johnny.

BOYLE.   I thought you were goin'?

MRS. BOYLE.   That's what has you as you are—you can't bear to be spoken to. Knowin' the way we are, up to our ears in debt, it's a wondher you wouldn't ha' got up to go to th' solicitor's an' see if we could ha' gettin' a little o' the money even.

BOYLE (*shouting*). I can't be goin' up there night, noon an' mornin', can I? He can't give the money till he gets it, can he? I can't get blood out of a turnip, can I?

MRS. BOYLE. It's nearly two months since we heard of the Will, an' the money seems as far off as ever. . . . I suppose you know we owe twenty poun's to oul' Murphy?

BOYLE. I've a faint recollection of you tellin' me that before.

MRS. BOYLE. Well, you'll go over to the shop yourself for the things in future—I'll face him no more.

BOYLE. I thought you said you were goin'?

MRS. BOYLE. I'm goin' now; come on, Mary.

BOYLE. Ey, Juno, ey!

MRS. BOYLE. Well, what d'ye want now?

BOYLE. Is there e'er a bottle o' stout left?

MRS. BOYLE. There's two o' them here still.

BOYLE. Show us in one o' them an' leave t'other there till I get up. An' throw us in the paper that's on the table, an' the bottle o' Sloan's Liniment that's in th' drawer.

MRS. BOYLE (*getting the liniment and the stout*). What paper is it you want—the *Messenger*?

BOYLE. *Messenger! The News o' the World!*

(MRS. BOYLE *brings in the things asked for and comes out again.*)

MRS. BOYLE (*at door*). Mind the candle, now, an' don't burn the house over our heads. I left t'other bottle o' stout on the table. (*She puts bottle of stout on table. She goes out with* MARY. *A cork is heard popping inside.*)

(*A pause; then outside the door is heard the voice of* JOXER *lilting softly:* "Me pipe I'll smoke, as I dhrive me moke . . . are you . . . there . . . More . . . aar . . . i . . . tee!" *A gentle knock is heard and, after a pause, the door opens, and* JOXER, *followed by* NUGENT, *enters.*)

JOXER. Be God, they must all be out; I was thinkin' there was somethin' up when he didn't answer the signal. We seen Juno an' Mary goin', but I didn't see him, an' it's very seldom he escapes me.

NUGENT. He's not goin' to escape me—he's not goin' to be let go to the fair altogether.

JOXER. Sure, the house couldn't hould them lately; an' he goin' about like a mastherpiece of the Free State counthry; forgettin' their friends; forgettin' God—wouldn't even lift his hat passin' a chapel! Sure they were bound to get a dhrop! An' you really think there's no money comin' to him afther all?

NUGENT. Not as much as a red rex, man; I've been a bit anxious this long time over me money, an' I went up to the solicitor's to find out all I could—ah, man, they were goin' to throw me down the stairs. They toul' me that the oul' cock himself had the stairs worn away comin' up afther it, an' they black in the face tellin' him he'd get nothin'. Some way or another that the Will is writ he won't be entitled to get as much as a make!

JOXER.   Ah, I thought there was somethin' curious about the whole thing; I've bin havin' sthrange dreams for the last couple o' weeks. An' I notice that that Bentham fella doesn't be comin' here now—there must be somethin' on the mat there too. Anyhow, who, in the name o' God, ud leave anythin' to that oul' bummer? Sure it ud be unnatural. An' the way Juno an' him's been throwin' their weight about for the last few months! Ah, him that goes a borrowin' goes a sorrowin'!

NUGENT.   Well, he's not goin' to throw his weight about in the suit I made for him much longer. I'm tellin' you seven poun's aren't to be found growin' on the bushes these days.

JOXER.   An' there isn't hardly a neighbour in the whole street that hasn't lent him money on the strength of what he was goin' to get, but they're after backing the wrong horse. Wasn't it a mercy o' God that I'd nothin' to give him! The softy I am, you know, I'd ha' lent him me last juice! I must have had somebody's good prayers. Ah, afther all, an honest man's the noblest work o' God!

(BOYLE *coughs inside.*)

JOXER.   Whisht, damn it, he must be inside in bed.

NUGENT.   Inside o' bed or outside of it he's goin' to pay me for that suit, or give it back—he'll not climb up my back as easily as he thinks.

JOXER.   Gwan in at wanst, man, an' get it off him, an' don't be a fool.

NUGENT (*going to the door left, opening it and looking in*).   Ah, don't disturb yourself, Mr. Boyle; I hope you're not sick?

BOYLE.   Th' oul' legs, Mr. Nugent, the oul' legs.

NUGENT.   I just called over to see if you could let me have anything off the suit?

BOYLE.   E-e-e-eh, how much is this it is?

NUGENT.   It's the same as it was at the start—seven poun's.

BOYLE.   I'm glad you kem, Mr. Nugent; I want a good heavy top-coat —Irish frieze, if you have it. How much would a top-coat like that be now?

NUGENT.   About six poun's.

BOYLE.   Six poun's—six an' seven, six an' seven is thirteen—that'll be thirteen poun's I'll owe you.

(JOXER *slips the bottle of stout that is on the table into his pocket.*
    NUGENT *rushes into the room, and returns with the suit on his arm;
    he pauses at the door.*)

NUGENT.   You'll owe me no thirteen poun's. Maybe you think you're betther able to owe it than pay it!

BOYLE (*frantically*).   Here, come back to hell ower that—where're you goin' with them clothes o' mine?

NUGENT.   Where am I goin' with them clothes o' yours? Well, I like your damn cheek!

BOYLE.   Here, what am I going to dhress meself in when I'm goin' out?

NUGENT.   What do I care what you dhress yourself in? You can put yourself in a bolsther cover, if you like. (*He goes towards the other door, followed by* JOXER.)

JOXER.   What'll he dhress himself in! Gentleman Jack an' his frieze coat!

(*They go out.*)

BOYLE (*inside*).   Ey, Nugent, ey, Mr. Nugent, Mr. Nugent! (*After a pause* BOYLE *enters hastily, buttoning the braces of his moleskin trousers; his coat and vest are on his arms; he throws these on a chair and hurries to the door on right.*)

BOYLE.   Ey, Mr. Nugent, Mr. Nugent!

JOXER (*meeting him at the door*).   What's up, what's wrong, Captain?

BOYLE.   Nugent's been here an' took away me suit—the only things I had to go out in!

JOXER.   Tuk your suit—for God's sake! An' what were you doin' while he was takin' them?

BOYLE.   I was in bed when he stole in like a thief in the night, an' before I knew even what he was thinkin' of, he whipped them from the chair, an' was off like a redshank!

JOXER.   An' what, in the name o' God, did he do that for?

BOYLE.   What did he do it for? How the hell do I know what he done it for? Jealousy an' spite, I suppose.

JOXER.   Did he not say what he done it for?

BOYLE.   Amn't I afther tellin' you that he had them whipped up an' was gone before I could open me mouth?

JOXER.   That was a very sudden thing to do; there mus' be somethin' behin' it. Did he hear anythin', I wondher?

BOYLE.   Did he hear anythin'?—you talk very queer, Joxer—what could he hear?

JOXER.   About you not gettin' the money, in some way or t'other?

BOYLE.   An' what ud prevent me from gettin' th' money?

JOXER.   That's jus' what I was thinkin'—what ud prevent you from gettin' the money—nothin', as far as I can see.

BOYLE (*looking round for bottle of stout with an exclamation*).   Aw, holy God!

JOXER.   What's up, Jack?

BOYLE.   He must have afther lifted the bottle o' stout that Juno left on the table!

JOXER (*horrified*).   Ah, no, ah, no! He wouldn't be afther doin' that, now.

BOYLE.   An' who done it then? Juno left a bottle o' stout here, an' it's gone—it didn't walk, did it?

JOXER.   Oh, that's shockin'; ah, man's inhumanity to man makes countless thousands mourn!

MRS. MADIGAN (*appearing at the door*).   I hope I'm not disturbin' you in any discussion on your forthcomin' legacy—if I may use the word—

an' that you'll let me have a barny for a minute or two with you, Mr. Boyle.

BOYLE (*uneasily*).   To be sure, Mrs. Madigan—an oul' friend's always welcome.

JOXER.   Come in the evenin', come in th' mornin'; come when you're assed, or come without warnin', Mrs. Madigan.

BOYLE.   Sit down, Mrs. Madigan.

MRS. MADIGAN (*ominously*).   Th' few words I have to say can be said standin'. Puttin' aside all formularies, I suppose you remember me lendin' you some time ago three poun's that I raised on blankets an' furniture in me uncle's?

BOYLE.   I remember it well. I have it recorded in me book—three poun's five shillin's from Maisie Madigan, raised on articles pawned; an', item: fourpence, given to make up the price of a pint, on th' principle that no bird ever flew on wan wing; all to be repaid at par, when the ship comes home.

MRS. MADIGAN.   Well, ever since I shoved in the blankets I've been perishing with th' cowld, an' I've decided, if I'll be too hot in th' nex' world aself, I'm not goin' to be too cowld in this wan; an' consequently, I want me three poun's, if you please.

BOYLE.   This is a very sudden demand, Mrs. Madigan, an' can't be met; but I'm willin' to give you a receipt in full, in full.

MRS. MADIGAN.   Come on, out with th' money, an' don't be jack-actin'.

BOYLE.   You can't get blood out of a turnip, can you?

MRS. MADIGAN (*rushing over and shaking him*).   Gimme me money, y'oul' reprobate, or I'll shake the worth of it out of you!

BOYLE.   Ey, houl' on, there; houl' on, there! You'll wait for your money now, me lassie!

MRS. MADIGAN (*looking around the room and seeing the gramophone*). I'll wait for it, will I? Well, I'll not wait long; if I can't get th' cash, I'll get th' worth of it. (*She catches up the gramophone.*)

BOYLE.   Ey, ey, there, wher'r you goin' with that?

MRS. MADIGAN.   I'm goin' to th' pawn to get me three quid five shillin's; I'll bring you th' ticket, an' then you can do what you like, me bucko.

BOYLE.   You can't touch that, you can't touch that! It's not my property, an' it's not ped for yet!

MRS. MADIGAN.   So much th' bether. It'll be an ayse to me conscience, for I'm takin' what doesn't belong to you. You're not goin' to be swankin' it like a paycock with Maisie Madigan's money—I'll pull some o' the gorgeous feathers out o' your tail! (*She goes off with the gramophone.*)

BOYLE.   What's th' world comin' to at all? I ass you, Joxer Daly, is there any morality left anywhere?

JOXER.   I wouldn't ha' believed it, only I seen it with me own two eyes. I didn't think Maisie Madigan was that sort of a woman; she has either a sup taken, or she's heard somethin'.

BOYLE. Heard somethin'—about what, if it's not any harm to ass you?

JOXER. She must ha' heard some rumour or other that you weren't goin' to get th' money.

BOYLE. Who says I'm not goin' to get th' money?

JOXER. Sure, I know—I was only sayin'.

BOYLE. Only sayin' what?

JOXER. Nothin'.

BOYLE. You were goin' to say somethin', don't be a twisther.

JOXER (*angrily*). Who's a twisther?

BOYLE. Why don't you speak your mind, then?

JOXER. You never twisted yourself—no, you wouldn't know how!

BOYLE. Did you ever know me to twist; did you ever know me to twist?

JOXER (*fiercely*). Did you ever do anythin' else! Sure, you can't believe a word that comes out o' your mouth.

BOYLE. Here, get out, ower o' this; I always knew you were a prognosticator an' a procrastinator!

JOXER (*going out as* JOHNNY *comes in*). The anchor's weighed, farewell, re . . . mem . . . ber . . . me. Jacky Boyle, Esquire, infernal rogue an' damned liar!

JOHNNY. Joxer an' you at it agen?—when are you goin' to have a little respect for yourself, an' not be always makin' a show of us all?

BOYLE. Are you goin' to lecture me now?

JOHNNY. Is mother back from the doctor yet, with Mary?

(MRS. BOYLE *enters; it is apparent from the serious look on her face that something has happened. She takes off her hat and coat without a word and puts them by. She then sits down near the fire, and there is a few moments' pause.*)

BOYLE. Well, what did the doctor say about Mary?

MRS. BOYLE (*in an earnest manner and with suppressed agitation*). Sit down here, Jack; I've something to say to you . . . about Mary.

BOYLE (*awed by her manner*). About . . . Mary?

MRS. BOYLE. Close that door there and sit down here.

BOYLE (*closing the door*). More throuble in our native land, is it? (*He sits down.*) Well, what is it?

MRS. BOYLE. It's about Mary.

BOYLE. Well, what about Mary—there's nothin' wrong with her, is there?

MRS. BOYLE. I'm sorry to say there's a gradle wrong with her.

BOYLE. A gradle wrong with her! (*Peevishly.*) First Johnny an' now Mary; is the whole house goin' to become an hospital! It's not consumption, is it?

MRS. BOYLE. No . . . it's not consumption . . . it's worse.

JOHNNY. Worse! Well, we'll have to get her into some place ower this, there's no one here to mind her.

MRS. BOYLE. We'll all have to mind her now. You might as well know now, Johnny, as another time. (*To* BOYLE.) D'ye know what the doctor said to me about her, Jack?

BOYLE.   How ud I know—I wasn't there, was I?

MRS. BOYLE.   He told me to get her married at wanst.

BOYLE.   Married at wanst! An' why did he say the like o' that?

MRS. BOYLE.   Because Mary's goin' to have a baby in a short time.

BOYLE.   Goin' to have a baby!—my God, what'll Bentham say when he hears that?

MRS. BOYLE.   Are you blind, man, that you can't see that it was Bentham that has done this wrong to her?

BOYLE (*passionately*).   Then he'll marry her, he'll have to marry her!

MRS. BOYLE.   You know he's gone to England, an' God knows where he is now.

BOYLE.   I'll folley him, I'll folley him, an' bring him back, an' make him do her justice. The scoundrel, I might ha' known what he was, with his yogees an' his prawna!

MRS. BOYLE.   We'll have to keep it quiet till we see what we can do.

BOYLE.   Oh, isn't this a nice thing to come on top o' me, an' the state I'm in! A pretty show I'll be to Joxer an' to that oul' wan, Madigan! Amn't I afther goin' through enough without havin' to go through this!

MRS. BOYLE.   What you an' I'll have to go through'll be nothin' to what poor Mary'll have to go through; for you an' me is middlin' old, an' most of our years is spent; but Mary'll have maybe forty years to face an' handle, an' every wan of them'll be tainted with a bitther memory.

BOYLE.   Where is she? Where is she till I tell her off? I'm tellin' you when I'm done with her she'll be a sorry girl!

MRS. BOYLE.   I left her in me sisther's till I came to speak to you. You'll say nothin' to her, Jack; ever since she left school she's earned her livin', an' your fatherly care never throubled the poor girl.

BOYLE.   Gwan, take her part agen her father! But I'll let you see whether I'll say nothin' to her or no! Her an' her readin'! That's more o' th' blasted nonsense that has the house fallin' down on top of us! What did th' likes of her, born in a tenement house, want with readin'? Her readin's afther bringin' her to a nice pass—oh, it's madnin', madnin', madnin'!

MRS. BOYLE.   When she comes back say nothin' to her, Jack or she'll leave this place.

BOYLE.   Leave this place! Ay, she'll leave this place, an' quick too!

MRS. BOYLE.   If Mary goes, I'll go with her.

BOYLE.   Well, go with her! Well, go, th' pair o' yous! I lived before I seen yous, an' I can live when yous are gone. Isn't this a nice thing to come rollin' in on top o' me afther all your prayin' to St. Anthony an' The Little Flower. An' she's a child o' Mary, too—I wonder what'll the nuns think of her now? An' it'll be bellows'd all over th' disthrict before you could say Jack Robinson; an' whenever I'm seen they'll whisper, "That's th' father of Mary Boyle that had th' kid be th' swank she used to go with; d'ye know, d'ye know?" To be sure they'll know—more about it than I will meself!

JOHNNY. She should be dhriven out o' th' house she's brought disgrace on!

MRS. BOYLE. Hush, you, Johnny. We needn't let it be bellows'd all over the place; all we've got to do is to leave this place quietly an' go somewhere where we're not known, an' nobody'll be the wiser.

BOYLE. You're talkin' like a two-year-oul', woman. Where'll we get a place ou' o' this?—places aren't that easily got.

MRS. BOYLE. But, Jack, when we get the money . . .

BOYLE. Money—what money?

MRS. BOYLE. Why, oul' Ellison's money, of course.

BOYLE. There's no money comin' from oul' Ellison, or any one else. Since you heard of wan throuble, you might as well hear of another. There's no money comin' to us at all—the Will's a wash out!

MRS. BOYLE. What are you sayin', man—no money?

JOHNNY. How could it be a wash out?

BOYLE. The boyo that's afther doin' it to Mary done it to me as well. The thick made out the Will wrong; he said in th' Will, only first cousin an' second cousin, instead of mentionin' our names, an' now any one that thinks he's a first cousin or second cousin t'oul' Ellison can claim the money as well as me, an' they're springin' up in hundreds, an' comin' from America an' Australia, thinkin' to get their whack out of it, while all the time the lawyers is gobblin' it up, till there's not as much as ud buy a stockin' for your lovely daughter's baby!

MRS. BOYLE. I don't believe it, I don't believe it, I don't believe it!

JOHNNY. Why did you say nothin' about this before?

MRS. BOYLE. You're not serious, Jack; you're not serious!

BOYLE. I'm tellin' you the scholar, Bentham, made a banjax o' th' Will; instead o' sayin', "th' rest o' me property to be divided between me first cousin, Jack Boyle, an' me second cousin, Mick Finnegan, o' Santhry," he writ down only, "me first an' second cousins," an' the world an' his wife are afther th' property now.

MRS. BOYLE. Now, I know why Bentham left poor Mary in th' lurch; I can see it all now—oh, is there not even a middlin' honest man left in th' world?

JOHNNY (to BOYLE). An' you let us run into debt, an' you borreyed money from everybody to fill yourself with beer! An' now, you tell us the whole thing's a wash out! Oh, if it's thrue, I'm done with you, for you're worse than me sisther Mary!

BOYLE. You hole your tongue, d'ye hear? I'll not take any lip from you. Go an' get Bentham if you want satisfaction for all that's afther happenin' us.

JOHNNY. I won't hole me tongue, I won't hole me tongue! I'll tell you what I think of you, father an' all as you are . . . you . . .

MRS. BOYLE. Johnny, Johnny, Johnny, for God's sake, be quiet!

JOHNNY.   I'll not be quiet, I'll not be quiet; he's a nice father, isn't he?
Is it any wondher Mary went asthray, when . . .

MRS. BOYLE.   Johnny, Johnny, for my sake be quiet—for your mother's
sake!

BOYLE.   I'm goin' out now to have a few dhrinks with th' last few
makes I have, an' tell that lassie o' yours not to be here when I come back;
for if I lay me eyes on her, I'll lay me han's on her, an' if I lay me han's on
her, I won't be accountable for me actions!

JOHNNY.   Take care somebody doesn't lay his han's on you—y'oul' . . .

MRS. BOYLE.   Johnny, Johnny!

BOYLE (*at door, about to go out*).   Oh, a nice son, an' a nicer daughter,
I have. (*Calling loudly upstairs.*) Joxer, Joxer, are you there?

JOXER (*from a distance*).   I'm here, More . . . ee . . . aar . . . i . . . tee!

BOYLE.   I'm goin' down to Foley's—are you comin'?

JOXER.   Come with you? With that sweet call me heart is stirred; I'm
only waiting for the word, an' I'll be with you, like a bird!

(BOYLE *and* JOXER *pass the door going out.*)

JOHNNY (*throwing himself on the bed*).   I've a nice sisther, an' a nice
father, there's no bettin' on it. I wish to God a bullet or a bomb had
whipped me ou' o' this long ago! Not one o' yous, not one o' yous, have
any thought for me!

MRS. BOYLE (*with passionate remonstrance*).   If you don't whisht,
Johnny, you'll drive me mad. Who has kep' th' home together for the past
few years—only me. An' who'll have to bear th' biggest part o' this
throuble but me—but whinin' an' whingin' isn't going to do any good.

JOHNNY.   You're to blame yourself for a gradle of it—givin' him his
own way in everything, an' never assin' to check him, no matther what he
done. Why didn't you look afther th' money? why . . .

(*There is a knock at the door;* MRS. BOYLE *opens it;* JOHNNY *rises on
his elbow to look and listen; two men enter.*)

FIRST MAN.   We've been sent up be th' Manager of the Hibernian
Furnishing Co., Mrs. Boyle, to take back the furniture that was got a
while ago.

MRS. BOYLE.   Yous'll touch nothin' here—how do I know who yous are?

FIRST MAN (*showing a paper*).   There's the ordher, ma'am. (*Reading.*) A chest o' drawers, a table, wan easy an' two ordinary chairs; wan
mirror; wan chestherfield divan, an' a wardrobe an' two vases. (*To his
comrade.*) Come on, Bill, it's afther knockin' off time already.

JOHNNY.   For God's sake, mother, run down to Foley's an' bring father
back, or we'll be left without a stick.

(*The men carry out the table.*)

MRS. BOYLE.   What good would it be? You heard what he said before
he went out.

JOHNNY.   Can't you thry? He ought to be here, an' the like of this
goin' on.

(MRS. BOYLE *puts a shawl around her, as* MARY *enters.*)

MARY. What's up, mother? I met men carryin' away the table, an' everybody's talking about us not gettin' the money after all.

MRS. BOYLE. Everythin's gone wrong, Mary, everythin'. We're not gettin' a penny out o' the Will, not a penny—I'll tell you all when I come back; I'm goin' for your father. (*She runs out.*)

JOHNNY (*to* MARY, *who has sat down by the fire*). It's a wondher you're not ashamed to show your face here, afther what has happened.

(JERRY *enters slowly; there is a look of earnest hope on his face. He looks at* MARY *for a few moments.*)

JERRY (*softly*). Mary!

(MARY *does not answer.*)

JERRY. Mary, I want to speak to you for a few moments, may I?

(MARY *remains silent;* JOHNNY *goes slowly into room on left.*)

JERRY. Your mother has told me everything, Mary, and I have come to you. . . . I have come to tell you, Mary, that my love for you is greater and deeper than ever. . . .

MARY (*with a sob*). Oh, Jerry, Jerry, say no more; all that is over now; anything like that is impossible now!

JERRY. Impossible? Why do you talk like that, Mary?

MARY. After all that has happened.

JERRY. What does it matter what has happened? We are young enough to be able to forget all those things. (*He catches her hand.*) Mary, Mary, I am pleading for your love. With Labour, Mary, humanity is above everything; we are the Leaders in the fight for a new life. I want to forget Bentham, I want to forget that you left me—even for a while.

MARY. Oh, Jerry, Jerry, you haven't the bitter word of scorn for me after all.

JERRY (*passionately*). Scorn! I love you, love you, Mary!

MARY (*rising, and looking him in the eyes*). Even though . . .

JERRY. Even though you threw me over for another man; even though you gave me many a bitter word!

MARY. Yes, yes, I know; but you love me, even though . . . even though . . . I'm . . . goin' . . . goin' . . . (*He looks at her questioningly, and fear gathers in his eyes.*) Ah, I was thinkin' so. . . . You don't know everything!

JERRY (*poignantly*). Surely to God, Mary, you don't mean that . . . that . . . that . . .

MARY. Now you know all, Jerry; now you know all!

JERR. My God, Mary, have you fallen as low as that?

MARY. Yes, Jerry, as you say, I have fallen as low as that.

JERRY. I didn't mean it that way, Mary . . . it came on me so sudden, that I didn't mind what I was sayin'. . . . I never expected this—your mother never told me. . . . I'm sorry . . . God knows, I'm sorry for you, Mary.

MARY. Let us say no more, Jerry; I don't blame you for thinkin' it's terrible. . . . I suppose it is. . . . Everybody'll think the same. . . . It's only as I expected—your humanity is just as narrow as the humanity of the others.

JERRY. I'm sorry, all the same. . . . I shouldn't have troubled you. . . . I wouldn't if I'd known . . . if I can do anything for you . . . Mary . . . I will. (*He turns to go, and halts at the door.*)

MARY. Do you remember, Jerry, the verses you read when you gave the lecture in the Socialist Rooms some time ago, on Humanity's Strife with Nature?

JERRY. The verses—no; I don't remember them.

MARY. I do. They're runnin' in me head now—

> An' we felt the power that fashion'd
> All the lovely things we saw,
> That created all the murmur
> Of an everlasting law,
> Was a hand of force an' beauty,
> With an eagle's tearin' claw.
>
> Then we saw our globe of beauty
> Was an ugly thing as well,
> A hymn divine whose chorus
> Was an agonizin' yell;
> Like the story of a demon,
> That an angel had to tell.
>
> Like a glowin' picture by a
> Hand unsteady, brought to ruin;
> Like her craters, if their deadness
> Could give life unto the moon;
> Like the agonizing horror
> Of a violin out of tune.

(*There is a pause, and* DEVINE *goes slowly out.*)

JOHNNY (*returning*). Is he gone?

MARY. Yes.

(*The two men re-enter.*)

FIRST MAN. We can't wait any longer for t'oul' fella—sorry, Miss, but we have to live as well as th' nex' man.

(*They carry out some things.*)

JOHNNY. Oh, isn't this terrible! . . . I suppose you told him everything . . . couldn't you have waited for a few days . . . he'd have stopped th' takin' of the things, if you'd kep' your mouth shut. Are you burnin' to tell every one of the shame you've brought on us?

MARY (*snatching up her hat and coat*). Oh, this is unbearable! (*She rushes out.*)

FIRST MAN (*re-entering*). We'll take the chest o' drawers next—it's the heaviest.

(*The votive light flickers for a moment, and goes out.*)

JOHNNY (*in a cry of fear*).   Mother o' God, the light's afther goin' out!

FIRST MAN.   You put the win' up me the way you bawled that time. The oil's all gone, that's all.

JOHNNY (*with an agonizing cry*).   Mother o' God, there's a shot I'm afther gettin'!

FIRST MAN.   What's wrong with you, man? Is it a fit you're takin'?

JOHNNY.   I'm afther feelin' a pain in me breast, like the tearin' by of a bullet!

FIRST MAN.   He's goin' mad—it's a wondher they'd leave a chap like that here be himself.

(*Two IRREGULARS enter swiftly; they carry revolvers; one goes over to JOHNNY; the other covers the two furniture men.*)

FIRST IRREGULAR (*to the men, quietly and incisively*).   Who are you— what are yous doin' here—quick!

FIRST MAN.   Removin' furniture that's not paid for.

IRREGULAR.   Get over to the other end of the room an' turn your faces to the wall—quick.

(*The two men turn their faces to the wall, with their hands up.*)

SECOND IRREGULAR (*to JOHNNY*).   Come on, Sean Boyle, you're wanted; some of us have a word to say to you.

JOHNNY.   I'm sick, I can't—what do you want with me?

SECOND IRREGULAR.   Come on, come on; we've a distance to go, an' haven't much time—come on.

JOHNNY.   I'm an oul' comrade—yous wouldn't shoot an oul' comrade.

SECOND IRREGULAR.   Poor Tancred was an oul' comrade o' yours, but you didn't think o' that when you gave him away to the gang that sent him to his grave. But we've no time to waste; come on—here, Dermot, ketch his arm. (*To JOHNNY.*) Have you your beads?

JOHNNY.   Me beads! Why do you ass me that, why do you ass me that?

SECOND IRREGULAR.   Go on, go on, march!

JOHNNY.   Are yous goin' to do in a comrade—look at me arm, I lost it for Ireland.

SECOND IRREGULAR.   Commandant Tancred lost his life for Ireland.

JOHNNY.   Sacred Heart of Jesus, have mercy on me! Mother o' God, pray for me—be with me now in the agonies o' death! . . . Hail, Mary, full o' grace . . . the Lord is . . . with Thee.

(*They drag out JOHNNY BOYLE, and the curtain falls. When it rises again the most of the furniture is gone. MARY and MRS. BOYLE, one on each side, are sitting in a darkened room, by the fire; it is an hour later.*)

MRS. BOYLE.   I'll not wait much longer . . . what did they bring him away in the mothor for? Nugent says he thinks they had guns . . . is me throubles never goin' to be over? . . . If anything ud happen to poor Johnny, I think I'd lost me mind . . . I'll go to the Police Station, surely they ought to be able to do somethin'.

(*Below is heard the sound of voices.*)

MRS. BOYLE.   Whisht, is that something? Maybe, it's your father, though when I left him in Foley's he was hardly able to lift his head. Whisht!

(*A knock at the door, and the voice of* MRS. MADIGAN, *speaking very softly:*)

Mrs. Boyle, Mrs. Boyle. (MRS. BOYLE *opens the door.*)

MRS. MADIGAN.   Oh, Mrs. Boyle, God an' His Blessed Mother be with you this night!

MRS. BOYLE (*calmly*).   What is it, Mrs. Madigan? It's Johnny—something about Johnny.

MRS. MADIGAN.   God send it's not. God send it's not Johnny!

MRS. BOYLE.   Don't keep me waitin', Mrs. Madigan; I've gone through so much lately that I feel able for anything.

MRS. MADIGAN.   Two polismen below wantin' you.

MRS. BOYLE.   Wantin' me; an' why do they want me?

MRS. MADIGAN.   Some poor fella's been found, an' they think it's, it's . . .

MRS. BOYLE.   Johnny, Johnny!

MARY (*with her arms round her mother*).   Oh, mother, mother, me poor, darlin' mother.

MRS. BOYLE.   Hush, hush, darlin'; you'll shortly have your own throuble to bear. (*To* MRS. MADIGAN.) An' why do the polis think it's Johnny, Mrs. Madigan?

MRS. MADIGAN.   Because one o' the doctors knew him when he was attendin' with his poor arm.

MRS. BOYLE.   Oh, it's thrue, then; it's Johnny, it's me son, me own son!

MARY.   Oh, it's thrue, it's thrue what Jerry Devine says—there isn't a God, there isn't a God; if there was He wouldn't let these things happen!

MRS. BOYLE.   Mary, Mary, you mustn't say them things. We'll want all the help we can get from God an' His Blessed Mother now! These things have nothin' to do with the Will o' God. Ah, what can God do agen the stupidity o' men!

MRS. MADIGAN.   The polis want you to go with them to the hospital to see the poor body—they're waitin' below.

MRS. BOYLE.   We'll go. Come, Mary, an' we'll never come back here agen. Let your father furrage for himself now; I've done all I could an' it was all no use—he'll be hopeless till the end of his days. I've got a little room in me sisther's where we'll stop till your throuble is over, an' then we'll work together for the sake of the baby.

MARY.   My poor little child that'll have no father!

MRS. BOYLE.   It'll have what's far betther—it'll have two mothers.

(*A rough voice shouting from below:*)

Are yous goin' to keep us waitin' for yous all night?

MRS. MADIGAN (*going to the door, and shouting down*).   Take your hour, there. take your hour! If yous are in such a hurry, skip off, then, for nobody wants you here—if they did yous wouldn't be found. For you're the same as yous were undher the British Government—never where yous are wanted! As far as I can see, the Polis as Polis, in this city, is Null an' Void!

MRS. BOYLE. We'll go, Mary, we'll go; you to see your poor dead brother, an' me to see me poor dead son!

MARY. I dhread it, mother, I dhread it!

MRS. BOYLE. I forgot, Mary, I forgot; your poor oul' selfish mother was only thinkin' of herself. No, no, you mustn't come—it wouldn't be good for you. You go on to me sisther's an' I'll face th' ordeal meself. Maybe I didn't feel sorry enough for Mrs. Tancred when her poor son was found as Johnny's been found now—because he was a Die-hard! Ah, why didn't I remember that then he wasn't a Die-hard or a Stater, but only a poor dead son! It's well I remember all that she said—an' it's my turn to say it now: What was the pain I suffered, Johnny, bringin' you into the world to carry you to your cradle to the pains I'll suffer carryin' you out o' the world to bring you to your grave! Mother o' God, Mother o' God, have pity on us all! Blessed Virgin, where were you when me darlin' son was riddled with bullets, when me darlin' son was riddled with bullets? Sacred Heart o' Jesus, take away our hearts o' stone, and give us hearts o' flesh! Take away this murdherin' hate, an' give us Thine own eternal love!

(*They all go slowly out.*)

(*There is a pause; then a sound of shuffling steps on the stairs outside. The door opens and* BOYLE *and* JOXER, *both of them very drunk, enter.*)

BOYLE. I'm able to go no farther. . . . Two polis, ey . . . what were they doin' here, I wondher? . . . Up to no good, anyhow . . . an' Juno an' that lovely daughter o' mine with them. (*Taking a sixpence from his pocket and looking at it.*) Wan single, solithary tanner left out of all I borreyed. . . . (*He lets it fall.*) The last o' the Mohicans. . . . The blinds is down, Joxer, the blinds is down!

JOXER (*walking unsteadily across the room, and anchoring at the bed*). Put all . . . your throubles . . . in your oul' kit bag . . . an' smile . . . smile . . . smile!

BOYLE. The counthry'll have to steady itself . . . it's goin' . . . to hell. . . . Where'r all . . . the chairs . . . gone to . . . steady itself, Joxer. . . . Chairs'll . . . have to . . . steady themselves. . . . No matther . . . what any one may . . . say . . . Irelan's sober . . . is Irelan' . . . free.

JOXER (*stretching himself on the bed*). Chains . . . an' . . . slaveree . . . that's a darlin' motto . . . a daaarlin' . . . motto!

BOYLE. If th' worst comes . . . to th' worse . . . I can join a . . . flyin' . . . column. . . . I done . . . me bit . . . in Easther Week . . . had no business . . . to . . . be . . . there . . . but Captain Boyle's Captain Boyle!

JOXER. Breathes there a man with soul . . . so . . . de . . . ad . . . this . . . me . . . o . . . wn, me nat . . . ive l . . . an'!

BOYLE (*subsiding into a sitting posture on the floor*). Commandant Kelly died . . . in them . . . arms . . . Joxer. . . . Tell me Volunteer Butties . . . says he . . . that . . . I died for . . . Irelan'!

JOXER. D'jever rade Willie . . . Reilly . . . an' his . . . own . . . Colleen . . . Bawn? It's a darlin' story, a daarlin' story!

BOYLE. I'm telling you . . . Joxer . . . th' whole worl's . . . in a terr . . . ible state o' . . . chassis!

CURTAIN

QUESTIONS

1. The first scene of *Juno and The Paycock*, involving Mary, Mrs. Boyle, and Johnny, establishes an effect of some seriousness and even an element of uneasiness or foreboding for Johnny before the hilarious scene involving "Captain" Boyle, Joxer, and Juno. How is the uneasiness established? What effect has this opening on the play as a whole?

2. Throughout the play comic scenes are alternated with serious ones. Note the chief examples. Analyze these examples to show how this intermeshing of serious and comic enhances the dramatic effect of each.

3. The major situation of the play revolves about a supposed inheritance that does not materialize. O'Casey sees both the comic and serious aspects of this situation and endeavors to present both. List as many devices as you can discover by which he brings out the comic aspects; the serious aspects.

4. Every major character in the play, with the possible exception of Johnny, has comic or ludicrous traits. Indicate the chief comic traits of character to be found in the portrayals of "Captain" Boyle, Joxer, Juno, and Maisie Madigan. Despite elements of the comic in her characterization, Juno is not ludicrous in the same way as are "Captain" Boyle and Joxer. Why not?

5. In rendering the characters of this play O'Casey was definitely concerned with certain comments upon and assessments of contemporary Irish characters. Yet his characterizations are sufficiently universalized to have meanings beyond the boundaries of Ireland. Point out any examples of this commentary upon human nature in general.

6. In the second scene of the play Jerry Devine's news from Father Farrell begins a minor comic complication. Trace this complication through the stages of its involvement to its crisis. Does it have a resolution? If so, what is it?

7. Where does the major complication revolving around the inheritance begin? What are the stages of its involvement to a crisis? What is the crisis? What is the resolution?

8. Note that the involvement of this major complication up to the crisis is largely comic, whereas the resolution is in a considerable measure serious. How is this resolution made probable?

9. There are indications in this play of O'Casey's conception of the admirable in human beings. What are they and where do they occur?

/\

:Y